D1426621

The progressive in 19th-century English

A process of integration

LANGUAGE AND COMPUTERS:
STUDIES IN PRACTICAL LINGUISTICS

No 54

edited by
Christian Mair
Charles F. Meyer
Nelleke Oostdijk

The progressive in
19th-century English
A process of integration

Erik Smitterberg

Amsterdam - New York, NY 2005

Online access is included in print subscriptions:
see www.rodopi.nl

The paper on which this book is printed meets the requirements of
"ISO 9706:1994, Information and documentation - Paper for documents -
Requirements for permanence".

ISBN: 90-420-1735-X (bound)
©Editions Rodopi B.V., Amsterdam - New York, NY 2005
Printed in The Netherlands

Table of contents

Table of contents   v

List of tables and figures   ix

Preface   xv

Chapter 1. Introduction   1

1.1 General background   1
1.2 Aim and scope   3
1.3 Plan of the study   5
1.4 Terminology   6
1.5 Analytical frameworks   8
    1.5.1 Corpus linguistics and the variationist approach   8
    1.5.2 Multi-feature/multi-dimensional approaches   11
    1.5.3 Applying the frameworks   13
1.6 Typographical and statistical conventions   14
    1.6.1 Typography   14
    1.6.2 Corpus citations   15
    1.6.3 Statistical conventions   15

Chapter 2. Material and data   17

2.1 Material   17
    2.1.1 Periodization   18
    2.1.2 Genre division   20
    2.1.3 Sampling setup and word count   22
2.2 The data: Retrieving and identifying progressives   24
    2.2.1 Defining the progressive and designing the retrieval
        process   25
    2.2.2 Post-processing the retrieval output: A discussion of
        doubtful cases   26
        2.2.2.1 Appositively used participles   26
        2.2.2.2 Predicative adjectival participles   28
        2.2.2.3 Gerunds   31
        2.2.2.4 BE *going to* + infinitive with future reference   32
        2.2.2.5 Progressives with nominal characteristics   34
    2.2.3 The progressives in the CONCE corpus   38

**Chapter 3. The frequency of the progressive in 19th-century
English**   39

3.1 Measuring the frequency of the progressive: A methodological
    discussion   39

3.1.1 Calculating the frequency of the progressive: A
       comparison of four coefficients   40
       3.1.1.1 The M-coefficient   40
       3.1.1.2 The K-coefficient   42
       3.1.1.3 The V-coefficient   44
       3.1.1.4 The S-coefficient   45
3.1.2 Comparing the M- and S-coefficients: A methodological
       perspective   48
3.1.3 Applying the model: Obtaining input data for the
       calculation of the S-coefficient   50
3.2 Frequency variation across genres, by gender, and in diachrony   54
     3.2.1 The status of the progressive in late Modern English
            grammar   54
            3.2.1.1 Previous research: A survey and discussion   54
            3.2.1.2 The concept of integration   57
     3.2.2 Diachronic variation in 19th-century English   58
     3.2.3 Genre variation   63
     3.2.4 Genre-specific frequency developments across the 19th
            century   66
            3.2.4.1 Debates   67
            3.2.4.2 Drama   68
            3.2.4.3 Fiction   69
            3.2.4.4 History   72
            3.2.4.5 Letters   73
            3.2.4.6 Science   74
            3.2.4.7 Trials   75
            3.2.4.8 Summary of results   76
     3.2.5 Gender-based variation in the frequency of the progressive   78
            3.2.5.1 "Sex" versus "gender"   78
            3.2.5.2 Variation in the frequency of the progressive
                     between women and men letter-writers   79
            3.2.5.3 A new parameter: Taking the sex of the addressee
                     into account   83
            3.2.5.4 Explanatory factors   85
3.3 Discussion of results   87

Chapter 4. M-coefficients and factor score analysis   **93**

4.1 Factor scores and the frequency of the progressive: A cross-
     genre comparison   94
4.2 Genre developments   98
4.3 Gender, M-coefficients, and co-occurrence patterns   105
4.4 Discussion of results   108

Chapter 5. Morphosyntactic variation in the verb phrase   **115**

5.1 Tense   116

5.2 The perfect progressive   121
5.3 Voice   123
5.4 Modal auxiliaries   133
5.5 Verb phrase patterns   138
5.6 The *being* + present participle construction   141
5.7 Discussion of results   143

Chapter 6. Variation with linguistic parameters   **147**

6.1 Main verbs   147
   6.1.1 Frequent main verbs in progressive verb phrases   148
   6.1.2 The development of BE and HAVE as main verbs in the
       progressive   156
6.2 Aktionsart   160
   6.2.1 Aktionsart typologies: A selective survey and discussion   160
   6.2.2 The progressive and situation types: An overview of the
       distribution in CONCE   167
   6.2.3 A diachronic account   174
   6.2.4 Variation with genre   177
6.3 Agentivity of subject   181
   6.3.1 The agentive/non-agentive distinction   181
   6.3.2 Agentivity and the progressive in previous research   183
   6.3.3 The progressive and agentivity: Evidence from the CONCE
       corpus   185
6.4 Modification by temporal adverbials   188
6.5 Clause type   194
6.6 Discussion of results   202

**Chapter 7. The not-solely-aspectual progressive: An analytical
         approach**   **207**

7.1 Progressives modified by adverbials of the ALWAYS type   210
7.2 Potentially experiential progressives   217
7.3 The interpretative progressive   227
7.4 Discussion of results   237

Chapter 8. Concluding discussion   **243**

8.1 Interrelating the results: The integration of the progressive   243
8.2 The secondary aims of the study: A selective overview   250
8.3 Suggestions for further research   251

References   **255**

Appendix 1. Primary material: The CONCE corpus   **271**

Appendix 2. Text-level codes used in CONCE   **277**

Appendix 3. Tests for statistical significance   **279**

List of tables and figures

Tables

Table 1   Some important 19th-century sociocultural events and developments (taken from Harvie 1992, Matthew 1992, and Görlach 1999)

Table 2   Description of the genres in CONCE (based on Kytö et al. 2000)

Table 3   The sampling setup per period aimed at for the genres in CONCE

Table 4   Word counts by period and genre in CONCE

Table 5   Progressives by period and genre in CONCE

Table 6   Finite non-imperative verb phrases, excluding BE *going to* + infinitive constructions with future reference, by period and genre in the S-coefficient subcorpus

Table 7   Finite progressive verb phrases by period and genre in the S-coefficient subcorpus

Table 8   M-coefficients per period in CONCE

Table 9   M'- and S-coefficients per period in the S-coefficient subcorpus

Table 10   M-coefficients by genre in CONCE

Table 11   M'- and S-coefficients by genre in the S-coefficient subcorpus

Table 12   M-coefficients by period and genre in CONCE

Table 13   The frequency of the progressive in Debates over the 19th century; "All" refers to figures for the whole CONCE corpus (M-coefficients) or for the whole S-coefficient subcorpus (S-coefficients and verb density ratios)

Table 14   The frequency of the progressive in Drama over the 19th century; "All" refers to figures for the whole CONCE corpus (M-coefficients) or for the whole S-coefficient subcorpus (S-coefficients and verb density ratios)

Table 15   The frequency of the progressive in Fiction over the 19th century; "All" refers to figures for the whole CONCE corpus (M-coefficients) or for the whole S-coefficient subcorpus (S-coefficients and verb density ratios)

Table 16   Word counts per period for the dialogue and non-dialogue subsamples of Fiction

Table 17   Progressives per period in the dialogue and non-dialogue subsamples of Fiction

Table 18   M-coefficients per period for the dialogue and non-dialogue subsamples of Fiction

Table 19   The frequency of the progressive in History over the 19th century; "All" refers to figures for the whole CONCE corpus (M-coefficients) or for the whole S-coefficient subcorpus (S-coefficients and verb density ratios)

Table 20   The frequency of the progressive in Letters over the 19th century;
                "All" refers to figures for the whole CONCE corpus (M-
                coefficients) or for the whole S-coefficient subcorpus (M'-
                coefficients, S-coefficients, and verb density ratios)

Table 21   The frequency of the progressive in Science over the 19th century;
                "All" refers to figures for the whole CONCE corpus (M-
                coefficients) or for the whole S-coefficient subcorpus (S-
                coefficients and verb density ratios)

Table 22   The frequency of the progressive in Trials over the 19th century;
                "All" refers to figures for the whole CONCE corpus (M-
                coefficients) or for the whole S-coefficient subcorpus (S-
                coefficients and verb density ratios)

Table 23a   Letters written by women: progressives and word counts per
                period

Table 23b   Letters written by men: progressives and word counts per period

Table 24a   Letters written by women in the S-coefficient subcorpus:
                progressives, word counts, finite progressives, and finite non-
                imperative verb phrases (excluding BE *going to* + infinitive
                constructions with future reference) per period

Table 24b   Letters written by men in the S-coefficient subcorpus:
                progressives, word counts, finite progressives, and finite non-
                imperative verb phrases (excluding BE *going to* + infinitive
                constructions with future reference) per period

Table 25a   Letters written by women: M-, M'-, and S-coefficients, and verb
                density ratios per period; "All" refers to figures for the whole
                CONCE corpus (M-coefficients) or for the whole S-coefficient
                subcorpus (M'-coefficients, S-coefficients, and verb density ratios)

Table 25b   Letters written by men: M-, M'-, and S-coefficients, and verb
                density ratios per period; "All" refers to figures for the whole
                CONCE corpus (M-coefficients) or for the whole S-coefficient
                subcorpus (M'-coefficients, S-coefficients, and verb density ratios)

Table 26   Progressives, word counts, and M-coefficients for the four
                subsamples of Letters, period 3, based on the sex of the letter-
                writer and addressee

Table 27   The order of the genres in CONCE with respect to M-coefficients
                and to Dimensions 1 (Involved vs. informational production), 2
                (Narrative vs. non-narrative concerns), 3 (Elaborated vs. situation-
                dependent reference), and 5 (Abstract vs. non-abstract
                information) (dimension scores taken from Geisler 2000)

Table 28   The ranking of the Debates genre, relative to the other genres, with
                respect to M-coefficients and to Dimensions 1, 2, 3, and 5
                (dimension scores taken from Geisler 2002)

Table 29   The ranking of the Drama genre, relative to the other genres, with respect to M-coefficients and to Dimensions 1, 2, 3, and 5 (dimension scores taken from Geisler 2002)

Table 30   The ranking of the Fiction genre, relative to the other genres, with respect to M-coefficients and to Dimensions 1, 2, 3, and 5 (dimension scores taken from Geisler 2002)

Table 31   The ranking of the History genre, relative to the other genres, with respect to M-coefficients and to Dimensions 1, 2, 3, and 5 (dimension scores taken from Geisler 2002)

Table 32   The ranking of the Letters genre, relative to the other genres, with respect to M-coefficients and to Dimensions 1, 2, 3, and 5 (dimension scores taken from Geisler 2002)

Table 33   The ranking of the Science genre, relative to the other genres, with respect to M-coefficients and to Dimensions 1, 2, 3, and 5 (dimension scores taken from Geisler 2002)

Table 34   The ranking of the Trials genre, relative to the other genres, with respect to M-coefficients and to Dimensions 1, 2, 3, and 5 (dimension scores taken from Geisler 2002)

Table 35a   Letters written by women: M-coefficients and dimension scores on Dimensions 1, 3, and 5 (dimension scores from Geisler 2001; 2003)

Table 35b   Letters written by men: M-coefficients and dimension scores on Dimensions 1, 3, and 5 (dimension scores from Geisler 2001; 2003)

Table 36   Non-finite progressives in CONCE by period and genre

Table 37   Finite progressives in CONCE by period and genre

Table 38   Present-tense progressives in CONCE by period and genre (percentages of all finite progressives in each subsample within brackets)

Table 39   Past-tense progressives in CONCE by period and genre (percentages of all finite progressives in each subsample within brackets)

Table 40   Perfect progressives in CONCE by period and genre (percentages of all progressives in each subsample within brackets)

Table 41   Active, passival, and passive progressives in CONCE per period (row percentages within brackets)

Table 42   Passive and passival progressives in Arnaud's database per period (row percentages within brackets)

Table 43   Active, passival, and passive progressives in CONCE by genre (row percentages within brackets)

Table 44   Progressive verb phrases with modal auxiliaries in CONCE by period and genre (percentages of all finite progressives in each subsample within brackets)

Table 45	The distribution of modal auxiliaries in progressive verb phrases per period
Table 46	The distribution of modal auxiliaries in progressive verb phrases by genre
Table 47	The distribution of modal auxiliaries in progressive verb phrases per period in Arnaud's database (row percentages within brackets)
Table 48	The distribution of finite progressive verb phrases across the parameters of tense and modal, perfect, and passive auxiliaries per period (column percentages within brackets)
Table 49	Main verbs with more than 20 occurrences in progressive verb phrases in CONCE (percentages of all progressive verb phrases in the material within brackets)
Table 50	The most frequent main verbs in progressive verb phrases in CONCE per period (percentages of all progressive verb phrases in each period subsample within brackets)
Table 51a	The most frequent main verbs in progressive verb phrases in the expository genres Debates, History, and Science (raw frequencies within brackets)
Table 51b	The most frequent main verbs in progressive verb phrases in the non-expository genres Drama, Fiction, Letters, and Trials (raw frequencies within brackets)
Table 52	The Aktionsart features of Vendler's typology (based on Brinton 1988: 28f.)
Table 53	The eleven situation types in Quirk et al.'s (1985) classification
Table 54	The seven situation types distinguished in the present study
Table 55a	The progressives in CONCE across the parameter of situation type (column percentages within brackets); 'future' situations included as a separate category
Table 55b	The progressives in CONCE across the parameter of situation type (column percentages within brackets); 'future' situations reclassified
Table 56a	The progressives in CONCE across the parameters of time and situation type (row percentages within brackets); 'future' situations included as a separate category
Table 56b	The progressives in CONCE across the parameters of time and situation type (row percentages within brackets); 'future' situations reclassified
Table 57a	The progressives in CONCE across the parameters of genre and situation type (row percentages within brackets); 'future' situations included as a separate category
Table 57b	The progressives in CONCE across the parameters of genre and situation type (row percentages within brackets); 'future' situations reclassified

Table 58   The diachronic distribution of human, quasi-human/animal, and
            inanimate subjects in Strang's (1982) analysis (row percentages
            within brackets)
Table 59   Progressives with non-agentive subjects in CONCE by period and
            genre (progressives occurring in 'stative' and 'stance' situations
            excluded from the counts; percentages of all progressives
            occurring in 'active', 'processive', 'momentary', and 'transitional'
            situations in each subsample within brackets)
Table 60   Progressives in CONCE modified by temporal adverbials by period
            and genre (percentages of all progressives in each subsample
            within brackets)
Table 61   Progressives modified by temporal adverbials in Fiction (CONCE)
            and in Scheffer's (1975) corpus of Present-Day English fiction
            (percentages of all progressives in each subsample within brackets)
Table 62   The progressives in CONCE by period and clause type (row
            percentages within brackets)
Table 63   The progressives in Debates by period and clause type (row
            percentages within brackets)
Table 64   The progressives in Drama by period and clause type (row
            percentages within brackets)
Table 65   The progressives in Fiction by period and clause type (row
            percentages within brackets)
Table 66   The progressives in History by period and clause type (row
            percentages within brackets)
Table 67   The progressives in Letters by period and clause type (row
            percentages within brackets)
Table 68   The progressives in Science by period and clause type (row
            percentages within brackets)
Table 69   The progressives in Trials by period and clause type (row
            percentages within brackets)
Table 70   ALWAYS-type adverbials modifying progressives in CONCE
Table 71   Progressives modified by ALWAYS-type adverbials by period and
            genre (percentages of all progressives in each subsample within
            brackets)
Table 72   Wright's (1994) diagnostics for the modal progressive
Table 73   Criteria used to select potentially experiential progressives
Table 74   Potentially experiential progressives in CONCE by period and genre
            (percentages of all progressives in each subsample within brackets)
Table 75   The order of the genres in CONCE with respect to the frequency of
            the potentially experiential progressive (M-coefficients) and to
            Dimensions 1 (Involved vs. informational production), 2
            (Narrative vs. non-narrative concerns), 3 (Elaborated vs. situation-
            dependent reference), and 5 (Abstract vs. non-abstract
            information) (dimension scores taken from Geisler 2000)

Table 76   Potentially experiential progressives modified by expressions of emotion by period and genre (percentages of all potentially experiential progressives in each subsample within brackets)
Table 77   Interpretative progressives by period and genre (percentages of all progressives in each subsample within brackets)

Figures

Figure 1   M-coefficients for period/genre subsamples in CONCE
Figure 2   M'-coefficients for period/genre subsamples in the S-coefficient subcorpus
Figure 3   S-coefficients for period/genre subsamples in the S-coefficient subcorpus

Preface

The topic of the present study is the use and development of the progressive in English during the 19th century. The study is a revised version of the doctoral thesis I presented at Uppsala University in 2002. Among other things, the chapter structure has been changed, and studies published since 2002, as well as a number of valuable comments I have received on the thesis text, have been taken into account.

I would like to start by thanking Professor Merja Kytö, who supervised my studies with great enthusiasm and perspicacity. Her unflagging support, constructive criticism, and scholarly example have been central to my work. I am also grateful to Professor Mats Rydén, who first suggested the topic of the original study to me; by taking an active interest in my work after his retirement, Professor Rydén has supported me literally beyond the call of duty. Many thanks are due to the members of the research seminar at the Department of English, Uppsala University. I would especially like to thank Dr Christer Geisler and Dr Peter Grund. Dr Geisler helped me with problems related to the tagging of corpora, factor score analysis, and statistical matters; Dr Grund's close readings of the chapters helped to give shape to my text. Outside the seminar, I am indebted to Dr Stefan Mähl for valuable suggestions concerning the history of the Germanic languages, and for helping me with a number of German references. In addition, I am very grateful to Professor René Arnaud and to my Faculty Examiner, Professor Marianne Hundt, for their highly valuable comments; Professor Arnaud deserves additional thanks for allowing me to use his impressive database. Donald MacQueen expertly checked my English, and made several suggestions that improved the final product; I am also indebted to Pamela Marston and Terry Walker for their comments on subsequent revisions.

On a more general note, the members of staff at the Department of English, Uppsala University, provided a highly stimulating working environment during my employment there. I would also like to thank the staff members at the Department of Humanities at Örebro University, the Department of Humanities and Social Sciences at the University of Gävle, and the Department of English at Stockholm University.

I thank the participants at the 10ICEHL and 11ICEHL conferences, in Manchester and Santiago de Compostela respectively, where some of my results were presented. Thanks are also due to Professor Josef Schmied, Professor Angela Hahn, and Dr Sabine Reich for helpful comments and suggestions; to Professor Raymond Hickey, who kindly let me use a beta version of the Corpus Presenter suite to double-check my collection of data; and to Professor David Denison, Dr Paloma Núñez Pertejo, and Nicholas Smith, who helpfully shared the results of their investigations with me.

I am pleased to acknowledge financial support from the Department of English at Uppsala University, Erik Tengstrands stiftelse, Svenska institutet, and Helge Ax:son Johnsons stiftelse. I would also like to express my gratitude to the

Faculty of Languages at Uppsala University for funding my research for four years, and to Örebro University for supplying me with a part-time research grant that gave me time to revise the thesis manuscript.

I am grateful to the series editors for including this study in the Language and Computers series, and to Eric van Broekhuizen at Rodopi for his much appreciated help regarding the preparation of camera-ready files; I am also indebted to David Minugh in this regard.

Finally, special thanks are due to my family and friends for their much appreciated support and involvement over the years. I am also grateful to them for occasionally reminding me that, since the idea that something is in progress will always imply incompletion anyway, this may be as good a time as any for a break.

Uppsala, 9 May, 2004
Erik Smitterberg

Chapter 1

Introduction

1.1 General background

The present work is a corpus-based study of the use and development of the progressive, e.g. *are playing* in *They are playing tennis*, in the 19th-century English of England (henceforth "English English"). The period 1800–1900 is of importance for the history of the English language in several ways. Tendencies and changes visible in previous centuries continued into the 1700s and 1800s, regarding for instance the gradual settling of the preterite and past participle forms (see e.g. Gustafsson 2002), the development of the BE *going to* + infinitive future expression (see e.g. Danchev and Kytö 1998), the BE/HAVE variation with intransitives (see e.g. Rydén and Brorström 1987; Kytö 1997), and, as is topical to the present study, the development of the progressive (see e.g. Mossé 1938). In addition, the 19th century was of crucial importance for the formation of many text categories that were to become prominent in Present-Day English, such as academic language and newspaper language.

Despite these promising research areas, the English language of the 19th century has received surprisingly little scholarly attention. Rydén (1979: 34) claims that one reason why the syntax of late Modern English has been neglected compared with that of early Modern English is the view that the former does not deviate conspicuously from Present-Day English syntax. In recent years, however, with the publication of such works as Bailey (1996), Romaine (1998), and Görlach (1999), interest in 19th-century English has increased. A further indication of this increase in interest was the *International Conference on the English Language in the Late Modern Period 1700–1900*, held at the University of Edinburgh in August–September, 2001. The development of diachronic corpora such as ARCHER (= A Representative Corpus of Historical English Registers), which spans the period 1650–1990, and CONCE (= A Corpus of Nineteenth-Century English), which focuses on the 1800s (see Chapter 2 for a description of the CONCE corpus), has also been important in this context.

The same state of affairs, by and large, holds for research on the progressive. Monographs devoted to the development of the progressive typically focus on periods that precede late Modern English (e.g. Nickel 1966; Erdmann 1871), though Present-Day English is sometimes also included in the discussion (e.g. Scheffer 1975). The period 1700–1900 is usually addressed in detail only in discussions of particular issues, such as the emergence of the passive progressive of the type *The house is being built* (which largely replaced the older type *The house is building*), and of the progressive of the verb BE.[1] Scheffer (1975: 250) even claims that there are no essential differences between the use of the 16th-century progressive and that of the present-day construction.

Moreover, despite the scholarly interest in the English progressive, there is still no study that deals with its development across the entire 19th century from an explicit cross-genre perspective.[2] Visser's (1973) and Denison's (1993; 1998) extensive and valuable surveys do not provide us with systematically quantified data from different genres; Arnaud (1973) includes several genres in his investigation, but does not focus on quantitative research in his analyses; and while the material used in Arnaud (1983; 1998; 2002) covers most of the 19th century, it only comprises private correspondence. In general, studies of the progressive tend to focus wholly or partly on genres where the construction is assumed to be relatively frequent, for instance personal letters, plays, and fiction. There are at least two reasons for doing so. First, when dealing with a low-frequency feature like the progressive, the researcher must choose the material for his/her study with the necessity of obtaining sufficient data in mind. Secondly, the progressive has been on the increase for over 500 years (see e.g. Aitchison 1991: 99f.), and as it has been hypothesized that this change first took place in informal language (see e.g. Dennis 1940), it makes sense to draw on colloquial and/or speech-related genres for data.

However, there are also good reasons for examining genres where the progressive is not expected to be frequent. It may be of interest to see with what other linguistic features the progressive tends to co-occur, and not to co-occur, in texts. Such comparative analyses are easier to carry out if a wide variety of genres are examined (see, for instance, Biber 1988 for a cross-genre analysis of the co-occurrence patterns of a large number of linguistic features). The inclusion of several genres in analyses also makes it easier for researchers to extrapolate from written to spoken language (see Rissanen 1986: 98). If genres from different parts of the written spectrum, from formal texts written to be read (e.g. academic prose) to informal speech-related texts (e.g. drama comedies), are included in the corpus, it becomes possible to study in detail how the use of the progressive varies with formality and medium.

---

1   Grammars from the 19th and early 20th centuries, e.g. Poutsma (1926), constitute another source of information on the late Modern English progressive.

2   Following practice established in e.g. Biber (1988), I will use the term "genre" throughout this study to refer to text categories established on extralinguistic grounds.

We also need more research on how the parameters of time and genre in combination affected the use of the progressive during the course of the 19th century. Studies carried out on the LOB, FLOB, Brown, and Frown corpora (e.g. Hundt and Mair 1999) have shown that sampling intervals of 30 years may be enough to detect linguistic change across genres and in diachrony; a similar investigation into 19th-century English could lead to interesting results. Arnaud's (1998) findings indicate that it may even be feasible to investigate the development of the progressive between adjacent decades, provided that the researcher has access to a sufficiently large and varied corpus.

1.2 Aim and scope

The main aim of the present study is to account for the use and development of the progressive in English English during the 19th century, using data from a wide spectrum of written genres, speech-related and non-speech-related. This main aim subsumes a number of secondary aims:

1. To discuss some relevant methodological issues, such as how the progressive should be defined and its frequency measured, and how quantitative, corpus-based methods can be used in order to supplement qualitative methodology.

2. To correlate the use of the progressive with the extralinguistic features of time, genre, and the sex of the language user. It is known that the frequency of the progressive varies with these features (see e.g. Arnaud 1998; Smitterberg 2000a), but the present study is expected to shed more light on how various combinations of extralinguistic features affect the incidence of the construction.

3. To analyse the make-up of progressive verb phrases in detail (insofar as this is possible given the low frequency of some types of progressives). The occurrence of modal, perfect, and passive auxiliaries in progressive verb phrases will be investigated; the study also includes an analysis of which main verbs are commonly used in the progressive.

4. To investigate what kinds of linguistic features co-occur with the construction, and how these features affect language users' interpretation of a given progressive. Special attention will be paid to progressives that express something beyond purely aspectual meaning (see e.g. Wright 1994; Rydén 1997; Hübler 1998). The investigations carried out within the scope of this secondary aim have in common a general pragmatic approach, in the sense that linguistic features in the near context will be used, alone and in combination, as a tool regarding the functional classification of progressives. In addition, close readings of individual instances will, where necessary, be used as a complementary method.

In trying to fulfil the main aim of this study, I will thus draw on several analytical frameworks (see Section 1.5). The results will shed more light on what I will refer to as an integration process, by which the progressive became an increasingly more important part of late Modern English grammar. This concept of an integration process combines, among other things, grammaticalization theory, the development of obligatory functions of the progressive, the increase in the frequency of the construction, and the diffusion of the progressive across linguistic and extralinguistic contexts. (See Section 3.2.1.2 for a detailed discussion of the term "integration".)

Given that a corpus-based methodology will be applied throughout this study, there are also areas relevant to the progressive which fall outside the scope of the present work. To begin with, no effort will be made to present an account of the progressive within the frameworks of formal semantics (see e.g. Dowty 1977), although I will comment on such analyses where appropriate. Nor will analyses be dealt with where the progressive is investigated within the framework of generative theory. Within the corpus-based paradigm, correlations between socioeconomic group and language use will not be explicitly touched upon in this study. There are several reasons for this, the most important one being the scarcity of texts produced by members of the lower socioeconomic groups. The corpus used for the present study was not designed primarily for dealing with socioeconomic variation, and historical texts which display socioeconomic stratification are also difficult to obtain. In order to analyse the correlation between language and society as a whole, we need texts from at least one genre where members of all socioeconomic groupings produce texts, which in turn presupposes near-universal literacy or access to spoken texts; in addition, if both men's and women's language are included in the investigation, there must be representatives from both sexes. Moreover, even if such data were available, it would be necessary to postulate a scale of social classification with which the data could be correlated. This would present a further problem, as English society changed over the 19th century, with the spread of industrialism and the increasing political influence of the middle classes. Consequently, the status of a member of a given socioeconomic group in 1800 would not correspond exactly to that of a member of the same group in 1900.[3] For the above reasons, variation with socioeconomic factors in the use of the progressive will not be dealt with explicitly.

Social network theory is another research area where the social situation of the people who produced the texts investigated is important (see e.g. Milroy 1992). It has been hypothesized (Denison 1998: 153ff.; Pratt and Denison 2000) that the social network around Robert Southey and Samuel Taylor Coleridge was

---

3   To some extent, the same objection can be raised when diachronic differences across the genre parameter are researched: the place of a genre within the system of all English genres will change as genres develop and disappear through the history of the English language. However, unlike socioeconomic groupings, genres are defined by criteria external to the genres themselves to a large extent; for instance, a text defined as belonging to the genre of fiction will usually remain a fiction text regardless of changes in the overall distribution of genres. In contrast, the place of people with a given occupation on the socioeconomic continuum may well change owing to changes internal to the continuum.

important for the development of the passive progressive, as in *The house is being built*, which largely replaced the older type *The house is building* (see Section 5.3). However, as the corpus used for the present study was not compiled with social networks in mind, the influence of such networks on the development of the progressive will not be accounted for in any systematic way.

Lastly, varieties other than English English will not be investigated. It would doubtless be valuable to extend the scope of the present study to deal with, for instance, Scottish English, Irish English, and transplanted varieties as well. However, limitations of time and material made it necessary to focus on one variety, and English English was chosen for two main reasons. First, most previous research has been carried out on this variety, which means that the results of the present study will be more comparable to those of other studies than if another variety had been chosen. Secondly, the choice was also governed by the availability of CONCE, a multi-genre, periodized corpus of 19th-century English English (see Section 2.1 for a description).

1.3   Plan of the study

The present study is organized in the following way. The remainder of Chapter 1 first states what practices will be followed as regards terminology. Then, some important analytical frameworks that will be applied in subsequent chapters are discussed. Finally, I address the use of abbreviations, the presentation of linguistic forms and examples, and the performance and presentation of statistical tests for significance.

Chapter 2 is devoted to the selection of material and data. The first part of the chapter introduces the CONCE corpus, which was used for the present work. The sampling set-up, periodization, and genre division of the corpus are discussed, and word counts for period, genre, and period/genre subsamples as well as for the whole corpus are given. The description of the corpus is followed by an account of how the data for the present study were collected. Special attention is paid to the definition of the progressive, the computerized retrieval process, the selection of relevant examples, and to various ways of classifying doubtful cases. The discussion concludes with an account of how many progressives were found in the CONCE corpus.

In Chapter 3, I first discuss four methods of measuring the frequency of the progressive, and state how these methods relate to variationist studies. Two frequency coefficients are selected for application to the data. Those two coefficients are then used to analyse the occurrence and development of the progressive in relation to the extralinguistic variables of time, genre, and sex. In this chapter, the occurrence of the progressive is analysed both from a variationist perspective (i.e. as part of a progressive/non-progressive paradigm) and as a linguistic feature in itself. I also discuss the concept of integration, and state how it will be applied throughout the rest of the study.

Chapter 4 compares some of the results obtained in Chapter 3 with the results of Geisler's (2000; 2001; 2002; 2003) factor score analyses. This comparison makes it possible to see which other linguistic features the progressive co-occurs with in the corpus, and to interpret these co-occurrences in terms of the functions of the construction.

In Chapters 5 through 7, I analyse variation in the use of the progressive with a number of linguistic features. The extralinguistic variables of time and genre are used as independent variables when the features in question are discussed. Chapter 5 deals with linguistic variation within the verb phrase. The features under scrutiny are tense, voice, and the presence of perfect and/or modal auxiliaries. In addition, a rare type of progressive verb phrase, the *being* + present participle construction, is dealt with.

Chapter 6 is devoted to an analysis of the progressives in the corpus in relation to five linguistic parameters which have been claimed to affect the distribution of the progressive in previous research. First, the distribution of main verbs in progressive verb phrases is investigated. I then consider the occurrence of the progressive in different situation types (based on binary values such as [±stative] and [±durative]) and in agentive vs. non-agentive contexts. Finally, I discuss the modification of the progressive by temporal adverbials and the occurrence of the progressive in main clauses and in different types of subordinate clauses.

In Chapter 7, the not-solely-aspectual functions of the progressive receive special attention (see Section 1.4 for a discussion of the term "not solely aspectual"). Three separate analyses of not-solely-aspectual progressives are carried out. The first involves the modification of the progressive by adverbials such as *always*. The second analysis focuses on the co-occurrence of the progressive with combinations of four linguistic features which may together prompt a not-solely-aspectual interpretation of a given progressive. The last analysis deals with the so-called interpretative progressive (see e.g. Ljung 1980).

The last chapter of the study provides a summary and a concluding discussion. An introductory discussion ties together the results presented, thus providing a unified account of the integration of the progressive into 19th-century English English. This discussion is followed by a statement of how the secondary aims of the present work have been addressed, and a presentation of some suggestions for further research.

1.4   Terminology

Most abbreviations, such as names of corpora, will be explained in full the first time they are used (some very common abbreviations, such as LOB, will not be explained). The same practice will be followed concerning terminology, i.e. linguistic terms whose meaning is not self-evident will be explained the first time they appear in the text. An exception to this practice is the discussion of how to define the progressive: since the progressive is the construction under scrutiny in the present study, this definition is discussed in detail in Section 2.2.

As verb phrases such as *are playing* in *They are playing tennis* are of special importance to this study, my choice of the term "the progressive" for this construction will be justified in the present section. A number of terms have been suggested for this verbal construction, among them "definite tense", "continuous form", "continuous tense", "BE + *ing* construction", "expanded form", and "periphrastic form" (for a detailed list see Visser 1973: 1920f.). I chose the label "progressive" for the main reason that it appears to be the commonest term for the construction in recent research (see e.g. Denison 1993, Wright 1994, Mair and Hundt 1995, Rydén 1997, Arnaud 1998, Denison 1998, Hundt and Mair 1999). My choice does thus not involve a commitment as regards the semantics of the progressive. I will therefore use the label "progressive" for the entire history of English, even though the expression of action in progress may not have been the most frequent reason for the use of the construction in Old and Middle English (see also Denison 1993: 371).

Two important terms that concern the functions of the progressive will also be explained here. Broadly speaking, I will discuss the functional distribution of the progressive in terms of "aspectual" and "not-solely-aspectual" functions. Progressives with aspectual functions will be taken to express imperfective aspect, in Comrie's (1976: 24) sense that imperfective aspect refers explicitly "to the internal temporal structure of a situation, viewing a situation from within". However, there are shades of imperfectivity that are not usually covered by the progressive; most importantly, there are restrictions on the occurrence of the progressive in stative and habitual situations. Nevertheless, in previous research, the English progressive has been referred to both as a marker of progressive aspect (see e.g. Comrie 1976: 25) and as a restricted marker of imperfective aspect (see Goossens 1994: 164ff.), and there are signs that the progressive is becoming less restricted concerning at least its occurrence in stative situations (see for instance Section 6.2 of the present study). I will therefore use the wider term "imperfective" to refer to the type of aspect covered by the progressive, although it should be borne in mind that the construction is not used for the entire imperfective spectrum.

As for the term "not solely aspectual", this term will be used for progressives that express something beyond purely aspectual meaning. For instance, the progressive has been claimed to express subjectivity, emotional involvement, and emphasis compared with the non-progressive (see e.g. Rydén 1997). However, it is doubtful whether any occurrence of the progressive, at least in Present-Day English, is wholly devoid of aspectual meaning, as an element of simultaneity, ongoing process, or temporariness will often be present even in examples where the main reason for using the progressive is non-aspectual. For this reason, I will use the more neutral term "not solely aspectual" rather than "non-aspectual" in the present study. However, by choosing the term "not solely aspectual" I do not commit myself to the position that aspectual functions of the progressive are semantically or diachronically prior to not-solely-aspectual functions.

Names for periods of the history of English will be used as follows: Old English refers to the period 700–1100, Middle English to the period 1100–1500, and Modern English to the period 1500–1960. When necessary, these periods will also be divided into "early" and "late" subperiods, so that early Modern English, for instance, covers the period 1500–1700. The term Present-Day English refers to the period from 1961, the year in which the texts that make up the Brown and LOB corpora were published, on. Where relevant, these terms will be supplemented with more exact references, such as "early 20th-century English".

1.5   Analytical frameworks

In the present section, some general methodological issues that are relevant to a study of the 19th-century progressive will be addressed briefly; detailed discussion of these issues as they relate to the concerns of the present study will be postponed to Chapters 3 through 7. I will first discuss to what extent the methodological frameworks of corpus linguistics and the variationist approach are applicable to research on the progressive. A subsection will then be devoted to multi-feature/multi-dimensional approaches, more specifically to the analyses that have been carried out in e.g. Biber (1988), Biber and Finegan (1997), and Geisler (2002; 2003).

1.5.1   Corpus linguistics and the variationist approach

In corpus-based studies of the progressive, instances of the construction are usually collected and then classified according to a number of linguistic parameters (e.g. tense), and extralinguistic parameters (e.g. genre). The main reason for using a corpus that consists of different genres is the expectation that language use may vary with the extralinguistic characteristics that define the genres and thus stratify the material. Similarly, it is expected that the use of the progressive may vary with the linguistic features investigated, such as tense, modification by temporal adverbials, and clause type. This approach is in line with the principle of ordered heterogeneity, as outlined in Weinreich, Labov, and Herzog (1968). For historical linguistics, this type of research presupposes the adoption of the so-called uniformitarian principle, which postulates that language was subject to the same kinds of factors in the past as today (see e.g. Romaine 1982: 122).

As Weinreich, Labov, and Herzog (1968: 188) state, however, "[n]ot all variability and heterogeneity in language structure involves change; but all change involves variability and heterogeneity". To be able to make credible hypotheses about what, if any, variation in the use of the progressive involves change, the dimension of time is added to the corpus set-up. This addition makes it possible to study the use of the progressive in diachrony, and to see how linguistic and extralinguistic features affect the occurrence of the construction over time. However, a statement concerning the frequency of the progressive in a text is dependent on both the researcher's definition of the progressive (see Section 2.2) and on his/her way of calculating the incidence of the progressive (see Section 3.1).

Within the field of diachronic syntax, many corpus-based studies make use of the so-called variationist approach. Research within this framework can be described as attempts "to describe and discuss development in terms of changing variant fields"; a variant field comprises "the pattern formed by the variants expressing one and the same meaning or relationship, and it should be defined not only by enumerating the variants and giving information on their proportion of occurrence, but also by discussing the factors, both internal and external, which affect the choice of the variant" (Rissanen 1986: 97). As syntactic change frequently consists of changes in the relative distribution of such variants within variant fields, a quantitative methodology is well suited to describing these changes. In many cases, it is possible to use the quantitative results of a study as input for statistical analyses in order to determine, for instance, what differences are statistically significant and what factors have the greatest effect on the distribution of variants.

Studies of the progressive typically incorporate many elements of the variationist approach: corpora are often used, and linguistic as well as extralinguistic factors are considered.[4] However, there is a difference between most studies of the progressive and variationist studies which has to do with the definition of a syntactic variant. As Rissanen (1986: 98) points out, "[t]he change of the variant in identical environments should not change the referential or descriptive meaning of the expression, and this requirement is much more problematic when dealing with syntactic than with phonological variables". The most obvious variant field for a study of the 19th-century progressive is that comprising the progressive/non-progressive paradigm.[5] However, the criterion that the referential meaning of a given sentence should not change when the variants are substituted for one another becomes problematic when variation between the progressive and the non-progressive is investigated. The not-solely-aspectual functions of the progressive may perhaps be said not to change the truth-conditional meaning of the non-progressive (see Wright 1994: 472); but claiming sameness of meaning for the non-progressive and progressives with aspectual functions is problematic, as different aspectual values will lead to different truth conditions. Romaine (1984) criticizes the wholesale adoption of

---

4   There are of course also studies of the progressive that are not corpus-based, or that use examples from natural languages which have not been taken from a corpus defined as a "systematic collection of speech or writing in a language or variety of a language" (Matthews 1997: 78).

5   Depending on the period in focus, there are other candidates as well. For instance, many researchers claim that the most common function of the Old English progressive was to add emphasis, intensity, and/or vividness to the verbal action (see e.g. Nehls 1988: 180; Rydén 1997: 422). In this period, it is possible that the progressive was rather an alternative to a combination of the non-progressive and other means of expressing these not-solely-aspectual functions.

the concept of the variable from the field of phonology to that of syntax, as non-phonological variables "may have social and stylistic significance (or what we may call 'stylistic' meaning) in a given case, but they always have cognitive meaning by definition" (Romaine 1984: 411). (See also Raumolin-Brunberg 1988: 140f. for further discussion of this issue.)

Another, related problem concerns the issue of how to exclude cases where there is no choice between the variants that make up the variant field under scrutiny. So-called knock-out factors, i.e. factors that make it impossible or near-impossible to use one of the variants, should be taken into consideration, so that only data from those areas of use where there is actual competition between the variants of a variant field are included in the counts. Decisions of this kind may be difficult to make even when the variant field only contains two variants, e.g. the progressive and the non-progressive. When a diachronic dimension is added, defining the variant field and selecting knock-out factors become even more problematic.

An alternative to studying the progressive from a variationist perspective is to consider the construction as a linguistic feature in itself. Within this framework, the researcher studies the progressive and factors that appear to influence its occurrence, but does not take into account the use of the non-progressive. On the one hand, this approach is methodologically safer than the variationist approach, insofar as no assumptions about substitutability and equivalence of referential meaning have to be made prior to the investigation. On the other hand, the researcher will not be able to certify either (a) that a change in the frequency of the progressive is mirrored by an opposite frequency development of the non-progressive, i.e. that a change in the frequency of one variant affects the relative distribution of variants, or (b) whether factors that influence the use of the progressive also influence the use of the non-progressive.

The decision whether to treat the progressive as a variant of a variant field or as a linguistic feature in itself has consequences for how the frequency of the progressive in texts should be calculated. If the progressive is regarded as part of a variant field, the frequency of the progressive should be related to that of the non-progressive. This would enable the researcher to test variation in the progressive/non-progressive distribution for statistical significance. However, there is a risk that the variant field constructed is not wholly valid for reasons stated above, and this may make the results less valuable.[6] In contrast, if the progressive is considered as a linguistic feature in itself, it is more logical to normalize its raw frequency to a given unit, typically a specific number of words, in order to make frequencies independent of text length. However, by failing to take into account the fact that the progressive is always a verb phrase, this method is less suitable for testing variation for statistical significance. (See Section 3.1 for further discussion of this issue.)

---

6   Another, more practical problem with this method is that all instances of verb phrases, not only progressives, have to be included in the counts.

In the present study, the progressive will be considered both in isolation and in a paradigmatic relation with the non-progressive, as regards frequency counts and their relation to the extralinguistic variables of time, genre, and sex. Owing to limitations of time, however, linguistic factors have only been coded for progressives, not for non-progressives. Nevertheless, it is to be hoped that this double perspective will make it possible to combine advantages of both approaches and thus obtain more reliable results.

1.5.2   Multi-feature/multi-dimensional approaches

In Biber (1988), the co-occurrence patterns of a large number of linguistic features were analysed.[7] The study included 67 linguistic features, which "have been associated with particular communicative functions and therefore might be used to differing extents in different types of texts" (Biber 1988: 72).[8] The progressive was not included as a feature in this analysis; as will be discussed below, however, in a later factor analysis, Biber (2003), the progressive was included. The incidence of the features included was counted in texts that had been chosen with the aim of representing "the range of communicative situations and purposes available" in Present-Day English in mind (Biber 1988: 65).[9] The normalized frequencies of these features were used as input to a factor analysis which turned "a large number of original variables, in this case the frequencies of linguistic features", into "a small set of derived variables, the 'factors' " (Biber 1988: 79) based on the co-occurrence patterns of the linguistic features.[10] Features that tended to co-occur, or not to co-occur, in texts loaded on the same factor in the analysis (Biber 1988: 79ff.).

The next step was to interpret the factors identified in the analysis. The theory behind the interpretation process is that linguistic features that co-occur in texts will have partly shared functions (Biber 1988: 91). Features with high (positive or negative) loadings on the factor are given more weight when the nature of the factor is interpreted, as they "are better representatives of the dimension underlying the factor" (Biber 1988: 81). In the end, six factors were considered to have sufficiently strong structures, so that their underlying functional dimensions could be interpreted with some certainty (Biber

---

7   Note that the description of the multi-feature/multi-dimensional approach given in this section is not intended to be exhaustive, or to explain the mathematical principles that underlie the analyses. I will focus only on the elements of the approach that are relevant to the present study.

8   One feature, that of split infinitives, was later dropped from the analysis owing to its low incidence in the texts examined (Biber 1988: 85n.).

9   The two corpora used in Biber's study were the LOB corpus and the London–Lund Corpus of Spoken English. In addition, a collection of professional and personal letters was included in the material (Biber 1988: 66).

10   The features of type/token ratio and word length were not normalized (Biber 1988: 75).

1988: 115). The interpretation was based on the functions of the features that loaded on the factors. The six dimensions were given the functional labels "Involved vs. informational production" (Dimension 1), "Narrative vs. non-narrative concerns" (Dimension 2), "Elaborated vs. situation-dependent reference" (Dimension 3), "Overt expression of persuasion" (Dimension 4), "Abstract vs. non-abstract information" (Dimension 5), and "On-line informational elaboration" (Dimension 6) (Biber 1988: 122; Biber and Finegan 1997: 258).[11] Features with positive and negative loadings load on opposite sides of the dimension: on Dimension 1, for example, a feature with a positive loading indicates involved production, while a feature with a negative loading is an indicator of informational production.

Of the six dimensions listed above, Dimensions 1, 3, and 5 are of special relevance to research on the progressive. These three dimensions distinguish "stereotypically oral (conversational)" from "stereotypically literate (written expository)" genres (Biber and Finegan 1997: 260): oral genres tend to be associated with involved production on Dimension 1, situation-dependent reference on Dimension 3, and/or non-abstract information on Dimension 5, whereas the opposite holds true for literate genres. Similarly, the progressive has been hypothesized to be common in genres which incorporate spoken, colloquial features, such as plays and personal letters (see e.g. Dennis 1940). The possibility of a connection between the progressive and Dimensions 1, 3, and 5 is further strengthened by the new factor analysis presented in Biber (2003), based on Present-Day spoken and written academic English, where the progressive loads as an oral feature on the dimension "Oral vs. literate discourse". This dimension is partly made up of linguistic features that loaded on Dimensions 1, 3, and 5 in Biber (1988). In addition, Dimension 2 is worth attention, as this dimension has been claimed to separate specialist and popular written genres (Biber and Finegan 1997: 271). Against this background, it can be hypothesized that the progressive will co-occur in texts with features that indicate involved production, narrative concerns, and situation-dependent reference, and that the construction will not co-occur with features indicative of informational production, elaborated reference, and abstract information.[12] Since Biber's dimensions are interpreted in functional terms, a comparison between (a) the frequency of the progressive, and (b) dimension scores for Dimensions 1, 2, 3, and 5 of the factor analysis, may shed new light on the functional load of the progressive. It makes sense to assume that the progressive shares some functions with the linguistic features with which it co-varies in texts.

The factor analysis in Biber (1988) focuses on Present-Day English, but since then factor score analyses have also been carried out on diachronic corpora,

---

11   There is some variation between studies concerning the labels. In the present study, I will use the labels given in Biber (1988), with the exception that, following Biber and Finegan (1997), "elaborated reference" rather than "explicit reference" will be used for Dimension 3.

12   There are no negative features on Dimension 2 and Dimension 5, i.e. features indicating non-narrative concerns and non-abstract information (Biber 1988: 102f.).

for instance the ARCHER corpus in Biber and Finegan (1997), and recently the CONCE corpus in e.g. Geisler (2002; 2003).[13] These studies show that the dimensions identified in Biber (1988) are also applicable to earlier stages in the history of English, such as the 19th century. Moreover, the results presented in these studies demonstrate that it is possible to study the development of genres on the dimensions even if the periodization of the corpora used is quite narrow. As was shown in Hundt and Mair (1999) and Smitterberg (2000a), and as will be further demonstrated in Chapter 3 of the present study, the same holds true for the frequency development of the progressive in late Modern and Present-Day English.

In Chapter 4, I will use results from Geisler's (2002; 2003) factor score analyses of CONCE to see what correlations can be attested between the frequency of the progressive and dimension scores on Dimensions 1, 2, 3, and 5. Dimension scores and normalized frequencies of the progressive will be used to rank genre and period/genre subsamples relative to one another. Similarities in rankings will be taken as evidence of co-variation among the linguistic features involved, and as indications of shared functional loads between the progressive and the linguistic features that load on the dimensions. By way of exemplification, if the same genre has both the highest frequency of progressives and the highest score on Dimension 1 ("Involved vs. informational production"), another genre has both the second highest frequency of progressives and the second highest score on Dimension 1, etc., it will be assumed that the progressive shares one or several functions with the linguistic features that were taken to indicate involved production in Biber's (1988) factor analysis. In addition to the functional interpretation, it is to be hoped that the findings will throw more light on how the functions of the progressive varied across the genre parameter in 19th-century English.

1.5.3   Applying the frameworks

In Sections 1.5.1–1.5.2, some elements of two important theoretical and methodological frameworks with a bearing on the present study have been presented. These frameworks will be applied in Chapters 3 through 7. The general framework of corpus linguistics is relevant to all of these chapters. The concept of variation between the progressive and the non-progressive will be particularly useful in Chapter 3. In Chapter 4, insights gained from Geisler (2000; 2001;

---

13   In the present study, the terms "factor analysis" and "factor score analysis" are used with different meanings. The former refers to an analysis where the factors themselves are defined on the basis of co-occurrence patterns among linguistic features. The latter term covers analyses where factor scores are computed for factors whose make-up, in terms of which linguistic features load on each factor, has been defined in a previous factor analysis. Where relevant, I will use the term "multi-feature/multi-dimensional" to cover both types of analyses.

2002; 2003) will be used to link information on the frequency of the progressive to hypotheses concerning the functions of the construction.

Where relevant, I will also incorporate elements from other analytical frameworks in the following chapters. For instance, the results of the present study will show that the genre parameter is an important conditioning factor regarding the use of the progressive. Part of this importance is due to differences between genres in terms of, for instance, production circumstances and the relationship between addresser and addressee. In connecting the results to such characteristics of individual genres, I will draw on historical pragmatic methodology (see e.g. Jacobs and Jucker 1993 for an introduction to historical pragmatics). When discussing some aspects of the development of the progressive, such as the increase in the frequency of the construction (see Chapter 3) and the emergence of the passive progressive (see Section 5.3), I will also have occasion to refer to grammaticalization theory (see e.g. Hopper and Traugott 1993). Historical pragmatics and grammaticalization theory are both relevant to my discussion of some subjective, not-solely-aspectual functions of the progressive in Chapter 7, as it has been proposed that the grammaticalization of a linguistic form leads to the occurrence of more speaker-centred functions of the form (see e.g. Traugott 1995).

1.6   Typographical and statistical conventions

1.6.1   Typography

In the present study, italics, underlining, small capitals, capitals, and single and double quotation marks have specific functions. Outside numbered examples, italics will be used to mark linguistic forms, e.g. *is working*, which are only intended to stand for the specific form quoted. However, spelling variants of the same word are considered to be variants of the same form, so that for example *is working* subsumes *is workin'* and *is workin*.

In numbered examples, italics will also be used to highlight progressives and potential progressives (see Section 2.2). Where relevant, underlining will be used in numbered examples to draw attention to linguistic features other than progressives, e.g. temporal adverbials that modify progressive verb phrases (for exemplification, see Section 1.6.2).

Small capitals will be used throughout to denote all the relevant linguistic forms of a superordinate linguistic form: BE *working*, for instance, will be taken to subsume forms such as *will be working*, *am working*, *has been workin'* etc. In abbreviations of proper nouns, small capitals will be used for abbreviations which are read out as words (e.g. CONCE /'kɒnsə/), whereas capitals will be used for abbreviations which are read out as initials (e.g. *OED* /'əʊ 'iː 'diː/).

Single quotation marks will be used around meanings of words or phrases; in addition, I will use single quotes around names of situation types in Chapter 6.

Double quotation marks, in contrast, will be used around quotations from secondary sources, and to draw attention to terms.

1.6.2   Corpus citations

Corpus citations will be given in the form they appear in CONCE. Codes for corpus citations in numbered examples are given within brackets immediately after each example, and take the following format: [Genre], [Author's surname], [first year of period]–[last year of period], [page number(s) in the edition cited]. By way of exemplification, consider the following citation from Charles Dickens's *David Copperfield*, with temporal clauses that modify the progressive underlined:

(1)   I *was taking* my coffee and roll <u>in the morning</u>, <u>before going to the Commons</u> – and I may observe in this place that it is surprising how much coffee Mrs. Crupp used, and how weak it was, considering – <u>when Steerforth himself walked in</u>, to my unbounded joy.
(Fiction, Dickens, 1850–1870, p. 251)

All texts in CONCE are listed, sorted by period, genre, and (where relevant) author's name, in Appendix 1.

When two or more authors with the same surname have been sampled in the same period/genre subsample, first names will be used in references to keep the texts apart. Debates texts have no author, as the texts in this genre consist of recorded speeches made by several different politicians from the Houses of Parliament; moreover, given that there is only one Debates text per period, there is no need for further subdivision below the period/genre subsample level. There is no author for the texts in the Trials genre either, but here the defendant's name will be used instead to keep texts from the same period/genre subsample apart.

1.6.3   Statistical conventions

Where relevant, the chi-square test will be used in order to determine whether differences between samples of data are statistically significant. A significance level of 0.05 will be used throughout the study. The test will not be applied to contingency tables where the expected frequency of any cell(s) is < 5. Most of the tests carried out will be based on quantitative information presented in tabular format. In these cases, I will only state in the main text whether the distribution of data is significant or not. Detailed information on raw frequencies, chi-square and p values, and degrees of freedom for each calculation will instead be presented in Appendix 3; in this Appendix, the tests performed are sorted according to the table on which each test is based. In the few cases where the chi-square test is applied to data that are not based on a table, chi-square values and degrees of freedom are given within brackets in the main text, along with the statement of whether or not the difference is statistically significant.

A few words on the requirements of statistical tests are in order in this context. The chi-square test requires that observations (for instance, progressive and non-progressive verb phrases) be independent of one another, i.e. the observations should be "separate and not linked in any way" (Woods, Fletcher, and Hughes 1986: 148). However, in corpus-based investigations, it is seldom possible to meet this requirement. To begin with, if the test is applied to test differences between groups of texts, it is likely that the different texts will contain varying numbers of observations, in which case texts with a large number of observations will have an undue influence on the group totals. Moreover, from a statistical point of view, the distribution of observations within each text cannot be considered independent, as it is possible that an informant's performance with respect to a linguistic variable (e.g. the progressive/non-progressive paradigm) in, for example, a private letter is dependent on his/her performance with respect to the same variable in another letter written the same day – or further on in the same letter (cf. Woods et al. 1986: 147ff.). In addition, a few writers contribute to more than one genre in CONCE, which may reduce the independence of distributions that are compared across the genre parameter. Although the chi-square will be used to test differences between samples despite these caveats, limitations such as these should be taken into account when the results of the tests are interpreted.

Furthermore, if the same samples are used to analyse the distribution of two different linguistic variables, the two variables are unlikely to be wholly independent (Woods et al. 1986: 149f.). By way of exemplification, there is likely to be some relation between the distribution of progressives and non-progressives (variable 1) in a given sample and the distribution of tenses and auxiliaries within the progressive paradigm (variable 2) in the same sample. Thus, if variation in the distribution of several variables is tested for significance using the same material, the samples (e.g. genre and period subsamples of CONCE) may "appear either more or less alike than they really are, depending on the relationship between the different variables" (Woods et al. 1986: 150).

A more general limitation on the use of statistical techniques to test variation between samples of data is the requirement that the sampling techniques should be random. In practice, this requirement can rarely be fulfilled, as limitations of time and financial resources often make it impossible to collect corpora based wholly on random sampling techniques. However, in this case the data can usually be treated as if randomly sampled, and the researcher then investigates the data further if an important result is obtained (Woods et al. 1986: 55). However, this way to proceed makes it important that the material on which the study is based be described in detail (Woods et al. 1986: 56). Part of the next chapter of the present work is thus devoted to a description of the CONCE corpus.

Chapter 2

Material and data

2.1   Material

The present study is based on data taken from a working version of the Corpus of Nineteenth-Century English (CONCE), compiled by Merja Kytö (Uppsala University) and Juhani Rudanko (University of Tampere).[1] CONCE is divided into three periods (1800–1830, 1850–1870, and 1870–1900), and seven genres (Debates, Drama, Fiction, History, Letters, Science, and Trials); the corpus comprises approximately 1 million words (for word counts, see Section 2.1.3 and Appendix 1). The corpus will be presented in some detail in this section, by way of background information. I will discuss the periodization, genre division, and sampling setup of CONCE, and comment on the relevance of the characteristics of the corpus to a study of the progressive. In this presentation, I will draw freely on the discussion in Kytö, Rudanko, and Smitterberg (2000).

The original aim of the CONCE project was to provide 19th-century English English follow-up material to the Diachronic Part of the Helsinki Corpus of English Texts (henceforth "the Helsinki Corpus"; see Kytö 1996, and Rissanen, Kytö, and Palander-Collin 1993), and thus make it possible to follow up research on early Modern English.[2] But CONCE was also designed to make it possible to compare the English English of the 19th century with other varieties, with Present-Day English, or with other corpora covering the 19th century, such as the ARCHER corpus and the Corpus of Late Modern English Prose.

---

1   In some analyses in Chapter 5, I will also use data taken from the corpus on which Arnaud (2002) based his study. I am indebted to Professor René Arnaud for giving me access to his data.

2   In order to reduce the influence of dialects other than English English on the distribution of linguistic features, an effort was made only to sample texts produced in England; texts containing a good deal of dialectal variation were also avoided. However, occasional dialectal features do occur in CONCE.

2.1.1   Periodization

The texts in CONCE are stratified into three periods: period 1 comprises texts produced between 1800 and 1830, period 2 texts produced between 1850 and 1870, and period 3 texts produced between 1870 and 1900.[3] The periodization makes it possible to study developments within the 19th century in a detailed manner; CONCE is thus in line with the recent interest in research on short-term diachronic change, exemplified by studies based on the LOB, Brown, FLOB, and Frown corpora (see e.g. Hundt and Mair 1999).[4] This possibility is of special relevance to studies of a feature such as the progressive, whose frequency has been shown to increase substantially over the 19th century (see Arnaud 1998).

As explained in Kytö et al. (2000), the periodization of CONCE was influenced to some extent by the availability of suitable texts within the financial resources available. Four main criteria, some of which were not applicable to all genres, were used to assess the suitability of candidates for inclusion in the corpus:

1.   Efforts were made to use the earliest possible editions of texts such as collections of letters, novels, plays, and trial proceedings.

2.   Debates and Trials texts were scrutinized to make sure that the dialogue format had been preserved when notes had been taken down. In addition, the title pages of trial proceedings were checked: phrases such as "verbatim report" and "complete report" were also considered indications of authenticity, although the truth of such statements is difficult to verify.

3.   In order to make it possible to correlate language and sex, where possible, the inclusion of women's voices was given priority, either as producers of texts (novels, collections of letters) or as speakers in texts (trial proceedings, novels, plays).

4.   The length of the texts was estimated before the texts were keyed in, so that, when possible, only texts that contained a sufficient number of words to fit the sampling frames were included.

---

3   The term "produced" has a slightly different meaning depending on which genre it is applied to. For Debates and Letters, the term refers to the actual production of the debates and the letters themselves. For the other genres, production should be taken to equal publication. (However, Trials texts were generally published shortly after the trials had taken place in order to maximize sales, so the difference between production and publication date is small for this genre.)

4   There are differences between the periodization principles used for the CONCE corpus and those used for the LOB, FLOB, Brown, and Frown corpora. Whereas the texts that constitute the four latter corpora were published within a single year, the texts that make up CONCE were produced within intervals of 20 or 30 years. Comparisons across periods will thus be less exact for CONCE, as texts need not be evenly distributed within each period. However, such approximations may be a useful middle ground for researchers who wish both to use suitable texts and to compare results from successive periods in the history of English.

For some genres, it proved difficult to obtain texts that met all of the above criteria for the entire 19th century, which influenced the delimitation of the periods.

The division of the CONCE corpus into periods also reflects a number of 19th-century historical events and developments of importance, an overview of which is given in Table 1.

Table 1. Some important 19th-century sociocultural events and developments (taken from Harvie 1992, Matthew 1992, and Görlach 1999)

Year	Event(s)
1825	Trade unions legalized
1832	The First Reform Bill
1833	The first important Factory Act restricting child labour; beginning of Oxford movement
1834	Slavery abolished; the Poor Law Amendment Act
1835–6	"Little" railway mania
1840	The penny post instituted
1844–5	Railway mania
1846	Corn Law abolished
1851	The Great Exhibition
1855	The final repeal of the Stamp Act of 1712
1867	The Second Reform Bill
1870	The Elementary Education Act; Married Women's Property Act extends the rights of women in marriage
1884–5	The Third Reform Bill

If the contents of Table 1 are compared with the periodization of CONCE, it becomes clear that period 1 largely pre-dates the great reforms of the 19th century. According to Görlach (1999: 158f.), the prose of the period 1800–1830 also stands out linguistically from the rest of the century, as certain 18th-century conventions were still influential in the first three decades. Period 2 follows some societal changes, e.g. the First Reform Bill and the introduction of the penny post, and encompasses others, e.g. the Second Reform Bill. By comparison, period 3 is more stable: Görlach (1999: 6) refers to the period 1870–1914 as "[l]ate Victorian imperialism and the last phase of global 'stability' ". However, reforms concerning the franchise and elementary education take place in this period, and for instance the expansion of the railway system continues.

It can of course be questioned whether, and to what extent, extralinguistic events such as those listed in Table 1 affect a given distribution of linguistic features in a corpus. However, it is possible that the increasing availability of basic education, as well as cheap newspapers and postage, affected the make-up of the reading public to such an extent that producers of written texts adapted the language of written genres directed to the reading public at large, such as novels, to these developments (see Biber and Finegan 1992; 1997). Altick (1957: 171) presents figures which indicate that the percentage of female literates increased from 54.8% in 1851 to 96.8% in 1900; the corresponding figures for males are 69.3% and 97.2%, respectively. In addition, the extension of the franchise brought about by the Reform Bills may have affected the make-up of official and political language, as it grew important to gain votes from groups that had recently become politically influential.

2.1.2   Genre division

In order to facilitate research on a wide spectrum of 19th-century English, the CONCE corpus was compiled with a cross-genre perspective in mind. The seven genres in CONCE – Debates, Drama, Fiction, History, Letters, Science, and Trials – are described in Table 2.

Table 2.   Description of the genres in CONCE (based on Kytö et al. 2000)

Genre	Characteristics
Debates	Recorded debates from the Houses of Parliament
Drama	Prose comedies or farces
Fiction	Novels
History	Historical monographs
Letters	Private, personal letters between relatives or close friends
Science	Monographs pertaining to the natural or social sciences
Trials	Recorded trial proceedings (chiefly in dialogue format)

Cross-genre studies are based on the hypothesis that extralinguistic differences between genres may affect the distribution of linguistic features in texts. There are several extralinguistic parameters with respect to which the seven genres in CONCE have different values, among them the following:

- Medium. Fiction, History, Letters, and Science texts were for the most part written to be read. In contrast, Drama texts were written to be spoken, and Debates and Trials texts constitute speech taken down. (However, claiming that Debates and Trials constitute actual speech is problematic for several reasons – see below.)
- Relation to publication. Texts from Drama, Fiction, History, and Science were produced for publication. Debates and Trials texts, although not aimed primarily at publication, were produced with all speakers (in Debates) or some speakers (in Trials) being aware of possible/certain publication. The texts in the Letters genre, however, were not produced for publication. Note that the basis for this classification is the probable level of awareness of the people who produced the texts. For Debates, the Members of Parliament can be assumed to have been aware that their speeches would undergo an editorial process and then be published. This is less certain for the Trials genre, where publication depended on such factors as whether publishers thought that they would profit from publishing accounts of the trial

proceedings. In many cases, the people testifying at the trials cannot have been certain that the proceedings were going to be published, and some witnesses may not even have been aware that the possibility existed, particularly if they were illiterate. Finally, as regards Letters, some letter-writers were aware of the possibility that their letters would be published, but it can be hypothesized that the privacy of the production circumstances of this genre, compared with those of Debates and Trials, still justifies classifying Letters apart from these two genres as regards relation to publication.

- Narrativity. Texts from Fiction and Trials contain passages where narrative elements dominate. Science, in contrast, is a genre where expository elements dominate. In the rest of the genres (Debates, Drama, History, and Letters), a mixture of the two can be found.

All of the genres in CONCE are important to a study of the progressive, but for different reasons. Drama, Fiction, and Letters are genres where the progressive is usually assumed to be relatively frequent, and all of them have been selected for studies of the construction focusing on one single genre (see Arnaud 1998 for Letters, Strang 1982 for Fiction, and Wright 1994 for Drama). One of the reasons for this is that these genres can be expected to contain spoken, colloquial features, either because they partly consist of writing intended to represent speech or because their production circumstances are so informal that spoken features can be found in the texts. This is of particular interest to a study of the progressive, as the results of several previous studies suggest that the increase in the frequency of the construction took place first in colloquial language and was later transferred to other genres (see e.g. Dennis 1940: 858ff.).

Debates and Trials give the researcher access to texts that consist of recorded speech, although several factors make it difficult to claim that Debates and Trials texts constitute actual speech. To begin with, texts belonging to both genres were in all probability affected by the editorial process that texts went through prior to publication in the 19th century (see e.g. Bailey 1996: 187f.). (Parts of the texts in Debates are rendered as indirect rather than direct speech, which further increases editorial presence.) Moreover, even if the recordings were truly verbatim, the speech situations in which the texts were produced were quite different from those in which 19th-century people usually spoke to one another. The texts in Debates comprise political speeches from the Houses of Parliament that may have been partly prepared in advance; in addition, Görlach (1999: 149) claims that 19th-century speeches were, in some cases, much further from colloquial speech than they are in Present-Day English. Nor is the courtroom situation in which the Trials texts were produced likely to be conducive to the production of conversation-like speech. These drawbacks notwithstanding, the inclusion in CONCE of Debates and Trials should give us a more many-faceted picture of how people used the progressive in 19th-century speech than would be possible if only plays and novels had been included.

The History and Science genres, which both belong to the hyper-genre of academic language, are relevant to a study of the progressive in the 19th century for two main reasons. First, Görlach (1999: 150) claims that scientific style "changed from somewhat personal accounts to impersonal, objective description" in the 19th century; in addition, based on a factor score analysis of the ARCHER corpus, Biber and Finegan (1997: 273) found that specialist expository genres have become more literate, and less oral, since the 17th century. As the progressive can be hypothesized to be more common in personal accounts that incorporate oral features than in literate, impersonal, objective descriptions, this genre development may, wholly or partly, counteract the general tendency towards an increase in the frequency of the construction through Modern English. Secondly, History and Science comprise formal texts that were written to be read. These genres are therefore valuable as counterparts to informal and/or speech-related genres if the researcher wishes to give as full as possible an account of the use of the progressive. It has been shown that the frequency of the progressive varies greatly with the formality of written genres in both 19th- and 20th-century English (Hundt and Mair 1999: 233; Smitterberg 2000a: 285ff.).

2.1.3   Sampling setup and word count

There is some variation among the genres in CONCE concerning both how many texts were included in each period/genre subsample and what word counts were targeted for individual texts. The setup aimed at is given in Table 3.

Table 3.   The sampling setup per period aimed at for the genres in CONCE

Genre	Sampling setup per period
Debates	1 text of 20,000 words = 20,000 words
Drama	3 texts of 10,000 words each = 30,000 words
Fiction	3 texts of 10,000 words each = 30,000 words
History	3 texts of 10,000 words each = 30,000 words
Letters	10 texts of 10,000 words each =100,000 words
Science	3 texts of 10,000 words each = 30,000 words
Trials	3 texts of 20,000 words each = 60,000 words
Total	26 texts containing a total of 300,000 words

As Table 3 shows, varying numbers of words per text were sampled for the seven genres. In order to give some emphasis to the genres that contain recorded speech (Debates and Trials), 20,000 words per text were sampled for these genres. However, only one text per period was sampled for the Debates genre: since all debates from the Houses of Parliament were printed in the same series, idiolectal influence is constrained through the sampling of several speakers' output within the same text rather than through the sampling of several texts. To some extent the same holds for Trials, as each text contains several speakers' output in this genre also. However, some Trials texts contain relatively few speakers, as the number of possible speakers in a Trials text is limited to the number of participants in a given trial. Moreover, since speakers in Trials texts are likely to represent the diversity of English English better than speakers in Debates texts, and since the direct-speech, dialogue format is more noticeable in Trials than in Debates, the former genre can be argued to be more central than Debates as a speech-related genre. For these reasons, Trials were sampled more extensively than Debates for each period.

The Letters genre was sampled more extensively than the other genres, and constitutes roughly a third of the entire corpus. There are several ways in which this focus on Letters can be useful for scholars interested in the progressive. Private letters are written texts that often contain colloquial and/or speech-related features owing to their informal, familiar nature; they thus form a middle ground between prototypical speech and prototypical writing. According to Görlach (1999: 149), letters also "reflect the social and functional relations between sender and addressee to a very high degree". Moreover, in CONCE, the Letters genre has been stratified into texts produced by women and texts produced by men, so that each period sample should contain five texts by women and five by men letter-writers. This makes it possible to study variation in the use of the progressive from yet another extralinguistic angle, viz. the sex of the letter-writer. Arnaud's (1998: 139f.) results indicate that the gender parameter influences the occurrence of the progressive: in his corpus of 18th- and 19th-century private correspondence, women used the progressive more than men. However, for results of gender-based studies based on Letters to be reliable, idiolectal influence had to be kept under control in both subgroups of the genre (i.e. letters written by women and by men), which made it necessary to include additional texts from this genre in the corpus.

There are two deviations from the setup in Table 3. First, period 3 lacks one text by a woman letter-writer (owing to a misleading period code discovered over the course of the compilation work); this period/genre subsample thus contains nine texts, four by women and five by men letter-writers. Secondly, owing to the lack of access to suitable texts of sufficient length it proved necessary to use four texts instead of three to reach the total period/genre word count aimed at for period 2 of the Trials genre.

A more detailed system of text-level codes was applied to CONCE than was used for the Helsinki Corpus. The word counts for the Helsinki Corpus exclude text segments coded as "foreign language", "editor's comment" or "our comment" (Kytö 1996: 168). Most headings could also be excluded from the Helsinki Corpus word counts. In addition to the above, the text-level codes in CONCE make it possible for the researcher to exclude the following text segments from the word counts: stage directions in Drama; indications of speakers in Debates, Drama, and Trials; and sender, date, and addressee information in Letters.[5] For the present study, word counts were calculated using this more

---

5   Indications of speakers have not been coded as such for the parts of the Debates genre that consist of indirect speech, as such indications are then, syntactically, part of the text proper.

detailed system of text-level codes.[6] An overview of the text-level codes is given in Appendix 2.

Table 4 presents the word counts down to the level of period/genre subsamples. The table shows that the total word count for the version of CONCE used in this study is 986,814.[7] (For word counts of each text in the corpus, see Appendix 1.)

Table 4.   Word counts by period and genre in CONCE

Period	Debates	Drama	Fiction	History	Letters	Science	Trials	**Total**
1	19,908	31,311	42,032	30,904	121,624	38,037	62,360	346,176
2	19,385	29,543	39,045	30,504	131,116	31,679	60,570	341,842
3	19,947	29,090	30,113	30,564	90,891	30,603	67,588	298,796
Total	59,240	89,944	111,190	91,972	343,631	100,319	190,518	986,814

2.2   The data: Retrieving and identifying progressives

Collecting progressives in a machine-readable corpus with the aid of retrieval software involves a number of decisions on the part of the researcher. Some of these decisions concern the instructions given to the computer program(s) used in the retrieval process; others relate to the manual post-processing of the retrieved output. In this section, some possible approaches to these decisions will be discussed, and the principles that were applied in the present work will be stated. I will first define the progressive, and describe the retrieval procedure used for this study. The second subsection will be devoted to cases where doubt may arise as to whether a find is a progressive or not; I will also state how these cases were dealt with in the present work. In both of these subsections, the discussion will be confined to cases with a bearing on the English English of the 19th century. In the final subsection, I will present the result of the search process, in terms of how many progressives were identified in each period, genre, and period/genre subsample, as well as in the entire CONCE corpus.

---

6   The computer program Hcount, the same program that was used to obtain word counts for the texts in the Helsinki Corpus, was used to calculate word counts for the texts in CONCE when they had been transferred to electronic format. The input values of the program were updated to conform to the more elaborate system of text-level codes described above.

7   If the same method is applied to CONCE as was used for the Helsinki Corpus, the total word count is 1,030,409. However, note that at the time when the data for the present study were collected, CONCE was still in compilation: the collection of texts had been frozen, but the second round of proof-reading had yet to be carried out. All word counts should therefore be considered approximate relative to those of the finalized version of the corpus.

2.2.1 Defining the progressive and designing the retrieval process

For the purposes of the present study, the progressive in 19th-century English is defined as a verb phrase of two or more words which contains a form of BE and a present participle; in this context, the term "verb phrase" stands for 'a verb with any auxiliaries' (Matthews 1997: 396). A further constraint on the progressive, which will be discussed in Section 2.2.2.4, is that a progressive verb phrase cannot include a *to*-infinitive following the present participle. Given this definition, every potential progressive in the corpus will contain the verb BE and a word ending in *-ing*. This fact formed the basis for the retrieval procedure.

The WordSmith Tools computer program was used to search for potential progressives in each period/genre subsample; in addition, extensive back-up checking was carried out with the Corpus Presenter program. The search strings used for the retrieval of present participles were **ing*, **in*, and **in'*. (Parts of CONCE had previously been examined with the WordCruncher program to see whether spelling variants from previous stages of English could be found in the corpus texts; the results were negative.) The various forms of BE were used as context words. The search parameters were set so that a form of BE had to occur no more than six words to the left of the word ending in *-ing* for the program to retrieve the combination. This means that a small number of progressives, with more than five words between the form of BE and the participle, might have passed undetected. In addition, possible progressives where the form of BE follows the present participle (as in *Going, were you?*), or where either the form of BE or the participle is absent (as in *Going?*), were not retrieved. However, the status of many such constructions is doubtful: for instance, they often lack a clear non-progressive alternative.

An alternative to this procedure would have been to look for only one of the forms, i.e. either all forms of BE or all forms in *-ing*. This method would have had the advantage that neither the relative position of BE and *-ing* nor the distance between them would have affected retrieval. However, given the high frequency of forms of BE as well as words ending in *-ing* in late Modern English, such a retrieval procedure would have been extremely time-consuming, and was consequently not selected for the present study.

The next step in the retrieval procedure was to go through the concordances and exclude all instances that were not progressives from the counts. Most of these were easy to exclude: for instance, in (2), *be* is not a progressive auxiliary but a main verb, and *lodging* is not a present participle but a noun.

(2)   Home-cook *would be* a better name for this *lodging*!
        (Letters, Thackeray Ritchie, 1870–1900, p. 251)

However, there were also more difficult cases. Given the importance of decisions concerning such potential progressives for the quantitative results, I will devote the following section to a discussion of five classes of doubtful cases.

2.2.2   Post-processing the retrieval output: A discussion of doubtful cases

In 19th-century English, there are chiefly three types of constructions whose surface structures may be identical to that of the progressive. In these cases, it is not always clear from the overall semantics of the situation whether or not a progressive reading is intended. The three types, illustrated with constructed, non-progressive examples, are:

- Appositively used participles, as in *I was in the kitchen, washing dishes.*
- Predicative adjectival participles, as in *This book is fascinating.*
- Constructions with BE + gerund, as in *To do so is taking a prudent step.*

In addition, there are two types of potential progressives whose status as progressives is doubtful. These two types, illustrated with constructed examples, are:

- BE *going to* + infinitive constructions with future reference, as in *I am going to play tennis tomorrow.*
- Potential progressives which incorporate nominal elements. There are three main variants: the form in *-ing* may be preceded by a (usually reduced) preposition, as in *What have you been a-doing?*; the verb phrase may govern an *of*-phrase rather than a direct object, as in *What have you been doing of?*; and the two types may be combined, as in *What have you been a-doing of?.*[8]

I will devote one subsection to each of the five types. In these subsections, I will discuss various ways in which constructions that are not progressives can be excluded when doubtful cases are dealt with. Parts of this account rely heavily on Denison (1993: 371–380) and Visser (1973: 1929–1934). The constructions taken up will be illustrated with corpus examples throughout. A general principle when dealing with doubtful cases was to include in the counts only constructions that could be classified as progressives with certainty: cases that were still unclear after close scrutiny were not included in the data.

2.2.2.1   Appositively used participles

Doubts as to whether a present participle is part of a progressive or used appositively may arise when a form of BE occurs in the near context of the participle. Syntactically, such an appositive participle is "head of a [verb phrase] which does not contain BE", and is thus not part of a progressive verb phrase (Denison 1993: 372). However, there is some variation in the way such constructions are treated by linguists. Most researchers seem to agree that

---

8   It can be argued that these constructions represent several different types. However, they are often claimed to have the same historical source, namely the amalgamation of the progressive and a construction with BE + preposition + gerund, as in *He was on hunting* (see Section 2.2.2.5). I will therefore treat them under the same heading in this chapter. For further examples of these types in late Modern English, with DO as well as other main verbs, see Visser (1973: 2002ff.).

examples such as (3), where the form of BE and the present participle are clearly not in the same clause, should not be classified as progressives.

(3)   Alice *is* here, *hoping* to get into her own pretty house next month.
      (Letters, Butler, May, 1870–1900, p. 231)

The surface dissimilarity between such appositively used participles and progressives becomes less obvious when no comma separates the clauses, as in (4). Nevertheless, in late Modern English, the presence of a locative element between BE and the participle, such as *in Town* in (4), often indicates that the example is not a progressive.[9] Examples like (4) were thus not included in the counts.

(4)   One of Mr. Montagu's Sons, who is an Ambleside Scholar, *is* now <u>in Town</u> *spending* his vacation.
      (Letters, Wordsworth, Mary [2], 1800–1830, p. 28)

When the clause containing BE is introduced by existential *there*, as in (5), there is some disagreement among scholars.

(5)   Had it been only the Holt vassalage, either their feeling would have been one with her own, or they would have made way for her, but <u>there</u> *were* some pert nursery maids *gaping* about with the children from Beauchamp, whence the heads of the family had been absent all the winter and spring, leaving various nurses and governesses in charge.
      (Fiction, Yonge, 1850–1870, p. I.101)

Scheffer (1975: 8) is of the opinion that cases like (5) should, in most cases, be classified as progressives. Denison (1993: 372), on the other hand, does not seem to consider such constructions as progressives. In accordance with the principle of including only convincing examples of progressives in the counts, the latter policy of excluding instances such as (5) was adopted for the present study. Nor were constructions in similar sentences introduced by *here*, such as (6), counted as progressives.

(6)   [$Brierly.$] <u>Here</u>'*s* a gentleman *waiting* for you, sir, on business.
      (Drama, Taylor, 1850–1870, p. 309)

---

9   Note, however, that a temporal adverbial, like *now* in (4), can interrupt a progressive verb phrase. Smith (2004: 183) argues that, in 18th-century English, the occurrence of long and/or multiple adverbials within progressive verb phrases is a sign of incomplete grammaticalization.

2.2.2.2   Predicative adjectival participles

A present participle, such as *interesting*, may be used adjectivally in both attributive (*They have an interesting theory*) and predicative (*Their theory is interesting*) positions. The latter pattern may cause problems when it is difficult to tell the progressive from a construction with BE + adjectival participle. Consider (7):

(7)   ... I often wish he was at School – but he is a sweet Boy & I think this journey will have made impressions upon him which *will be lasting*, & he will be better for it hereafter –
(Letters, Wordsworth, Mary [1], 1800–1830, p. 184)

In (7), *will be lasting* can be seen either as verb phrase (*will be*) + adjectival complement (*lasting*) or as a progressive of the verb LAST. In the absence of an adverbial of duration, e.g. *for several years*, or some other linguistic indication of a verbal use of *will be lasting*, the former classification was chosen for examples like (7), which was thus excluded from the counts.

There are several tests listed in Denison (1993: 373–379) and Visser (1973: 1931–1934) that can be used to determine which of the possible interpretations is more likely. If, in the progressive reading, the verb phrase is used transitively, the most obvious test is to see if there is an object or not. Thus, with verbs that have no intransitive uses, such as INTEREST, the present participle can usually be assumed to be adjectival if it occurs without an object, as in (8):

(8)   During the conversation between Mrs. Overall and Crackenthorpe, which began at length *to be* rather *interesting*, inasmuch as it gave the lady an opportunity to descant, and that too upon a subject with which she was intimately connected; Miss Engleheart had been accompanying Miss Palmer in the beautiful English song of "Bid me discourse."
(Fiction, Hook, 1800–1830, pp. I.241–I.242)

It is therefore chiefly intransitive uses of progressives that can be difficult to tell from structures with BE + adjectival present participle.

For cases where there is ambiguity between an intransitive progressive verb phrase and a BE + adjective construction, the presence of adverbs of degree such as *so* and *too* may indicate that the participle is adjectival (Visser 1973: 1932f.). Consider (9):

(9)   I am better this morning, only still my head feels like a jelly, and I *am* so *trembling* and weak I can hardly hold myself upright.
(Letters, Jewsbury, 1850–1870, p. 357)

Owing to the presence of *so*, as well as the following adjective *weak* and the comparative clause *I can hardly hold myself upright*, in (9), the possibility that *trembling* was adjectival could not be excluded, and *am trembling* was thus excluded from the counts. However, there are also cases where the presence of *so* was not considered a sufficiently strong indication that the participle was adjectival. Consider (10):

(10)   We *are* so *longing* to get well for our boy's holidays, he writes by every post, "On the 21st I arrive at Euston. Send me the journey money at once. Please be well in time."
        (Letters, Thackeray Ritchie, 1870–1900, p. 221)

In (10), the overall semantics of the situation were indicative of a verbal use of *longing*; *are ... longing* was consequently classified as a progressive despite the presence of *so*.

        Visser (1973: 1934) also mentions the prefixes *un-* and *forth-* as indicators of adjectival status. However, this criterion should not be understood as valid for all cases. Visser mentions e.g. *unfeeling, unforgiving,* and *forthgiving,* and states that the absence or obsolescence of the verbs UNFEEL, UNFORGIVE, and FORTHGIVE indicates that such participles should be considered adjectival. But applying this criterion systematically to all the relevant participles would mean that for instance progressives of UNDO (as in *He was undoing the clasp*) would be considered impossible.

        In other cases, doubt may arise as to whether there is a non-progressive corresponding to a given progressive. Consider (11):

(11)   [$Hawkshaw.$] Oh dear no – I like to work single-handed – but don't be excited. Take it coolly, or you may frighten the bird.
        [$Goes to desk, L.$]
        [$Mr. Gibson.$] Easy to say take it coolly! I *haven't been thief catching* all my life. [$Exit GIBSON into his room, R.$]
        (Drama, Taylor, 1850–1870, p. 312)

There is no entry for a verb THIEF-CATCH in *OED*; nevertheless, *haven't been thief catching* was classified as a progressive in the present study, as it seems to be a variant – probably intended to be humorous – of *haven't been catching thieves,* which has a corresponding non-progressive variant *haven't caught thieves.* (The overall semantics of the example also indicate a verbal use of *thief catching.*) Jespersen (1909–1949: 220) lists a number of other cases where what may be progressives lack obvious non-progressive counterparts. Most of these are like BE *thief catching* in that the constituent which would usually be the object of the verb phrase is instead placed before the present participle and made part of the verb phrase, e.g. BE *holiday-taking* for BE *taking a holiday.*

        Co-ordination is also mentioned as a possible test: if the present participle is co-ordinated with a noun or adjective, this may indicate that the participle has adjectival status. However, both Denison (1993: 378) and Visser (1973: 1933) consider this test to be less than wholly reliable, as the same instance of BE frequently acts both as a main verb and as a progressive auxiliary, with the complement of the main verb and the verbal (progressive) participle co-ordinated. Still, in cases like (12), where *ailing* and the adjective *unable* are co-ordinated, the test may provide an indication that *ailing* should not be seen as part of a progressive. (The same type of co-ordination can be observed in example 9 above.)

(12)   As I do not see that you were present at the memorial service to Ld Winchester yesterday it has occurred to me that you *may be ailing*, & unable to go out?
(Letters, Hardy, 1870–1900, p. 134)

Although *may be ailing* in (12) was not included in the counts, in these cases decisions were made example by example rather than according to a general principle of excluding participles that were co-ordinated with a noun or an adjective.

These tests notwithstanding, the researcher is frequently forced to rely on close readings of individual instances when trying to distinguish between adjectival and verbal participles. Such close readings are inherently partly subjective, as they are based on general semanto-pragmatic impressions rather than syntactic characteristics. Denison (1993: 377) discusses "the (rather unsafe) equations verb = action, adjective = state"; Visser (1973: 1933; italics original) lists cases where the participle "*refers to a natural or innate quality or property*". Some BE + -*ing* combinations can have both verbal and adjectival readings, which may be difficult to distinguish. For instance, consider the two cases of BE *ailing* in (13):

(13)   Just before he went to Shrewsbury *had* he *been* at all *ailing*? Not to my knowledge. – When he came back from Shrewsbury he at once said he *was ailing*, did he not? That he was poorly.
(Trials, Palmer, 1850–1870, p. 43)

In (13), *had ... been ... ailing* is modified by *at all*, which makes an adjectival interpretation likely, as *at all* occurs between the form of BE and the present participle; *was ailing* is parallel to the BE + adjective structure *was poorly* in the next sentence. However, it could be argued that the presence and position of *at all* do not rule out a progressive interpretation of *had ... been ... ailing*, and that *was poorly* (which is not uttered by the same speaker as *was ailing*) need not be structurally parallel to *was ailing*. In such cases, which remained doubtful even after close inspection, the general strategy to include only convincing progressives in the data was followed, and neither *had ... been ... ailing* nor *was ailing* was thus included in the counts.

2.2.2.3   Gerunds

The term "gerund" is often used "for verb forms with a noun-like role ... e.g. English *fighting* is traditionally a gerund in *Fighting used to be fun*" (Matthews 1997: 145). This gerund is formally identical with the present participle that is part of the English progressive in the 19th century. Consequently, there are cases where the structure BE + *-ing* may be either a progressive or a construction where BE is a linking verb followed by a gerund. The difference between the two interpretations when the construction is BE *being* is discussed by Denison (1993: 396); as Denison points out, Visser (1973: 1956) includes what look like clear instances of BE + gerund in his examples of progressives.

In most cases, the syntactic ambiguity between a progressive and a BE + gerund interpretation is not problematic, as the overall semantics of the situation make clear which reading is intended. Consider (14):

(14)   ... What suddenly cheered me up just now *was thinking* what prizes I have drawn in Life, what dear, dear prizes.
        (Letters, Thackeray Ritchie, 1870–1900, p. 173)

Syntactically, (14) can be analysed in two different ways:
- [What suddenly cheered me up just now] [was thinking] [what prizes I have drawn in Life] (the progressive interpretation).
- [What suddenly cheered me up just now] [was] [thinking what prizes I have drawn in Life] (the BE + gerund interpretation).

For (14), however, only the latter classification is possible semantically, as the subject is incapable of thought and thus cannot be the subject of a verb phrase with THINK as main verb.

However, the identity in form between the progressive and the BE + gerund construction may occasionally make the two difficult to tell apart, as in (15):

(15)   "I don't mean that – it was yellow hair."
        "Nonsense."
        "That's *insulting* me. I know it was yellow. Now whose was it? I want to know."
        (Fiction, Hardy, 1870–1900, p. II.121)

In (15), the semantic difference between a progressive ([That]['s insulting] [me]) and a BE + gerund ([That]['s] [insulting me]) interpretation is smaller than in (14). For instance, a non-progressive verb phrase with the same main verb as that of the progressive interpretation (*That insults me*) may be possible in (15), but is unlikely in (14) owing to the incompatibility of the subject with the verb THINK. Nevertheless, owing to general semantic considerations, the BE + gerund interpretation was considered more likely in (15), which was thus excluded from the counts. In similar cases, where the choice between a progressive classification and a BE + gerund classification may be based partly on subjective judgement, the general policy of including only convincing progressives in the counts was followed.

2.2.2.4   BE *going to* + infinitive with future reference

In late Middle and early Modern English, a new construction referring to future time developed. Formally, this construction consisted of a progressive of the verb GO followed by a *to*-infinitive, as in *I am going to read the book tomorrow*. Many scholars claim that the first likely instance hitherto attested dates from the 15th century (Danchev and Kytö 1998: 147f.; see also Núñez Pertejo 1999). It is often difficult to say whether the futurity sense or the movement sense (≈ BE *going in order to* + infinitive) of BE *going to* + infinitive constructions is more prevalent in early Modern English: many examples seem to admit both readings, or possibly a combination of the two. Danchev and Kytö (1998: 155) point to the difficulty of trying to "fix a cut-off point of grammaticalisation … which would appear to be a rather artificial endeavour" (see Section 3.2.1 for a discussion of the term "grammaticalization" in connection with the progressive).

Given that the use of BE *going to* + infinitive constructions with future reference was becoming established in late Modern English (see e.g. Strang 1982: 438), it is important to state whether they should be counted as progressives in the present study. Since previous research on this issue will inform my own decision, I will provide a short survey of various researchers' views on this matter. Scheffer (1975: 82) counts BE *going to* + infinitive constructions with future reference as progressives. Although he admits that it is arguable that these constructions are progressives "only in a formal sense", Scheffer claims that excluding them would make comparisons with previous research difficult, since other grammarians classify progressives and BE *going to* + infinitive constructions with future reference together. Strang (1982: 438) also appears to include all BE *going to* + infinitive constructions in her counts, as she states that one of her samples includes "18,000 words from Clarissa, accounting for 11 examples, of which one is a quotation from her sister, while two are instances of *be going to*, which is much better established by 1700 than *be+ing* in general". Elsness (1994: 18) includes all instances of BE *going to* + infinitive in his counts of early Modern English progressives, though he does admit that the construction is not a clear-cut progressive (Elsness 1994: 12). Nurmi (1996: 154), in contrast, states that her figures differ from Elsness's because Elsness defined the progressive in broader terms; BE *going to* + infinitive constructions with future reference were omitted from Nurmi's counts. Ota (1963: 94) excluded BE *going to* + infinitive constructions from his discussion of the progressive/non-progressive paradigm in 20th-century American English. Similarly, Mair and Hundt (1995: 114) explicitly exclude instances of BE *going to* + infinitive with future reference from their counts of progressives. Their reason for doing so is that the increase in frequency of this construction would blur the picture of the development of the progressive itself. Nor do Biber et al. (1999: 472) include instances of "the semi-modal *be going to*" in their counts of progressives of GO.

Many scholars apparently count all BE *going to* + infinitive constructions as progressives. This in itself constitutes an argument for following the same strategy: as Scheffer (1975: 82) points out, it is difficult to compare results reached in different studies if the same method has not been applied when the raw frequency of the progressive has been determined. On the other hand, there are at least two strong arguments for excluding instances of BE *going to* + infinitive with future reference from the counts. The first of these arguments builds on the one given in Mair and Hundt (1995): if the development of the progressive is being investigated, marginal progressives should preferably be excluded from the counts, as they need not have the same occurrence pattern as the progressives themselves. Including marginal cases in the counts may distort the quantitative picture both in diachrony and across genres. The BE *going to* future construction is more common in imaginative than in informative genres in Present-Day English (Berglund 1997: 17); it is a reasonable hypothesis that this genre diversity existed in 19th-century English as well. Since the progressive is usually hypothesized to be more common in imaginative than in informative genres to begin with, one probable effect of including BE *going to* + infinitive constructions with future reference in the counts is that cross-genre frequency differences would be exaggerated.

The second reason for excluding BE *going to* + infinitive constructions concerns the relation between the progressive and the non-progressive. A progressive of a verb should be related to a non-progressive of the same verb (see also Section 2.2.2.2); but no such relationship holds between *I am going to sell my house* (in the future-reference sense of BE *going to* + infinitive) and *I go to sell my house*. This argument is perhaps not wholly valid for early Modern English, where BE *going to* + infinitive with future reference was a new construction and was still closely related to the progressive of GO. However, Strang's (1982: 438) comment (quoted above) that BE *going to* + infinitive was better established in 1700 than the progressive in general suggests that in late Modern English it makes little sense to speak of BE *going to* + infinitive constructions with future reference as progressives.

The policy followed in the present study was to go through all instances of BE *going to* + infinitive manually to see in which examples the futurity sense was predominant and in which the movement sense was felt more strongly.[10] Only members of the latter group were included in the counts of progressives. This decision reflects the constraint added to the definition of the progressive in Section 2.2.1. When the movement sense is predominant, the *to*-infinitive should be analysed as part of an infinitival clause of purpose, and thus not as part of the

---

10   A potential problem inherent in this procedure is that, by dividing instances of BE *going to* + infinitive into future and non-future, the researcher is creating a binary distinction out of what is in effect a semanto-pragmatic continuum. In practice, however, the two variants were easy to tell apart in most cases; moreover, the possibility of excluding all instances which could not with certainty be classified as progressives was still there.

verb phrase containing BE *going*; the instance then matches the definition of the progressive. In contrast, when the future sense is more pronounced, the *to*-infinitive rather contains the main verb of a verb phrase in which BE *going* acts as a (semi-)auxiliary; since the verb phrase thus includes the *to*-infinitive, these instances were excluded from the counts. By way of exemplification, consider (16) and (17):

(16)   Oh, it made the place one calls the heart feel as it *was going* to ache.
(Letters, Coleridge, 1800–1830, p. 467)

(17)   I found in talking to one of the boys, aged about 16, that he was being brought up for a calico printer; or designer, but had never seen calico printing, so as we *were going* to see the Schwabe's print-works – and had a place in carriage I offered to take him, and you can't think what a commotion of talking on the fingers there was directly among all the children.
(Letters, Gaskell, 1850–1870, p. 150)

The BE *going* in (16) was considered to be a future-in-the-past auxiliary and thus excluded from the counts, as the subject does not appear to be compatible with movement. The structure in (16) can be roughly given as [*it*] [*was going to ache*]. In contrast, the BE *going* in (17) was counted as a progressive, as the presence of a mode of transportation ("carriage") indicates that the movement sense is intended. The structure in (17) is thus rather [*we*] [*were going*] [*to see the Schwabe's print-works*].

2.2.2.5   Progressives with nominal characteristics

According to many scholars, the present-day progressive has been influenced by a construction with BE + preposition + gerund, as in *He was on hunting*, where the preposition has subsequently been reduced to *a-* and finally deleted.[11] The frequency of the progressive appears to have been low in early Middle English (Mossé 1938, II: 30ff.). In addition, some scholars claim that the functions of the Old English progressive with BEON/WESAN + present participle in *-(i)ende* were different from those of the present-day progressive (see e.g. Bybee, Perkins, and Pagliuca 1994: 132, 135).[12] For these reasons, among others, it has even been

---

11   Nehls (1988: 189) uses the term "deverbal noun" for the form following the preposition before 1300, after which time "gerund" is used. I will refer to this pattern as the "BE + preposition + gerund construction" throughout, although gerunds with verbal properties may not have developed until well into the Middle English period (see Fischer 1992: 252f.). The form typically ended in *-ung* or *-ing* in Old English, depending on, among other things, what verb class it was derived from and on dialectal differences (Nehls 1988: 192n.).

12   In a few cases, WEORÞAN + *-(i)ende* is also attested (Mitchell 1985: 272).

claimed that the present-day progressive has developed from the BE + preposition + gerund construction rather than from the Old English progressive. This is the line taken by Bybee et al. (1994), and by Braaten (1967: 173ff., referring to Dal 1952), who emphasizes the influence of Celtic languages on the development of the BE + preposition + gerund construction (see Mittendorf and Poppe 2000 for formal and functional correspondences between the BE + preposition + gerund construction and a similar construction in Middle Welsh).

However, there are several counterarguments to this theory. First, several scholars see continuity in the use of the progressive from Old English into later periods (see e.g. Åkerlund 1911: 101; Kisbye 1963: 61f.; Scheffer 1975: 218ff.), which would argue against a theory of replacement. Secondly, the frequency of the BE + preposition + gerund construction, and of the construction with *a-*, appears never to have been very high (see Mossé 1938, II: 127f.; van der Gaaf 1930: 201; Goedsche 1932: 476). Thirdly, the transition from *be on hunting* via *be a-hunting* to *be hunting* is disputed: as Mossé (1938, II: 123) points out, the preposition *in* was more common than *on* in Middle English BE + preposition + gerund constructions, and *in* is less likely than *on* to be reduced to *a-*, a reduced form which also occurs relatively late. According to Denison (1993: 400), recent studies tend to argue for the Old English progressive as the main source of the present-day progressive (which of course does not exclude influence of the BE + preposition + gerund construction on the progressive).[13]

In the BE + preposition + gerund construction, the preposition and gerund are not originally part of the verb phrase containing BE, and *He was on hunting* would thus not be classified as a progressive in 19th-century English. However, there are cases where weaker indications of a nominal element may remain, which makes the resulting construction ambiguous between a progressive and a gerundial reading.[14] In these cases, the element *a-* occurs before the *-ing* form, as in (18). The element *a-* is often linked to the *-ing* form by a hyphen, as in (18),

---

13   Bybee et al. (1994: 132) also argue that "the preponderance of locative sources for progressives in other languages would suggest a locative source for the English Progressive as well" (i.e. the BE + preposition + gerund construction). However, Bybee et al. (1994: 130f.) admit that progressive markers with a BE-auxiliary and a non-finite verb form can sometimes be seen as locative, since either or both of these verb forms may have a locative origin. The original meaning of the verb BE in Old English appears to have been locative, viz. 'to occupy a place', with more generalized meanings such as 'to exist' derived from the former (*OED*; see also Wright 1986: 108ff.). Moreover, as Bybee et al. point out, expressions of the type "X is a Y", where the main verb is encoded as a nominal, have been cited as an origin of progressive constructions (see Heine 1994: 269ff.), and Nickel (1967) considered such a construction, with BE + agent noun, to be the most important source of the Old English progressive (see also Nickel 1966). Hewson and Bubenik (1997: 348) see the development of a progressive marker as a natural development in Germanic languages, considering the characteristics of time and tense representation in this language family.

14   Bolinger (1971a–b) claims that there are still indications in Present-Day English that the progressive has nominal elements, owing to its being derived from the BE + preposition + gerund construction.

but may also be written as a separate word, or together with the *-ing* form without a hyphen.

(18)   [$Mrs. Willoughby.$] Heart, my dear – which I wish it had been his heart I found in his right-'and pocket as I *was a-mending* his best trowsers last night, which it was a short pipe, which it is nothing but the truth, and smoked to that degree as if it had been black-leaded, which many's the time when he've come in, I've said, "Sam," I've said, "I smell tobacco," I've said.
(Drama, Taylor, 1850–1870, pp. 289–290)

Some instances, e.g. (19), have a further indication of nominal status, viz. an *of*-phrase where a direct object would be expected. The origin of this *of*-phrase is believed to be the Old English genitive complement of nouns (Visser 1973: 1995).

(19)   "O, if you please, mum," she begins, "I thought I'd better step up with it, as it might be of consequence. It came when I *was a-cleaning* of myself, and I didn't lose a hinstant putting on my hout-door things before I started to bring it."
(Fiction, Braddon, 1870–1900, p. III.103)

In intransitive constructions, the *a-* + *-ing* construction may also appear without either an *of*-phrase or a direct object, as in (20):

(20)   [$Mrs. Willoughby.$] Oh – Robert! I suppose by the way he*'s a-goin' on*, Robert's your brother – leastways, if he ain't your brother –
(Drama, Taylor, 1850–1870, p. 290)

In a fourth variant with nominal characteristics, the *a-* element is absent, but the *-ing* form is followed by an *of*-phrase where a direct object would follow the non-progressive (e.g. *when I was cleaning of myself* versus *when I cleaned myself*). No clear examples of this variant were attested in CONCE, although it does occur in 19th-century English (see e.g. Visser 1973: 2003f.). As can be seen from (18)–(20), these constructions chiefly occur in colloquial contexts: the clear majority are found in Drama texts. According to Visser (1973: 1996, 2002), the *a-* before the *-ing* form came to be considered nonstandard in the early 20th century, roughly a century later than the use of an *of*-phrase instead of a direct object.

As these constructions can be said to retain traces of nominal elements, there is some doubt concerning their progressive status. Different opinions have also been voiced in previous research. Scheffer (1975: 103) appears to consider constructions such as (18)–(20) variants of progressives in Present-Day English. Fanego (1996: 102f.) counts early Modern English instances of *-ing* forms preceded by *a-* as gerunds, but does not give gerund status to cases where an *of*-phrase, instead of a direct object, follows *-ing* forms which are not preceded by an *a-* element (as in *when I was cleaning of myself*). Also focusing on early Modern English, Elsness (1994: 12ff.) adopts a wide definition of the progressive and includes *-ing* forms preceded by *a-* and followed by *of-*phrases in his counts (in fact, even some *-ing* forms preceded by full prepositions are included). Arnaud (1998: 127) treats some 19th-century instances of *-ing* form + *of-*phrase (instead of a direct object) as adjectival, but also states that *of-*phrases, rather than direct objects, may follow proper progressives.

If the line is taken that the 19th-century progressive is a continuation of the Old English progressive with BEON/WESAN + *-(i)ende*, it can be argued that constructions such as (18)–(20) are not progressives, as they do not have the same origin. However, as stated above, many scholars argue that the progressive and the BE + preposition + gerund construction influenced each other, during the Middle and/or early Modern English period; Nehls (1988: 184), for instance, refers to this process as "functional blending". This would mean that, in the 19th century, these two constructions were more or less equivalent from a functional perspective, and that differences were stylistic rather than syntactic. The tendency for the forms with *a-* to occur in colloquial contexts may be revelatory of such stylistic grading.

Furthermore, it is doubtful whether the *a-* should be seen as a full preposition, and thus an indication that the *-ing* form is nominal, in 19th-century English. In cases where the *a-* form occurs without either an *of-*phrase or a direct object (as in *I am a-singing*), there is thus only a weak indication that the *-ing* form is nominal; and when a direct object follows the *-ing* form (as in *I am a-singing a song*), there is a clear syntactic indication that the construction is verbal (the direct object), but only a vague indication that it is nominal (the reduced preposition). In the opposite case, where there is no *a-* before the *-ing* form but where an *of-*phrase instead of a direct object follows (as in *I am singing of a song*), the nominal indication is also weak, since no determiner or preposition precedes the *-ing* form.[15] Finally, the rarity of the variants illustrated in (18)–(20), as well as the apparent stylistic restrictions on their occurrence, suggests that they did not constitute a generally available alternative to the 19th-century progressive: less than 20 instances of the three variants attested in CONCE were found altogether.

Against this background, I classified forms such as (18), (19), and (20) as progressives in the present study. However, note that this choice is only intended to be valid for 19th-century English: in earlier periods, before the hypothesized functional blending of the variants, this solution may not be advisable.

---

15   It can be argued that the construction in (19), *when I was a-cleaning of myself*, displays
      clearer signs of being nominal. However, as mentioned above, the prepositional status of *a-* is
      doubtful.

2.2.3   The progressives in the CONCE corpus

After all combinations of BE and *-ing* that were not convincing progressives had been excluded from the counts, the progressives were saved into new concordance files. Each progressive was turned into an entry in a Microsoft Access database. Progressives which shared part of their verb phrase with a previous progressive, such as *was ... dancing* in *He was singing and dancing*, were given a special code in the database. Constructions like *He was singing and dancing* were counted as one instance of the progressive, as the choice of whether or not to use a progressive is influenced by the previous progressive(s) in the verb phrase. Only the first progressive (*was singing* in the above example) was included in the counts. The same principle was followed in cases where two or more forms of BE were followed by a single present participle, as in *I am, and will be, singing.* In cases such as these, only the first complete combination (*am ... singing* in the example) was included in the counts. However, progressives such as *was ... dancing* and *will be singing* above were kept in the database, as they could still be of value in qualitative investigations.

After these selection processes, the total number of progressives in CONCE was 2,440. The period/genre breakdown is given in Table 5.[16]

Table 5.   Progressives by period and genre in CONCE

Period	Debates	Drama	Fiction	History	Letters	Science	Trials	Total
1	12	37	88	10	246	26	178	597
2	11	108	126	37	423	24	171	900
3	30	117	69	66	386	35	240	943
Total	53	262	283	113	1,055	85	589	2,440

These progressives served as input for the quantitative analyses in the present study. In these analyses, linguistic and extralinguistic features were coded for each progressive in the Microsoft Access database; aggregates were grouped and computed in Access and transferred to Microsoft Excel, where the calculations were carried out.

---

16   The figures in Table 5 differ somewhat from those presented in Smitterberg (2000a). Since Smitterberg (2000a) was written, the Trials and Debates genres have been included in CONCE. In addition, one Drama text and one Letters text have been added to the corpus, and one Letters text removed (see Section 2.1.3). Finally, after a second round of back-up checking, some additional progressives were entered into the database, and a few cases which had previously been classified as progressives were on second reading reclassified as doubtful and excluded from the counts.

Chapter 3

The frequency of the progressive in 19th-century English

Previous quantitative research on the development of the progressive indicates that the frequency of the construction has been increasing ever since the late Middle English period (see e.g. Nehls 1988: 190), and still continues to increase in Present-Day English (see e.g. Mair and Hundt 1995). As will be made clear in Section 3.2, this increase in frequency is an important indication that the progressive was, and is, becoming more fully integrated into English grammar. Considering the weight given to frequency data in this respect, it is important to discuss how the frequency of the progressive is best measured. The first section of the present chapter is devoted to such a discussion. I will consider four ways in which the frequency of the progressive can be measured. Two of these will form the basis for the presentation of my results in Section 3.2, where I analyse variation in the frequency of the progressive with the extralinguistic variables of time, genre, and sex. The chapter concludes with Section 3.3, which contains a summary and discussion of the results reached, and their implications for the integration of the progressive into late Modern English grammar.

3.1 Measuring the frequency of the progressive: A methodological discussion

The present section is organized as follows. In Section 3.1.1, I will take up three different methods (viz. the M-, K-, and V-coefficients) that have been used by scholars to measure the frequency of the progressive. I will also present a fourth method designed by myself, the S-coefficient, and discuss the advantages and drawbacks of the four methods. Based on the outcome of the discussion, the M- and S-coefficients will be selected for use in Section 3.2; the M-coefficient will also be used in Chapter 4. In Section 3.1.2 will follow a methodological discussion of how the M- and S-coefficients relate to each other. This discussion will also be connected with the general question, discussed in Section 1.5.1, of whether to investigate the frequency of the progressive from a variationist standpoint or as a linguistic feature in itself. The S-coefficient has not previously been used in research and requires more preparatory work as regards processing the material than does the M-coefficient: I will therefore devote Section 3.1.3 to an applied discussion of the work involved in obtaining the raw frequencies necessary to calculate the S-coefficient. The relevant raw frequencies will be given at the end of Section 3.1.3.

3.1.1   Calculating the frequency of the progressive: A comparison of four coefficients

It is common practice in research on the progressive to normalize the raw frequencies of progressives (also referred to as N_{PROG} in what follows) to some type of coefficient (see Section 2.2 for an overview of how N_{PROG} was determined). This makes it possible to compare frequency results from different studies, and also from different subsamples in the researcher's own corpus. As pointed out in Section 1.5.1, two main methods are used when the raw frequency of the progressive is normalized. If the progressive is analysed as a linguistic feature in itself, the raw frequencies are related to the number of words in the texts on which the study is based. If the progressive is analysed as part of a progressive/non-progressive paradigm, the raw frequency of the construction is instead related to the number of verb phrases (with possible extra modifications, such as knock-out factors which make it impossible or near-impossible to use the progressive or the non-progressive). Sections 3.1.1.1–3.1.1.4 will be devoted to an examination of some ways in which these two methods can be applied to data when the raw frequency of the progressive is normalized.

3.1.1.1   The M-coefficient

The commonest way of measuring the frequency of the progressive appears to be the so-called M-coefficient (M after Mossé). The M-coefficient normalizes the raw frequency of the progressive to occurrences per 100,000 words, and is thus a variant of the typical occurrences/words normalization procedure. The following formula is used to obtain the M-coefficient for a given text:

$$M = N_{PROG} / N_{WORD} \times 100,000$$

In the formula, N_{WORD} equals the number of words in the text in question.

The M-coefficient has three main advantages. First, the fact that it is the most frequent way of normalizing the raw frequency of the progressive means that results based on the M-coefficient are comparable to those reached in many other studies.[1] Moreover, as most researchers normalize the frequency of the linguistic features they investigate to a given number of words, the normalized frequencies of the progressive can also be compared with frequency data on other features.

---

1   See, however, comments in Section 2.2 on differences between scholars' classifications of progressives.

Secondly, the M-coefficient is a fairly objective unit in that it depends for its calculation on only two definitions, viz. that of what constitutes a progressive and that of what constitutes a word. Although there is some disagreement on how the former should be defined (see Section 2.2), the replicability of the calculation procedure is increased if the criteria used in the definition of the progressive are specified. As regards the latter, many retrieval programs define a word as a unit consisting of one or several character/s (excluding punctuation marks, spaces etc.) separated by one or several punctuation marks, spaces etc.[2]

The fact that computer software can be used to retrieve word counts brings us to yet another advantage of the M-coefficient: it can be calculated relatively easily and quickly. The researcher only needs two types of input data for each text – the raw frequency of progressives and the word count – in order to calculate the relevant M-coefficients. This advantage is of importance especially when a large number of texts are examined.

However, from a variationist perspective there are drawbacks associated with the use of the M-coefficient. Most importantly, the M-coefficient does not reflect the fact that the progressive is not a possible substitute for any word in English, but only for non-progressive verb phrases.[3] In other words, the raw frequency of the progressive in a text is related to a number of slots (all the words in the text), but the progressive can only fill a minority of these slots (the words in the text that form verb phrases). This can become a problem because the number of verb phrases per words in texts frequently varies both across genres and in diachrony. For instance, formal written genres in CONCE, such as Science, can be expected to have few verb phrases per number of words compared with speech-related genres such as Drama. The M-coefficient for Drama would thus be higher than the M-coefficient for Science, even if both genres had the same number of progressives per number of verb phrases. To the extent that the relation between the number of progressives and the number of verb phrases gives a better picture of the occurrence of the progressive in texts than the relation between the number of progressives and the number of words, this is a problem inherent in the use of the M-coefficient. Moreover, formal written genres often have both few verb phrases per number of words and low frequencies of progressives, whereas the opposite is true of many spoken or speech-related genres. The effect of the M-

---

2   Older studies, however, are based on manual word counts, something which might affect results, as the total is often estimated from e.g. words/line and lines/page ratios rather than counted. More recent studies may also make use of manual, approximate word counts if they are not based on machine-readable corpora: Arnaud (1998: 126), for instance, used a method where "[t]he number of words was carefully estimated from random samples".

3   This generalization is not without exceptions. First, as will be discussed further in Section 3.1.1.4, there are verb phrases that take the progressive very rarely, e.g. imperative verb phrases in Present-Day English. Secondly, we cannot know with certainty that language users choose between progressive and non-progressive verb phrases only: for not-solely-aspectual progressives, for instance, it is conceivable that the choice may rather involve using the progressive or, say, an expression of emphasis. In the majority of cases, however, it is probable that the above generalization holds.

coefficient is thus often to exaggerate cross-genre differences in frequencies of progressives.

A further, related, drawback concerns the possibility of testing variation between samples of text for statistical significance using, for instance, the chi-square test. There are problems associated with using differences between samples in the two units that underlie the M-coefficient, viz. the raw frequency of the progressive and the total word count, as input for chi-square tests. The chi-square test is typically used for distributions of nominal data where the categories are different realizations of an underlying trait (Reynolds 1984: 10): for instance, a verb phrase (the underlying trait) can be either progressive or non-progressive (the two categories). In contrast, it makes less sense to say that a word can either be a progressive or another word, because this categorization has little bearing on how language users build sentences. Moreover, the categories in a nominal scale should be mutually exclusive (Reynolds 1984: 10). Since a progressive verb phrase can theoretically be between two and five words long, it is difficult to apply the chi-square test to frequencies of progressives and word counts in texts without taking into account the length, in number of words, of the progressive verb phrases in each text. One solution in this respect would be to test variation between samples in the number of words that are part of progressives and the number of words that are not. Even so, however, a significant result may simply reflect, for instance, a difference between the texts in the number of verb phrases per words.[4]

Despite the above-mentioned disadvantages connected with the use of the M-coefficient, I will base frequency counts in the present study primarily on this normalizing procedure, given that the M-coefficient is easy to calculate and that the results of the present study will then be comparable with those of previous research. However, I will also complement the use of the M-coefficient by applying an additional normalizing coefficient, which takes the relation between the progressive and the verb phrase into account. I now turn to a survey of three possible additional coefficients, the K-, V-, and S-coefficients.

3.1.1.2   The K-coefficient

Because of the above-mentioned drawbacks associated with the use of the M-coefficient, researchers have devised alternative ways of measuring the frequency of the progressive. The K-coefficient, devised by Nickel (1966), is the best-known alternative in this respect. Unlike the M-coefficient, the K-coefficient takes into account the connection between the progressive and verb phrases. It is computed for a text by dividing the number of progressives by the total number

---

4   Virtanen (1997) uses the chi-square test in this way, but also recognizes that a safer method would be to compare the number of finite progressives with the number of finite non-progressives. See also Mair and Hundt (1995: 114n.) for a discussion of the problems involved in using raw frequencies of progressives and words when comparing the frequency of the progressive in different samples.

of verb phrases, excluding those which cannot appear in the progressive. The formula is as follows:

$$K = N_{PROG} / (N_{VERB} - N_{NOPROG}) \times 10,000$$

In this formula, N_{VERB} stands for the total number of verb phrases in a text and N_{NOPROG} for the number of those verb phrases in which the progressive is considered impossible.[5]

By relating the number of slots the progressive fills to the number of slots the construction can fill, the K-coefficient takes so-called knock-out factors into account: verb phrases that cannot take the progressive, and where choice consequently does not exist, are excluded from the counts. (See Section 3.1.1.4 for examples of potential knock-out factors in this respect.) Thus, the K-coefficient gives the researcher an indication of the probability of a progressive occurring in a given text.

A further advantage of using the K-coefficient is that the number of progressives can be compared with the number of non-progressives that could be progressives; the latter number equals $(N_{VERB} - N_{NOPROG}) - N_{PROG}$. As progressives and non-progressives where the progressive would be possible can be considered alternative realizations of the same variable, viz. verb phrases that can take the progressive, this relationship is a safer basis for statistical analysis than the number of progressives and the number of words in texts, i.e. the data on which the M-coefficient is based.[6]

However, there are also problems associated with the use of the K-coefficient. To begin with, in order to decide whether or not a progressive would be possible in a given verb phrase, the researcher would – at least in theory – have to go through all non-progressive verb phrases in his/her corpus and classify them accordingly (Sume 1995: 11). Quirk et al. (1985: 198n.) claim that fewer than 5% of all verb phrases in Present-Day English are in the progressive. Even 5% is likely to be too high a figure for the 19th century, considering the increase in frequency throughout Modern English that is reported in the literature (see e.g. Dennis 1940). Nevertheless, let us assume, for the sake of illustration, that the 2,440 progressives in CONCE constitute exactly 5% of all verb phrases in the corpus. In theory, the corpus would then contain 46,360 (= (2,440 / 0.05) – 2,440) non-progressive verb phrases that the researcher would need to examine in order to ascertain whether they could take the progressive or not. With access to a tagged corpus and/or the results of pilot studies, it may be possible to exclude many of these verb phrases automatically or semi-automatically, by taking into account for instance that some verbs very rarely occur in the progressive (see e.g.

---

5   Nickel's (1966: 18) own formula does not explicitly include the elimination of verb phrases where the progressive is not possible. However, Nickel (1966: 18n.) states in a footnote that such verb phrases can be deducted from the dividend, and other studies (e.g. Scheffer 1975; Sume 1995) often include this deduction process in the calculation of the K-coefficient.

6   It is usually taken for granted that there are no knock-out factors in the other direction, i.e. that all verb phrases can be non-progressive. However, as the progressive is becoming increasingly more frequent in English, this matter may deserve further investigation as regards Present-Day English.

Biber et al. 1999: 472); but the number of verb phrases that would have to be examined manually would still be large.

The methodology involved in the calculation of the K-coefficient raises additional questions. Decisions as to whether a progressive is possible or not will inevitably involve subjective and theory-dependent decisions. Thus, scholars may disagree on what the value of ($N_{VERB} - N_{NOPROG}$) should be in a given text even if their value for N_{PROG} is the same; consequently, their K-coefficients would differ. There is therefore a risk that, compared with the M-coefficient, the use of the K-coefficient decreases the comparability of studies. Furthermore, decisions concerning the possibility of a verb phrase taking the progressive may be difficult to make in diachrony. For instance, the combination of perfect and progressive marking is not attested until late Middle English (see Section 5.2), but taking this factor into account would entail deciding for each text whether or not the progressive would be available in perfect verb phrases. First and last attestations may be of some help in making decisions; but as the historical linguist lacks access to many important genres, such as spontaneous conversation, these indications are not wholly reliable. (Nor can it be regarded as certain that a given type of progressive is available in all genres and contexts because it has been attested in one particular genre and context.) Finally, there is a risk of circular reasoning involved in making decisions about changes in the make-up of the progressive paradigm when such changes are simultaneously the object of study. For the above reasons, the K-coefficient was not considered suitable for the present study.

3.1.1.3   The V-coefficient

Sume (1995: 11) introduces the V-coefficient (V for "verb") as a compromise between the M- and K-coefficients. The V-coefficient relates the number of progressives in a text to the number of verb phrases, and is calculated as follows:

$$V = N_{PROG} / N_{VERB} \times 10,000$$

As knock-out factors are not taken into account by the V-coefficient, it is less precise than the K-coefficient. Nevertheless, the V-coefficient has a number of advantages. Like the K-coefficient, it relates the number of progressives to the number of verb phrases, thus neutralizing differences between samples in ratios of the number of verb phrases to the number of words; but it lacks the subjective features involved in obtaining N_{NOPROG} for the K-coefficient. Moreover, if the researcher has access to a tagged corpus, the number of verb phrases in the texts under scrutiny can be obtained automatically (if not, the K- and V-coefficients share the problem that the corpus must be gone through manually in search of verb phrases).

As the V-coefficient takes into account the fact that the progressive only occurs in verb phrases, the data on which it is based are better suited as input to, for instance, the chi-square test than are those used to calculate the M-coefficient. When testing differences between samples in this way, the researcher adopts a variationist stance, and considers the progressive and the non-progressive as the two variants of the verb phrase. However, the V-coefficient does not reflect the fact that the progressive is only marginally possible in some verb phrases, for instance imperative verb phrases in Present-Day English. Results of tests for significance based on the data used to calculate the V-coefficient should therefore be interpreted with some caution.

The V-coefficient keeps some of the advantages of the K-coefficient while lacking its drawbacks; at the same time, provided that the researcher has access to a corpus that has been tagged with high recall and precision, it is nearly as easy to calculate as the M-coefficient. It is thus a valuable methodological tool for studies on the progressive. However, considering the detailed output offered by modern taggers, it may be possible to refine the methodology even more, at least for an investigation of late Modern English.

3.1.1.4   The S-coefficient

The present section is devoted to the introduction of a new normalization coefficient, the S-coefficient, for raw frequencies of the progressive.[7] As with the K- and V-coefficients, the corpus on which the study is based must be tagged for the S-coefficient to be easily calculated. The calculation of the S-coefficient was constructed to be applicable chiefly to the progressive in late Modern English, and was adapted to the level of detail in the tagged output. In the present section, my discussion will be limited to how the S-coefficient is calculated and what types of verb phrases are included in and excluded from the counts. An overview of the tagging procedure itself, problems associated with it, and of the process by which the raw frequencies of the relevant features were retrieved, will instead be given in Section 3.1.3.

Ideally, the S-coefficient should include the advantages of both the K- and the V-coefficient, while sharing as few of their drawbacks as possible. In my discussion, I will start out from the V-coefficient, and then consider possible ways in which the precision of this frequency measure can be enhanced further without introducing too time-consuming analyses or affecting the objectivity of the procedure. Since the calculation of N_{PROG} and N_{VERB} has already been discussed in Section 2.2 and in Sections 3.1.1.2–3.1.1.3, I will start from types of verb phrases where the progressive rarely occurs in the Modern English period.

There are a number of syntactic and semantic contexts where the progressive is sometimes claimed to be impossible in Modern English verb phrases (see e.g. Nehls 1974: 150ff.). These contexts include demonstrations (as in *I take this hat*), performatives (as in *I name this ship* Elizabeth), simple imperatives (with a few exceptions, such as *be going* and *be packing* in early

---

7   Similar frequency measures have been used by, for instance, Buyssens (1968) and Arnaud (1973), but these studies used slightly different criteria regarding what constructions were included in the counts.

Modern English), and stative situations.[8] Such verb phrases are all included when the V-coefficient is calculated, but can be excluded from the calculation of the K-coefficient. On the one hand, removing such verb phrases from the counts would restrict the analysis more to those contexts where choice between the progressive and the non-progressive exists, and thus improve the methodology from a variationist viewpoint. On the other hand, such claims are problematic for two main reasons, which were touched on in Section 3.1.1.2: they are to some extent theory-dependent and thus subjective, especially as regards the issue of what constitutes a stative situation; and in order to evaluate some of them, it would be necessary to go through a large number of verb phrases manually.

Concerning at least one of the contexts listed above, it is possible to refine the methodology of the V-coefficient without time-consuming manual checking of a large number of verb phrases, and without introducing subjective decisions into the analysis. Imperative verb phrases, unlike performatives, demonstrations, and stative situations, can be identified automatically using modern part-of-speech taggers. As CONCE has been tagged using the EngCG–2 tagger, it would thus be possible to refine the frequency counts of the V-coefficient one step further automatically by removing imperative verb phrases from the counts. However, before this removal of imperatives is carried out, it must be ascertained whether the hypothesis that the progressive does not occur in the imperative mood in 19th-century English is valid.

To test whether progressives occurred in the imperative in CONCE, I checked the 2,440 progressives included in the counts for mood. No simple imperatives were found. However, one imperative with DO-periphrasis was attested, viz. (21):

(21)   *Don't be having* tooth-ache and *lying* awake this week as a preparation for enjoying London.
(Letters, Eliot, 1850–1870, p. 103)

Given that only one instance was attested, progressive imperatives with DO-periphrasis appear to be quite rare in late Modern English. As Allen (1966) shows, the same holds true for 20th-century American English. In Allen's corpus of 4,800 verb phrases, no progressive imperatives with DO-periphrasis were attested (Allen 1966: 207). Nevertheless, the occurrence of imperative progressives with DO-periphrasis in CONCE is a problem for a methodology that involves the automatic exclusion of imperative verb phrases from the data, since the EngCG–2 tagger, which was used for the present study, does not separate simple imperatives from imperatives with DO-periphrasis. However, the latter type turned out to be rare in CONCE. In order to see whether imperative verb phrases in CONCE frequently incorporated *do*, I ran searches for all possible or

---

8   Söderlind (1951: 90) also found a progressive imperative of JOG in his investigation of verb syntax in John Dryden's prose; Núñez Pertejo (2001: 341) lists a progressive imperative of WALK from the Helsinki Corpus.

certain imperatives in a subset of 20 texts from period 1.[9] New searches were then run to find all instances of *do* for which the tagger did not exclude an imperative interpretation. Of the 1,032 possible or certain imperative verb phrases identified by the tagger for the 20 texts in period 1, 78 incorporated the form *do*, corresponding to *c.* 8% of all possible or certain imperatives in these 20 texts. However, in some of these 78 cases *do* was the main verb and not an auxiliary, and in these cases the progressive would not be substitutable for the non-progressive. On the basis of these figures, I excluded all imperatives from the counts, as the small discrepancy resulting from the exclusion of imperatives with DO-periphrasis (where the progressive cannot be excluded) was unlikely to affect the overall results.[10]

Moreover, non-finite verb phrases – progressive and non-progressive – were excluded from the calculation of the S-coefficient. A verb phrase was considered non-finite in this context if it did not contain a finite form of either a main verb or one of the modal or primary auxiliaries. Constructions such as *He forgot to leave*, where *to leave* is not preceded by an auxiliary proper, were counted as two verb phrases, one finite (*forgot*) and one non-finite (*to leave*). There were several reasons for this decision. To begin with, non-finite progressives are rare in the material: only 44 non-finite progressives were attested in the entire CONCE corpus. It also appears that the non-finite paradigm may be an area where variation between the progressive and the non-progressive is influenced partly by other factors than those operating on finite verb phrases. In verb complementation, for example, the first choice often seems to be between a *to*-infinitive and a present participle (e.g. *She continued to read* vs. *She continued reading*) rather than between a progressive and a non-progressive *to*-infinitive (e.g. *She continued to be reading* vs. *She continued to read*). In addition, the near-disappearance of the *being* + present participle construction (see Section 5.6) makes the progressive/non-progressive paradigm more asymmetrical in non-finite verb phrases. Moreover, the EngCG–2 tagger does not separate bare infinitives (e.g. *go* in *I must go there tomorrow*) from *to*-infinitives (e.g. *to go* in *I have to go there tomorrow*), which means that finite verb phrases that also contain bare

---

9   This subset corresponds to all texts in the S-coefficient subcorpus belonging to period 1 (see Section 3.1.3 and Appendix 1 for information on the S-coefficient subcorpus). Before the search was run, all cases where the tagger could not decide whether a word was an imperative verb form or another finite verb form had been disambiguated manually (see Section 3.1.3 for an account of this disambiguation procedure).

10   The progressive is also possible following some imperatives of LET, e.g. *let the missing man's warm bath be waiting for its master* (Drama, Pinero, 1870–1900, p. 133). However, the imperative form *let* itself does not occur in the progressive. For the purposes of the present study, the remaining part of the imperative construction (*wait/be waiting*) was classified as a non-finite verb phrase and thus, as will be made clear, excluded from the counts.

infinitive forms would be counted twice if infinitives were included in the retrieval procedure.[11]

Finally, BE *going to* + infinitive constructions with future reference were excluded from the counts of finite verb phrases. As pointed out in Section 2.2.2.4, these constructions were excluded from the counts of progressive verb phrases. However, since there is no choice between a progressive and a non-progressive variant of BE *going to* + infinitive constructions with future reference, they should not be classified as non-progressives either.

The S-coefficient is thus calculated for a text on the basis of five figures: the number of finite progressives (N_{FINPR}), the number of finite verb phrases (N_{FINVP}), the number of imperative verb phrases (N_{IMPVP}), the number of BE *going to* + infinitive constructions with future reference (N_{BGT}), and a normalization coefficient. As an English finite verb phrase has one finite verb form only, the number of finite verb forms and the number of imperative verb forms were taken to equal N_{FINVP} and N_{IMPVP}, respectively. For the sake of convenience, I will use 100 as the normalization coefficient, instead of 100,000 (as with the M-coefficient) or 10,000 (as with the K- and V-coefficients). The S-coefficient thus becomes a percentage of all finite non-imperative verb phrases (excluding BE *going to* + infinitive constructions with future reference) that are in the progressive. The S-coefficient is calculated for a given text using the following formula:

$$S = N_{FINPR} / (N_{FINVP} - (N_{IMPVP} + N_{BGT})) \times 100$$

Since the S-coefficient is related to the V-coefficient, it has largely the same advantages and drawbacks. However, as the frequency of imperative and non-finite verb phrases, and of BE *going to* + infinitive constructions with future reference, may vary across the genre parameter, it is to be hoped that excluding these types of verb phrases from the counts will increase the reliability of the S-coefficient, as compared to the V-coefficient, from a cross-genre perspective. It should be noted, however, that the S-coefficient was designed for a study of late Modern English. In Old English, for instance, the progressive occurred in the imperative mood, which means that another coefficient would have to be used.

3.1.2   Comparing the M- and S-coefficients: A methodological perspective

As mentioned above, in the present study the frequency of the progressive will be analysed both from a variationist perspective (that is, in relation to the frequency

---

11   In theory, this problem could have been solved, but the solutions would in turn have involved potential drawbacks. Only infinitives immediately preceded by *to* could have been included in the counts, but split infinitives would then have been excluded from retrieval. Alternatively, modal auxiliaries could have been excluded from the retrieval procedures and infinitives included, but this solution would probably have increased the error rate in the output, as modals can be retrieved (semi-)lexically to a greater extent than infinitives. Moreover, neither of these solutions solves the more serious problem of different constraints influencing the distribution of progressives and non-progressives in finite and non-finite verb phrases.

of the non-progressive) and from a non-paradigmatic perspective, where the progressive is seen as a linguistic feature in itself (and the raw frequency is instead related to the number of words in each text). The former perspective corresponds to the S-coefficient, the latter to the M-coefficient.

By way of recapitulation, the main reasons for using the M-coefficient are (a) that it is widely used in previous research, (b) that it is comparatively objective, and (c) that it is easy to calculate and can thus be applied to the entire CONCE corpus. The most important motivation for using the S-coefficient, in contrast, is methodological. The progressive can only occur in verb phrases: the S-coefficient, which takes this constraint into account, relates the raw frequency of the progressive to the number of slots it could potentially fill in a more realistic way than does the M-coefficient.[12] It is to be hoped that the application of the S-coefficient to the material can help to assess the extent to which the results are influenced by the fact that the M-coefficient does not take the number of verb phrases in texts into account. For instance, if two texts have the same S-coefficient but different M-coefficients, this result may indicate that, since the M-coefficient does not take the distribution of verb phrases across texts into account, it is not wholly reliable as an indicator of the frequency of the progressive in texts that differ considerably with respect to this distribution.

The information needed to calculate the S-coefficient also makes it possible to calculate the frequency of non-progressive finite non-imperative verb phrases, excluding BE *going to* + infinitive constructions with future reference. This frequency is calculated by subtracting the number of finite progressives, the number of imperatives, and the number of BE *going to* + infinitive constructions with future reference, from the number of finite verb phrases, i.e. (N_{FINVP} − ($N_{IMPVP} + N_{BGT} + N_{FINPR}$)). If these non-progressive verb phrases and the finite progressives in the material are treated as the two possible variants of finite non-imperative verb phrases, excluding BE *going to* + infinitive constructions with future reference, differences between samples in the distribution of these two variants can be tested for statistical significance. It is thus possible to see which differences in S-coefficients represent statistically significant variation.

Two caveats should be mentioned in this context. First, the S-coefficient is not based on exactly the same raw frequencies of progressives as is the M-coefficient, as non-finite progressives are excluded from the calculation of the former. Thus, differences between the two coefficients in a given text may be due to factors other than the relation between, on the one hand, the number of finite

---

12   On the other hand, the M-coefficient may give a better picture than the S-coefficient of the impact of the progressive on language users. When reading or listening to a text, language users will probably form their judgement of how frequent the progressive is in the text on the basis of the number of progressives per number of words rather than per number of verb phrases. (Other factors, such as how quickly the text is processed, also enter into the discussion.) In this way, the M- and S-coefficients can be said to complement each other: the S-coefficient describes the use of the progressive better from the viewpoint of the linguist studying the status and development of the construction, while the M-coefficient is valuable in that it may approximate the impact the use of the progressive in a given text has on a language user.

non-imperative verb phrases (BE *going to* + infinitive constructions with future reference excluded) and, on the other hand, the number of words.[13] Secondly, although finite non-imperative verb phrases (excluding BE *going to* + infinitive constructions with future reference) are either progressive or non-progressive, the semantics of an individual situation are frequently incompatible with those of the progressive or the non-progressive. This incompatibility arises because the progressive/non-progressive paradigm constitutes a syntactic variable, whose variants, unlike those of phonological variables, differ in meaning (see the discussion in Section 1.5.1). However, despite the latter caveat, the S-coefficient can be assumed to take into account an approximation of what occurrence potential finite progressives have in a given text, which makes the S-coefficient a valuable complement to the M-coefficient.

As pointed out above, the calculation of the S-coefficient is time-consuming if the researcher does not have access to a tagger that assigns word classes to the words in the corpus. Moreover, it is often necessary to complement the automatic tagging procedure with some manual checking and editing, especially when taggers developed for use on Present-Day English texts are applied to historical corpora: changes in lexicon, morphology, and syntax between the period covered by the corpus and Present-Day English may cause errors in the tagging process. Some features of the method used to extract data from the tagged version of CONCE have a bearing on the results that were obtained and used as input for the calculation of the S-coefficient. An applied overview of the procedures related to selecting texts, post-processing the tagged output, and extracting data will therefore be given in the next section.

3.1.3   Applying the model: Obtaining input data for the calculation of the S-coefficient

The calculation of S-coefficients for the texts in CONCE was made possible after the corpus had been part-of-speech tagged using Conexor's EngCG–2 tagger (see Karlsson et al. 1995 for an introduction to the Constraint Grammar framework). As the tagger is intended primarily for Present-Day English, parts of the tagged output were checked manually to see whether it would be possible to use automatic tagging, in combination with software that counted the incidence of the relevant tags, to obtain the number of finite non-imperative verb forms (i.e. $N_{FINVP} - N_{IMPVP}$) for each text.[14] Extracts from the beginning of each text in CONCE were chosen: all in all, 32,176 words, or roughly 3% of the whole corpus, were checked manually.

---

13   A further difference is that the calculation of S-coefficients was restricted to parts of CONCE (see Section 3.1.3 for a discussion of this issue).

14   I am indebted to Dr. Christer Geisler for tagging the CONCE corpus, as well as for devising and running Perl scripts that automatically counted the tags whose frequency in CONCE was needed to calculate N_{FINVP} and N_{IMPVP}.

As confirmed by the checking round, there are two ways in which the tagged output from EngCG–2 may require manual post-editing. First, the error rate must be considered. In this context, a word is considered to be erroneously tagged only if none of the suggested output readings is correct. Consider (22):

(22) To_TO live_Vinf cheap_A , – to_TO save_Vinf the_DET crushing_ING expense_N of_PREP furnishing_ING a_DET house_N ; – sound_Vpres_Vimp , good_A , mercantile_A motives_Npl !
(Letters, Southey, 1800–1830, p. 56)

In (22), as in other examples of the tagged output, each word is followed by the tag(s) assigned to it, and each tag is preceded by an underscore. There are two errors in (22). With one suggested output reading, the tagger claims that *cheap* is an adjective (coded as "A") when it is used as an adverb ("ADV"); with two suggested output readings, the tagger suggests that *sound* is either a verb in the present tense ("Vpres") or an imperative ("Vimp") when it is in fact used as an adjective. Only *c.* 1.3% of all words in the manually checked parts of the corpus were classified erroneously.[15] This was considered a tolerable error rate, and errors were left uncorrected.

In other cases, the tagger presents several possible output readings, one of which is correct. For example, when in doubt whether a given form is a verb in the past tense ("Vpast") or a past participle ("EN"), the tagger frequently gives both alternatives, as in (23), where *neglected* is a past participle, and in (24), where *sat* is a verb in the past tense. In (23) and (24), the output is thus ambiguous but not erroneous. (There are also cases where more than two possible output readings are given.)

(23) I_P must_Vmod write_Vinf , or_Cc I_P shall_Vmod have_Vinf delayed_EN it_Pobl till_Cs delay_N has_Vpres made_EN the_DET thought_N painful_A as+of_PREP a_DET duty_N neglected_EN_Vpast .
(Letters, Coleridge, 1800–1830, p. 456)

(24) Her_Pgen expressive_A eyes_Npl were_Vpast two_Ncard stars_Npl whose_DETwh beams_Npl were_Vpast love_N ; hope_N and_Cc light-heartedness_N sat_EN_Vpast on_PREP her_Pgen cloudless_A brow_N .
(Fiction, Shelley, 1800–1830, p. I.249)

In the manually checked parts of CONCE, *c.* 2.5% of all words had been given more than one output reading; Geisler (2002: 250ff.) found that ambiguous tags represented *c.* 2% of the tagged version of CONCE. These figures do not in

---

15 The tagger occasionally combines several words into a compound phrase and assigns one tag to the whole compound. For instance, the phrase *once or twice* is analysed as a compound adverb (coded as "once+or+twice_ADV"). In this context, the term "words" should be taken also to encompass such compound phrases.

themselves call for alarm, but it turned out that a large proportion of all ambiguities included at least one alternative which was a finite, non-imperative verb form, and at least one alternative which was not. The tag "_EN_Vpast" was particularly frequent, probably because EngCG–2 cannot process the type of context which is often necessary to disambiguate between a past-tense reading and a past-participle reading. If nothing had been done to remedy the situation, the counts of finite verb forms in CONCE would have been too high, as the tag "_EN_Vpast" would have been counted as an instance of "_Vpast", including non-finite forms such as *neglected* in (23) in the counts. Alternatively, ambiguous tags could have been ignored, but this would have reversed the misrepresentation: no words coded as, for instance, "_EN_Vpast" would have been included in the counts, excluding e.g. *sat* in (24). To solve this problem, I disambiguated manually all words that had been assigned at least one alternative corresponding to a finite, non-imperative verb form and at least one alternative corresponding to any other category.

Since the manual disambiguation process is time-consuming, limitations of time made it necessary to restrict the calculation of S-coefficients to roughly half of the CONCE corpus. Texts were chosen with the aims of maximizing the diachronic spread of the results, keeping all genres represented, and including both women and men letter-writers. A total of 20 texts from period 1 and 20 texts from period 3 were selected. The entire period samples of CONCE were used for these two periods, with the exception that only four Letters texts from each period were included. Two texts written by women and two by men letter-writers were selected for each period. For period 1, the two letter collections whose first letter was dated the closest to 1800 by women and men letter-writers respectively were selected; for period 3, letter collections beginning with letters dated as close to 1900 as possible were selected.[16] (For an overview of the texts selected, see Appendix 1.) This subsample of CONCE, for which S-coefficients were calculated, will be referred to as "the S-coefficient subcorpus" henceforth.

As a result of this restriction, differences in text selection will make the M- and S-coefficients less comparable when texts from Letters and/or period 2 are included in the calculation of M-coefficients. To solve this problem, alternative M-coefficients will be calculated for the texts that make up the S-coefficient subcorpus only. In the interest of clarity, such M-coefficients will be referred to as "M'-coefficients" in what follows.

Searches for all ambiguous tags that contained at least one tag representing a finite, non-imperative verb form and at least one tag representing some other category were run on the tagged texts. When such an ambiguity was found, it was

---

16   However, only one letter collection per letter-writer was included in the S-coefficient subcorpus. There is material from two collections of letters written by Samuel Butler in CONCE, but only one of the two collections (the one beginning with the letter closer to 1900) was selected. Note that the selection was based on a preliminary version of CONCE.

disambiguated manually.[17] When all 40 texts had been gone through, the frequency of single output readings that marked finite, non-imperative verb forms, and of ambiguous tags whose alternatives only comprised tags marking finite, non-imperative verb forms, was obtained using Perl scripts (see note 14). The resulting frequencies were added up for each text. All instances of BE *going to* + infinitive constructions with future reference were then subtracted from these totals.[18] These calculations resulted in text-specific values for the frequency of finite non-imperative verb phrases, excluding BE *going to* + infinitive constructions with future reference, i.e. $(N_{FINVP} - (N_{IMPVP} + N_{BGT}))$. Table 6 presents the results for the S-coefficient subcorpus.

Table 6.   Finite non-imperative verb phrases, excluding BE *going to* + infinitive constructions with future reference, by period and genre in the S-coefficient subcorpus

Period	Debates	Drama	Fiction	History	Letters	Science	Trials	Total
1	1,830	3,849	4,569	2,489	5,991	3,021	8,763	30,512
3	1,909	3,605	3,538	2,806	4,498	2,616	9,865	28,837
Total	3,739	7,454	8,107	5,295	10,489	5,637	18,628	59,349

The remaining statistic needed for the calculation of the S-coefficient is the number of finite progressive verb phrases, i.e. N_{FINPR}. This information is given in Table 7.

Table 7.   Finite progressive verb phrases by period and genre in the S-coefficient subcorpus

Period	Debates	Drama	Fiction	History	Letters	Science	Trials	Total
1	11	37	86	10	84	23	176	427
3	29	114	69	66	145	32	234	689
Total	40	151	155	76	229	55	410	1,116

---

17   A small number of ambiguous tags proved impossible to disambiguate. These tags were left as they were, which means that the actual number of finite verb forms in the texts is likely to be slightly lower than that reached through the automatic counting procedure. However, the cases where disambiguation was impossible were so few that the influence of this factor on the results can be assumed to be negligible.

18   BE *going to* + infinitive constructions with future reference were selected from the concordance files which were previously used to find potential progressives in the material (see Section 2.2).

3.2   Frequency variation across genres, by gender, and in diachrony

In this section, I will investigate variation in the frequency of the progressive with the extralinguistic variables of time, genre, and the sex of the letter-writer. In other words, the frequency of the progressive, expressed as M- or S-coefficients, will be used as a dependent variable, with the extralinguistic variables as independent variables. In addition, variation in S-coefficients between subsamples of the corpus will be tested for statistical significance. As pointed out in Section 3.1, it is likely that differences between the M- and S-coefficients will chiefly be due to different ratios of the number of finite non-imperative verb phrases (excluding BE *going to* + infinitive constructions with future reference) to the number of words in the texts examined. I will therefore devote some space to commenting on differences in such ratios.

In previous research, developments in the frequency of the progressive have been linked to the grammaticalization of the construction and the obligatorification of its aspectual functions. Before I present my results, I will therefore survey briefly how the development which led to the progressive becoming a more integrated part of English grammar has been accounted for by scholars. I will also present my own perspective on this development, and describe how this perspective will be applied in Chapters 3 through 7.

3.2.1   The status of the progressive in late Modern English grammar

3.2.1.1   Previous research: A survey and discussion

In many ways, the progressive was a well-established feature of the English language by 1800. Its paradigm was similar, though not identical, to that of Present-Day English; moreover, the frequency of the progressive had been increasing ever since the late Middle English period. Finally, most functions of the progressive attested in Present-Day English were present in the language of 1800.[19] Over the 19th century, the paradigm was to become identical to that of Present-Day English, and the progressive was to become near-obligatory to express ongoing action and frame-time in non-stative situations. Most importantly for the purposes of the present chapter, the frequency of the construction would also continue to rise.

This frequency increase has been linked to the integration of the progressive into the English language. Strang (1982: 432), for instance, drawing for data on narrative prose, suggests that what corresponds to an M-coefficient of *c.* 270–330 represents "the maturity" of the progressive. Variation above this

---

19   Possible exceptions include the use of the past progressive to indicate that events in narrative passages are described from a given character's point of view, discussed in Ehrlich (1990), as well as the use of the progressive as a foregrounding device in conversational narrative taken up in Couper-Kuhlen (1995).

level of frequency is, she claims, due to idiosyncratic writing strategies rather than to the development of the English language. Strang claims that this stage was reached in the middle of the 19th century in what she refers to as "standard literary English" (1982: 432); she believes, however, that different types of English reached the same stage at different times.

The picture outlined above has also led scholars to construct hypotheses as regards how the progressive went from being an optional verbal periphrasis with a formally active passive (the passival progressive) to being a construction with obligatory functions and a symmetric passive (the passive progressive). Denison (1993: 440ff.) centres on the syntactic implications of these changes, and on their connections with the phenomenon of grammaticalization. From a syntactic point of view, grammaticalization of the progressive would mean that progressive BE changed "from being head of its phrase to a modifier of the lexical head" (Denison 1993: 441). Denison places this postulated development in the late Modern English period, and links it to the near-disappearance of the *being* + present participle construction and the appearance of the passive progressive (for which see Chapter 5). Before the reanalysis, the verb phrase of a sentence such as *The house is being built* would consist of *is* as main verb plus a typically resultative complement *being built*: the verb phrase would thus not express passive progressive meaning (Denison 1993: 441). Denison also considers it possible that the reanalysis contributed to the near-loss of the *being* + present participle construction, as "it was now the only construction where the first auxiliary verb (the one which determines the syntax of the whole group) had the same morphology as the lexical verb" (Denison 1993: 442).

From a semantic point of view, grammaticalization is usually considered to involve generalization and bleaching of semantic content. Traugott (1982) hypothesizes that, in the process of delexicalization, semantic changes tend to go from more to less concrete, from less to more personal, and from propositional to textual to expressive content.[20] Many of these changes would match a postulated development of not-solely-aspectual functions of the progressive from aspectual functions. Moreover, if we accept that the syntactic reanalysis of the progressive took place in late Modern English, Wright's (1994) claim that the progressive had not-solely-aspectual functions in early Modern English would be in line with Brinton's (1988: 161) statement that "[t]he acquisition of syntactic features associated with full auxiliary status lags behind the semantic developments ... and seems to be dependent in part upon the age and frequency of the construction".[21] However, the existence of not-solely-aspectual functions of the progressive even in Old English (see Nehls 1988; Rydén 1997) presents a

---

20   The term "personal" is used by Traugott (1982: 253) in the sense 'anchored in the context of the speech act, particularly the speaker's orientation to situation, text, and interpersonal relations'.

21   Brinton (1988) focuses on the development of aspectualizers in English, not on the development of the progressive. However, she claims that the study is relevant to research on grammaticalization as a semantic process in general (Brinton 1988: 162).

problem for this view, as it does not seem likely that there should be a time lag of some 1,000 years between semantic and syntactic developments.[22] Moreover, it makes sense to assume that the increase in the frequency of the progressive should accompany the transition from lexical to grammatical in grammaticalization; but the progressive has been on the increase from late Middle English onwards (see e.g. Nehls 1988: 190), which makes it necessary to account for why this increase should precede the syntactic developments. Results which will be presented in Chapter 7 imply that the frequency increase cannot be accounted for solely with reference to the development and/or increase in frequency of not-solely-aspectual functions. (However, the interaction between the progressive and other linguistic features throughout the history of English may have obscured what would otherwise have been a clearer case of grammaticalization.)

Nehls (1988) approaches the integration of the progressive into late Modern English grammar from yet another angle. Focusing on the aspectual functions of the progressive, he (1988: 175) considers a language to have acquired the category of (imperfective vs. perfective) aspect when the following three criteria are met:

- The verbal paradigm has systematic morphological devices to express the two aspects.
- Answers to the questions "What are you doing?" and "What is happening?" (Nehls 1988: 175) must contain the imperfective form.
- Utterances "where one event is in progress and a second event impinges so to speak on the first event" (Nehls 1988: 174), as in *They were leaving when I arrived*, must contain both the imperfective and the perfective form.

Nehls (1988: 188f.) postulates that these three criteria were met in English around the middle of the 19th century.

If Nehls's hypotheses concerning the development of verbal aspect in English are accurate, we might expect either of two possible developments concerning the frequency of the 19th-century progressive. If the change from optional to obligatory aspectual marking was sudden, we should see a relatively marked increase in frequency for all genres at roughly the same time in the middle of the century. In contrast, if the change takes more time, it would be likely to manifest itself as an increase in the first half of the 19th century (the middle of an S-curve of diffusion), followed by a flattening-out effect as the last vestiges of optional aspectual marking are slowly eroded. Either way, it is also probable that we would see a reduction of frequency differences across genres, as the establishment of a more or less categorical grammatical rule may be expected to reduce situational usage differentiation (although there may be cross-genre

---

22   If the line is taken that the origin of the late Middle English and Modern English progressive is the construction BE + preposition + gerund, as in *He was on hunting*, rather than the Old English progressive (see Section 2.2.2.5), the not-solely-aspectual functions of the Old English progressive become less relevant to the discussion. This would decrease the time lag between the semantic and syntactic developments to *c.* 500 years.

differences in the number of verb phrases where the progressive would be obligatory, and even in the timing of the change from optional to obligatory aspectual marking).[23] In other words, to some extent Nehls's (1988) hypotheses are testable.

Another way of testing such a hypothesis would be to go through all non-progressives in a corpus to see if a point is reached when no non-progressives occur that would have to be in the progressive if Nehls's hypotheses were true. However, there are several reasons why this approach is unsuitable. First, the number of non-progressive verb phrases that would have to be gone through would be very large. Secondly, judgements as to whether or not a progressive would be required in a given sentence are to some extent theory-dependent and subjective. Lastly, even if no non-progressives that would require a progressive could be found, this would not constitute more than weak support for Nehls's hypotheses: as Rydén (1979: 22) points out, "[t]he non-existence of a certain syntactic feature in the texts examined does not of course mean that it was considered ungrammatical and that it was never used; it may just have never happened to be written down (owing to very low frequency or for other reasons) or it may simply have eluded discovery by the examiner".

3.2.1.2   The concept of integration

Further research is needed concerning how the progressive interacted with other features in Old, Middle, and early Modern English, and how this interaction affected the functional distribution of the construction. More research is also necessary in order to make clear the connection between the progressive and the processes of grammaticalization and obligatorification in late Modern English. Moreover, there are other areas that are relevant to the development of the progressive in the 19th century and that should be looked into, such as diffusion across genres and linguistic parameters (e.g. clause type, situation type, and auxiliary combinations in the verb phrase). Many of these developments enter into discussions of grammaticalization as well, as increased syntactic applicability often occurs together with the semantic bleaching characteristic of many grammaticalization processes.

Since quantitative analyses of the distribution of the progressive across such linguistic and extralinguistic parameters are central to the present study, I prefer the wider term "integration" to "grammaticalization" with reference to my own results (although the latter term will be used in discussions of previous research). The term "integration" should be taken to cover aspects of both

---

23   It is possible that both the timing of the increase and the decrease in cross-genre differences in the frequency of aspectual progressives may be partly counteracted by developments concerning the not-solely-aspectual functions of the construction. However, aspectual functions can be expected to account for the majority of the occurrences of the progressive in 19th-century English, so the two changes should still manifest themselves in the quantitative results.

grammaticalization and obligatorification; it focuses, however, on other, related areas, such as the formal expansion of the progressive across the English verb phrase, the extension of the progressive to new types of situations and subjects, and the general increase in the frequency of the construction. In this way, it is possible to discuss the integration of the progressive into English grammar from a quantitative position. Integration is thus seen as a process, and as a relative rather than an absolute notion: while a feature can be more or less fully integrated into one language variety than into another, there is no cut-off point prior to which the feature is not integrated and beyond which it is integrated.[24]

It is possible for the integration of a linguistic feature into a language variety to be influenced by both linguistic and extralinguistic factors. The integration of the progressive into late Modern English grammar will be investigated from different perspectives in Chapters 3–7. In the present chapter, the chief aspect of the concept of integration which will be analysed is that of frequency: an increase in frequency over the 19th century will be taken to indicate that the progressive became more fully integrated into English grammar during this period, and in that sense a less marked feature. In Chapter 4, I will establish a bridge between frequency and function, when frequency results for corpus subsamples are compared with dimension scores on four of Biber's (1988) dimensions of variation. In Chapters 5 and 6, the integration of the progressive will be discussed with reference to the distribution of the construction over the verbal paradigm and to the co-occurrence of the progressive with other linguistic features and contexts. Finally, in Chapter 7, I will focus on the integration of three types of not-solely-aspectual progressives.

3.2.2   Diachronic variation in 19th-century English

In what follows, I will present results pertaining to the frequency development of the progressive in CONCE. Results for individual genres will be conflated in this section; genre-specific variation will be the topic of Section 3.2.3. However, I will still comment on cross-genre variation when I compare the results of my investigation with what has been reported in previous research, as one source of differences in this respect may be the genre distribution of the corpora used.

Previous research on the development of the progressive across the 19th century has shown that the construction increased substantially in frequency during this period. Although Mossé's (1938, II: 271f.) data are not stratified into period subsamples, his results still indicate an increase in the frequency of the progressive over the 19th century. Arnaud (1998: 131), focusing on private letters, finds that the M-coefficient more than doubled in the period 1787–1880: it

---

24   To some extent, grammaticalization can also be seen as a continuum rather than a binary variable. However, in Denison's (1993) account the syntactic grammaticalization of the progressive involves the distinction between BE and the notionally most salient verb as head of the verb phrase; syntactic grammaticalization thus appears to be a binary distinction at least on the level of each progressive verb phrase.

was *c.* 140 at the beginning of the period investigated, and *c.* 330 at the end of the same period, amounting to an increase of *c.* 136%.[25] Dennis (1940: 839) divides each century into three periods (for the 19th century, 1800–1832, 1833–1865, and 1866–1899), and measures the frequency of the progressive in terms of occurrences per 500 or 1,000 lines of text. Her overall results for the British English part of her corpus indicate an increase of 185% between the periods 1766–1799 and 1866–1899 (there are 20 occurrences in the former period and 57 in the latter). In a recent study based on the ARCHER corpus, Hundt (2004b: 115) found that the frequency of the progressive in British English, as measured in M-coefficients and including *going + to*-infinitive constructions, increased from 103 in the period 1750–1799, via 128 in the period 1800–1849, to 233 in the period 1850–1899. All sets of data thus indicate a more than doubled frequency from the late 18th to the late 19th century. However, Arnaud's, Dennis's, and Hundt's results regarding the rate of increase within this period are not in unison. Whereas Arnaud's data indicate a fairly even increase between 1787 and 1880, Dennis's results rather point to a jump somewhere around the year 1800, followed by a flattening of the curve, and Hundt's data imply a pronounced increase between the first and second half of the 19th century itself.

Dennis's results are in agreement with an account of the progressive that postulates a grammaticalization of the construction in the 18th century, followed by an S-curve of diffusion flattening out when the progressive has become (near-)obligatory to express imperfective aspect. However, the low raw frequencies may indicate that Dennis's samples are too small for differences between adjacent periods to be considered reliable: for instance, her results indicate a small decrease in the overall frequency of the progressive in British English between the periods 1733–1765 and 1766–1799 (Dennis 1940: 861).

Dennis (1940), Arnaud (1998), and Hundt (2004b) are highly valuable studies in their own right. However, as regards the collection and quantification of material and data, there is still a need for more research on the frequency of the 19th-century progressive. Arnaud's results need not be generalizable to English as a whole, as he only includes private letters in his corpus; moreover, the number of words per text was estimated rather than counted (something which is, however, understandable considering the large corpus, *c.* 10 million words [Arnaud 1998: 124]). Dennis includes both verse and prose in her corpus, and both formal and informal genres, but her samples are comparatively small, and are based on counting the number of lines in the texts that constitute her corpus. This means that typographical factors such as typeface and page size will have affected her calculations, and that her results are difficult to compare to those of other scholars. Hundt (2004b), in contrast, uses electronic corpora with exact word counts. However, the importance of developments within the 19th century indicated by Arnaud's, Dennis's, and Hundt's results, as well as the discrepancies in the rate of increase attested in the three studies, indicates that a

---

25   Arnaud (1998) does not provide tables giving the exact M-coefficients for his subperiods; instead, the coefficients have to be estimated from figures.

study of the development of the progressive within the 19th century based on an electronic corpus with a narrower periodization would be a valuable complement to previous research.

When M-coefficients are calculated for the three period subsamples of CONCE, the picture obtained is in rough accordance with what Arnaud (1998), Dennis (1940), and Hundt (2004b) found. The M-coefficients are given in Table 8.

Table 8.   M-coefficients per period in CONCE

Period	M-coefficient
1	172
2	263
3	316
1–3	247

Since period 1 in CONCE begins later than the first period Arnaud (1998) studied, it is not surprising that the M-coefficient for period 1 is higher than the earliest M-coefficient (*c.* 140) obtained by Arnaud (1998: 131). It may seem surprising that the frequency for period 3 in CONCE is lower than that (*c.* 330) obtained for Arnaud's final period (1865–1880), as period 3 in CONCE covers a partially later time span (1870–1900). However, this can probably be explained partly by the fact that private letters, the only genre included in Arnaud's corpus, constitute a genre where the progressive increased considerably in frequency over the 19th century compared with most other genres in CONCE (see Smitterberg 2000a: 286 and Section 3.2.4). In contrast, ARCHER does not focus on private letters to the same extent as CONCE, which may help to explain why the frequencies in Table 8 are higher than Hundt's (2004b) results. Another factor that may be at work is the difference in periodization between the corpora used: texts from the period 1850–1900 constitute roughly half of Hundt's (2004b) 19th-century sample, whereas texts from the same period make up about two thirds of CONCE. Because the frequency of the progressive clearly increases in diachrony, a relative emphasis on the latter half of the 19th century is likely to lead to higher normalized frequencies.

The results in Table 8 show that the frequency of the progressive in the entire CONCE corpus did not quite double from period 1 to period 3. In contrast, Arnaud's (1998), Dennis's (1940), and Hundt's (2004b) results, given above in this section, point to a more than doubled frequency. This difference between the present study and those carried out by Arnaud, Dennis, and Hundt has several possible explanations. First of all, since period 1 comprises texts produced between 1800 and 1830 and period 3 texts produced between 1870 and 1900, the mean difference between a text from period 1 and a text from period 3 is 70 years.[26] In contrast, Arnaud's first and last periods are 1787–1804 and 1865–1880 respectively, with a mean difference of 77 years;[27] the mean difference between Hundt's first and last periods (1750–1799 and 1850–1899) is 100 years. Dennis's study gives an indication that even such relatively small differences in the time span covered by different corpora may be important: if her (1940: 859) results for British English in the periods 1800–1832 and 1866–1899 are compared (instead of those for 1766–1799 and 1866–1899 as above), the increase is from 43 to 57 occurrences, i.e. 33%, instead of the 185% stated above. (See also above for questions concerning the reliability of Dennis's results.) Secondly, as pointed out above, the Letters genre is one of the genres where the progressive increases most over the 19th century. Thus, a corpus consisting of letters only, like Arnaud's, will be likely to show a more pronounced increase over this period than will a multi-genre corpus.

As for the rate of increase, the CONCE data indicate that the progressive increased in frequency at a fairly even pace in 19th-century English. The difference between periods 1 (1800–1830) and 2 (1850–1870) is 38 M-coefficient units bigger than that between periods 2 and 3 (1870–1900); but the two former periods are also further apart in diachrony, so this distribution is to be expected. The rate of increase between the mid years of periods 1 (1815) and 2 (1860) is 2.02 M-coefficient units per year; that between the mid years of periods 2 and 3 (1885) is 2.12 units per year. However, as will be shown in Section 3.2.4, this even development is not attested in all of the individual genres.

If we turn to a comparison of the M- and the S-coefficient, as was pointed out above, the main reason for differences between the two coefficients is that the texts differ in terms of the ratio of the number of finite non-imperative verb phrases (excluding BE *going to* + infinitive constructions with future reference) to the number of words, i.e. $(N_{FINVP} - (N_{IMPVP} + N_{BGT})) / N_{WORD}$. I will refer to this ratio as the "verb density" ratio in what follows, as the ratio gives a rough indication of how many finite verb phrases occur in a text of a given length. However, the term "verb density" covers more ground than the formula accounts for, as imperative and non-finite verb phrases, as well as BE *going to* + infinitive constructions with future reference, are excluded from the ratio. The verb density ratio was designed to reflect the frequency of verb phrases whose realization, as progressive or non-progressive, affects the value of the S-coefficient, and should only be taken as an approximation of the frequency of verb phrases in texts.

As pointed out in Section 3.1.3, in order to obtain M-coefficients that are based on the same selection of texts as the S-coefficients, M'-coefficients were calculated based on the texts in the S-coefficient subcorpus only (that is, the

---

26   This mean difference reflects a purely mathematical mean, that is, the difference between the mid years of each period: $(1870 + 1900) / 2 - (1800 + 1830) / 2 = 3770 / 2 - 3630 / 2 = 1885 - 1815 = 70$. The texts need not be evenly distributed across the subperiods, however.

27   Arnaud (1998) also uses a more fine-grained periodization for some analyses; I focus here on the periods that underlie the frequency figures referred to above.

calculations included periods 1 and 3 only, and only four Letters texts per period). Table 9 presents the results.

Table 9.   M'- and S-coefficients per period in the S-coefficient subcorpus

Period	M'-coefficient	S-coefficient	Verb density
1	158	1.40	0.110
3	286	2.39	0.117
1, 3	218	1.88	0.114

The increase in S-coefficients from period 1 to period 3 is statistically significant: random variation in frequency among texts can thus be ruled out as a possible cause of the development attested.[28] As for the total figures, it appears that roughly 2% of all finite non-imperative verb phrases (excluding BE *going to* + infinitive constructions with future reference) are in the progressive. This result corresponds well with findings reported by Arnaud (1973: 590); Arnaud found that the frequency of the progressive was rarely higher than 3% of the frequency of the non-progressive in his 19th-century corpus.

If we relate the two accounts of the frequency development of the progressive afforded by the M'- and S-coefficient to each other by expressing them as percentage changes between periods 1 and 3, the following picture emerges: the S-coefficient increased by 71% between periods 1 and 3, whereas the M'-coefficient increased by 81%.[29] The main reason for this discrepancy is that the verb density ratio has not remained constant in diachrony: it is 0.110 in period 1, but 0.117 in period 3. The increasing ratios imply that the English language as a whole became more "verby" over the 19th century: the number of finite non-imperative verb phrases (excluding BE *going to* + infinitive constructions with future reference) in a given text from the beginning of the century will thus tend to be lower than in an equally long text from the end of the century. As a result, the overall occurrence potential of the progressive in texts increased from 1800 to 1900. In addition, the change in verb density ratios may indicate that English sentence structure shifted towards a greater proportion of finite clauses over the century. I will return to this issue when I deal with the development of the progressive in individual genres in Section 3.2.4. First, however, a few words on frequency results for genre totals are in order.

---

28   As pointed out in Section 1.6.3, the chi-square test for statistical significance with a 0.05 significance level will be used throughout the present work; chi-square and p values, and degrees of freedom, are given in Appendix 3.

29   The percentages are calculated by dividing the difference in frequency between periods 1 and 3 by the frequency of the progressive in period 1, and multiplying the resulting quotient by 100. For the S-coefficients in Table 9, the calculation is thus $(2.39 - 1.40) / 1.40 \times 100 \approx 71$. In all calculations carried out on the basis of information presented in tables, exact figures have been used throughout the present study. This occasionally leads to seeming discrepancies between results presented in table format and in the main text.

3.2.3   Genre variation

The genre variable has long been known to be important to the development of the progressive. For instance, Dennis (1940: 860) starts out from the assumption that, ceteris paribus, the frequency of the progressive will be higher in colloquial texts, and Biber et al. (1999: 462) show that, in Present-Day English, the progressive is several times more common in conversation than in academic prose. However, the verb density ratio is also likely to vary across the genre parameter, with formal expository genres such as History and Science having lower ratios than speech-related and/or informal genres such as Drama and Letters. Thus, we would expect the comparison of M- and S-coefficients to reveal cross-genre differences.

The M-coefficients for the genres in CONCE are given in Table 10.[30]

Table 10.   M-coefficients by genre in CONCE

Genre	M-coefficient
Debates	89
Drama	291
Fiction	255
History	123
Letters	307
Science	85
Trials	309
All genres	247

As is demonstrated in Table 10, there is considerable variation in the frequency of the progressive across the genre parameter. The speech-related genres Trials and Drama and the informal written genre Letters have the highest M-coefficients; Fiction, which contains a mix of written narrative and constructed dialogue, forms a middle ground, although the M-coefficient is closer to that of Drama than to that of History; and the formal, speech-related genre Debates, together with the written, formal genres History and Science, has the lowest normalized frequencies.

The two genres that are partly based on recorded speech, viz. Debates and Trials, have widely different M-coefficients: Trials have the highest M-coefficient of all genres, whereas Debates have the second lowest. This dissimilarity may be due to such factors as differences regarding the formality of the occasion, the probability of publication of the proceedings and the speakers' awareness of this

---

30   In most tables in Chapters 3 through 7, the genres are listed in alphabetical order, as I do not wish to group genres together on the presupposition that the linguistic make-up of some genres should be similar because they share extralinguistic characteristics. On a few occasions, however, when it has been necessary to split tables into subtables, I have grouped the expository (Debates, History, Science) and the non-expository (Drama, Fiction, Letters, Trials) genres together, in the interest of clarity.

probability, the extent to which it may have been possible for speakers to prepare parts of the texts in advance, and the editing process that texts from the two genres went through when being transferred into writing. Whatever the factors behind the variation, these results point to the importance of considering more specific genre characteristics in addition to medium when research on the progressive is being carried out. The findings are also in line with Biber's (1988: 161) finding for Present-Day English that none of the dimensions of variation identified in his analysis "defines an absolute spoken/written distinction".

History and Science, the two written expository genres in CONCE, are also clearly distinct with respect to their M-coefficients, though both have comparatively low normalized frequencies: History has a higher M-coefficient than Science. One reason for this may be that History includes more narrative features than Science: it has been shown that narrative concerns may distinguish specialized from popular written genres (Biber and Finegan 1997: 271). I will return to this matter in Chapter 4. In addition, Biber (1988: 171) takes academic prose (an umbrella term that would encompass both Science and History) in Present-Day English as an example of a genre that includes "several well-defined sub-genres, and the variation within the genre is due in part to variation among the sub-genres". This intra-genre variation may also help to explain why the two genres differ with respect to the frequency of the progressive.

If we turn to comparisons between M'- and S-coefficients, differences in verb density ratios can be expected to be quite pronounced across the genre parameter. We can therefore expect a good deal of variation between M'- and S-coefficients and, as mentioned in Section 3.1, we can also expect this variation to lead to cross-genre differences being less pronounced when the S-coefficient is used than when the M'-coefficient is used. The results for the S-coefficient subcorpus are presented in Table 11.

Table 11.   M'- and S-coefficients by genre in the S-coefficient subcorpus

Genre	M'-coefficient	S-coefficient	Verb density
Debates	105	1.07	0.094
Drama	255	2.03	0.123
Fiction	218	1.91	0.112
History	124	1.44	0.086
Letters	258	2.18	0.117
Science	89	0.98	0.082
Trials	322	2.20	0.143
All genres	218	1.88	0.114

As Table 11 shows, there are substantial differences in verb density ratios across the genre parameter: in fact, the ratio is 75% higher for the genre with the highest value (Trials) than for the genre with the lowest value (Science). As was shown in Table 10, these were also the genres with the highest and lowest M-coefficients respectively in CONCE as a whole. Table 11 shows that this also holds true when only the S-coefficient subcorpus is drawn on for data, regardless of whether the M'- or the S-coefficient is used. In fact, the overall order of the genres in terms of the frequency of the progressive is the same regardless of the coefficient used.

However, given that the verb density ratio is considerably higher in Trials than in Science, there are more slots which can be filled by progressives in the former genre. It can therefore be expected that the difference, expressed as a percentage, between the two genres will be lower when calculations are based on the S-coefficient than when the M'-coefficient is used, and this is also the case: the cross-genre difference is 262% when the M'-coefficient is used but only 126% when the S-coefficient is employed. This clearly shows the tendency of the M-coefficient to indicate greater cross-genre differences in the frequency of the progressive than the S-coefficient.

The findings provide further support for the theory that the progressive is more common in non-expository than in expository genres. From a linguistic point of view, expository genres can be expected to have long and elaborated noun phrases and a high proportion of non-finite clauses compared with non-expository genres. These characteristics will lower the verb density ratio for an expository genre; and genres that have low verb density ratios will, on the whole, have fewer slots that can be filled by progressives than genres with high ratios. As was shown above, however, differences in verb density ratios do not account for all of the frequency variation between expository and non-expository genres: the expository and non-expository groups are still easily distinguished when the S-coefficient, which takes differences in verb density ratios into account, is used.

The chi-square test was applied to the data to see whether the variation attested in the distribution of progressive and non-progressive finite non-imperative verb phrases (excluding BE *going to* + infinitive constructions with future reference) was significant across the genre parameter. The test revealed that the differences were significant when computed for all genres together. However, when differences between adjacent genres were tested, only one of the differences was statistically significant, viz. that between Fiction and History. Fiction is the non-expository genre with the lowest S-coefficient and History the expository genre with the highest S-coefficient; the significant difference between these two thus further emphasizes the importance of the expository/non-expository divide for the distribution of the progressive in texts.

These results also point to the importance of using large and varied corpora and of being cautious when interpreting one's results. If two samples differ with respect to verb density ratios, even substantial differences between them in M-coefficients, such as that between Letters and Trials in Table 11 (a difference of 64 M-coefficient units), may turn out not to be significant when the S-coefficient is applied to the same data. (However, the M'- and S-coefficients differ with respect to parameters other than verb density ratios as well, since non-finite progressives were not included in the calculation of the latter.) As will become clear in the next section, this also holds true for developments within individual genres.

3.2.4   Genre-specific frequency developments across the 19th century

As previous research has shown, the genre parameter is important in diachronic analyses of the progressive. Dennis (1940) shows that the incidence of the progressive is higher in informal prose texts than in verse texts or formal prose texts, although frequency increases can be noted in most genre types (and in both British and American English) over the 19th century. (See, however, Section 3.2.2 for a critique of Dennis's methodology.) Hundt and Mair (1999: 236), looking at the development of a number of linguistic features – among others the progressive – in the Brown, LOB, Frown, and FLOB corpora, claim that their "findings require a model in which grammatical change is seen as mediated through genre". I will devote the present section to accounting for the development of the progressive in the genres of CONCE. Table 12 and Figure 1 show the development over the century, as measured in M-coefficients.

Table 12.   M-coefficients by period and genre in CONCE

Period	Debates	Drama	Fiction	History	Letters	Science	Trials	All genres
1	60	118	209	32	202	68	285	172
2	57	366	323	121	323	76	282	263
3	150	402	229	216	425	114	355	316
1–3	89	291	255	123	307	85	309	247

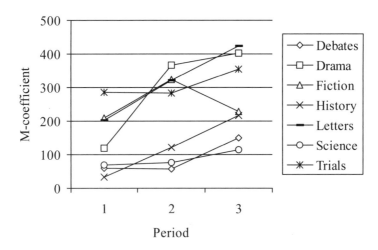

Figure 1.   M-coefficients for period/genre subsamples in CONCE

Table 12 and Figure 1 show that the division between two groups of genres, one non-expository group comprising Drama, Fiction, Letters, and Trials, and one expository group comprising Debates, History, and Science, appears to be present in diachrony as well. In none of the periods is there any overlap of M-coefficients between these two genre groups. In contrast, there is considerable diachronic overlap within both groups: in fact, the order of the genres within either group changes within every period.

The results do not appear to support Nehls's hypothesis concerning an overall obligatorification of aspectual progressives in the middle of the century, if we take decreased genre diversity in the frequency of the progressive to be a likely result of this process. The genre diversity increases rather than decreases over the century: the difference between the genres with the highest and lowest frequencies is 253 M-coefficient units in period 1 (Trials and History), and 310 in period 3 (Letters and Science). The apparent increase in genre diversity as regards the frequency of the progressive is interesting, as this result correlates with findings reported in Biber and Finegan (1997). Biber and Finegan (1997: 273) found that "the specialist expository registers in ARCHER – medical prose, science prose, and legal prose – have followed a consistent course towards ever more literate styles"; conversely, popular written genres, such as Letters and Fiction, have gone towards the oral end of the continuum during the 19th and 20th centuries. This lends support to the hypothesis that the progressive is an oral rather than a literate feature, as the construction is decidedly more common in popular than in specialized genres.

In what follows, I will comment on the results for individual genres in more detail. In these sections, M-coefficients will be complemented by S-coefficients and verb density ratios in order to present a more comprehensive account of the development of each genre. As the S-coefficient subcorpus, apart from its excluding period 2 entirely, is identical with the entire corpus in all genres but Letters, there is no need for presenting separate M- and M'-coefficients with the exception of this one genre.

3.2.4.1   Debates

The results for the Debates genre as regards M-coefficients, S-coefficients, and verb density ratios are given in Table 13.

Table 13.   The frequency of the progressive in Debates over the 19th century; "All" refers to figures for the whole CONCE corpus (M-coefficients) or for the whole S-coefficient subcorpus (S-coefficients and verb density ratios)

Period	M-coefficient	S-coefficient	Verb density
1	60	0.60	0.092
2	57	–	–
3	150	1.52	0.096
All	89	1.07	0.094

As Table 13 shows, in terms of M-coefficients there is a small decrease between periods 1 and 2, followed by a substantial increase (almost a trebling) between periods 2 and 3. This development may seem surprising: as periods 1 and 2 are separated by 20 years, whereas periods 2 and 3 are adjacent, more pronounced differences could be expected between the first two periods in CONCE than between the last two periods.

However, there may be text-internal explanations for this seeming discrepancy. In all samples for period 1, and most samples for period 2, the debates are presented as indirect speech. In period 3, conversely, direct speech is the norm in all samples. It is possible that this switch from indirect to direct speech brought with it a reduction in editorial interference, so that the printed text became more similar to what was actually said in the debates. Given that the progressive appears to have been characteristic of speech-related language in 19th-century English, such a trend may in turn have contributed to an increase in the frequency of the construction. Concerning S-coefficients, there is a clear and statistically significant increase between periods 1 and 3. Owing to the diachronic increase, however slight, in verb density ratios, we might expect the S-coefficients to indicate a somewhat smaller increase in the frequency of the progressive than the M-coefficients, but in fact there is a slight difference in the other direction: the S-coefficient increases by 153% between periods 1 and 3, the M-coefficient by 150%. The reason for this difference is the distribution of non-finite progressives in Debates. Both period 1 and period 3 have a non-finite progressive, but since there are 12 progressives in period 1 and 30 in period 3 altogether, the removal of one progressive from the period 1 sample affects the period frequency more, thus lowering the S-coefficient for period 1 and counteracting the influence of changing verb density ratios.

3.2.4.2   Drama

Developments for the Drama genre are given in Table 14.

Table 14.   The frequency of the progressive in Drama over the 19th century; "All" refers to figures for the whole CONCE corpus (M-coefficients) or for the whole S-coefficient subcorpus (S-coefficients and verb density ratios)

Period	M-coefficient	S-coefficient	Verb density
1	118	0.96	0.123
2	366	–	–
3	402	3.16	0.124
All	291	2.03	0.123

The Drama genre shows a more expected and straightforward development, with a huge increase in M-coefficients between periods 1 and 2 followed by a smaller but still considerable increase between periods 2 and 3. This clear increase is not due to the Drama genre tending towards higher verb density ratios, i.e., the chief reason why the M-coefficients increase is not that Drama texts contain more and more slots that the progressive can fill. Drama has a very high ratio even in period 1 – only Trials have a higher ratio – and the verb density ratio in Drama remains almost exactly the same through the century.

If Trials can be considered the genre in CONCE that is the closest to actual speech, the results thus imply that the imitation of speech in the Drama texts approaches the actual speech of the period in terms of verb density ratios. Although, as pointed out in Section 2.1.2, it cannot be taken for granted that the linguistic characteristics of Trials texts are similar to those of actual 19th-century speech, the relative lack of change in verb density ratios between periods 1 and 3 in Drama, which indicates that Drama texts did not develop towards more speech-like imitation in this respect over the 19th century, strengthens this implication. One reason for the lack of development may be that the texts were already sufficiently close to speech. Another possible reason is that there existed conventions as to how imitated speech in Drama (and perhaps, as will become clear in the next section, Fiction) should be represented in the 19th century.

Since the verb density ratio remains stable across the century in Drama, the rate of increase is similar for the M- and S-coefficients. The M-coefficient increases by 240% and the S-coefficient by 229% between periods 1 and 3, a difference of eleven percentage points which is chiefly due to three non-finite progressives in period 3. But regardless of how the frequency of the progressive is measured, it more than trebles in Drama across a time span of less than a century. The increase in S-coefficients is statistically significant.

3.2.4.3 Fiction

Fiction is the only genre to show a substantial decrease in frequency between two periods: the frequency of the progressive is 94 M-coefficient units higher in period 2 than in period 3, and the frequency in period 3 is only 20 M-coefficient units higher than that in period 1. The figures are given in Table 15.

Table 15.   The frequency of the progressive in Fiction over the 19th century; "All" refers to figures for the whole CONCE corpus (M-coefficients) or for the whole S-coefficient subcorpus (S-coefficients and verb density ratios)

Period	M-coefficient	S-coefficient	Verb density
1	209	1.88	0.109
2	323	–	–
3	229	1.95	0.117
All	255	1.91	0.112

This decrease is contradictory to expectations, against the background of the progressive being common in non-expository genres and increasing significantly in frequency in the corpus as a whole. I will therefore devote some space to accounting for a possible reason behind this development.

My hypothesis was that the distribution of dialogue and narrative passages, and different patterns concerning the occurrence of the progressive in these two subsamples of Fiction, might influence the period results. To test this hypothesis, I divided all Fiction texts into dialogue and non-dialogue. The presence of quotation marks was used as the main indicator of dialogue, which means that direct thought, indirect speech, free indirect speech, and free indirect thought were coded as dialogue or non-dialogue depending chiefly on the presence or absence of quotation marks. This may be considered a crude division, especially as regards the classification of direct thought, which "is often presented without quotation marks to distinguish it from [direct speech] presented with them" (Short 1996: 313). However, owing to the relative scarcity of this mode of presentation in the corpus texts, this factor is unlikely to affect results in any substantial way. The word counts for the two subsamples of the Fiction genre are presented in Table 16.

Table 16.   Word counts per period for the dialogue and non-dialogue subsamples of Fiction

Period	Dialogue	Non-dialogue
1	12,816	29,216
2	10,702	28,343
3	12,642	17,471
Total	36,160	75,030

As is seen in Table 16, the subsamples are relatively large, although there is of course more variation in dialogue/non-dialogue distribution within individual texts. The word count in each slot was thought sufficient for the present analyses.

After the Fiction texts had been divided into dialogue and non-dialogue subsamples, the progressives were classified according to which of the two subsamples they came from.[31] The results of the classification are given in Table 17.

---

31   Following the typology used in Short (1996), I considered all instances of the progressive occurring in direct speech, the one progressive occurring in direct thought, and two progressives occurring within quotation marks in free indirect speech part of the dialogue subsample. The non-dialogue subsample comprised the rest of the progressives occurring in free indirect speech, as well as all progressives occurring in indirect speech, narrator's representation of speech, narrator's representation of speech acts, free indirect thought, indirect thought, narrator's representation of thought, narrator's representation of thought acts, and narrator's representation of action.

Table 17. Progressives per period in the dialogue and non-dialogue subsamples of Fiction

Period	Dialogue	Non-dialogue
1	31	57
2	28	98
3	35	34
Total	94	189

As Table 17 shows, there appeared to be a sufficient number of progressives in each slot for basing conclusions on normalized frequencies.

Using the data in Tables 16 and 17, I calculated separate sets of M-coefficients for the dialogue and non-dialogue subsamples. The results of these computations are presented in Table 18.

Table 18. M-coefficients per period for the dialogue and non-dialogue subsamples of Fiction

Period	Dialogue	Non-dialogue
1	242	195
2	262	346
3	277	195
1–3	260	252

The overall figures for the two subsamples are almost identical: 260 for dialogue and 252 for non-dialogue, as measured in M-coefficient units. Thus, the results do not indicate that there are inherent differences between dialogue and non-dialogue in the frequency of the progressive. However, when we look at the diachronic development of the two subsamples, differences do emerge. While the dialogue subsample exhibits very similar M-coefficients across the century, with a small increase which is to be expected considering the overall development of the progressive in CONCE, the figures for the non-dialogue subsample rise drastically between periods 1 and 2, but fall just as abruptly again between periods 2 and 3, so that there is no increase over the century as a whole. Although word counts for dialogue and non-dialogue samples of individual texts are in some cases too low to form the basis for reliable conclusions, the results do not indicate that unexpectedly high or low frequencies of progressives in any one text underlie this unexpected development in the non-dialogue subsample. The non-dialogue sample that stands out most clearly is that from Jane Austen's *Emma* in period 1, with a very high M-coefficient (648); but this text obviously does not affect the size of the unexpected decrease between periods 2 and 3.

The results thus indicate that most of the variation in the frequency of the progressive that Fiction exhibits over the 19th century is due to variation within the non-dialogue subsample. These findings are interesting for several reasons. To begin with, they show that it is important to consider the dialogue/non-dialogue proportions of Fiction texts included in corpora on which studies of the progressive are based. Moreover, they point to the possibility (mentioned previously in Section 3.2.4.2 in connection with the Drama genre) that there existed some type of implicit convention for how speech should be represented in 19th-century fictional texts, in contrast to narrative passages in Fiction, whose language may have been subject to different constraints. The similarity between dialogue in Fiction and Drama is only partial in this respect: in Drama, the verb density ratio, rather than the frequency of the progressive, is constant across time; and the frequency of the progressive is lower in dialogue in Fiction than it is in Drama. Nevertheless, considering that such lack of variation in diachrony is found in one genre and one subsample of a genre that consist of constructed speech, it would be an interesting research question to investigate the possible existence of implicit conventions in 19th-century fictional representations of speech and what characteristics these possible conventions may have had.

In the Fiction genre in its entirety, there is a noticeable trend towards higher verb density ratios over the 19th century (from 0.109 to 0.117), which means that the occurrence potential of the progressive is likely to have increased between periods 1 and 3. This development accounts for the difference between the M- and S-coefficients in the increase in the frequency of the progressive: the M-coefficients show an increase of 9%, the S-coefficients an increase of 4%. The increase in S-coefficients is not statistically significant.[32]

3.2.4.4   History

The History genre shows a clear development: among the expository genres, it goes from having the lowest M-coefficient in period 1 to having the highest M-coefficient in period 3. (See Section 4.2 for a possible relation between this increase and the narrative nature of History texts.) Information on the frequency development of the progressive in this genre, including verb density ratios and S-coefficients, is given in Table 19.

Table 19.   The frequency of the progressive in History over the 19th century; "All" refers to figures for the whole CONCE corpus (M-coefficients) or for the whole S-coefficient subcorpus (S-coefficients and verb density ratios)

Period	M-coefficient	S-coefficient	Verb density
1	32	0.40	0.081
2	121	–	–
3	216	2.35	0.092
All	123	1.44	0.086

32   Note that, as these statistics do not take period 2 into account, much of the variation in frequency across the century in Fiction is not apparent from the percentages.

Table 19 shows that only a minor part of the increase in frequency is due to a change in verb density ratios between periods 1 and 3. The M-coefficient increases by 567% between these periods, the S-coefficient by 485% – quite dramatic increases against the general background of less than doubled M-coefficients for all genres taken together between periods 1 and 3. As will be shown in Section 3.2.4.6, Science, the other genre in CONCE that consists of academic prose, does not exhibit any such pronounced increase in the frequency of the progressive. The increase in S-coefficients for History is statistically significant.

3.2.4.5   Letters

For the Letters genre, the make-up of the table presenting the results of the analyses differs slightly from those presented for the other genres. Two separate sets of M-coefficients are given in Table 20: the set labelled "M-coefficient" is based on all Letters texts in the relevant subsamples; the other, labelled "M'-coefficient", is based on the S-coefficient subcorpus.

Table 20.   The frequency of the progressive in Letters over the 19th century; "All" refers to figures for the whole CONCE corpus (M-coefficients) or for the whole S-coefficient subcorpus (M'-coefficients, S-coefficients, and verb density ratios)

Period	M-coefficient	M'-coefficient	S-coefficient	Verb density
1	202	165	1.40	0.115
2	323	–	–	–
3	425	387	3.22	0.119
All	307	258	2.18	0.117

As Table 20 shows, the M'-coefficient is lower than the M-coefficient in both period 1 and period 3. For period 1, this is to be expected. The progressive increases in frequency in Letters over the 19th century, and the Letters texts that are part of the S-coefficient subcorpus in period 1 are those whose first letters are dated closest to 1800. Consequently, other things being equal, the M'-coefficient should be lower than the M-coefficient. For period 3, in contrast, the result is unexpected, as the Letters texts in the S-coefficient subcorpus for this period are those whose first letters are dated closest to 1900. The M'-coefficients for period 3 might thus be expected to be higher than the corresponding M-coefficients. However, selecting Letters texts for the S-coefficient subcorpus based on the dating of their first letter only is not a wholly reliable method of determining which text contains the earliest or latest letters as a whole, which may affect the figures. In addition, it is likely that idiosyncratic characteristics of individual letter-writers influence the results in this respect.

In terms of M-coefficients, the Letters genre shows a clear and consistent increase, not unlike that of History, but with higher frequencies overall. The rate of increase in Letters is relatively constant over the century. A comparison of the M'- and S-coefficients shows that the former increase by 135% between periods 1 and 3, while the latter increase by 130%. The main reason for this difference between the rates of increase is that the verb density ratio changes over the century, from 0.115 to 0.119. However, even though the increase in S-coefficients is slightly lower than that in M-coefficients, it is still statistically significant.

3.2.4.6   Science

As shown in Table 21, Science exhibits a comparatively modest increase in the frequency of the progressive.

Table 21.   The frequency of the progressive in Science over the 19th century; "All" refers to figures for the whole CONCE corpus (M-coefficients) or for the whole S-coefficient subcorpus (S-coefficients and verb density ratios)

Period	M-coefficient	S-coefficient	Verb density
1	68	0.76	0.079
2	76	–	–
3	114	1.22	0.085
All	85	0.98	0.082

The frequency of the progressive is similar in periods 1 and 2, and even the increase between periods 2 and 3 is small compared with those found in other genres. Across the whole century, the M-coefficients for periods 1 and 3 show an increase of 67%, the S-coefficients an increase of 61%.

The chi-square test showed that the increase between periods 1 and 3 was not statistically significant. In other words, Science is best analysed as stable in terms of frequency developments during the 19th century. There are several possible reasons for this lack of change. Görlach's (1999: 150) statement that "scientific style ... changed from somewhat personal accounts to impersonal, objective description" in the 1800s ties in with Biber and Finegan's (1997) findings that specialized written genres developed towards more literate styles in the 19th and 20th centuries. Although, as shown by Geisler (2002: 269), this tendency is not manifest in the CONCE texts, it may still have counteracted the general trend towards an increasing use of the progressive in English.[33] When

---

33   Note, however, that the Science texts come from several academic disciplines, such as the social sciences and chemistry, though the genre has not been stratified to include texts from these disciplines in even proportions. As these disciplines are linguistically distinct (Geisler 2002: 270), it may be the case that differences between them cancel one another out and result in what appears to be linguistic stability.

verb density ratios are considered, there is a small tendency towards higher ratios from period 1, when the ratio is 0.079, to period 3, when the ratio is 0.085.

3.2.4.7   Trials

As demonstrated in Table 10, Trials pattern together with the non-expository written genres Drama, Fiction, and Letters, rather than with the expository genres Debates, History, and Science, as regards the frequency of the progressive. Detailed information on the development of the progressive in Trials is given in Table 22.

Table 22.   The frequency of the progressive in Trials over the 19th century; "All" refers to figures for the whole CONCE corpus (M-coefficients) or for the whole S-coefficient subcorpus (S-coefficients and verb density ratios)

Period	M-coefficient	S-coefficient	Verb density
1	285	2.01	0.141
2	282	–	–
3	355	2.37	0.146
All	309	2.20	0.143

The M-coefficient for Trials does not increase between periods 1 and 2 (there is even a small decrease), but then increases by 73 between periods 2 and 3. The M-coefficient for period 1 is remarkably high – in fact, Trials is the only genre subsample from period 1 that has a higher M-coefficient than the mean value for the corpus as a whole (247); but the Trials genre is overtaken by Drama, Letters, and Fiction in period 2, though it passes Fiction again in period 3. This result is partly unexpected: to the extent that Trials can be expected to approach unmonitored speech more closely than popular written genres such as Drama and Letters, the progressive – a feature hypothesized to be conversational – should be more frequent in Trials than in the other genres. However, it may be that the speech-related nature of the Trials texts, which would promote a high frequency of progressives, is partly counteracted by the relative formality of the speech situation in this genre. Moreover, there may be extralinguistic explanations for the unexpected development of the progressive in Trials between periods 1 and 2. The majority of the Trials texts in periods 1 and 3 deal with violent crime, while this is not true for the texts from period 2; it is possible that the subject matter of the trials affects the distribution of linguistic features, such as the progressive, in the texts. The progressive has been claimed to have emphatic, subjective connotations compared with the non-progressive, and trial proceedings dealing with violent crime may well contain a larger number of linguistic features with such emotional connotations. (See Chapter 4 for further indications in this respect.)

Looking at the verb density ratio in Trials, we can see that the ratio increases, albeit not by much, between period 1 (where the ratio is 0.141) and period 3 (0.146). However, more research is needed to ascertain whether differences such as the above in verb density ratios are substantial enough to be important. Owing partly to this increase in verb density ratios in Trials, the S-coefficient does not increase as much as the M-coefficient between periods 1 and 3: the M-coefficient increases by 24%, the S-coefficient by 18%. The increase in S-coefficients is not statistically significant, despite the fact that there is a corresponding increase of 70 M-coefficient units between periods 1 and 3.

3.2.4.8   Summary of results

In Sections 3.2.4.1–3.2.4.7, I have presented results concerning the development of the progressive in the seven genres in CONCE. To some extent, the findings conformed with the expected picture of an increase in frequency in all genres, and a clear division between expository and non-expository genres. No genre exhibited an overall decrease in frequency from period 1 to period 3, regardless of whether the M- or the S-coefficient was used; and non-expository genres tended to have higher frequencies than expository genres. However, the addition of the S-coefficient to the analysis showed that the clarity of this picture is to some extent an effect of the normalization procedure, and thus indicated that it may not be wholly safe to rely on the number of words in texts as the only norm to which raw frequencies of progressives are normalized. Some genres, both expository (Science) and non-expository (Fiction, Trials), did not exhibit a statistically significant increase in S-coefficients between periods 1 and 3, in spite of the fact that the increases in M-coefficients were sometimes substantial; in the case of Fiction, the distribution of dialogue and non-dialogue appeared to be important in this respect.

Interestingly, the order of the genres in period 3 changed when the S-coefficient was used instead of the M-coefficient, and the effect of this change was that the expository/non-expository division became somewhat less neat. Figures 2 and 3 below show the development of the seven genres in the S-coefficient subcorpus in terms of M'- and S-coefficients respectively.

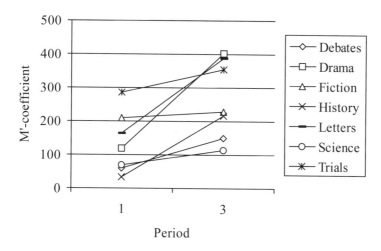

Figure 2. M'-coefficients for period/genre subsamples in the S-coefficient subcorpus

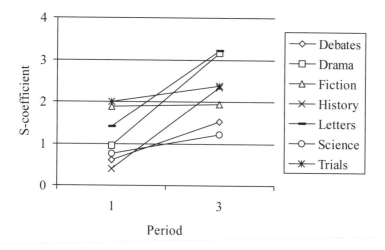

Figure 3. S-coefficients for period/genre subsamples in the S-coefficient subcorpus

As shown in Figures 2 and 3, the order of the genres as regards the frequency of the progressive in period 3 turns out to be dependent on the method of calculation used. If the M'-coefficient is used, the progressive is commonest in Drama, followed by Letters, Trials, Fiction, History, Debates, and Science; but if the S-coefficient is used, the progressive is more common in Letters than in Drama, and more frequent in History than in Fiction. The latter difference is of special interest, as it means that the split between expository and non-expository genres is clear-cut only when the M-coefficient is used. In other words, differences in calculation between the M'- and S-coefficients may affect the order of genres with respect to the frequency of the progressive even across the expository/non-expository split. However, as shown in Table 11, the difference in S-coefficients between History and Fiction is still the biggest of all frequency differences between adjacent genres in CONCE in the S-coefficient subcorpus as a whole. Moreover, this difference was the only one between adjacent genres in CONCE that turned out to be statistically significant.

3.2.5   Gender-based variation in the frequency of the progressive

Numerous studies have shown that women and men differ as regards their use of language (see e.g. Chambers 1995 for exemplification). There is as yet no consensus, however, concerning how such differences should best be interpreted (see Culpeper and Kytö 2000 for a survey of the three main directions that studies of women's and men's language have taken). In the present section, women's and men's use of the progressive in 19th-century private letters will be discussed in the light of some theoretical frameworks that have been proposed in previous research. In order to present a fuller picture, I will also consider the question of whether the addressee is male or female.[34] Before I present the results of these analyses, however, I will devote a subsection to a discussion of the terms "sex" and "gender", and state how they will be used in the present study.

3.2.5.1   "Sex" versus "gender"

There is some disagreement between scholars on what the independent variable with "female/women" and "male/men" as variants should be called. Many recent studies refer to this variable as "gender", although "sex" is also used (see e.g. Milroy 1992). In the present study, both terms will be used, but with different meanings. I will refer to the variable itself as "sex", on a par with other extralinguistic bases for classification that function as independent variables, such as time and genre. "Gender", on the other hand, will be used to refer to the socioculturally constructed identities that can be classified as female and male

---

34   As pointed out in Chapter 1, no attempt has been made to classify the speakers and writers in CONCE into socioeconomic groups. However, even if the letter-writers had been classified on this parameter, it would be difficult to claim sameness of socioeconomic status for men and women in 19th-century England: as Romaine (1999: 174) points out, "[i]f men and women do not really have equal status, then comparisons drawn between the classes do not have equal validity for men and women". See also Milroy (1994: 134) for a critique of the way in which women have been assigned socioeconomic status in sociolinguistic studies.

(though in this context "female" and "male" should be understood as the endpoints of a continuum rather than as binary values). In other words, "sex" will be used as a classificatory and "gender" as an interpretative variable. In particular, I will refer to connections between female and male "gender styles" and the distribution of linguistic features; these gender styles start out from the language in female or male speaker/listener and reader/writer environments.

The decision to use both "sex" and "gender" as terms was based on the assumption that the name of the independent variable should reflect the variants that constitute alternative realizations of the variable, rather than the factors that can be hypothesized to lie behind the variation attested in the distribution of the variants of the dependent variable (i.e. the progressive and the non-progressive). Linguistic variation between men and women is, in most cases, considered to be influenced chiefly by social rather than directly biological factors. (Exceptions include men's lower average vocal pitch and greater susceptibility to aphasia – see e.g. Chambers 1995: 105ff.) Differences between the language of men and women are thus attributed to correspondences between biological sex and sociocultural gender, not to any language-constraining characteristics of language users' biological sex as such. However, in linguistic investigations language users are typically classified according to their biological sex rather than their socioculturally constructed gender identity; the present study is no exception. There are at least two reasons for doing so. First, as stated above, gender is best realized as a continuum with "female" and "male" as endpoints and speakers occupying positions somewhere in between these endpoints; biological sex, in contrast, is by and large a binary variable suitable for discrete classification and quantification (see, however, Romaine 1999: 43ff. for criticism of treating sex as a straightforward binary variable). Secondly, it would in many cases be difficult to find the data necessary to classify a given language user as regards his/her place on the gender continuum, or even to reach agreement on what should constitute such data.

3.2.5.2 Variation in the frequency of the progressive between women and men letter-writers

Previous research has shown that there are gender-based differences in the frequency of the progressive in 19th-century English: in Arnaud's (1998: 139ff.) material, women letter-writers consistently displayed higher frequencies of progressives than men letter-writers.[35] This result forms the background for a

---

35   One interesting result, not mentioned explicitly by Arnaud but clear from his results, is that the difference between women and men, with respect to the frequency of the progressive, decreased when the addresser and addressee were on an intimate footing. Arnaud distinguishes three degrees of intimacy: for the lowest degree, the difference (in M-coefficient units) was 55; for the mid degree, 48; and for the highest degree, 17. The assignment of degrees of intimacy "was based essentially on biographical data, supported by features such as the frequency of the letters and promptings from the text (terms of endearment, forms of address, etc.)" (Arnaud 1998: 130).

similar investigation of the CONCE corpus, where the Letters genre has been stratified into letters written by women and by men (see Section 2.1.3 for a presentation of the sampling strategies). Table 23a–b presents raw frequencies of progressives and word counts for these two subsamples of Letters.

Table 23a. Letters written by women: progressives and word counts per period

Period	Progressives	Word count
1	158	69,271
2	241	62,340
3	245	50,154
Total	**644**	**181,765**

Table 23b. Letters written by men: progressives and word counts per period

Period	Progressives	Word count
1	88	52,353
2	182	68,776
3	141	40,737
Total	**411**	**161,866**

Using the data in Table 23a–b, it is possible to calculate the relevant M-coefficients for letters written by women and men. To be able to calculate the corresponding M'- and S-coefficients, I also computed raw frequencies of finite progressive verb phrases, finite non-imperative verb phrases (excluding BE *going to* + infinitive constructions with future reference), and word counts for women and men letter-writers in the S-coefficient subcorpus. These raw frequencies are presented in Table 24a–b.

Table 24a. Letters written by women in the S-coefficient subcorpus: progressives, word counts, finite progressives, and finite non-imperative verb phrases (excluding BE *going to* + infinitive constructions with future reference) per period

Period	Progressives	Word count	Finite progressives	Verb phrases
1	59	30,308	57	3,603
3	101	21,071	100	2,466
Total	**160**	**51,379**	**157**	**6,069**

Table 24b. Letters written by men in the S-coefficient subcorpus: progressives, word counts, finite progressives, and finite non-imperative verb phrases (excluding BE *going to* + infinitive constructions with future reference) per period

Period	Progressives	Word count	Finite progressives	Verb phrases
1	27	21,856	27	2,388
3	45	16,657	45	2,032
Total	**72**	**38,513**	**72**	**4,420**

Using the data in Tables 23–24, I calculated M-, M'-, and S-coefficients, as well as verb density ratios, for the relevant subsamples of the Letters genre. The results of these calculations are given in Table 25a–b.

Table 25a. Letters written by women: M-, M'-, and S-coefficients, and verb density ratios per period; "All" refers to figures for the whole CONCE corpus (M-coefficients) or for the whole S-coefficient subcorpus (M'-coefficients, S-coefficients, and verb density ratios)

Period	M-coefficient	M'-coefficient	S-coefficient	Verb density
1	228	195	1.58	0.119
2	387	–	–	–
3	488	479	4.06	0.117
All	**354**	**311**	**2.59**	**0.118**

Table 25b. Letters written by men: M-, M'-, and S-coefficients, and verb density ratios per period; "All" refers to figures for the whole CONCE corpus (M-coefficients) or for the whole S-coefficient subcorpus (M'-coefficients, S-coefficients, and verb density ratios)

Period	M-coefficient	M'-coefficient	S-coefficient	Verb density
1	168	124	1.13	0.109
2	265	–	–	–
3	346	270	2.21	0.122
All	**254**	**187**	**1.63**	**0.115**

The results in Table 25 are in accordance with Arnaud's findings: in every period, women use the progressive more than men, and the overall difference is one of 100 M-coefficient units. Moreover, the difference appears to increase in diachrony: it is 60 M-coefficient units in period 1, 122 in period 2, and 142 in period 3. As far as frequency is concerned, women are thus ahead of men as regards the integration of the progressive into late Modern English.

There are no major changes in the picture when the M'- and S-coefficients are added to the discussion. The total difference in S-coefficients between women's and men's letters is statistically significant, as are the differences between periods 1 and 3 for both women and men letter-writers. Women's and men's letters are thus further apart than the Letters genre as a whole is from either Drama or Trials, since the differences between Letters and these two genres were not statistically significant (see Section 3.2.3). While women's letters have a higher S-coefficient than Trials, men's letters have a lower S-coefficient than Fiction (cf. Table 11). The results as expressed in S-coefficients are also similar to those expressed in M-coefficients in that the difference between women's and men's use of the progressive increases in diachrony: the difference is 0.45 S-coefficient units in period 1 and 1.84 in period 3, with an overall difference of 0.96 units. In fact, whereas the difference in S-coefficient units between women and men letter-writers in period 3 is statistically significant, the difference in period 1 is not. (However, note that each period sample in the S-coefficient subcorpus includes only two texts produced by women and two by men, and whereas the chi-square test is useful when it comes to excluding random variation, systematic variation caused by idiolectal characteristics within individual texts is not compensated for. This factor is normally constrained by the sampling of additional texts per subsample.)

One of the reasons for this increase in gender-based differentiation is that the development in verb density ratios is different for women and men letter-writers. The texts produced by women exhibit almost no change on this parameter. In contrast, the texts produced by men change substantially: the verb density in letters written by men increases by 12% between periods 1 and 3. In comparison with the corresponding M'-coefficients, these differences in verb density between women and men lead to lower S-coefficients for women in period 1 and for men in period 3.

In sum, the results indicate (1) that there is a difference between women's and men's use of the progressive in 19th-century private letters, (2) that this difference consists in the progressive being more frequent in women's than in men's letters,[36] and (3) that this difference increases, or becomes significant, during the course of the century. As mentioned above, these results imply that men lagged behind women concerning the integration of the progressive into English grammar. Before turning to a discussion of the possible reasons behind the differences, I will take the analysis one step further by presenting results where the sex of both the letter-writer and the addressee has been taken into account in the classification of the data.

---

36   Many studies start out from the implicit assumption that female usage (in this case, the higher frequency of progressives in letters written by women) is what has to be explained, presumably because it is seen as deviating from an implicit male norm. While the present study also starts out from women's use of the progressive, no such assumption underlies this decision: it is equally valid to ask oneself why men letter-writers use fewer progressives than women letter-writers as vice versa. The choice of direction in comparisons was motivated solely by a wish on my part to facilitate comparison with previous research.

3.2.5.3 A new parameter: Taking the sex of the addressee into account

In the preceding section, it was shown that there were significant gender-based differences in the frequency of the progressive in Letters: women letter-writers used more progressives than men. Against this background, the sex of the recipient of the letter may also be of interest. If comparatively high frequencies of progressives are characteristic of women's letters, and low frequencies characteristic of men's letters, in 19th-century English, such differences may be even more pronounced when the recipient of the letter is of the same sex as the letter-writer.

The texts in Letters are classified according to the sex of the letter-writer; the sex of the addressee, in contrast, was not taken into account systematically in the compilation of the corpus.[37] Consequently, it was necessary to go through each Letters text manually in a classification process in which letters with female and male recipients were saved to separate files. Owing to limitations of time, only parts of the Letters genre could be analysed in this fashion. Period 3 was selected, since this period manifested the most pronounced gender-based differences with respect to the sex of the letter-writer (see Section 3.2.5.2). New M-coefficients were calculated for the four relevant subsamples of Letters, period 3: women writing to women, women writing to men, men writing to women, and men writing to men. (Since the S-coefficient subcorpus is too small for results based on it to be reliable when the addressee parameter is taken into account, results in the form of M'- and S-coefficients will not be given in this section.) Table 26 presents the results for the four subcorpora of Letters, period 3.

Table 26. Progressives, word counts, and M-coefficients for the four subsamples of Letters, period 3, based on the sex of the letter-writer and addressee

Letter-writers	Addressees	Progressives	Word count	M-coefficient
Women	Women	61	12,362	493
Women	Men	184	37,792	487
Men	Women	91	23,909	381
Men	Men	50	16,828	297

The findings support the indications in Section 3.2.5.2 that the sex of the letter-writer is an important factor in the distribution of the progressive: the biggest difference (106 M-coefficient units) between two adjacent subsamples is that between letters from women to men and letters from men to women. However, the results also indicate that the sex of the recipient is a relevant parameter, especially as regards men letter-writers: there is a difference of 83 M-coefficient units between the subsample consisting of letters from men to women and that consisting of letters from men to men. In contrast, the difference between the

---

37   As pointed out in Chapter 2, the present study is based on a preliminary version of CONCE.

subsample consisting of letters from women to women and that consisting of letters from women to men is only 7 units.[38]

A few caveats should be mentioned in connection with the results presented above. First, the two subsamples that consist of letters where the writer and the addressee are both women or both men are quite small. (Moreover, the subsample consisting of letters from women to women contains material from two corpus texts only; idiosyncratic influence thus cannot be ruled out for this subsample.) Results for these subsamples should therefore be treated with some caution, although the raw frequencies of progressives are relatively high, as the construction is comparatively common in Letters overall. Secondly, there are other addressee-related factors which may affect the frequency of the progressive in a letter. Arnaud (1998), for instance, shows that the level of intimacy between letter-writer and addressee is relevant to the discussion. In addition, the addressee need not have been the only person for whom a given letter was intended. Letters to a family member may have been read aloud to the whole family; marriage and other family ties could thus have affected the target group of a letter. It is possible, even likely, that letter-writers took circumstances such as these into account when, consciously or unconsciously, selecting the stylistic level of a given letter.

Despite these caveats, the consistency of the results presented above implies that the sex of the letter-writer and that of the addressee affect the frequency of the progressive in texts. Interestingly, men seem to adapt more than women to the sex of the addressee in this respect. Two hypotheses, both of which have implications for the development of the progressive, can be formulated on the basis of this result. First, as pointed out in Section 3.2.5.2, women seem to have been in the forefront of the integration process, as the progressive is significantly more frequent in letters written by women than in letters written by men. Since the progressive was more fully integrated in women's letters to begin with, regardless of the sex of the addressee, it is possible that the frequency of the construction in women's letters was close to a "saturation point" in 19th-century English: there may have been fewer non-progressive verb phrases that could take a progressive, and thus cause a further increase in the frequency of the construction, when a woman wrote a letter to another woman.

Secondly, the fact that men used fewer progressives when writing to other men than when writing to women has potential implications for our interpretation of the occurrence of the construction in genres outside private letters. The expository genres in CONCE – Debates, History, and Science – are all characterized by low overall frequencies of progressives in comparison with the non-expository genres. In the 19th century, these expository genres were also characterized by male speakers and writers, since careers as politicians, historians, and scientists were, by and large, not available to women. To the extent that results for Letters can be generalized to other genres, some of the

---

38   As pointed out in Section 3.2.2, results presented in the running text are based on exact figures rather than on figures that have been rounded off before being given in tables.

cross-genre differences in the frequency of the progressive discussed in the present chapter may thus be a result of men dominating as speakers and writers in certain genres but not in others. The language in Debates, History, and Science would then be more or less indicative of a male gender style.[39]

Against this background, however, we might also expect the frequency of the progressive in Drama and Trials to be lower than the frequency of the progressive in Letters, since all writers of Drama texts in CONCE are men, and since women could not assume the part of lawyers (and, in most cases, expert witnesses such as physicians) in Trials. But these two genres differ from the expository genres in having women participants: there are women characters in Drama (and in Fiction), and women lay witnesses in Trials. Furthermore, Drama, Fiction, and Trials texts all had audiences consisting of both women and men. Theatres were visited – and novels read – by members of both sexes, and women could both attend trials and read published accounts of the proceedings afterwards.

By way of speculation, it is even possible that some of the difference in the frequency of the progressive between History, on the one hand, and the two other expository genres Debates and Science, on the other hand, can be attributed to audience-related factors. As will be made clear in Chapter 4, the high score for History on Dimension 2, "Narrative vs. non-narrative concerns", in Geisler's (2002) factor score analysis of CONCE may indicate that History was a more popular and less specialized expository genre than Debates and Science. A piece of history writing may also have had a larger share of female readers than a scientific work or an account of parliamentary proceedings; this factor may have influenced the distribution of the progressive. However, the importance of the sex of the addressee(s) should not be exaggerated, and results for the Letters genre cannot safely be claimed to be valid for the language as a whole.

3.2.5.4   Explanatory factors

Results presented in Sections 3.2.5.2–3.2.5.3 indicate that there is a consistent pattern of variation in the frequency of the progressive with the sex of the letter-writer and addressee in Letters: the likelihood of a high frequency of progressives in a private letter increases if the letter-writer is a woman, as well as if the addressee is a woman. In this light, it is possible that a high frequency of progressives is characteristic of a female gender style, and a low frequency of a male gender style. This raises the question of what further characteristics these gender styles have. This issue, among others, will be addressed in Chapter 4, where I will compare the frequency of the progressive with dimension scores resulting from Geisler's (2000; 2001; 2002; 2003) factor score analyses of the CONCE corpus. However, the distribution of the progressive in Letters is likely to

---

39   Within the historical framework, the concept of male and female styles has previously been used by e.g. Palander-Collin (1999a), in her discussion of gender-based differences in the distribution of *I think* (see also Chapter 4).

be the result of several factors. In what follows, I will examine some other theories on gender-based variation in language and discuss whether they are applicable to the 19th-century progressive.

Most research into gender-based differences has indicated that women use more standard forms than men. This finding has been attributed to the unequal power structure of the societies investigated by many scholars: for instance, Romaine (1999: 174), referring to Eckert (1993), suggests that "[w]omen may be using linguistic means as a way to achieve status that is denied to them through other outlets such as occupation". Romaine (1999: 128) also discusses how the ability to speak properly became a type of social capital during the Victorian era. It thus seems likely that the avoidance of features considered to be non-standard would have constituted social capital for 19th-century English women to a higher extent than for men.

However, for this analytical framework to be applicable to the data presented above, the progressive must have stylistic values that can be fitted onto a scale of perceived correctness. Some variants of the 19th-century progressive were indeed stylistically stigmatized, namely those involving the sequence BE *being* (for which see Chapters 5 and 6), and possibly what was felt by some speakers of English English to be an overuse of the progressive in Scottish English and Irish English. However, progressives containing BE *being* constitute only a small subset of all progressives, and CONCE focuses on English English, so these factors are unlikely to have affected the results in any substantial way. Moreover, if this factor had been influential, and the progressive had had non-standard connotations, the predicted result would rather have been the opposite from what was found: we would have expected men, rather than women, to use the progressive more. Thus, stylistic judgements concerning the acceptability of the progressive do not appear to play an important role when it comes to accounting for the differences in the data.

Labov (2001) presents some interesting hypotheses with a bearing on the present investigation. According to Labov (2001: 292), "[i]n linguistic change from below, women use higher frequencies of innovative forms than men do", but also "conform more closely than men to sociolinguistic norms that are overtly prescribed" (Labov 2001: 293). These statements can be connected with the results presented in this chapter. Apart from a few parts of the progressive paradigm that received overt, negative prescriptive evaluation (see above), the general increase in the frequency of the progressive can probably be regarded as a change from below, taking place largely below the level of social awareness. In addition, since the results presented in the present chapter have shown that the progressive is encroaching on the non-progressive, the progressive can be seen as the more innovative feature. The results for Letters in CONCE thus match Labov's (2001) hypothesis, which would predict that women should use more progressives than men because the progressive is, by and large, an innovative feature whose incidence increases as a result of change from below.

In recent years, attempts have been made to explain gender-based differentiation within the framework of social network theory, according to which weak network ties constitute a promising channel for the diffusion of linguistic change (see e.g. Milroy 1992). Arnaud (1998: 142f.) hypothesizes that middle- and upper-class women may have been influenced by servants from, for example, Ireland and Scotland, in whose dialects the progressive was more frequent; the women would have had more contact with these servants, and thus been more influenced, than the men. It is possible that these two theories can be combined. If we accept that the progressive was more common in Scottish English and Irish English than it was in standard English English, servants in middle-class and upper-class households could have carried linguistic change over to the middle- and upper-class women with whom they were in contact via weak network ties. It must be emphasized that these hypotheses are merely speculative, however. For example, we would need an answer to the questions of why women would pick up a higher frequency of progressives from their servants, and of how these women would be able to maintain a higher frequency of the construction without at the same time adopting stylistically stigmatized progressives.[40]

The hypotheses presented in this section can only hint at possible causes for the linguistic variation between men and women attested in the data. More research is needed, especially as regards other linguistic differences between women and men letter-writers in CONCE, including the normative evaluation of the linguistic features involved. However, the consistency of the results and the possibility of linking them to established theories on gender-based variation in language seem to be good starting-points for such further research.

3.3   Discussion of results

In this chapter, the progressive has been analysed in terms of its variation in frequency with the extralinguistic factors time, genre, and gender. Two different ways of measuring the frequency of the progressive were used: the M-coefficient, which relates the raw frequency of progressives to the number of words in a given

---

40   One possible answer to the latter question is presented in Chambers (1995), in an account where differences in linguistic behaviour between men and women are partly determined by sex rather than gender. Chambers (1995: 135) starts out from the hypothesis that women have a statistical advantage in language skills and can "use a larger repertoire of variants and command a wider range of styles than men of the same social groups even though gender roles are similar or identical" (Chambers 1995: 137). Though Chambers's hypothesis still needs to be correlated with linguistic facts in specific cases, it ties in with the possible causes mentioned above for why women use the progressive more than men. Women's greater verbal skills may well make them better than men at (a) picking up differences between their own speech and that of other people with whom they formed weak network ties, and (b) adopting some of these differences (e.g. a more frequent use of the progressive) into their own speech without simultaneously adopting stylistically stigmatized usage (e.g. the passive progressive). However, the hypothesis does not explain why men, who would not be as good at picking up stylistic differences, would adapt their usage in private letters more than women to the sex of the addressee (although, as stated above, characteristics of the sampling procedure may make the results unreliable in this respect). Moreover, since Victorian women and men cannot be taken to have had similar gender roles, the hypothesis need not be applicable to 19th-century English.

text, and the S-coefficient, which relates the raw frequency of finite progressives to the number of finite non-imperative verb phrases (excluding BE *going to* + infinitive constructions with future reference). Differences between the two coefficients were commented on and analysed in terms of differing verb densities among texts.

With time as the only independent variable, the results showed that the progressive increased considerably in frequency over the 19th century, though not quite so much as other scholars have reported. It is likely that some of this discrepancy is due to the fact that many previous studies have not included genres like Science, where the progressive is expected not to be frequent; differences in sample sizes and periodization may also be of importance. The results also indicated that the verb density in English as a whole increased over the 19th century, which implies that there were more slots that could be filled by progressives at the end of the century than at the beginning.

When, instead, genre was used as the sole independent variable, the genres in CONCE split into an expository and a non-expository group with respect to the frequency of the progressive. This split has previously been noted by Geisler (2002) in his factor score analysis of CONCE (see Chapter 4). The four non-expository genres (Drama, Fiction, Letters, and Trials) exhibited higher frequencies of progressives than the three expository genres (Debates, History, and Science). Moreover, the difference in S-coefficient units between the closest members of the two groups, Fiction and History, was the only difference between two adjacent genres in the corpus that was statistically significant.

The next step was to consider time and genre together as independent variables. Against the background of what has been reported in previous research, we might expect that frequency increases should be visible in all genres and that the division of the genres into an expository and a non-expository group should remain intact. However, most previous research has been based on methods where frequencies have been normalized to a given number of words, such as the M-coefficient, and it turned out that the addition of the S-coefficient to the analysis made the picture more complex. Some increases, as measured in S-coefficients, were not statistically significant; there was also overlap between the two groups of genres in period 3 when the S-coefficient was used.

As was mentioned in Section 3.1, one effect of the M-coefficient is to exaggerate differences in the frequency of the progressive between expository and non-expository genres, in terms of actual occurrences compared with potential occurrences: expository genres tend to have lower verb density ratios, and thus fewer slots that can be filled by progressives, than non-expository genres. For instance, in the CONCE corpus as a whole, History has a lower verb density ratio than Fiction (0.086 vs. 0.112), and this difference affects the results: the S-coefficient takes into account the fact that there are more slots that can be filled by progressives in Fiction than in History. The same tendency is visible within individual period subsamples. In period 1, if results are based on the M-coefficient, the progressive is 782% more common in the genre with the highest frequency (Trials) than in that with the lowest (History); but if the S-coefficient is used, this difference is only 400%.[41] In other words, nearly half of the difference in the frequency of the progressive across the genre parameter in period 1 can be accounted for partly in terms of differences in verb density.

Despite the differences between the M- and S-coefficients regarding results for period, genre, and period/genre subsamples, however, the most pronounced trends in the material were the same. These trends include the overall increase in the frequency of the progressive and the general tendency for expository and non-expository genres to form two separate groups. Moreover, the widespread use of the M-coefficient in research on the progressive and the small amount of work involved in calculating it make it a useful tool, in spite of its drawbacks. The results thus point to the value of complementing, rather than replacing, the M-coefficient with other normalization procedures.

An analysis of verb density ratios showed that the overall ratio increased from 0.110 to 0.117 between periods 1 and 3, an increase of 6%. There was a good deal of cross-genre variation: for instance, in Drama the ratio was 0.123 in period 1 and 0.124 in period 3, while in Science the ratio increased from 0.079 to 0.085. Low verb density ratios may indicate high frequencies of non-finite clauses and complex noun and prepositional phrases, and thus imply a comparatively elaborated sentence structure. In this respect, the results point to expository genres having a more complex sentence structure than non-expository genres: whereas all expository genres had verb density ratios of < 0.1, all non-expository genres had ratios of > 0.1. The diachronic results for the entire corpus thus imply that, in this respect, the English language as a whole tended towards a slightly less elaborated sentence structure across the 19th century.

The final extralinguistic parameter investigated was gender. This variable also had a significant influence on the occurrence of the progressive: women used more progressives than men in private letters, and the difference appeared to increase across the century (in fact, there was no statistically significant gender difference in period 1). However, men's letters changed more regarding verb density ratios, exhibiting higher ratios towards the end of the century, whereas women's letters displayed no change on this parameter. The addressee also influenced the frequency of the progressive, so that letters written to women were characterized by higher frequencies of progressives compared with letters written to men.

In Section 3.2.1, the relation of the frequency of the progressive to the concepts of grammaticalization, obligatorification, and integration was discussed. On the one hand, the regular diachronic increase in frequency of the progressive, reported on in Section 3.2.2, may be taken as an indirect indication of grammaticalization and/or obligatorification, as wider syntactic applicability and obligatory functions can be expected to lead to a higher frequency of a construction undergoing change. On the other hand, when the genre parameter was added to the analysis in Section 3.2.4, it turned out that the expected decrease

---

41   As the order of the genres changes in period 3 depending on whether the M- or the S-coefficient is used, this calculation was carried out for period 1 only.

in cross-genre frequency differences did not appear; conversely, the gaps in frequency across the genre parameter became more pronounced in diachrony. The analysis of gender differences in the frequency of the progressive in Section 3.2.5 also indicated that differences increased rather than decreased with time. These results may be linked to Biber and Finegan's (1997) claim that differences in linguistic make-up between expository and non-expository genres appear to have increased during the 19th and 20th centuries; I will return to this issue in Chapter 4.

Moreover, regarding the genre parameter, the increases in frequency did not take place at the same time in all genres: in Trials, it appeared that the steepest part of the expected S-curve of diffusion had already been passed in 1800, so that there was no significant increase across the century; in Drama, the increase was the most pronounced during the first half of the century, with a subsequent levelling out; in Debates, History, and Letters the increase was either more even across the century or more pronounced in the period 1850–1900; and in Fiction and Science (as in Trials) the frequency did not appear to increase significantly at all (although Fiction showed an unexpected decrease between periods 2 and 3). It is thus difficult to link the results to theories on the grammaticalization and/or obligatorification of the progressive in English as a whole.

What the results do indicate, however, is that the progressive became more fully integrated into the English language over the 19th century, although the process of integration neither began at the same time nor developed at the same pace in all genres (or for women and men). If we disregard the unexpected development of the Fiction genre, it is possible to hypothesize an integration process which first reached spoken non-expository genres, then spread to speech-related, non-expository written genres, and finally reached expository genres, speech-related or non-speech-related.[42] Such a development would be in line with suggestions that the progressive was a spoken, colloquial feature which gradually spread to written genres. As both the expository/non-expository continuum and the medium parameter seem to be important to the distribution of the progressive, it may be worthwhile including both expository and non-expository, and both speech-related and written genres, in studies of other linguistic features exhibiting variation and undergoing change. In addition, both women's and men's language deserve consideration. Such requirements place great demands on the primary material used for linguistic studies (see Raumolin-Brunberg 2002: 104f. for further discussion of extralinguistic parameters), if the researcher wishes to give as complete as possible a picture of the development of the linguistic feature/s under scrutiny.

---

42   We do not, of course, have access to the actual speech of the 19th century. However, given the clear patterns attested in the data and the wide spectrum of written genres covered by CONCE, the extrapolation to 19th-century speech seems credible (see also Rissanen 1986: 98).

The frequency variable is of great interest to studies of most linguistic features, including the progressive. However, another important factor is the functional distribution of the feature under scrutiny; in the case of the progressive, previous research indicates that the division into aspectual and not-solely-aspectual groups of functions is of particular importance in this respect (see, for instance, Rydén 1997). The next chapter will be devoted to an investigation of how the methodological tool of multi-feature/multi-dimensional analysis can help to build a bridge between statements concerning the frequency of the progressive and hypotheses on the functions of the construction.

Chapter 4

M-coefficients and factor score analysis

In the present chapter, I will place the frequency of the progressive in a wider context by relating it to the frequency and co-occurrence patterns of other linguistic features. I will use the M-coefficients that were presented in Chapter 3 to compare the frequency of the progressive in CONCE with dimension scores, obtained by Geisler (2000; 2001; 2002; 2003), on dimensions of variation that resulted from Biber's (1988) factor analysis (for a brief introduction to the factor analysis, see Section 1.5.2). This comparison will make it possible to see whether, for instance, high frequencies of progressives are likely to co-occur with high frequencies of features characteristic of involved or informational production. The results of the comparison will thus shed new light on the functional distribution of the 19th-century progressive.

Drawing for data on the CONCE corpus, Geisler has computed dimension scores, based on Biber's (1988) factor analysis, for Dimensions 1 ("Involved vs. informational production"), 2 ("Narrative vs. non-narrative concerns"), 3 ("Elaborated vs. situation-dependent reference"), and 5 ("Abstract vs. non-abstract information"). As regards the types of variation the dimensions describe, Dimensions 1, 3, and 5 "can be considered 'oral'/'literate', in that they distinguish between stereotypically oral (conversational) registers at one pole, and stereotypically literate (written expository) registers at the other pole" (Biber and Finegan 1997: 260). Dimension 2 "reflects a split between specialist and popular written registers" (Biber and Finegan 1997: 271), a split which appears to have become more marked through late Modern English.

As pointed out in Section 1.5.2, the progressive is included in the factor analysis presented in Biber (2003), but not in that presented in Biber (1988), on which Geisler's (2000; 2001; 2002; 2003) analyses are based. However, in Biber's (2003) analysis, the progressive loads as an oral feature on the dimension "Oral vs. literate discourse", which indicates that there may be a connection between the progressive and the "oral" features that load on Dimensions 1, 3, and 5. As the highly specialized Science genre has the lowest frequency of progressives in CONCE (see Section 3.2.3), the popular/specialist continuum reflected by Dimension 2 may also be relevant to the distribution of the progressive. In order to pursue these connections further, I will compare the way text samples in CONCE pattern with respect to these four dimensions of variation and with respect to the frequency of the progressive. The results of this comparison will be presented in three sections: the first section, 4.1, will focus on variation between genres in their entirety; the second, 4.2, will be devoted to developments within genres; and the third, 4.3, will address variation between women and men letter-writers.[1] Section 4.4 provides a concluding discussion of the results reached.

Data regarding dimension scores for the text samples have been taken from Geisler (2000; 2001; 2002; 2003). In the factor score analysis, raw frequencies of linguistic features were related to word counts of text samples. In the interest of consistency, comparisons between frequencies of progressives and dimension scores will therefore be based on the M- rather than the S-coefficient, as the M-coefficient also relates the frequency of the progressive to the number of words in texts.

In what follows, I will focus both on the order of the text samples relative to one another and on differences and similarities between developments in M-coefficients and dimension scores. I will use the two types of results to provide further support for the relationships that can be established between the progressive and the dimensions of variation.

4.1   Factor scores and the frequency of the progressive: A cross-genre comparison

In this section, I will present an analysis of how the frequency of the progressive in the genres in CONCE correlates with dimension scores obtained by Geisler (2000) on four of Biber's (1988) dimensions of variation. The aim of the comparison is to investigate whether any links between the frequency of the progressive in a given genre and the scores for the genre on the four dimensions can be established, and whether such links can be given a functional interpretation. Correlations established in analyses of the comparatively large genre samples will also be used as background for more fine-grained analyses when the parameters of time and gender are added to the investigation in Sections 4.2–4.3.

The results for the genre samples are given in Table 27.

---

1   Results regarding Dimension 2 will not be used in Section 4.3. Geisler's (2001; 2003) analyses also cover Dimension 4 ("Overt expression of persuasion"); this dimension is not included in comparisons in the present study.

Table 27. The order of the genres in CONCE with respect to M-coefficients and to Dimensions 1 (Involved vs. informational production), 2 (Narrative vs. non-narrative concerns), 3 (Elaborated vs. situation-dependent reference), and 5 (Abstract vs. non-abstract information) (dimension scores taken from Geisler 2000)

M-coeff.	Dim. 1	Dim. 2	Dim. 3	Dim. 5
Trials	Drama	Trials	Letters	Drama
(309)	(13.28)	(3.79)	(–2.38)	(–2.40)
Letters	Trials	Fiction	Trials	Trials
(307)	(11.24)	(1.98)	(–1.92)	(–2.30)
Drama	Letters	History	Drama	Fiction
(291)	(3.92)	(–0.34)	(–1.83)	(–1.12)
Fiction	Fiction	Debates	Fiction	Letters
(255)	(–2.42)	(–0.66)	(–1.53)	(–0.83)
History	Debates	Drama	Science	Debates
(123)	(–8.64)	(–1.05)	(2.23)	(1.79)
Debates	Science	Letters	History	History
(89)	(–8.93)	(–1.56)	(3.00)	(2.93)
Science	History	Science	Debates	Science
(85)	(–19.41)	(–5.52)	(3.89)	(4.32)

In multi-feature/multi-dimensional analyses, the genres are typically presented so that a high ranking corresponds to a high dimension score, in this case involved production, narrative concerns, elaborated reference, and abstract information. However, as the results show, the progressive rather appears to correlate with the latter pole of the continuum on Dimensions 3 and 5, i.e. with situation-dependent reference and non-abstract information. In order to clarify the presentation, the order of the genres on Dimensions 3 and 5 has therefore been reversed. Consequently, a high ranking for a genre in Table 27 corresponds to comparatively low dimension scores on Dimensions 3 and 5, and indicates that the genre tends towards situation-dependent reference and non-abstract information.

As can be seen from Table 27, on Dimensions 1, 3, and 5, which were labelled oral/literate by Biber and Finegan (1997), the genre patterns show great similarities to that provided by the M-coefficient: the non-expository genres Drama, Fiction, Letters, and Trials are consistently closer to the oral poles of the dimensions than the expository genres Debates, History, and Science. In other words, high frequencies of progressives appear to correlate positively with high frequencies of linguistic features that indicate involved production and situation-dependent reference, and negatively with features that indicate informational production, elaborated reference, and abstract information.[2]

---

2   Dimensions 2 and 5 contain no negative features, i.e. no linguistic features whose presence indicates non-narrative concerns or non-abstract information.

On Dimension 1, the features that indicate involved production "can be characterized as verbal, interactional, affective, fragmented, reduced in form, and generalized in content" (Biber 1988: 105); the features include private verbs and contractions. In contrast, the features that indicate informational production, such as nouns and prepositions, "are associated with communicative situations that require a high informational focus and provide ample opportunity for careful integration of information and precise lexical choice" (Biber 1988: 105). Dimension 1 is also a very powerful dimension in the analysis (Biber 1988: 104). The emotional, not-solely-aspectual functions of the progressive may explain why the construction appears to co-occur with features indicating involved production; the general stylistic preference for progressives in colloquial genres, which can be expected to contain more involved production, is perhaps also influential.

Dimension 3, "Elaborated vs. situation-dependent reference", is less powerful than Dimension 1, although it also has both positive and negative features with salient loadings. However, the scores on this dimension appear to match the M-coefficients closely, in terms of the order of the genres. In part, this similarity may be accounted for by the imperfective, aspectual functions of the progressive. Whereas many of the features that indicate elaborated reference are relative clauses, the features indicating situation-dependent reference are all adverbials or adverbs (see Biber 1988: 102). Biber (1988: 110) points out that place and time adverbials "often serve as deictics that can only be understood by reference to an external physical and temporal situation". Similarly, although aspect is usually considered to be non-deictic (Lyons 1977: 687), progressives in sentences such as *It is raining* or *It was raining when I arrived* depend for their reference on when 'now' or *when I arrived* happens. There is thus a partial connection between the occurrence of temporal adverbials and that of progressives (see also Section 6.4). Rydén (1997: 421) also mentions "situational/attitudinal immediacy and awareness" as characteristic of the progressive. A frequent function of adverbials is to modify or describe the action expressed by the verb phrase. Since the progressive is always a verb phrase, an overall connection between progressives and adverbials can be expected. In contrast, nominalizations, which load as a feature indicating elaborated reference on Dimension 3, are likely to reduce the number of verb phrases in texts by packing the information into a sequence of noun phrases.

Dimension 5 is an even less powerful factor; moreover, no negative features load on this dimension. The positive features include conjuncts and passives (Biber 1988: 103). Consequently, abstract information is the marked end of Dimension 5, and a low score on the dimension only indicates that the genre is stylistically unmarked in this respect (Geisler 2002: 265). Against this background, the results presented in Table 27 corroborate hypotheses that the progressive is rare in formal, technical discourse.

On Dimension 2, finally, there are greater differences in the order of the genres compared to their order with respect to M-coefficients. In other words, the features that indicate narrative concerns, such as past tense verbs and third-person pronouns, do not covary with the progressive to the same extent as the features loading on Dimensions 1, 3, and 5. Drama and Letters are not marked for narrativity, unlike Trials and Fiction, the other two genres with a relatively high frequency of progressives. Among the expository genres, Debates and, in particular, History show tendencies towards narrative concerns. However, as with Dimension 5, since there are no negative features on Dimension 2, narrative concerns constitute the marked alternative on this dimension, and a low dimension score only shows that a genre is unmarked with respect to narrativity (see Geisler 2002: 259). These differences notwithstanding, there are also some similarities between the genre patterns obtained for Dimension 2 and for the frequency of the progressive, especially as regards the expository genres. The comparatively narrative nature of History may contribute to this genre having higher frequencies of progressives than the other expository genres, Debates and Science. High scores on Dimension 2 indicate that a written genre is popular rather than specialized (Biber and Finegan 1997: 271); given the association of the progressive with colloquial language, the construction should be more frequent in popular than in specialized written genres.

The similarity between the relative order of the genres with respect to, on the one hand, inverted dimension scores on Dimension 3 and, on the other hand, M-coefficients is supported by a consideration of the actual M-coefficients and dimension scores. As pointed out in Section 3.2.3, the M-coefficients identify two distinct groups of genres: a non-expository group comprising Drama, Fiction, Letters, and Trials, and an expository group comprising Debates, History, and Science.[3] For both groups, the between-group difference in M-coefficients is bigger than the within-group differences. This is also the pattern that we find on Dimensions 3 and 5 (Geisler 2002: 264f.), though the order of the genres within these groups differs. (However, since Dimension 5 contains no features indicating non-abstract information, correlations with this dimension can only demonstrate that the progressive is not characteristic of abstract information.) In contrast, on Dimension 1, although there is no overlap between expository and non-expository genres, the contrast between the groups is less clear; moreover, Fiction, the non-expository genre with the lowest dimension score, is closer to the expository genre Debates than to the non-expository genre Letters. On Dimension 2, finally, as pointed out above, no expository vs. non-expository grouping can be established, and the biggest differences are those which separate Trials and Fiction, with narrative concerns, and Science, with non-narrative concerns, from the middle group; Trials and Fiction are also distinct from each other (Geisler 2002: 259).

The results presented above imply that the 19th-century progressive was frequent in genres where the incidence of linguistic features indicating involved production and situation-dependent reference was also relatively high, and where linguistic features indicating informational production, elaborated reference, and

---

3   In addition, the S-coefficients for genre totals also showed that the only significant difference between two adjacent genres was that between Fiction, the non-expository genre with the lowest S-coefficient, and History, the expository genre with the highest S-coefficient.

abstract information were comparatively infrequent. To a lesser extent, the progressive also seems to have correlated with features indicating narrative concerns. These findings are in line with descriptions of the functional load of the progressive that encompass both aspectual and not-solely-aspectual functions, such as Scheffer (1975) and Rydén (1997). As will become clear in the next section, there are also indications that the relative distribution of these functions may differ across the genre parameter.

4.2   Genre developments

In addition to the comparison of genre totals, Geisler's (2002) factor score analysis of the CONCE corpus makes it possible to relate the development of the progressive in the genres in CONCE to the development of the genres on Dimensions 1, 2, 3, and 5. On each dimension, the developments of a given genre relative to the others in the corpus can be matched against the developments of the same genre as regards the frequency of the progressive. This analysis adds a diachronic dimension to the investigation of genre totals carried out in Section 4.1. Moreover, it becomes possible to see whether there is variation across the genre parameter concerning which dimension matches the development of the progressive most closely.

In what follows, I will present the results for each genre with respect to the frequency of the progressive and the four dimensions investigated in Geisler (2002). The entry in a cell in these tables corresponds to the order of the genre relative to the other genres in CONCE on the dimension in question, or concerning the frequency of the progressive, in each period subsample.[4] By way of exemplification, in Table 28, the entry "6th" for Debates on Dimension 3 in period 3 means that Debates is the genre that exhibits the sixth most situation-dependent reference in this period: there are thus five genres that display more situation-dependent reference and one that exhibits less situation-dependent reference (and, consequently, more elaborated reference) than Debates in period 3.

Table 28.   The ranking of the Debates genre, relative to the other genres, with respect to M-coefficients and to Dimensions 1, 2, 3, and 5 (dimension scores taken from Geisler 2002)

Period	M-coeff.	Dim. 1	Dim. 2	Dim. 3	Dim. 5
1	6th (60)	6th (−11.37)	3rd (1.30)	7th (4.96)	5th (1.64)
2	7th (57)	6th (−9.70)	4th (0.57)	7th (3.68)	5th (1.28)
3	6th (150)	5th (−4.84)	6th (−3.86)	6th (3.01)	5th (2.43)

---

4   As with Table 27, the order of the genres has been reversed for Dimensions 3 and 5 to facilitate comparison with the development of the progressive: high rankings on these dimensions thus correspond to situation-dependent reference and non-abstract information respectively.

On Dimension 1, the Debates genre changes towards involved production (Geisler 2002: 257). This change is the most pronounced between periods 2 and 3, when both the position of Debates relative to the other genres and the dimension scores for Debates exhibit change. This increase parallels the increase in frequency of the progressive. Similarly, on Dimension 3, Debates exhibit a development from elaborated to situation-dependent reference over the 19th century (Geisler 2002: 264f.), though the similarity between the dimension scores and the M-coefficients is less pronounced in this case. In contrast, on Dimension 2 Debates become less narrative over the 19th century (Geisler 2002: 261), especially between periods 2 and 3. It is likely that the developments on both Dimension 1 and Dimension 2 are largely due to the switch from indirect to direct speech, and to the accompanying shift from the past to the present tense, that took place in the latter half of the century. Past-tense verbs are one of the most important features of texts that display narrative concerns, and present-tense verbs are indicators of involved production. The shift to first-person from third-person pronouns is also relevant in this context (Geisler 2002: 256f.). On Dimension 5, finally, the Debates genre is stable relative to the other genres as far as the order of the genres is concerned, and the change in dimension scores is not statistically significant (Geisler 2002: 267). In sum, the use of the progressive in Debates seems to be linked to how situation-dependent references are and, especially, how involved the production is. The results lend support to the hypothesis that the shift from indirect to direct speech should have made the Debates genre more oral and less literate, as high scores on Dimensions 1 and low scores on Dimension 3 are characteristic of oral genres.

The results for Drama are given in Table 29.

Table 29. The ranking of the Drama genre, relative to the other genres, with respect to M-coefficients and to Dimensions 1, 2, 3, and 5 (dimension scores taken from Geisler 2002)

Period	M-coeff.	Dim. 1	Dim. 2	Dim. 3	Dim. 5
1	4th (118)	1st (11.79)	4th (−0.36)	2nd (−1.87)	2nd (−1.83)
2	1st (366)	1st (13.63)	5th (−1.08)	2nd (−1.91)	1st (−2.73)
3	2nd (402)	1st (15.23)	5th (−2.08)	4th (−1.70)	1st (−2.99)

The Drama genre exhibits a constant increase in the frequency of the progressive; but the figures in Letters increase even more between periods 2 and 3, and this genre thus passes Drama in the latter period. Nevertheless, the overall picture of the progressive in Drama is one of high and increasing frequencies in diachrony. In this respect, the development of the progressive in Drama resembles the development of the genre on Dimension 5. Drama presents the least abstract information of all genres in CONCE in periods 2 and 3, but is second to Trials in period 1 (when Trials also have a higher frequency of progressives); there is thus a diachronic trend on Dimension 5 which roughly parallels that of the frequency of the progressive. The dimension scores, which indicate a drift towards less abstract information (Geisler 2002: 267), support the correlation. On Dimension 1, Drama displays the most involved production of the genres in CONCE in all three periods; the change in dimension scores is not statistically significant (Geisler 2002: 257). In contrast, compared with the other genres, Drama tends towards less narrative concerns, though the change in dimension scores is only marginally significant (Geisler 2002: 259ff.). Relative to the other genres in CONCE, Drama also moves towards somewhat more elaborated reference over the 19th century, but the differences in dimension scores are not statistically significant (Geisler 2002: 264f.). Consequently, Dimensions 1, 2, and 3 do not match the M-coefficients for Drama as closely as Dimension 5. The progressive in Drama thus does not seem to be a feature characteristic of abstract information. The results for Fiction are given in Table 30.

Table 30.   The ranking of the Fiction genre, relative to the other genres, with respect to M-coefficients and to Dimensions 1, 2, 3, and 5 (dimension scores taken from Geisler 2002)

Period	M-coeff.	Dim. 1	Dim. 2	Dim. 3	Dim. 5
1	2nd (209)	4th (−4.94)	2nd (2.01)	4th (−0.33)	3rd (−0.27)
2	2nd (323)	4th (−1.39)	1st (2.26)	3rd (−1.38)	3rd (−1.49)
3	4th (229)	4th (−0.91)	2nd (1.66)	1st (−2.87)	3rd (−1.59)

As commented on in Section 3.2.4.3, part of the development of the progressive in Fiction, viz. the drop in frequency between periods 2 and 3, is unexpected. If only the order of the genres is taken into consideration, however, the development looks more straightforward: Fiction goes from being the genre with the second highest frequency of progressives to being that of the four non-expository genres with the lowest frequency of the construction. This development is not paralleled by any one similar development along Dimensions 1, 2, 3, or 5. Fiction does not change to a statistically significant degree on Dimension 1, where it is the least involved of the four non-expository genres (Geisler 2002: 255ff.). On Dimension 2, Fiction is the second most narrative genre after Trials except in period 2, where the order is reversed (if only just, and seemingly owing to a drop in narrative concerns in Trials rather than any independent development in Fiction – cf. Table 34). The results in M-coefficients and dimension scores on Dimension 2 are similar in the sense that Fiction exhibits an increase between periods 1 and 2 but a decrease between periods 2 and 3 on both parameters; but as the change on Dimension 2 is not statistically significant (Geisler 2002: 259), this similarity need not be meaningful. On Dimension 3, Fiction goes from having the most elaborated to having the most situation-dependent reference of the four non-expository genres; again, however, the difference in dimension scores is not statistically significant (Geisler 2002: 264f.). Finally, Fiction is stable relative to the other genres with respect to Dimension 5, though the dimension scores indicate a significantly less abstract information focus in diachrony (Geisler

2002: 267f.). It thus seems as though other factors may influence the occurrence of the progressive in the Fiction genre (see Section 3.2.4.3 for a discussion of the possible influence of dialogue/non-dialogue distribution and implicit conventions for the presentation of fictional dialogue). It should also be remembered that the frequency of the progressive in Fiction, as measured in S-coefficients, did not exhibit a statistically significant increase between periods 1 and 3 (see Section 3.2.4.3).

In History, a clearer pattern of correspondence can be established with Dimension 2. Table 31 presents the results.

Table 31. The ranking of the History genre, relative to the other genres, with respect to M-coefficients and to Dimensions 1, 2, 3, and 5 (dimension scores taken from Geisler 2002)

Period	M-coeff.	Dim. 1	Dim. 2	Dim. 3	Dim. 5
1	7th (32)	7th (−22.13)	6th (−1.77)	6th (2.66)	6th (2.00)
2	5th (121)	7th (−18.15)	3rd (0.85)	6th (2.24)	6th (2.67)
3	5th (216)	7th (−18.17)	3rd (−0.31)	7th (4.23)	7th (4.18)

The History genre exhibits a clear increase in the frequency of the progressive through the three periods in CONCE. Against the background given in Section 4.1, this would lead us to expect the genre to move towards involved production, situation-dependent reference, and/or non-abstract information as well. However, the data do not support such a hypothesis. History is the most informational and, thus, the least involved genre in all periods, and it also displays an abstract information focus throughout the 19th century; the genre does not develop significantly on either dimension (Geisler 2002: 257, 268). Moreover, the genre moves towards more elaborated (i.e. less situation-dependent) reference over the 19th century as a whole, in terms of both its dimension scores (Geisler 2002: 264f.) and its position relative to the other genres. On Dimensions 1, 3, and 5, History is thus stable or moves in the opposite direction from what could be expected in a genre where the progressive is on the increase. The only development which appears to co-occur with an increasing frequency of progressives is that on Dimension 2, where History displays a clear trend towards more narrative concerns between periods 1 and 2 (Geisler 2002: 261), when it also passes Debates and Science with respect to the frequency of the progressive. Given the relatively modest overall correlation in CONCE between M-coefficients and dimension scores on Dimension 2, it is slightly surprising that the progressive in History seems to covary most closely with features that indicate narrative concerns. However, as pointed out in Section 4.1, Biber and Finegan's (1997: 271) finding that Dimension 2 "reflects a split between specialist and popular written registers" may help to explain this correlation. CONCE includes three expository genres: Debates, History, and Science. If the concept of written genres can be extended to include all expository genres regardless of medium, it makes sense to assume that Debates and Science are more specialized genres than

History, in the sense that the former were aimed at a narrower audience. The progressive in History may then have been part of a stylistic/narrative group of features that differentiated popular and specialized expository genres.

For Letters, the results are given in Table 32.

Table 32.   The ranking of the Letters genre, relative to the other genres, with respect to M-coefficients and to Dimensions 1, 2, 3, and 5 (dimension scores taken from Geisler 2002)

Period	M-coeff.	Dim. 1	Dim. 2	Dim. 3	Dim. 5
1	3rd (202)	3rd (2.96)	5th (−1.12)	3rd (−1.46)	4th (−0.05)
2	3rd (323)	3rd (4.86)	6th (−1.94)	1st (−3.05)	4th (−1.33)
3	1st (425)	3rd (3.62)	4th (−1.51)	2nd (−2.45)	4th (−0.97)

The frequency of the progressive in Letters increases throughout the century, as shown in Section 3.2.4.5; in period 3, the Letters genre is even the genre with the highest frequency of progressives. However, the connection between the frequency of the progressive and the dimension scores is problematic. The texts in the Letters genre do not exhibit any clear trends on Dimension 1, where the genre is the third most involved (after Trials and Drama) in all periods; nor do the dimension scores indicate any significant development (Geisler 2002: 257). Nor do the dimension scores change significantly either on Dimension 2, where Letters belong to the middle group of genres (also comprising Debates, Drama, and History) throughout the 19th century (Geisler 2002: 259), or on Dimension 3, on which Letters and the other non-expository genres display the most situation-dependent reference (Geisler 2002: 264). On Dimension 5, finally, the position of the Letters genre is stable relative to that of the other genres, but the dimension scores display a significant trend towards a less abstract style (Geisler 2002: 267f.). It thus seems as though the increase of the progressive in Letters is partly independent of genre developments on the four dimensions investigated, although some similarity with Dimension 5 can be noted. I will return to the Letters genre in Section 4.3, where the development of the progressive in letters written by women and men will be compared with the results of a factor score analysis that takes the sex of the letter-writer into account (Geisler 2003).

The results for Science are given in Table 33.

Table 33.   The ranking of the Science genre, relative to the other genres, with respect to M-coefficients and to Dimensions 1, 2, 3, and 5 (dimension scores taken from Geisler 2002)

Period	M-coeff.	Dim. 1	Dim. 2	Dim. 3	Dim. 5
1	5th (68)	5th (−10.72)	7th (−5.24)	5th (2.61)	7th (4.70)
2	6th (76)	5th (−9.29)	7th (−5.45)	5th (0.87)	7th (4.35)
3	7th (114)	6th (−6.88)	7th (−5.86)	5th (2.82)	6th (3.93)

Science has the highest frequencies of progressives of the three expository genres in period 1; but it is passed by History in period 2 and by Debates in period 3, making it the genre in CONCE with the lowest frequency of progressives at the end of the 19th century. In addition, when the S-coefficient was used to measure the frequency of the progressive in Science in periods 1 and 3, the analysis showed that there was no statistically significant increase. Similarly, Science does not change to a statistically significant degree on any of the four dimensions investigated by Geisler (2002: 269). If we only consider the relative order of the genres in CONCE, the dimension that matches the development of the progressive best is Dimension 1, on which Science goes from being the third to the second most informational genre over the century. As for the other dimensions of variation, on Dimension 2 Science is clearly the least narrative genre in CONCE in all three periods. On Dimension 3, Science is closest to situation-dependent reference of all expository genres in CONCE throughout the century. Relative to the other genres, Science is thus stable with respect to these two dimensions. On Dimension 5, finally, Science is the genre with the most abstract situation focus in periods 1 and 2, but is passed by History in this respect in period 3; however, neither History nor Science displays a statistically significant development on this dimension.

Görlach (1999: 150) suggests that scientific writing changed from more to less personal styles over the 19th century. If this holds true, one reason why the progressive is rare in Science may be that it was associated with other linguistic features which were also indicative of involved production, viz. those that load on Dimension 1. This association of the progressive with involved production may have led to the construction being considered less suitable for scientific writing.[5] However, as Geisler's (2002) results indicate that Science is, in fact, stable with respect to the dimensions of variation across the 19th century, no such trend towards a less personal style can be ascertained.

Finally, the results for Trials are given in Table 34.

Table 34. The ranking of the Trials genre, relative to the other genres, with respect to M-coefficients and to Dimensions 1, 2, 3, and 5 (dimension scores taken from Geisler 2002)

Period	M-coeff.	Dim. 1	Dim. 2	Dim. 3	Dim. 5
1	1st (285)	2nd (6.78)	1st (4.20)	1st (–3.00)	1st (–2.55)
2	4th (282)	2nd (11.25)	2nd (2.24)	4th (–0.25)	2nd (–2.04)
3	3rd (355)	2nd (15.16)	1st (4.43)	3rd (–2.05)	2nd (–2.24)

The analysis of S-coefficients indicated that the frequency of the progressive in Trials did not increase significantly between periods 1 and 3. Relative to the other

---

5   There are also other possible reasons for this scarcity of progressives. One reason may be that Science texts often deal with the discovery of general principles, such as natural laws, which are rarely expressed using progressive verb phrases (though here one might also expect variation among subgenres, such as the social and the natural sciences).

genres, Trials have the highest normalized frequency of progressives of all genres in period 1, but are passed by all the other non-expository genres in period 2, when the frequency of the progressive actually decreases slightly. Trials pass Fiction again in period 3, owing partly, however, to the unexpected decrease in the frequency of the progressive in the latter genre. This development links Trials with Dimensions 2 and 3. On Dimension 2, there is a statistically significant drop in dimension scores in period 2 (Geisler 2002: 261), where Fiction also passes Trials (if only just); this drop is reversed in period 3. On Dimension 3, the order of Trials relative to the other genres also indicates a trend towards elaborated reference in period 2, where the Trials genre is in fact the non-expository genre that exhibits the most elaborated reference. This trend is also reversed in period 3, but only partially, and the result is that the order of the Trials genre is the same relative to the other genres with respect to Dimension 3 and to the frequency of the progressive. The development of Trials on Dimension 3 is not statistically significant (Geisler 2002: 264). Consequently, Trials are stable with respect to both the frequency of the progressive and the dimension scores on Dimension 3, possibly a further indication of a connection between them.

The correlations with Dimensions 1 and 5 are less clear. On Dimension 1 Trials texts are among the most involved in all three periods, and become significantly more involved over the century (Geisler 2002: 257). On Dimension 5, the Trials genre exhibits the least abstract information in period 1, but is passed by Drama in periods 2 and 3; however, the dimension scores do not change significantly (Geisler 2002: 268). The most likely hypothesis seems to be that the progressive in Trials co-occurs with linguistic features that express situation-dependent reference and narrative concerns.

The results reported in the present section indicate that high frequencies of progressives correlate, positively and negatively, with the frequency of different sets of co-occurring linguistic features (i.e. the features that load on the four dimensions investigated). In addition, the results of the analyses imply that the nature and strength of the correlations depend on which genre in CONCE is being investigated. In fact, each genre in CONCE appears to have its own pattern in this respect. For Debates, the most pervasive correspondences seem to be with involved production and situation-dependent reference on Dimensions 1 and 3; for Drama, with non-abstract information on Dimension 5; for History, with narrative concerns on Dimension 2; for Science, with involved production on Dimension 1; and for Trials, with narrative concerns on Dimension 2 and situation-dependent reference on Dimension 3. For Fiction and Letters, it proved more difficult to discern a clear pattern, although minor similarities with Dimension 5 (for Letters) could be noted. As will be shown in Section 4.4, it is possible to interpret these apparent cross-genre differences in the material from a functional point of view.

4.3   Gender, M-coefficients, and co-occurrence patterns

In the present section, I will compare the distribution of the progressive, as measured in M-coefficients, with the results Geisler (2001; 2003) reached when calculating factor scores for Dimensions 1 ("Involved vs. informational production"), 3 ("Elaborated vs. situation-dependent reference"), and 5 ("Abstract vs. non-abstract information") of Biber's (1988) factor analysis for women and men letter-writers in CONCE. In Sections 4.1–4.2, Geisler's (2000; 2002) results for Dimension 2 ("Narrative vs. non-narrative concerns") were also included in the investigation. However, Dimension 2 will be left out of the present comparison, as results reached in Section 4.2 indicated that dimension scores for Dimension 2 do not correlate with the frequency of the progressive in Letters. As the sex of the addressee was not included as a parameter in Geisler (2003), only the sex of the letter-writer will be taken into account in the following analysis.

Table 35a–b presents results for the two subsamples of Letters concerning the frequency of the progressive and dimension scores on the three dimensions investigated. As mentioned above, high M-coefficients can be expected to correlate with involved production on Dimension 1, situation-dependent reference on Dimension 3, and non-abstract information on Dimension 5. In order to clarify these expected correlations, I will italicize the higher M-coefficient, as well as the dimension score closer to involved production, situation-dependent reference, and non-abstract information in each period subsample and for the total figures when Table 35a and Table 35b are compared.

Table 35a. Letters written by women: M-coefficients and dimension scores on Dimensions 1, 3, and 5 (dimension scores from Geisler 2001; 2003)

Period	M-coefficient	Dimension 1	Dimension 3	Dimension 5
1	*228*	*2.68*	−2.28	0.16
2	*387*	*8.89*	−3.09	*−1.11*
3	*488*	2.75	−3.47	−2.03
1–3	*354*	*4.79*	−2.88	−0.88

Table 35b. Letters written by men: M-coefficients and dimension scores on Dimensions 1, 3, and 5 (dimension scores from Geisler 2001; 2003)

Period	M-coefficient	Dimension 1	Dimension 3	Dimension 5
1	168	1.33	−0.38	*−0.27*
2	265	1.32	−2.32	−1.05
3	346	*5.31*	−1.68	−0.51
1–3	254	2.38	−1.51	−0.65

If there is a positive correlation between the frequency of the progressive and the dimension scores on any of the three dimensions included in the comparison, we would expect similar patterns concerning the M-coefficient and the scores on the relevant dimension in Table 35a–b. However, there are no clear parallels between the frequency of the progressive in these two subsamples and developments on any one of the dimensions.[6] Instead, it may be possible to link the difference between women and men letter-writers' use of the progressive to a combination of some developments on Dimensions 1, 3, and 5. The results presented in Sections 4.1–4.2 indicated that a multi-functional account of the 19th-century progressive is advisable to describe the use of the construction. It was hypothesized that Dimension 1 (and, perhaps, 5) may correlate with the not-solely-aspectual functions of the progressive, while Dimension 3 correlates with the aspectual functions of the construction. The Letters genre is one of the genres where the progressive was most fully integrated as regards frequency, and a high degree of integration can be expected to correlate with the presence of aspectual as well as not-solely-aspectual progressives in texts. Thus, both these types of functions of the progressive should be present in the data yielded by Letters.

The dimension scores from Geisler (2003) indicate no consistent development on Dimension 1: women's letters are slightly more involved than men's in period 1, much more involved in period 2, but more informational in period 3, when men's letters suddenly become considerably more involved. The developments are statistically significant for both women and men (Geisler 2003: 94). On Dimension 3, women's letters have more situation-dependent reference throughout. However, the difference between women and men on this dimension displays no consistent trend. Women's letters exhibit consistently more situation-dependent reference for every period, a trend which is marginally significant; the development of men's letters towards more situation-dependent reference is statistically significant, but the trend is not consistent (Geisler 2003: 98f.). Finally, on Dimension 5, we find a development which resembles that of the progressive: women's letters become consistently and significantly less abstract in information focus across the century compared with men's letters, which display no significant change (Geisler 2003: 102f.).[7] But unlike the distribution of the progressive, on Dimension 5 men's letters start out as displaying less abstract information; they are not passed by women letter-writers until period 2, and there is no substantial difference between the subsamples until the end of the century. Moreover, the overall difference between women and men letter-writers was not statistically significant for Dimension 5, which separates this dimension from Dimensions 1 and 3 (Geisler 2003: 92).

Against the background of these results, it can be hypothesized that Dimensions 1, 3, and 5 correlate cumulatively with the distribution of the progressive. In period 1, women letter-writers use more involved production than men and have more situation-dependent reference, but their letters are slightly more abstract in information focus. In period 2, differences between women and men on Dimensions 3 and 5 are not pronounced (although women letter-writers

---

6   The same result was reached for the Letters genre in its entirety (see Section 4.2).

7   As shown in Section 4.2, Dimension 5 was also the dimension whose dimension scores seemed to correlate best with the frequency of the progressive in Letters as a whole.

use more situation-dependent reference and their information focus is somewhat less abstract), but there is a considerable difference on Dimension 1, where women's letters are much more involved than men's. In period 3, finally, men's letters are in fact more involved than women's, but this unexpected result is perhaps compensated for by clear differences in the other direction on Dimensions 3 and 5: women's letters exhibit more situation-dependent reference and less abstract information than men's letters. Thus, the cumulative impression of women's and men's letters on Dimensions 1, 3, and 5 results in a picture that resembles the development of the progressive in these two subcorpora more closely than if only one dimension is singled out.

There is some indirect support from previous research for the above interpretation of the complex co-occurrence pattern. First, Biber and Finegan (1997: 260) identify Dimensions 1, 3, and 5 as signifying a split between oral and literate genres: the former will tend towards involved production, situation-dependent reference, and non-abstract information, while the latter tend towards informational production, elaborated reference, and abstract information. Moreover, Biber (2003) presents a new multi-feature/multi-dimensional analysis with a slightly different set of features that includes the progressive. The study is based on a corpus consisting of spoken and written academic Present-Day English. In this analysis, one very powerful dimension is called "Oral vs. literate discourse": this dimension "shows an absolute difference between spoken and written registers in the university context" (Biber 2003: 63). Many features that load on this dimension also load on Dimensions 1, 3, and 5 in Biber's (1988) analysis; Biber (2003: 63) even claims that this dimension "actually collapses three major oral/literate dimensions from the 1988 analysis (Dimensions 1, 3, and 5)".[8] Significantly, the progressive also loads as an oral feature on this dimension (Biber 2003: 56). Although the range of genres represented is limited, Biber's (2003) results thus provide support for the hypotheses (a) that Dimensions 1, 3, and 5 in Biber (1988) can, in some cases, be treated as a cumulative whole, and (b) that the progressive would load as an oral feature on such a cumulative dimension.[9] As the progressive is more frequent in non-expository and oral genres than in expository and literate genres, it makes sense that women's letters, where the progressive is more frequent, are, on the whole, closer than men's letters to the oral poles of Dimensions 1, 3, and 5 (see Table 35a–b), although the difference on Dimension 5 is not statistically significant (Geisler 2003: 102).

In Section 3.2.5.4, it was suggested that a high frequency of progressives in private letters may have been one indicator of a female gender style in 19th-century English. If there is such a female gender style, it appears that it is partly

---

8   Features that indicate involved production or situation-dependent reference load as oral features; features that indicate informational production, elaborated reference, or abstract information load as literate features.

9   However, each of Dimensions 1, 3, and 5 "has an independent set of defining linguistic features, and ... identifies a unique set of relations among the full range of registers" in Biber and Finegan's (1997) analysis (Biber and Finegan 1997: 260).

composed of linguistic features that load on Dimensions 1, 3, and 5, making women letter-writers' language more involved in production, more situation-dependent in reference, and less abstract in information focus than that of men letter-writers, although there is a good deal of variation along each of these dimensions. This pattern would support the hypothesis, presented in Section 3.2.5.3, that a male gender style (based on, among other things, predominantly male speaker/writer and listener/reader communities) may have dominated expository genres in the 19th century. The expository genres Debates, History, and Science all tend towards informational production, elaborated reference, and abstract information compared with the non-expository genres (see Geisler 2002).

Geisler (2003) also presents information on which individual linguistic features in the factor score analysis are used significantly more by men and women respectively. Among the features that are significantly more frequent in men's letters, we find prepositions, attributive adjectives, and nominalizations. Texts with high frequencies of these features tend to present information by means of complex noun and prepositional phrases rather than full clauses with verb phrases; such texts thus contain fewer possible slots where the progressive can appear.[10] Women's letters, in contrast, display higher frequencies of features such as emphatics, past-tense verbs, private verbs, time adverbs, and infinitives. As will be shown in Section 6.4, temporal adverbs frequently modify progressive verb phrases; infinitives and past-tense verbs are used to form verb phrases, and thus help to create slots where the progressive can appear. The higher frequency of emphatics in women's letters may correlate with the emotional, not-solely-aspectual functions of the progressive. This correlation may help to explain why private verbs, many of which are rare in the progressive, are more common in women's than in men's letters. States denoted by private verbs, e.g. BELIEVE and SUPPOSE, are often inherently subjective in that they "can only be subjectively verified" (Quirk et al. 1985: 202); similarly, the progressive has been shown to have subjective, not-solely-aspectual connotations (see e.g. Wright 1995).

4.4   Discussion of results

In this chapter, the frequency of the progressive, as expressed in M-coefficients, has been compared with the results Geisler (2000; 2001; 2002; 2003) reached when computing dimension scores, based on Biber's (1988) factor analysis, for different subsamples of CONCE. The dimensions identified in Biber (1988) characterize different types of discourse in the sense that they "are interpreted in terms of the situational and cognitive functions most widely shared by the co-occurring linguistic features, and in terms of the relations among registers along

---

10   The verb-phrase-related features that are significantly more common in men's than in women's letters are passives, prediction modals, and suasive verbs (Geisler 2003: 102, 104). As will be shown in Chapter 5, progressive verb phrases that contain modal and passive auxiliaries are comparatively infrequent. In addition, some suasive verbs, such as PRONOUNCE and PROPOSE, are rare in progressive verb phrases.

each dimension" (Biber and Finegan 1997: 258). Since the interpretations given to the different dimensions are thus based partly on functional considerations, there may be connections between the functions of the progressive and the functions of the features that load on these dimensions. If, for instance, both the progressive and the features that indicate situation-dependent reference are common in a given text, they may express related functions.

The results for the genre samples in their entirety, presented in Section 4.1, showed that the progressive appeared to co-occur with features indicating involved production and situation-dependent reference, and not to co-occur with features indicating informational production, elaborated reference, and abstract information. To a lesser extent, the progressive also co-occurred with features indicating narrative concerns. These results were interpreted as indications of the multifunctionality of the progressive: in particular, aspectual progressives should be common in texts with a good deal of situation-dependent reference, and not-solely-aspectual progressives should be frequent in texts tending towards involved production.

The next step, in Section 4.2, was to consider the development of each genre in CONCE with respect to, on the one hand, M-coefficients and, on the other hand, Dimensions 1, 2, 3, and 5 in Geisler's (2002) factor score analysis. In this context, the results based on the entire genre samples were used as interpretative tools. The results of the comparison confirmed the general tendency, established in Section 4.1, for comparatively high M-coefficients to be attested in samples displaying involved production, narrative concerns, situation-dependent reference, and non-abstract information. However, there was a great deal of variation across the genre parameter as regards which dimension(s) correlated most closely with the frequency of the progressive. Patterns of co-occurrence could be established between M-coefficients and all of the four dimensions investigated: with Dimension 1 in Debates and Science; with Dimension 2 in History and Trials; with Dimension 3 in Debates and Trials; and with Dimension 5 in Drama (and perhaps Letters).

This variation can be interpreted as pointing further to the multifunctionality of the progressive discussed in Section 4.1. Although most uses of the progressive imply aspectual values, the construction also has functions involving, inter alia, subjectivity, emotion, intensity, and emphasis (see for instance Scheffer 1975, Wright 1994, and Rydén 1997). Differences between genres in the relative distribution of these functions may cause the co-occurrence patterns of the progressive and the four dimensions investigated to exhibit cross-genre variation. High frequencies of not-solely-aspectual progressives can be expected to correlate with involved production and not to correlate with abstract information, which may help to explain the patterns found in Debates, Drama, and Science (and perhaps Letters). Similarly, high frequencies of aspectual progressives may well correlate with situation-dependent reference; such correlations may account for the patterns attested in Debates and Trials. The co-occurrence patterns with Dimensions 1, 3, and 5 would also be strengthened by the general tendency of the progressive to occur more often in genres that incorporate spoken and/or colloquial features, since these dimensions also form an oral/literate continuum.

The correspondence in History and Trials between M-coefficients and narrative concerns on Dimension 2 is less straightforward. As stated above, for History the pattern can probably be explained in terms of Dimension 2 separating specialist and popular written genres. The progressive would then be more frequent in History than in Science because 19th-century history writing was less specialized than the academic subgenres represented in Science. The correspondence in Trials is more difficult to interpret, but can perhaps be accounted for in terms of differences within the Trials genre concerning the types of texts selected in the different periods. As pointed out in Section 3.2.4.7, the Trials texts from period 2 (when the score drops on Dimension 2) do not deal with as dramatic subject matter overall as do the texts from periods 1 and 3. It is possible that this shift in subject matter manifests itself as a decrease in both narrative concerns and the frequency of the progressive: narrative reports of vivid events such as murders may contain both features that indicate narrative concerns and a relatively large number of progressives. However, in this context it is surprising that the dimension score for Trials on Dimension 1 is not affected by these changes of subject matter; Trials display a consistent, and statistically significant, trend towards more involved production on Dimension 1.

When the gender parameter was added to the discussion in Section 4.3, correlations between the frequency of the progressive and dimension scores in women's and men's letters proved difficult to establish when the dimensions were considered in isolation. However, when Dimensions 1, 3, and 5 were considered cumulatively, the results matched the frequency of the progressive better. This result further emphasizes the multifunctionality of the progressive, and implies that a comprehensive account of its functions must treat both the aspectual and the not-solely-aspectual uses of the construction.

In Section 3.2.5, it was hypothesized that female and male gender styles may lie behind some of the variation between women and men letter-writers in the frequency of the progressive: a comparatively high frequency of progressives would then be characteristic of a female gender style. Such a female gender style would, on the whole, contain comparatively high frequencies of linguistic features indicating involved production and situation-dependent reference, and comparatively low frequencies of features indicating informational production, elaborated reference, and abstract information. This assumption was supported by a look at some of the individual linguistic features that, Geisler (2003) found, were more common in women's and men's letters respectively: for instance, women letter-writers used adverbs more than men, whereas nominalizations were more common in men's letters.

Palander-Collin (1999a) reached partly similar results when she investigated the distribution of *I think* in 17th-century letters. Palander-Collin found that women use this feature more than men, and linked this structured variation to differences between women's and men's letters regarding frequencies of other linguistic features, which load on Dimension 1 of Biber's (1988) factor analysis (her results were not compared to those of an entire factor score analysis, however). The results show that women use these features, as well as *I think*, more than men, and Palander-Collin (1999a: 247ff.) draws the conclusion that *I think* can be seen as an indicator of involved style.

There are of course differences between *I think* and the progressive as linguistic features; Palander-Collin's study also covers a period prior to that in focus in the present work. Nevertheless, the use of the two constructions has parallels which indicate that similar differences in gender styles may underlie the attested differences between women's and men's language in the frequency of *I think* and the progressive. First, both *I think* and the progressive have functions connected to politeness and face-saving. Starting out from Brown and Levinson's (1987) classification, Palander-Collin (1999a: 230) discusses cases where *I think* is used in politeness strategies. The progressive can also be used as part of politeness strategies: it can function as a less direct variant than the non-progressive in requests, thus expressing negative politeness, and perhaps also as a positive politeness strategy when the progressive indicates intensity of feeling.[11] Secondly, the social distance between the addresser and addressee may affect the use of *I think* as well as the progressive. Palander-Collin (1999b) found that the frequency of *I think* was higher in 16th-century letters written to close family members than in letters to more distant acquaintances. (This difference is not attested in Palander-Collin 1999a: 240, however.) Similarly, in Arnaud's (1998) corpus of late Modern English letters, the frequency of the progressive grew with increasing degrees of intimacy for both women and men (Arnaud 1998: 140ff.).[12]

More research is needed before the more frequent use of the progressive by women than by men letter-writers can be attributed to differences in gender styles. Moreover, the concept of gender styles does not constitute an ultimate answer to the question of why gender-based variation in language occurs. For instance, if politeness strategies account for some of the gender-based differences in the frequency of the progressive, the question of why women use more

---

11   Positive politeness strategies communicate (partial) similarity between one's own wants and the addressee's wants (Brown and Levinson 1987: 101); the strategies are thus directed towards the addressee's positive face, i.e. the want of every "competent adult member" of a society that his/her wants "be desirable to at least some others" (Brown and Levinson 1987: 62). Brown and Levinson (1987: 102) include attention to the addressee's interests and the assertion of concern for his/her wants in their chart of positive politeness strategies. Negative politeness strategies focus on the addressee's negative face, i.e. "his want to have his freedom of action unhindered and his attention unimpeded" (Brown and Levinson 1987: 129). Hedges and conventional indirectness are both among the negative politeness strategies listed by Brown and Levinson (1987: 131).

12   Arnaud (1998) divided his letters into three degrees of intimacy, where degree one corresponded to "the family circle and 'bosom friends' ", degree two to "friends and relations in a more general sense", and degree three to "more distant connections" (Arnaud 1998: 129). As pointed out in Section 2.1.2, the Letters genre in CONCE includes letters written to family or close friends only, in order to obtain stable stratified subsamples where this variable does not affect results. Consequently, no classification of the letters in CONCE into degrees of intimacy was attempted in the present study.

politeness strategies still remains. Variables such as status and power are likely to be crucial in this respect. Romaine (1999: 168) points out that "the onus is on the subordinate person in an encounter to be polite … What is universal about politeness is acting deferentially to the person perceived as higher in status or power"; if a female gender identity is linked to political, social, and economic subordination relative to a male gender identity in the community under scrutiny, it is likely that female language-users will employ more linguistic features that can function as (part of) politeness strategies than will male language-users. However, the distribution of the progressive in Letters is likely to be the result of several factors (see Section 3.2.5.4 for some suggestions in this respect).

Some caveats should be mentioned as regards (a) the comparison of the order of subsamples of CONCE relative to other subsamples and (b) the interpretation of the results. To begin with, I have not systematically taken into account which particular genres are ranked above and below each genre in the tables: this means, for instance, that a genre has been considered stable if it occupies the same ranking relative to the other genres, even though the genres above and below it may have changed places. Moreover, the progressive itself was not included in Biber's (1988), Biber and Finegan's (1997), or Geisler's (2000; 2001; 2002; 2003) multi-feature/multi-dimensional analyses. The above investigations, where parallels have been established between the functions of the features that load on Biber's dimensions and the functions of the progressive, should therefore be treated with some caution: despite the co-occurrence patterns established, we do not know whether the progressive would load on one or several of the dimensions of variation. However, as mentioned above, some indirect support for the correlations established with Dimensions 1, 3, and 5 can be found in Biber (2003), where the progressive loaded as an oral feature on Dimension 1 ("Oral vs. literate discourse") of a new multi-feature/multi-dimensional analysis. This dimension incorporates many of the features loading on Dimensions 1, 3, and 5 in Biber's (1988) analysis.

The consistency of the results, and the extent to which they match what would be expected in the light of previous research, point to the value of complementing frequency analyses by making comparisons with multi-feature/multi-dimensional approaches. Such comparisons can provide researchers with an important link between frequency and function. The results of the above investigations lend support to theories of the progressive that encompass both aspectual and not-solely-aspectual functions, and suggest that variables such as genre and gender affect the distribution of these two groups of functions.

The connections established in this chapter between Biber's dimensions of variation and the frequency of the progressive also shed more light on the integration of the progressive into late Modern English. As the progressive correlated both with involved production on Dimension 1 and with situation-dependent reference on Dimension 3, both aspectual and not-solely-aspectual functions of the progressive appear to have been important in the integration process. In addition, in Section 3.3 it was hypothesized that this integration process was mediated through the parameters of medium and subject matter, so that speech-related and non-expository genres were affected first. The fact that high frequencies of progressives correlated with the oral ends of Dimensions 1, 3, and 5, as well as with the popular (as opposed to specialized) end of Dimension 2, supports this hypothesis.

In Chapter 3, an account was given of how the frequency of the progressive varied with time, genre, and gender in 19th-century English; in the present chapter, this account has been linked to the functions of the construction. The results of the analyses point to extralinguistic variables as being of great importance for the integration of the progressive into English grammar. However, many studies of the progressive have also discussed different linguistic contexts where the construction occurs. Examining the distribution of the progressive in such linguistic contexts may give us further evidence that the construction was becoming more fully integrated into 19th-century English. For instance, Denison (1993; 1998) and Warner (1993; 1995; 1997) both consider the emergence of the passive progressive important in their accounts; Denison also mentions the extension of the progressive to inanimate subjects. Other possible indicators include the extent to which the progressive is modified by temporal adverbials, the occurrence of the progressive in stative situations, and the combination of the progressive with other auxiliaries, e.g. modal and perfect, in the same verb phrase. Analyses of features such as these constitute the topics of the next two chapters.

Chapter 5

Morphosyntactic variation in the verb phrase

It was shown in Chapter 3 that, in terms of overall frequency, the progressive became more integrated into English grammar during the 19th century, although there was a good deal of variation across the genre parameter. However, the frequency of a construction is only one way of looking at its degree of integration in the language under scrutiny. Another way of investigating this process is to consider the formal expansion, if any, of the construction within the paradigm of which the construction is a part. For the Modern English progressive, the most relevant paradigm of this kind is the verb phrase.

In this chapter, the occurrence patterns of the progressive within the verb phrase will be analysed. I will focus on the combination of the progressive with four important formal features of the late Modern English verb phrase: tense (present vs. past), the perfect, the active and passive voice, and modal auxiliaries. These four features may affect the occurrence and functional distribution of the progressive by, for instance, encoding additional formal and semantic complexity. In what follows, these features will first be investigated one by one, in isolation, and then, in a separate section, in the ways they combine in complex verb phrases. The patterns that these features exhibit in progressive verb phrases will also be considered in relation to the extralinguistic parameters of time and genre. Throughout the chapter, the focus will be on the occurrence of the different patterns within the progressive paradigm rather than on variation between the progressive and the non-progressive. Finally, a section will be devoted to a low-frequency pattern that is relevant to a study of the progressive in 19th-century English, viz. the *being* + present participle construction, as in *Being teaching, I could not attend the meeting.*

As in all chapters of the present study, the main source of data is the CONCE corpus. However, some variants of progressives were very rare in 19th-century English, among them progressives that incorporate passive or modal auxiliaries. Since a one-million-word corpus cannot be expected to yield sufficient data for an analysis of such variants, I will use an additional data source. Professor René Arnaud kindly let me use his database of progressives, based on a corpus of private letters written between 1787 and 1880. This corpus comprises *c.* 10 million words, and formed the basis for the investigations carried out in Arnaud (1998) and Arnaud (2002). Where relevant, I have recoded Arnaud's data in accordance with the classificatory criteria used in the present study. The most important changes in this respect concern periodization: the relevant progressives in Arnaud's database have been reclassified according to what period in the CONCE framework they belong to. Since the periods covered by CONCE and by Arnaud's database do not match exactly, I have added the period labels "0" for progressives attested before 1800 and "1b" for progressives attested between 1830 and 1850. (A consequence of this recoding is that there will be relatively few progressives in Arnaud's database that match period 3 in CONCE, as this period starts in 1870 and Arnaud's corpus does not include letters written after 1880.) In addition, Arnaud includes progressives in his data that share part of their verb phrase with a previous progressive, e.g. *was ... dancing* in *He was singing and dancing*, whereas such instances were excluded from the counts in the present study (see Section 2.2.3); I have conformed Arnaud's data to match my criteria in this respect. More detailed changes to the coding scheme will be commented on in the sections where I deal with specific parts of the progressive paradigm. In these sections, data from CONCE and from Arnaud's corpus will be presented in separate tables.[1]

5.1   Tense

The progressive has occurred in both the present and the past tense ever since Old English (see Mitchell 1985: 272f.). It can thus be expected that the 19th-century progressive should be well established in both tenses. However, from a functional perspective the tense parameter is still of interest to research on the progressive: for instance, it was suggested by Hatcher (1951) that the progressive/non-progressive opposition is not the same in different tense forms.[2] From a cross-genre perspective, it is also possible that different tenses correlate with a high overall frequency of the progressive itself; this, in turn, may indicate that the progressive is more integrated in the present than in the past tense in some genres but the other way around in others, if the distribution of functions that the present and past progressives carry varies across the genre parameter.

In this section, the terms "present" and "past" cover all verb phrases that include a present or past finite verb form; that is, *I am writing a novel, I have been writing a novel*, and *The novel may be being written* would all be classified as present-tense progressives. Progressive verb phrases that do not have a finite verb form are classed as "non-finite" in this respect. (For a more detailed breakdown of finite occurrences of the progressive into different tense forms, see Section 5.5.)

---

1   Since there is some overlap between the letters that make up Arnaud's corpus and those which constitute the Letters genre in CONCE, it is not advisable to calculate cumulative results for the two corpora.

2   Hatcher (1951: 263f.) also argues for a more fine-grained division within each tense.

Before the distribution of present and past progressives can be discussed, it is necessary to remove non-finite, or [–tense] progressive verb phrases, as in (25) below, from the total counts. As stated in Section 3.1.1.4, the number of non-finite progressives in CONCE is 44. The period/genre breakdown is given in Table 36.

Table 36.   Non-finite progressives in CONCE by period and genre

Period	Debates	Drama	Fiction	History	Letters	Science	Trials	Total
1	1	–	2	–	5	3	2	13
2	1	–	4	–	3	2	6	16
3	1	3	–	–	2	3	6	15
Total	3	3	6	–	10	8	14	44

As shown in Table 36, there seems to be little overall development in the distribution of non-finite progressives: non-finite progressives account for roughly 2% of all progressive verb phrases in all periods. In all genres but Science, the raw frequencies of non-finite progressives are either too low to be reliable or account for less than 5% of all progressive verb phrases. In Science, however, non-finite progressives make up 9% of all progressive verb phrases. Non-finite progressives in Science appear to be used mostly in contexts where the content of the proposition is hedged or made hypothetical in one way or another, as in (25):

(25)   Examples have been given of animals which seem *to be oscillating* between the possession and loss of particular teeth, the first premolar of the Badgers, p1 of some species of Otter, &c.
(Science, Bateson, 1870–1900, p. 271)

It is possible that the use of non-finite progressives after verbs such as SEEM and APPEAR, as in (25), where the content is hedged by the verb phrase containing SEEM, has given the non-finite progressive a connotation of uncertainty or non-categoricalness. Charleston (1955: 275) claims that non-finite progressives are used for similar reasons after e.g. SEEM, WANT, and FAIL.[3]

The number of finite progressive verb phrases in CONCE per period and genre is given in Table 37.

---

3   Charleston (1955: 275) also argues that progressive verb phrases incorporating auxiliaries other than progressive BE have a similar effect. In addition, note a similar use of finite progressives in Present-Day English to make "the speaker's attitude more tentative and perhaps more polite" (Quirk et al. 1985: 202), as in *I am hoping you will come.*

Table 37.   Finite progressives in CONCE by period and genre

Period	Debates	Drama	Fiction	History	Letters	Science	Trials	Total
1	11	37	86	10	241	23	176	584
2	10	108	122	37	420	22	165	884
3	29	114	69	66	384	32	234	928
Total	50	259	277	113	1,045	77	575	2,396

The next step is to see how many, and what percentage of the progressives in Table 37 are in the present and the past tense respectively. The raw figures for present progressives, together with what percentage of the finite progressives in each subsample are present progressives, are given in Table 38; Table 39 presents the corresponding figures for past progressives.

Table 38.   Present-tense progressives in CONCE by period and genre (percentages of all finite progressives in each subsample within brackets)

Period	Debates	Drama	Fiction	History	Letters	Science	Trials	Total
1	–	30	20	2	184	17	31	284
		(81%)	(23%)	(20%)	(76%)	(74%)	(18%)	(49%)
2	3	81	24	2	342	19	47	518
	(30%)	(75%)	(20%)	(5%)	(81%)	(86%)	(28%)	(59%)
3	19	99	31	2	290	26	37	504
	(66%)	(87%)	(45%)	(3%)	(76%)	(81%)	(16%)	(54%)
Total	22	210	75	6	816	62	115	1,306
	(44%)	(81%)	(27%)	(5%)	(78%)	(81%)	(20%)	(55%)

Table 39.   Past-tense progressives in CONCE by period and genre (percentages of all finite progressives in each subsample within brackets)

Period	Debates	Drama	Fiction	History	Letters	Science	Trials	Total
1	11	7	66	8	57	6	145	300
	(100%)	(19%)	(77%)	(80%)	(24%)	(26%)	(82%)	(51%)
2	7	27	98	35	78	3	118	366
	(70%)	(25%)	(80%)	(95%)	(19%)	(14%)	(72%)	(41%)
3	10	15	38	64	94	6	197	424
	(34%)	(13%)	(55%)	(97%)	(24%)	(19%)	(84%)	(46%)
Total	28	49	202	107	229	15	460	1,090
	(56%)	(19%)	(73%)	(95%)	(22%)	(19%)	(80%)	(45%)

As shown in Tables 38 and 39, a little more than half of all finite progressive verb phrases in CONCE incorporate a present-tense verb form. It is difficult to discern any clear diachronic trends in the material. In Letters, Science, and Trials, there is an increase in present-tense progressives between periods 1 and 2, an increase which is partly or wholly neutralized by a decrease between periods 2 and 3. (The same pattern is discernible in the total figures.) As regards Trials, it is possible that differences between period 2 and the other periods in the types of proceedings that make up the texts influence the tense distribution of progressive verb phrases (see Section 3.2.4.7 for a discussion of these differences). In contrast, in Fiction and Drama there is a decrease in the percentage of present-tense progressives between periods 1 and 2 but an increase between periods 2 and 3. Debates and History, finally, display a more straightforward trend, with a development towards a higher percentage of present-tense progressive verb phrases in Debates and towards a lower percentage in History (though raw frequencies are too low for results to be conclusive). For Debates, the clear development from period 1 to period 3 is likely to be a consequence of the shift from indirect to direct speech (see also Section 3.2.4.1). A comparison with Fitzmaurice's (2004a: 147) investigation of the progressive in 17th-century and 18th-century English implies that the present tense accounts for a larger share of all progressives across time in Fiction (perhaps indicating a shift towards more present-tense dialogue at the expense of past-tense narrative) and Drama, while the percentage for Letters is more stable (no other genres were included in both Fitzmaurice 2004a and the present investigation).

The genre totals indicate that a high proportion of past progressives is a relatively good indicator that a genre has narrative concerns, as measured by the position of the genre on Dimension 2 of Biber's (1988) factor analysis. The four genres where more than 50% of all finite progressive verb phrases are in the past tense – Debates, Fiction, History, and Trials – are also the genres that exhibited the highest scores on Dimension 2 in Geisler's (2002) factor score analysis of CONCE. This may seem an expected result, given that past-tense verbs are one of the most important linguistic features loading on Dimension 2. However, it turns out that the parallel does not hold true as clearly for present progressives and the dimension on which present-tense verbs load most saliently, viz. Dimension 1. The second most involved genre, Trials, tends to have past rather than present progressives; and the second least involved genre, Science, tends to have present rather than past progressives. There are several possible reasons for this discrepancy. First, it is possible for a genre to exhibit both involved production on Dimension 1 and narrative concerns on Dimension 2, as evidenced by Trials. Secondly, there are more linguistic features that load on Dimension 1 than on Dimension 2, and whereas past-tense verbs have the highest loading on Dimension 2 in Biber's (1988) factor analysis, present-tense verbs have only the fourth highest loading on Dimension 1 (Biber 1988: 89). Thus, the past tense is a stronger indicator of narrative concerns than the present tense is of involved style.[4] Lastly, the functional load of the progressive may be different in the

---

4   In addition, the feature of present-tense verbs loads saliently as a negative feature on Dimension 2 in addition to loading as a positive feature on Dimension 1, while the feature of past-tense verbs does not load on Dimension 1. However, frequencies of present-tense verbs

present and the past. Wright (1994) hypothesizes that present-tense occurrence is one of several linguistic features that may indicate to language users that a given progressive is non-aspectual. If this is true, we would expect not-solely-aspectual progressives to be more common in the present than in the past. Thus, present progressives would have more diverse readings, aspectual and not-solely-aspectual, while past progressives would tend to have a more homogeneous set of chiefly aspectual functions, and be likely to function as background markers in narrative.[5] Against this background, it is likely that past-tense progressives are more marked for narrative concerns than present-tense progressives are for involved production, and this matches the data.

The correlation between the frequency of the progressive and its distribution across the tense variable also offers some interesting, to some extent genre-specific results. In the two genres that display the most narrative concerns (and high proportions of past progressives), Fiction and Trials, the frequency of the progressive seems to correlate with a high proportion of past progressives. In Fiction, the progressive is the most frequent in period 2, which is also the period with the highest proportion of past progressives; in Trials, the small decrease in the frequency of the progressive between periods 1 and 2 correlates with a decrease in the proportion of past progressives. For the other genres, however, this correlation is not apparent, and Debates even appear to exhibit the opposite development, with a substantial increase in frequency coupled with decreasing percentages of past progressives. (However, this trend cannot be verified owing to the low raw frequencies of present progressives in periods 1 and 2 of the Debates genre.) A possible explanation for these results is that the Trials genre shows a drop towards non-narrative concerns in period 2; in the same period, Fiction shows a small tendency towards more narrative concerns (see Section 4.2). It is possible that the progressive has so clearly defined functions in narrative genres that, in these texts, a drop in the frequency of the progressive will often accompany a decrease in narrative concerns, and, conversely, frequencies will tend to rise when texts exhibit clear narrative concerns.[6] However, at least in Fiction the change on Dimension 2 is too small for this to be the only reason

---

were not used in the computation of factor scores for Dimension 2 in Biber (1988), as each feature was only included "in the factor score of the factor on which it had the highest loading (in terms of absolute magnitude, ignoring plus or minus sign" (Biber 1988: 93).

5   However, Wright's (1994) investigation is only intended to cover one type of not-solely-aspectual progressives, viz. what Wright calls the "modal" progressive: the feature of tense need not be important for other not-solely-aspectual functions of the progressive. Moreover, since present-tense occurrence is only one of five diagnostics (see Section 7.2) for the modal progressive postulated by Wright, past progressives can also be modal if they meet several of the other criteria. The hypothesized difference between the present and the past as regards aspectual and not-solely-aspectual functions of the progressive is thus quantitative, not qualitative.

6   Provided that the proportion of all past-tense verb phrases that are progressives remains constant in diachrony, it is also possible that the percentage of past progressives and the factor score on Dimension 2 are both manifestations of the same underlying feature, viz. the frequency of past-tense verbs in texts.

behind the frequency variation (see also the discussion in Section 3.2.4.3 concerning the proportions of dialogue and non-dialogue in Fiction). More research is needed on how the functions of the progressive interact with the tense variable.

5.2   The perfect progressive

In the present section, I will use the term "perfect progressive" to cover all progressive verb phrases that include a past participle of BE, e.g. *has been being built* in *The house has been being built for four years now* and *had been reading* in *I had been reading a book.* Perfect progressives have been attested since the 14th century; Visser (1973: 2415) considers them to be "a well-established and not infrequently used idiom" roughly a century later. This should mean that perfect progressives were also quite fully integrated into 19th-century English, except perhaps in combination with other auxiliaries in the same verb phrase; the proportion of all progressive verb phrases that are perfect progressives can thus be expected to be relatively constant in diachrony.

The distribution of perfect progressive verb phrases across the parameters of time and genre in CONCE is given in Table 40, together with what percentage of all progressives in each sample are perfect progressives. (As non-finite progressive verb phrases can appear in the perfect, percentages were based on all progressives in CONCE, not just on finite progressive verb phrases.)

Table 40.   Perfect progressives in CONCE by period and genre (percentages of all progressives in each subsample within brackets)

Period	Debates	Drama	Fiction	History	Letters	Science	Trials	Total
1	–	8	15	–	37	4	23	87
		(22%)	(17%)		(15%)	(15%)	(13%)	(15%)
2	–	11	16	4	83	5	22	141
		(10%)	(13%)	(11%)	(20%)	(21%)	(13%)	(16%)
3	6	6	9	2	74	1	18	116
	(20%)	(5%)	(13%)	(3%)	(19%)	(3%)	(8%)	(12%)
Total	6	25	40	6	194	10	63	344
	(11%)	(10%)	(14%)	(5%)	(18%)	(12%)	(11%)	(14%)

As Table 40 shows, no consistent diachronic trends are discernible in the material as a whole. Nor does the percentage of all progressive verb phrases that are perfect progressives correlate, positively or negatively, with the overall frequency of the progressive. The most interesting result may be the comparatively high percentage of perfect progressive verb phrases in Letters. In this genre, present perfect progressives are often used to denote an activity that had not yet been finished, or a state that still obtained, at the time the letter was being written, as in (26):

(26)   And now I've begun this letter I remember it can't go tomorrow because of the Post, and I'*ve been scribbling* or *talking* since 8 this morning and will go to bed & say my prayers for my dearest children.
(Letters, Thackeray, 1850–1870, p. 34)

These meanings of present perfect progressives are compatible with Quirk et al.'s (1985: 210ff.) suggestions that perfect progressives express temporary situations or habits leading up to the present, with a possible implication that the situation or habit may continue beyond the present. Sometimes, however, the perfect progressive is also used to denote activities that were finished or states that no longer obtained. Consider (27):

(27)   Presently the carriage stopt; she looked up; it was stopt by Mr. and Mrs. Weston, who were standing to speak to her. There was instant pleasure in the sight of them, and still greater pleasure was conveyed in sound – for Mr. Weston immediately accosted her with,
"How d'ye do? – how d'ye do? – We *have been sitting* with your father – glad to see him so well. ...."
(Fiction, Austen, 1800–1830, pp. II.76–77)

In (27), the Westons are no longer sitting with the character's (Emma's) father, since they are now standing to speak to her. Perfect progressives may have the implications that the situation denoted by the verb phrase had limited duration and/or that its effects are still apparent (Quirk et al. 1985: 210ff.). As regards the first option, however, the main verb in (27) is SIT, and "the limitation of duration is weak" with verbs such as SIT and STAND (Quirk et al. 1985: 211). The latter interpretation, in contrast, seems possible in (27), since the progressive is followed by a comment on Emma's father's health. It is also possible that the progressive *have been sitting* has a not-solely-aspectual function, considering that other possible indicators of emotional colouring can be found in the context of the progressive verb phrase (*instant pleasure, still greater pleasure*, a repeated greeting, and *glad to see him so well*). (See Chapter 7 for a more detailed account of some not-solely-aspectual functions of the progressive in 19th-century English.)
        If we look at the period and genre parameters in combination, we find that, in the genres where the perfect progressive is represented in all period/genre subsamples, the percentage of perfect progressives decreases over the century in Trials, Drama, and Fiction; Letters and Science exhibit no clear pattern, although the percentage decreases sharply in Science between periods 2 and 3. However, owing to the low raw frequencies of perfect progressives in Science, these results should be treated with caution.

5.3   Voice

One of the most conspicuous developments in late Modern English grammar is the introduction of verb phrases that contain the sequence BE *being*. The availability of this sequence made it possible to combine progressive and passive marking formally, as in (28); the same sequence is used to form the progressive of BE (for which see Section 6.1.2.) Before this, progressive verb phrases with passive meaning had been formed using a construction that was semantically passive although it lacked formal passive marking, as in (29).

(28)   Then I *was being ushered* into one of these boxes, and found myself saying something as I sat down, and people about me crying "Silence!" to somebody, and ladies casting indignant glances at me, and – what! yes! – Agnes, sitting on the seat before me, in the same box, with a lady and a gentleman beside her, whom I didn't know.
(Fiction, Dickens, 1850–1870, p. 255)

(29)   They went in; and while the sleek, well-tied parcels of "Men's Beavers" and "York Tan" *were bringing* down and *displaying* on the counter, he said – "But I beg your pardon, Miss Woodhouse, you were speaking to me, you were saying something at the very moment of this burst of my amor patriæ. Do not let me lose it. I assure you the utmost stretch of public fame would not make me amends for the loss of any happiness in private life."
(Fiction, Austen, 1800–1830, pp. II.103–II.104)

Following Visser (1973), I will refer to the type in (28) as "passive" and to the type in (29) as "passival" (see Denison 1993: 389–391 for an account of the history of the passival progressive). Given that the gradual substitution of the passive for the passival progressive is one of the most important syntactic developments that took place during the 19th century, a good deal of attention has been paid to this replacement process in previous research.

Apart from a few possible early Modern English instances, attested by Elsness (1994: 15) and Nakamura (1998) among others, the formal combination of passive and progressive marking, as in (28), is not attested until the late 18th century: the first attested instance that is not subject to doubt dates from 1772 (Denison 1998: 152). Most early instances have been attested in texts not intended for publication, such as private letters (Visser 1973: 2426f.). Before the introduction of the passive progressive, the passival progressive was used instead; and this passival progressive continued to be used alongside the new construction over the 19th century.[7] Despite widespread stylistic condemnation of the

---

7   There were also other options with similar meanings. A passive non-progressive could be used, as in *The house is built* (Denison 1998: 151), or a paraphrase could be employed, as in e.g. *The house is under construction*.

sequence BE *being* (for exemplification see Visser 1973: 2427ff.), the passive progressive gained in frequency and replaced the passival progressive in many contexts during the 19th century.[8] However, as Hundt (2004b: 83f.) points out, passival progressives still occur in Present-Day English, especially with a restricted range of verbs such as PRINT in *The book is printing*. As the progressive has combined with modal auxiliaries since Old English and with perfect auxiliaries since Middle English, the questions of why it took so much longer for the combination of progressive and passive marking to develop and why the passival progressive was used instead have been the topic of a great deal of research.

Scheffer (1975: 260) links the use of BE + present participle of transitive verbs with passive meaning (i.e. the passival progressive) to that of BE + past participle of intransitive verbs with active meaning (i.e. the perfect formed with BE), and claims that these forms "could thrive when the language had not yet developed rigid rules for the use of [HAVE] as an auxiliary of tense and [BE] as one of voice, and when it was still possible to feel some uncertainty about the passive or active character of the participles".[9] Scheffer also thinks, as does Visser (1973: 2007), that BE + preposition + gerund constructions such as *The house is in building*, where the preposition was subsequently reduced to *a-* and omitted, contributed to the development of the passival progressive. According to Scheffer (1975: 260), both the passival progressive and the use of BE as a perfect auxiliary fell out of use as a result of literary English becoming "more formalized". Scheffer (1975: 262f.) claims that the development of the passive progressive was dependent on the previous development of the passive gerund and participle *being* in e.g. *being built*, and also lists some possible intermediate stages; Visser (1973: 2426) also mentions these constructions, but appears to give more weight to the development of explicit passive marking in e.g. *The house is to be let* from *The house is to let*.

Denison (1998) links the development of the passive progressive to the grammaticalization of the progressive. He also connects the appearance of the passive progressive with the subsequent development of progressives of BE, and claims that the sequence BE *being* was avoided "because it was felt that the progressive of the verb BE itself ... was an impossibility" (Denison 1998: 151). In Denison's account, the syntactic aspect of the grammaticalization of the progressive involved a change in the status of progressive BE "from being head of its phrase to a modifier of the lexical head", so that after the grammaticalization

---

8   However, only a century earlier the passival progressive, the construction which was now being replaced by the passive progressive, had itself attracted some negative stylistic evaluation (Rissanen 1999: 218).

9   Similarly, Denison (1998: 156) states that there was "a partial analogy" between, on the one hand, the formal identity of the active and passival progressive, and, on the other hand, that of the passive non-progressive (as in *The house was built*) and the active perfect with BE as auxiliary (as in *Jim was arrived*). In both cases, "a single surface pattern of BE + participle would be interpreted either as passive or as active according to the transitivity of the lexical verb and the potential agentiveness of the subject" (Denison 1998: 156).

process the passive progressive in e.g. *The house was being built* was "the progressive of BUILD rather than of passive BE" (Denison 1998: 155). Before the postulated reanalysis, the structure of a passive progressive would have been main verb BE + *being* + past participle; but the pattern *being* + past participle was typically, Denison (1998: 156) claims, "resultative in meaning rather than durative", and thus inappropriate, and, owing to the absence of progressives of BE, there were no other BE *being* sequences to support it. Dorodnikh (1989: 110) also takes semantic factors into account, and hypothesizes that the late appearance of the passive progressive was due to semantic incompatibility between the static nature of the passive and the dynamic nature of the progressive.

As regards the reason for the progressive being reanalysed at this time, Denison lists both linguistic and extralinguistic factors. He hypothesizes a connection between the reanalysis and the full regularization of the use of DO, which left progressive BE as the only operator complemented by another verb that was not yet a full auxiliary.[10] This may have led to systemic pressure on progressive BE to be grammaticalized (Denison 1998: 157). Denison also presents an innovative account of the diffusion of the passive progressive in terms of network analysis (Denison 1998: 152ff.; further elaborated in Pratt and Denison 2000). It is claimed that most of the early passive progressives that have been attested "are from Southey or from writers he would have known and/or corresponded with" (Denison 1998: 153), and hypothesized that the passive progressive may have been "seized on by the young iconoclasts of the Southey/Coleridge circle in a kind of radical experimentation" (Denison 1998: 154). The passival progressive would then have declined for two main reasons: as the progressive increased in frequency it also occurred more frequently with non-human subjects, making it more difficult to tell active and passival progressives apart; and the construction was no longer necessary once the passive progressive had become established (Denison 1998: 150). Åkerlund (1914: 337) argues that the wider range of verbs that the passive progressive could occur with contributed to the replacement of the passival by the passive progressive.

Denison also discusses the development of the passive progressive from a syntactico-semantic standpoint. He (1993: 440) argues that passive progressives "provide useful meaning distinctions and – most important – fill a systemic gap in the patterning of English verbs, so that active and passive become symmetrical at every point in the extended paradigm". To this might be added that the passive progressive, though symmetrical, is different from all other progressives – including the passival progressive – in that the main verb, and the final verb form in the verb phrase, is not a present participle. It is possible that this formal difference was another factor that delayed the introduction of the passive progressive.

---

10   However, Hundt's (2004b: 97) investigation shows that periphrastic DO increased steadily in frequency in the period 1650–1949, which may argue against the complete regularization of this construction taking place in the late 18th century.

Warner (1997), in contrast, claims that neither the need for making semantic oppositions explicit nor the patterning of the syntactic paradigm was central to the development of the passive progressive.[11] Instead, he claims that "the extension of the English verbal group was due in the first instance to formal factors" (Warner 1997: 186). Within Warner's framework, the introduction of the passive progressive is dependent on "the reinterpretation of the morphosyntactic category of *being*" (Warner 1997: 174), and a formal factor, viz. "the availability of the relevant morphosyntactic categories of auxiliaries", is given priority over functional factors (Warner 1997: 162).[12]

In Warner's account, BE underwent a change between 1750 and 1800, from being "inflected according to the general verbal paradigm, though largely suppletive" to having all its forms "stated in the lexicon without falling under the scope of any rule of formation (whether directly or as a suppletive item)" (Warner 1997: 166). After this reanalysis, only non-auxiliary verbs displayed verbal inflection. However, as *being* was still transparent in its make-up (*be* + *ing*), this form went from having auxiliary to having non-auxiliary status. Since BE was subcategorized for taking non-auxiliary complements, after the reanalysis BE *being* was predicted by the same subcategorization that had previously made it impossible, and the passive progressive appeared (Warner 1997: 166f.). (For the consequences of such a reanalysis for the development of progressives of BE and HAVE, see Section 6.1.2.)

In this study, when presenting results concerning the distribution of the progressive across the voice parameter, in most cases I will treat active, passival, and passive progressives as three separate categories. However, I will occasionally group passival and passive progressives together and compare their total incidence with that of active progressives. Doing so might present a skewed picture of the situation, as it has been hypothesized that the passive progressive developed partly out of a need for less ambiguous constructions than the passival progressive, and thus had a wider range of application. For instance, passive progressives have been hypothesized to be more compatible than passival progressives with *by*-agents and agentive subjects. In contrast, passival progressives might have occurred in, for instance, perfect verb phrases (as in *The house has been building*) more easily than passive progressives (as in *The house has been being built*). On the one hand, passival and passive progressives may thus not be fully equivalent from a variationist perspective; on the other hand, given the similarity of their functions, the two constructions can probably be

---

11   Warner expresses his analysis in terms of Head-Driven Phrase Structure Grammar. There are some empirical differences between his accounts (specifically Warner 1995 and Warner 1997). In what follows, I will focus on the account presented in Warner (1997).

12   As Warner (1997: 174) himself admits, however, functional factors may be relevant to the issue of the diffusion of BE *being*. For instance, he claims that one of the reasons why the sequences *be being* and *been being* are rarely recorded is that "since these constructions encode several oppositions, they demand a highly specialized context; they are therefore infrequent and tend to sound clumsy and odd as citations" (Warner 1997: 173).

treated as roughly equivalent (see Hundt 2004b for a fuller discussion of this issue).

Seven progressives in CONCE were excluded from the counts of active, passive, and passival progressives. A few of these were indeterminate between an active and a passival reading, as in (30):

(30)   At this momentous crisis, the green grocer (acting waiter) returned with two pots of Meux and Co.'s Entire, upon the tops of which stood heads, not a little resembling the whipped stuff upon the raspberry creams, – open goes the door again, puff goes the wind, and off go the "heads" of the porter pots, into the faces of the refined Major Overall, and his adorable bride, who *was disrobing* at the foot of the stairs.
       (Fiction, Hook, 1800–1830, p. I.227)

Hundt (2004b: 105ff.) discusses differences between passival, mediopassive, and ergative progressives. No attempt was made to separate these groups in the present study: progressives where the verb was used ergatively were generally classified as active, as in (31):

(31)   But this reunion only strengthened their aristocratic and exclusive tendencies, and widened the breach which *was* steadily *opening* on questions such as Parliamentary Reform between the bulk of the Whigs and the small fragment of their party which remained true to the more popular sympathies of Chatham.
       (History, Green, 1870–1900, p. IV.284)

However, some progressives that were indeterminate between a passival and an ergative/mediopassive reading, e.g. *is selling* and *will be selling* in (36), were excluded from the counts.[13]

(32)   Whilst 100l. capital in 5 per cent. stock *is selling* for 95l., an exchequer bill of 100l., *will be* sometimes *selling* for 100l. 5s., for which exchequer bill, no more interest will be annually paid than 4l. 11s. 3d: ...
       (Science, Ricardo, 1800–1830, p. 414)

Owing to the low raw frequencies of passival and passive progressives, results will only be presented for period and genre subsamples. The results for the three periods in CONCE are given in Table 41.

---

13   As Hundt (2004b: 107) points out, the categories "passival", "ergative", and "mediopassive" are not wholly discrete; scholars may thus disagree on the status of individual cases. For instance, Hundt classifies a sentence such as *These books sell well* as mediopassive, while Denison (1993: 390) discusses ergative uses of the verb SELL. For the purposes of the present study, I focused on excluding ambiguous cases and on making the classification internally consistent.

Table 41.   Active, passival, and passive progressives in CONCE per period (row percentages within brackets)

Period	Active	Passival	Passive	Total
1	588 (99%)	4 (1%)	1 (0%)	593
2	885 (99%)	5 (1%)	8 (1%)	898
3	925 (98%)	1 (0%)	16 (2%)	942
Total	2,398 (99%)	10 (0%)	25 (1%)	2,433

As Table 41 shows, the percentage of active progressives does not change much over the 19th century (the small decrease is not statistically significant). Despite the low raw frequencies, however, the diachronic trend concerning the distribution of passival and passive progressives is quite clear. The passival progressive is more common in period 1, but the passive progressive is more frequent in period 2 and dominates the scene almost completely in period 3. The table also indicates that the passive progressive was slightly more common at the end of the 19th century than the passival was at the beginning. Similarly, Hundt's (2004b: 104) results show that, in the period 1850–1899, the passive progressive was more common than the passival had ever been. This difference may be an indication of the greater applicability of the passive progressive compared with the passival progressive. It has been claimed that the passival progressive occurred predominantly with inanimate subjects, whereas the passive progressive lacked this restriction (see Section 6.3 for a discussion of animacy, agentivity, and the progressive). Owing to the passive and passival progressives' being two rare linguistic features, the data afforded by CONCE do not allow definite conclusions in this respect, but it deserves to be pointed out that only one of the passival progressives in the material has an animate subject, viz. (33):

(33)   [$Q.$] That he was never near your person out of doors, but when you *were* taken off the poney and *putting on*?
(Trials, Bowditch, 1800–1830, p. 43)

Moreover, in (33), the co-ordination of the passival progressive with the passive non-progressive *were taken* removes the potential ambiguity between an active and a passival reading of *were putting on*. Of the 25 passive progressives, five have animate subjects. Of these five, the subject is the pronoun *I* in three cases, *he* in one case, and in (34) the subject is animate by extension:

(34)   [$MR. SPEAKER:$] Members sitting on Committees have had their attention drawn in the usual way, by the ringing of the bell, to the fact that the House *was being counted* with a view to form a quorum.
(Debates, 1870–1900, p. IV.1181)

Since the raw frequencies of passive and passival progressives in CONCE are low, I will complement the picture by presenting figures taken from Arnaud's database. As it was necessary to reanalyse the data in order to make the two databases comparable concerning the classification of doubtful cases, I will only present results for passival and passive progressives in what follows. The period distribution is given in Table 42.[14]

Table 42. Passive and passival progressives in Arnaud's database per period (row percentages within brackets)

Period	Passival	Passive	Total
0	4 (100%)	–	4
1	48 (86%)	8 (14%)	56
1b	42 (65%)	23 (35%)	65
2	16 (27%)	43 (73%)	59
3	–	14 (100%)	14
Total	110 (56%)	88 (44%)	198

As pointed out above, the passival and passive progressive are not absolutely equivalent from a variationist perspective. Nevertheless, Table 42, where the incidence of passival and passive progressives is juxtaposed for each period subsample, can give us a useful indication of when the quantitative change from passival to passive progressives took place.

Despite the differences between the cross-genre make-up of CONCE and the focus on private letters in Arnaud's corpus, the results from the two corpora match each other quite well: in both Table 41 and Table 42, the passival progressive dominates in period 1, but the passive progressive has passed it in frequency in period 2, and appears to be almost the only option in period 3. The differences that exist can probably be attributed to period- and genre-specific constraints. Overall, Arnaud's analysis focuses on an earlier period than the present study, which accounts for the passival progressive being more common in his material than in CONCE. Moreover, Arnaud's corpus only includes private letters, whose subject matter may influence the distribution: in particular, passival progressives with PRINT as main verb, a pattern which may still occur in Present-Day English, are common in Arnaud's material.

The extra time spans covered by Arnaud's corpus give us valuable information on the distribution at the beginning, and in the middle, of the change. Before 1800, no passive progressives are attested in Arnaud's material. Period 1b, i.e. 1830–1850, is characterized by a more even distribution between passive and passival progressives than any other period. It appears that, at least in private

---

14 Arnaud has classified some progressives that might have an ergative or mediopassive interpretation, e.g. progressives of SELL similar to that in example (32), as passival. In order to make his figures comparable with mine, I excluded these progressives from Arnaud's counts.

letters, the period 1830–1870 would be of special relevance to further qualitative and quantitative research on the change from passival to passive progressive marking, since factors that affect the distribution of both forms can be discussed. Hundt's (2004b) results also indicate that the 18th century may be a fruitful period to study. According to Hundt (2004b: 104), the frequency of the passival progressive started to decrease before the passive progressive was introduced, but the negative prescriptive reaction to the passive progressive may have limited this decline at first.

Visser (1973: 2016) claims that the frequency of the passival progressive continued to be high in 19th-century prose, and that it is not clear that the introduction of the passive progressive had any effect on the frequency of the passival variant. The findings presented in Tables 41 and 42 do not support these claims.[15] The passival progressive appears to be quite rare in the second half of the century, and the distribution of the passival and passive progressive indicates that the increase in the frequency of the latter at least correlates well with the decrease in frequency of the former. The data seem to agree better with Denison's (1998) hypotheses on the social network around Robert Southey and Samuel Taylor Coleridge promoting the rise of the passive progressive. The only passive progressive in period 1 in CONCE, (35), comes from Letters; the author is Sara Hutchinson, a member of the network:

(35)   I was down stairs today while my room *was being put* in order; & tho' walking ½ a doz times the length of the dining room heated me as much as one of your reapers would have been under a July sun, yet I am no worse for it & am able to sit up great part of the day.
(Letters, Hutchinson, 1800–1830, p. 315)

In Arnaud's material, period 1 yields three passive progressives by Thomas Macaulay, two by Samuel Taylor Coleridge, and one each by Sara Hutchinson, Robert Southey, and Elizabeth Barrett Browning. The progressives by Coleridge, Hutchinson, and Southey support Denison's theory, whereas the other instances are less straightforward. However, Pratt and Denison (2000: 417) do not claim that the passive progressive was invented by the Southey network, but rather that it "was already a general if 'unrespectable' form in speech, possibly dialectally restricted, but was rarely written (except in private letters or trashy novels or newspapers?)"; thus, examples by other writers do not disprove the hypothesis.[16]

---

15   However, Visser's classification of passival progressives seems to be broader than that adopted in the present study, and this may have influenced his results. For instance, Visser (1973: 2017f.) includes an instance of BE *selling* that would be excluded from my counts of passival progressives.

16   As far as Macaulay is concerned, Pratt and Denison (2000: 415) note that Mary Meeke, writing under a pseudonym, is the likely author of a Gothic novel containing an early (1801) instance of the passive progressive, and that she is generally reported to have been "Macaulay's favourite 'bad' novelist". It is possible that Macaulay was first influenced by

After the period breakdown presented above, I now turn to a cross-genre comparison. The results for the different genres in CONCE are given in Table 43.

Table 43. Active, passival, and passive progressives in CONCE by genre (row percentages within brackets)

Genre	Active	Passival	Passive	Total
Debates	48 (91%)	1 (2%)	4 (8%)	53
Drama	260 (99%)	2 (1%)	–	262
Fiction	278 (99%)	1 (0%)	2 (1%)	281
History	109 (97%)	–	3 (3%)	112
Letters	1,042 (99%)	4 (0%)	7 (1%)	1,053
Science	74 (89%)	–	9 (11%)	83
Trials	587 (100%)	2 (0%)	–	589
Total	2,398 (99%)	10 (0%)	25 (1%)	2,433

Many researchers have hypothesized that the passive progressive would, at first, occur chiefly in colloquial conversation and in written texts that were not intended for publication (see e.g. Visser 1973: 2426), and most early examples have indeed been attested in private letters. This may seem surprising, as conversation and informal writing can be expected to contain comparatively few passive clauses in general. However, the overall frequency of passive verb phrases in a genre need perhaps not correlate positively with innovations within the passive paradigm: new types of passive marking need thus not develop in genres with many passives. Moreover, the heavy prescriptive criticism that the passive progressive attracted may help to explain this distribution: passive progressives may have been more acceptable in texts not intended for publication (e.g. private letters) and, possibly, in texts intended to represent speech (e.g. plays). However, it is also possible that further investigation of genres that can be expected to contain a great many passive constructions, such as academic prose, will reveal additional instances of passive progressives; Hundt (2004b: 109), for instance, found that the earliest passive progressives in ARCHER come from journals and religious texts, not private letters.

Nevertheless, against the background sketched above, it may seem surprising that the percentage of passive progressives should be the highest in the expository genres Science, Debates, and (to a lesser extent) History, and the lowest in Trials and Drama, with Fiction and Letters forming a middle ground. However, it must be emphasized that, owing to the low raw frequencies, the results should be treated with considerable caution. Moreover, a closer look at the periodization of the occurrences clarifies the picture somewhat. The passive progressive occurs eight times in period 2 in CONCE: of these eight occurrences,

---

passive progressives occurring in speech and in popular novels, but later reacted to this pattern; as Arnaud (2002) points out, Macaulay used the passive progressive himself until the 1830s, but then reverted to the passival progressive.

two are from Fiction, four from Letters, and two from Science. In period 3, in contrast, four of the 16 passive progressives are from Debates, three from History, two from Letters, and no fewer than seven from Science. It thus seems that the passive progressive spread first to informal and/or speech-related written genres, and then in the last third of the century to formal spoken and written genres (however, both of the passive progressives in Fiction are in fact from narrative passages, not from dialogue). It seems reasonable to assume that History and Science contain more passive clauses overall than other genres, so this factor may also have contributed to the occurrence of the passive progressive in these two genres. It is also possible that the need for lexical and syntactic precision was more felt in especially Science than in other genres, and that this functional motivation accounts for some of the occurrences.

It is more difficult to explain the distribution of the passive progressive in Debates, Drama, and Trials. As mentioned above, the passive progressive was frowned upon by 19th-century prescriptivists (see Visser 1973: 2427ff. for exemplification), and it has been hypothesized that it spread from speech and informal writing to formal writing. Against this background, we might expect that the construction would occur in Debates and Trials, and especially in the latter, although the formality of the speech situation may have kept down the incidence. However, the overall frequency of non-active progressives in Trials is very low – two passival occurrences; the comparative scarcity of non-active progressives in this genre means that a larger sample would be needed for the results to be reliable. The same holds true for Drama. However, it is still an unexpected result that Trials and Drama both yield two passival progressives but no passive progressives.[17]

As regards Debates, all passive progressives occur in period 3, which may reflect a decrease in editorial intervention (note that the chief mode of speech representation shifted from indirect to direct speech between periods 2 and 3) and/or in the need felt by speakers to avoid passive progressives in formal situations. It is likely that the passive progressive had become more accepted by the late 19th century, as indicated by its occurrence in formal written genres such as History and Science. Conversely, the formality of the speech situation in Debates and Trials, and the certainty of publication of Drama and Fiction texts, may have kept down the frequency of the passive progressive at least in the first half of the 19th century. But as mentioned above, the raw frequency of non-active progressives is too low for the results to be reliable. I will return to the cross-genre distribution of the passive progressive in Section 6.3, in connection with a discussion of the occurrence of the progressive with agentive and non-agentive subjects.

Before leaving the distribution of the progressive across the voice parameter, I will briefly comment on some passival progressives found in CONCE.

---

17   Early passive progressives have been attested in plays, however: Pratt and Denison (2000: 413) present a 1790 instance, discovered by Linda van Bergen, from a comedy in the Chadwyck-Healey *Literature Online* database.

Apart from (33) above, which has an animate subject, there are two instances worth commenting on. In (36), we find a passival progressive with a following *by*-agent, a combination that has been noted by for instance Denison (1998: 149) as rare but possible:

(36) A German Edition *is preparing* by very good Naturalist: & I hear of some foreign Reviews coming out.
      (Letters, Darwin, 1850–1870, p. VIII.118)

An even more striking example is (37), where the *being* + present participle pattern (see Section 5.6) co-occurs with the passival progressive:

(37) Mr. H. Thornton, adverting to the late collection of the Income Tax in Scotland, the duties of 1806 *being* only *collecting*, as appeared, in 1809, supposed that this circumstance might be owing to the rents being sooner collected in England than in Scotland.
      (Debates, 1800–1830, pp. XV.439–XV.440)

In Present-Day English, the nonfinite clause containing the progressive in (37) would correspond most closely to a finite clause with an explicit subordinator and a passive progressive (e.g. *... since the duties of 1806 were only being collected ...*).

5.4   Modal auxiliaries

The progressive and modal auxiliaries could occur in the same verb phrase as early as Old English (Visser 1973: 2412), and continued to do so in Middle English (Scheffer 1975: 220). However, the combination does not appear to have been frequent in the 1700s: Strang (1982: 440) claims that progressives with modal auxiliaries were rarer than perfect progressives at the beginning of the 18th century. For 19th-century English, we might thus expect either a continued low frequency of progressives with modal auxiliaries, or an increase in frequency as these types of verb phrases become more fully integrated into English. The period/genre breakdown is given in Table 44. (As modal auxiliaries only have finite forms in late Modern English, percentages concern the proportion of the finite progressive verb phrases in each sample that contain modals.)

Table 44.   Progressive verb phrases with modal auxiliaries in CONCE by period and genre (percentages of all finite progressives in each subsample within brackets)

Period	Debates	Drama	Fiction	History	Letters	Science	Trials	Total
1	1	1	7	–	15	3	4	31
	(9%)	(3%)	(8%)		(6%)	(13%)	(2%)	(5%)
2	–	3	2	1	12	5	–	23
		(3%)	(2%)	(3%)	(3%)	(23%)		(3%)
3	3	1	2	–	4	1	–	11
	(10%)	(1%)	(3%)		(1%)	(3%)		(1%)
Total	4	5	11	1	31	9	4	65
	(8%)	(2%)	(4%)	(1%)	(3%)	(12%)	(1%)	(3%)

As demonstrated in Table 44, progressive verb phrases with modal auxiliaries are quite rare in CONCE: they account for only 3% of all finite progressives in the material. Moreover, progressives that contain a modal auxiliary account for a lower percentage of all finite progressives in diachrony, and this decrease is statistically significant. There are several possible reasons for the decrease. First, it may be the case that the use of modal auxiliaries decreased generally in 19th-century English.[18] This hypothesis is supported by Grund and Walker's (forthcoming) investigation of the subjunctive in adverbial clauses in CONCE. Grund and Walker found that the percentage of verb phrases that incorporated modal auxiliaries decreased in favour of indicative and subjunctive verb phrases. Secondly, it has been claimed that the progressive itself has not-solely-aspectual functions that are related to modality (see e.g. Wright 1994 and Stubbs 1996); and as will be shown in Chapter 7, the not-solely-aspectual functions of the progressive appear to have gained ground in late Modern English. It is thus possible that, in some contexts, speakers felt less need for explicit modal marking when the progressive already expressed partly modal values. However, Smith's (2002: 319) investigation showed that progressive verb phrases with modal auxiliaries account for c. 6% of all progressives in the FLOB corpus, and that there has been an increase in the percentage of all progressives that include modal auxiliaries between the LOB and FLOB corpora. Moreover, Smith (2003: 715f.) shows that this increase takes place in spite of the fact that the frequency of modal auxiliaries in non-progressive verb phrases decreases during the same

---

18   Before the use of modals in progressive verb phrases can be correlated with the frequency development of modal auxiliaries in general, it may be necessary to analyse the kind of modality expressed by verb phrases with modal auxiliaries in the material example by example, as the progressive frequently changes the meaning of such verb phrases. For instance, Palmer (1979: 54) remarks that *She can't come on Monday* "would normally be interpreted as dynamic rather than epistemic", whereas in *She can't be coming on Monday* "an epistemic interpretation can be strongly suggested". Similarly, the progressive is claimed to exclude volitional uses of WILL and deontic uses of SHALL (Palmer 1979: 133f.). (See below, however, for examples from CONCE with MAY that do not appear to follow postulated present-day restrictions.)

period. Despite the differences in corpus make-up between CONCE and the corpora used by Smith, this apparent reversal of the 19th-century trend indicates that an investigation of early 20th-century English would be of great value in this respect.

The genre breakdown reveals that History contains the smallest number of modals in progressive verb phrases. However, History writing can perhaps be expected to contain relatively few modal auxiliaries in general, as it deals largely with events that have taken place in the past, and more rarely with hypothetical events. Against this background it may seem surprising that Science, another factual genre, contains the highest percentage of progressives with modal auxiliaries; but in Science, such constructions often occur as part of hypothetical statements expressing cause and effect, sometimes explicitly conditional, as in (38):

(38)   If it were otherwise – if its exports exceeded its imports – bullion *would be flowing* towards it; other countries *would be paying* part of their debts to it in gold, and no grounds for a prohibition of the export of bullion would have existed.
(Science, Goschen, 1850–1870, p. 72)

In the discussion of the distribution of the individual modal auxiliaries, which now follows, I will only consider period and genre subsamples, owing to the low raw frequencies of progressive verb phrases with modals. Moreover, when presenting results based on CONCE, I will treat the modal auxiliaries as other verbs in the sense that a (strictly non-existent) base form will be taken to subsume the present and past forms of the auxiliary: thus, CAN will be taken to subsume *can* and *could* (as well as contracted forms). Similarly, Denison (1993: 337n.) argues that it is justifiable to treat for instance *can* and *could* as "different tenses of a single lexeme CAN". The results for the period subsamples are given in Table 45.

Table 45.   The distribution of modal auxiliaries in progressive verb phrases per period

Period	CAN	MAY	MUST	SHALL	WILL	Total
1	1	7	5	6	12	31
2	1	4	4	8	6	23
3	–	2	2	6	1	11
Total	2	13	11	20	19	65

Although the low raw frequencies make definite conclusions impossible to draw, the results in Table 45 suggest that all modals in progressive verb phrases decreased over the 19th century, with the exception of SHALL, whose frequency seems more stable. As could be expected, the two modals that are often used to express future time in progressive verb phrases, i.e. SHALL and WILL, account for more than half (60%) of all occurrences. At the same time, progressive verb phrases that contain WILL decrease quite sharply in frequency over the century: there are 12 in period 1, 6 in period 2, and only 1 in period 3. This may be connected to developments concerning other means of expressing future time in English (see Section 6.2 for a discussion of progressives referring to the future without the aid of modal auxiliaries). In contrast, Smith's (2003: 715) study of the LOB and FLOB corpora shows that, in late 20th-century English, WILL is by far the commonest modal auxiliary in progressive verb phrases. If the results in Table 45 are indicative of a trend regarding the frequency of WILL in progressive verb phrases, this trend must thus have been reversed between 1900 and 1961.

The results for genre subsamples are given in Table 46.

Table 46.   The distribution of modal auxiliaries in progressive verb phrases by genre

Genre	CAN	MAY	MUST	SHALL	WILL	Total
Debates	–	2	–	–	2	4
Drama	–	2	2	1	–	5
Fiction	2	2	5	2	–	11
History	–	–	–	1	–	1
Letters	–	3	3	15	10	31
Science	–	1	1	1	6	9
Trials	–	3	–	–	1	4
Total	2	13	11	20	19	65

Table 46 shows that MAY is the modal auxiliary that occurs in the largest number of genres: it is only absent in History, the genre with the smallest number of modals in progressive verb phrases. Moreover, the use of MAY in some progressive verb phrases in periods 1 and 2 seems to differ from its use in Present-Day English. Consider (39):

(39)   If an estate of five thousand a year has a mortgage upon it of two thousand, two families, both in very good circumstances, *may be living* upon the rents of it, and both have considerable demands for houses, furniture, carriages, broad cloth, silks, cottons, &c.
(Science, Malthus, 1800–1830, p. II.362)

In (39), the non-progressive might be expected in Present-Day English, as the sense seems to be rather that it is possible for two families to live on the rents of the mortgage (the dynamic reading) than that it is possible that two families are in fact living on these rents (the epistemic reading). Another unexpected instance is (40):

(40)   Just write him a line that he *may* not *be expecting* anything from me, and
       tell him that I am of your persuasion, and will not let myself be tempted,
       by the chance of its being accepted in some quarter and of being paid for,
       to publish what I should certainly have been sorry to invent.
       (Letters, Jewsbury, 1850–1870, p. 364)

It seems more sensible to interpret (40) in terms of deontic permission than in
terms of epistemic possibility; but in Present-Day English "[t]he perfective and
progressive aspects are normally excluded when the modals express 'ability' or
'permission', and also when *shall* or *will* expresses 'volition'" (Quirk et al.
1985: 235). It is possible that part of the apparent decrease in the frequency of
progressive verb phrases with modal auxiliaries over the 19th century is due to
increased constraints in diachrony on what meanings a given combination of a
modal auxiliary and a progressive in the same verb phrase could express.
However, the low raw frequencies of such combinations make it impossible to
draw any definite conclusions, and the progressive verb phrases with other modal
auxiliaries in the material seem more straightforward.
       Another finding that stands out in Table 46 is the preponderance of SHALL
in Letters. However, this is due to most letters in this genre being written in the
first person, and SHALL usually either expresses future (with *shall*) or future-in-
the-past (with *should*), as in (41):

(41)   We *shall be having* a Box of Tea from Mr. Twining's very soon, in which
       might be sent the piece of carpetting you have had so long in your
       possession – if you will please to direct it to us and send it to them.
       (Letters, Wordsworth, Mary [2], 1800–1830, p. 30)

There are also cases where SHALL is part of conditional constructions in the
material. In contrast, WILL typically expresses future or future-in-the-past with
third-person subjects, as in (42):

(42)   ... – I fear we shall have no 1/2 years rent to receive in Aug: from
       Stockton, which was the source whence I meant to draw Miss Weir's pay
       for D., for Sarah tells me she has had a deduction of £33 for Legacy duty
       & when our rent-day arrives there will be the same black account given to
       us, no doubt — Surely a mine *will be springing* for us before long.
       (Letters, Wordsworth, Mary [1], 1800–1830, p. 250)

Given that so few progressives in CONCE co-occur with modals, I will also
present results taken from Arnaud's database. Table 47 shows the period
distribution of the different modal auxiliaries in progressive verb phrases in
Arnaud's material; since his results are based on a larger number of progressives,

the two forms of each modal (except MUST, which has only the form *must*) are given separately in the table.[19]

Table 47.   The distribution of modal auxiliaries in progressive verb phrases per period in Arnaud's database (row percentages within brackets)

Period	can	could	may	might	must	shall	should	will	would	Total
0	2	–	3	2	1	8	6	6	–	28
	(7%)		(11%)	(7%)	(4%)	(29%)	(21%)	(21%)		
1	4	3	17	14	39	27	47	57	13	221
	(2%)	(1%)	(8%)	(6%)	(18%)	(12%)	(21%)	(26%)	(6%)	
1b	10	6	35	17	36	42	33	57	12	248
	(4%)	(2%)	(14%)	(7%)	(15%)	(17%)	(13%)	(23%)	(5%)	
2	1	2	18	8	24	24	21	39	8	145
	(1%)	(1%)	(12%)	(6%)	(17%)	(17%)	(14%)	(27%)	(6%)	
3	–	–	–	2	2	3	5	3	1	16
				(12%)	(12%)	(19%)	(31%)	(19%)	(6%)	
Total	17	11	73	43	102	104	112	162	34	658
	(3%)	(2%)	(11%)	(7%)	(16%)	(16%)	(17%)	(25%)	(5%)	

Since Arnaud's material is not evenly distributed across the period subsamples, it is not possible to draw any conclusions about the incidence of modal auxiliaries in progressive verb phrases across time. If the different forms are compared, however, it may be noted that the majority are the most frequent in period 1b, but that *must*, *should*, and *would* have higher raw frequencies in period 1, and *will* has the same raw frequency in periods 1 and 1b. The overall distribution of the modals confirms the findings presented in Table 46: *shall/should* together account for 216 instances, *will/would* for 196, *may/might* for 116, *must* for 102, and *can/could* for 28. Likewise, the overall distribution of modal auxiliaries in 19th-century progressive verb phrases appears to be roughly the same in CONCE and in Arnaud's corpus: in Table 44 it was shown that 3% of all progressives (and of all progressives in Letters) contain (cardinal) modal auxiliaries; and Arnaud (2002) states that less than 4% of the progressives in his corpus, consisting only of private letters, contain modals (including both cardinal and marginal modal auxiliaries).

5.5   Verb phrase patterns

The discussion in Sections 5.1–5.4 has been confined to the interaction of the progressive with the parameters of tense, perfect auxiliaries, voice, and modal auxiliaries, in isolation. In the present section, a survey will be given of how the

---

19   Apart from the cardinal modal auxiliaries *can, could, may, might, must, shall, should, will,* and *would*, Arnaud also includes marginal modals in his classification; I have reanalysed his data to cover only the cardinal modal auxiliaries.

progressives in the data interact with these four features in combination to form verb phrases that may be between two and five words in length. As the combinations of auxiliaries that occur in progressive verb phrases may be relevant to a discussion of the diachronic integration of the progressive into late Modern English grammar, I will present cumulative results for period subsamples. Since modals only occur in finite verb phrases, the analysis will be confined to finite progressives. Moreover, the status of passival progressives is unclear concerning the complexity of progressive verb phrases, as their passive meaning does not correspond to any formal marking: passival progressives were thus excluded from the counts. Finally, progressives that could not be classified with certainty on all of the four parameters in Table 48 were not included in the counts. By way of exemplification, one verb phrase that would meet the criteria on each row will be given in the final column of the table; this verb phrase is always in the third person singular, the main verb is SING, and the modal auxiliary (if present) is WILL.

Table 48. The distribution of finite progressive verb phrases across the parameters of tense and modal, perfect, and passive auxiliaries per period (column percentages within brackets)

Tense	Mod.	Perf.	Pass.	Period 1	Period 2	Period 3	Example
Pres.	–	–	–	208 (36%)	391 (45%)	399 (43%)	*is singing*
Pres.	+	–	–	21 (4%)	12 (1%)	6 (1%)	*will be singing*
Pres.	–	+	–	53 (9%)	105 (12%)	90 (10%)	*has been singing*
Pres.	–	–	+	–	4 (0%)	7 (1%)	*is being sung*
Pres.	+	+	–	–	1 (0%)	–	*will have been singing*
Pres.	+	–	+	–	–	–	*will be being sung*
Pres.	–	+	+	–	–	–	*has been being sung*
Pres.	+	+	+	–	–	–	*will have been being sung*
Past	–	–	–	255 (44%)	321 (37%)	385 (42%)	*was singing*
Past	+	–	–	7 (1%)	7 (1%)	4 (0%)	*would be singing*
Past	–	+	–	30 (5%)	29 (3%)	25 (3%)	*had been singing*
Past	–	–	+	1 (0%)	4 (0%)	9 (1%)	*was being sung*
Past	+	+	–	2 (0%)	3 (0%)	1 (0%)	*would have been singing*
Past	+	–	+	–	–	–	*would be being sung*
Past	–	+	+	–	–	–	*had been being sung*
Past	+	+	+	–	–	–	*would have been being sung*

As demonstrated in Table 48, there are no clear signs of progressive verb phrases becoming formally more complex over the 19th century, with the exception of the passive progressive (discussed in Section 5.3). In fact, the percentage of all progressives in the material that incorporate no modal, perfect, or passive auxiliaries increases over the century: it is 80 in period 1, 81 in period 2, and 85 in period 3, an increase which is not, however, statistically significant. Nevertheless, the results imply that the integration of the progressive spread first to formally simple areas, where the formal and semantic influence of other auxiliaries does not complicate the picture.

It is difficult to ascertain whether this trend is still visible in Present-Day English. Scheffer (1975: 53ff.) investigated the use of the progressive in a 375,000-word corpus consisting of six 20th-century novels. The progressives were classified according to what type of verb phrase they occurred in; of the 2,468 progressive verb phrases, 36% were what Scheffer refers to as "verbs in the present progressive" and 50% "verbs in the preterite progressive". Applying the same restrictions on inclusion in the counts as those for Table 48 to the Fiction genre in CONCE, we find that 19% of the progressives in this genre are present-tense verb phrases with no perfect, modal, or passive auxiliary; past progressives with no modal, perfect, or passive auxiliaries account for 61% of all progressives in Fiction. If we disregard the difference in distribution between the present and the past tense and group the figures together to obtain totals for progressive verb phrases without modal, perfect, or passive auxiliaries, these are 81% in Fiction in CONCE and 86% in Scheffer's corpus.[20] This continuity ties in with Mair and Hundt's (1995: 116) claim that, in Present-Day English, most of the ongoing increase in the frequency of the progressive "is due to a greater incidence of already established and frequent uses". In contrast, Smith's (2002: 319) results indicate that 78% of all progressives in the LOB corpus, and 76% of all progressives in the FLOB corpus, are past or present progressives with no perfect, modal, or passive auxiliary. These lower percentages may indicate that the trend is being reversed in late 20th-century English, but differences in genre selection and sampling frames make definite conclusions impossible to draw.

If we compare the distribution of present-tense and past-tense progressives without modal, perfect, or passive auxiliaries, the picture becomes even more complex. The CONCE data reveal no clear trends: both types account for between *c.* 35% and *c.* 45% of all progressives in each period. In contrast, Smith (2002) found that present-tense progressives without modal, perfect, or passive auxiliaries increase markedly in frequency in late 20th-century English, while their past-tense counterparts decrease. Again, however, differences in corpus make-up and sampling frames preclude any definite conclusions here.

From a qualitative perspective, there is a slight tendency in CONCE for past progressives to occur in more complex verb phrases than present progressives do:

---

20   There are differences in the classification procedures that need to be taken into account in this context, however. Unlike the present study, Scheffer's counts include some constructions that may be appositively used participles, and also BE *going to* + infinitive constructions with future reference. Moreover, Scheffer (1975: 54) classifies the verbs in the progressive in his material as "present", "preterite", "perfect", "pluperfect", "future", "pret. future", "perf. future", "plup. future", "imperative", "infinitive", or "perf. infinitive". It is not clear, for instance, how modals other than SHALL and WILL enter into his classification. Comparisons between Scheffer's results and those of the present study should thus be treated with caution.

there are past progressive verb phrases that contain both modal and perfect auxiliaries in all three periods, while for the present tense this combination is missing in periods 1 and 3; in addition, the passive progressive occurs only in the past tense in period 1. Owing to the low raw frequencies of such complex verb phrases, however, these differences could be a mere accident of the sampling (see also Rydén 1979: 22). Moreover, when the same issue is regarded from a quantitative viewpoint, the picture is in fact reversed: in period 1, 26% of all present-tense progressive verb phrases, vs. 14% of all past-tense progressive verb phrases, incorporate one or several auxiliaries in addition to progressive BE; in period 2, 24% vs. 12%; and in period 3, 21% vs. 9%. This difference seems mainly to be due to the relative stability in diachrony of the percentage of present perfect progressives.

Finally, the passive progressives in the corpus do not combine with perfect and/or modal auxiliaries in any of the three periods, which means that at least six cells per period are empty in Table 48. This is not surprising, as, according to Warner (1997: 170), the earliest attested instances of passive progressives where *being* is preceded by a non-finite form of BE date from the period 1910–1920 (but cf. Section 6.1.2 for an example from CONCE with a progressive of BE).[21] Visser (1973: 2446) goes so far as to claim that passive progressives with perfect or modal auxiliaries have "not yet reached the status of a generally recognized idiom in Standard English", and Palmer (1988: 32f., 95) voices doubts concerning the patterns HAVE *been being taken* and WILL *have been being taken* (see also Hundt 2004b: 98f. regarding the rare occurrence of complex passive progressives). However, Warner (1997: 173) seems to claim that such phrases are at least marginally possible.

5.6   The *being* + present participle construction

Both Denison (1993) and Warner (1997) note the near-absence in Present-Day English of progressives containing the sequence *being* + present participle, as in (43).[22] Previous research indicates that the construction went out of regular use in early 19th-century English.

---

21   However, Warner (1997: 171ff.) claims that progressives with *be being* and *been being* may have been possible in 19th-century colloquial English. He lists several factors in support of this claim, including the following: our limited access to historical speech; the general scarcity of *be being* and *been being* even in Present-Day English; the possibility that prescriptive hostility to BE *being*, which would have affected formal genres to a higher extent than colloquial genres, was even more pronounced when the form of BE was non-finite; and the inclusion of such patterns in paradigms in grammars.

22   Example (43) has previously been noted by Denison (1985: 157).

(43)   At last he was persuaded to move on from the front of the Crown; and *being* now almost *facing* the house where the Bateses lodged, Emma recollected his intended visit the day before, and asked him if he had paid it.
(Fiction, Austen, 1800–1830, p. II.100)

CONCE yields too few data for it to be possible to present a detailed analysis of the *being* + present participle construction. However, because of its potential importance to the general development of the progressive, I will present the data available together with a short survey of some relevant research on this topic. I will also use Arnaud's database to obtain further examples of the *being* + present participle construction.

Denison (1993: 394) states that "[t]he syntagm *being* + V*ing* should occur when a finite progressive is turned into a gerundial or present participial construction" and that "[t]he *being* + V*ing* pattern had some currency at least from the mid-sixteenth century to the early nineteenth"; Warner (1997: 180) presents a couple of 15th-century examples. As pointed out above, this pattern seems to be almost absent from Present-Day English, although isolated examples can still be attested (Denison 1993: 411n.). The reasons behind the near-disappearance of this pattern are not entirely clear. Since the progressive paradigm has developed towards completion and towards symmetry with the non-progressive paradigm (consider for instance the development of the perfect progressive in Middle English and the passive progressive in late Modern English), it seems odd that the *being* + present participle construction should disappear from the language. As Denison (1993) points out, owing to its near-absence in Present-Day English, finite progressives such as *While I was examining the patient* ...lack nonfinite counterparts.

In contrast to the present-day situation, there was more freedom in the use of this construction in at least the early 19th century. Jane Austen has been noted by e.g. Phillipps (1970: 115f.) for her frequent use both of the progressive in general and of the *being* + present participle construction; Raybould (1957: 176) also comments on the "interesting examples of expanded gerunds" that can be found in Austen's works. Austen seems to have been one of the last authors to use the *being* + present participle construction regularly (Denison 1998: 204). As Denison (1985: 158) points out, the tendencies to extend the progressive/non-progressive contrast to the entire English verbal paradigm and to avoid the *being* + present participle pattern would counteract one another. Phillipps (1970: 115) hypothesizes that "[t]he quasi-conjunctive use of *being* meaning 'since' or 'because' (still found in substandard English)" may have been an influence favouring the use of *being* + present participle.

The evidence yielded by CONCE, though scarce, supports the observations of previous research. Apart from (43) given above, there is one more occurrence of *being* + present participle in a progressive, viz. (37) (also cited in Section 5.3):

(37) Mr. H. Thornton, adverting to the late collection of the Income Tax in Scotland, the duties of 1806 *being* only *collecting*, as appeared, in 1809, supposed that this circumstance might be owing to the rents being sooner collected in England than in Scotland.
(Debates, 1800–1830, pp. XV.439–XV.440)

The two instances of *being* + present participle in CONCE have several common characteristics. To begin with, (43) and (37) both occur in period 1, i.e. in the early part of the 19th century, when the pattern was still current. (CONCE thus yields no evidence of *being* + present participle constructions after 1830.) Moreover, in both examples one or several words occur between the two forms in *-ing*, something which, Bolinger (1979: 55) claims, increases the acceptability of the construction.[23]

There are also interesting aspects of the individual instances. Example (43) comes from Jane Austen's novel *Emma*. The fact that the only *being* + present participle construction in a written genre in CONCE comes from a text written by Austen supports the claims that she was one of the last people to use the construction regularly in writing. The second example, (37), is remarkable in that it combines a *being* + present participle construction and a passival progressive (see Denison 1993: 394f. for further instances of this pattern; see also Section 5.3). Thus, in (37), the two progressive constructions that largely disappeared in the course of the 19th century are combined.

Turning to Arnaud's database for further exemplification, I found four additional examples of the *being* + present participle construction.[24] One comes from period 1, but the other three (the latest of which is from 1840) belong to period 1b. (The example belonging to period 1 comes from Sir Walter Scott; of the instances belonging to period 1b, one comes from William Wordsworth and two from Jane Welsh-Carlyle.) This result may help to post-date the availability of the *being* + present participle construction, at least in informal language.

5.7   Discussion of results

This chapter has focused on variation in the use of the progressive with morphosyntactic features inherent in the verb phrase. The analysis was restricted to variation within the progressive paradigm; differences between progressive and non-progressive verb phrases were not commented on. Where possible, the data were stratified according to the extralinguistic features of time and genre.

---

23   According to Denison (1985: 157), (43) also meets another criterion mentioned by Bolinger (1979: 55), namely that "one or both of the *-ing*s is lexicalized as a non-verb (and processed directly)".

24   Arnaud also included instances of the type *having been* + present participle. These were excluded from the counts in the present study, as it does not seem that the same restrictions apply to such instances. Nor are constructions with *having been* + present participle grouped together with *being* + present participle constructions by Denison (1993: 394).

Separate sections were devoted to the features of tense, the perfect, voice, and the presence of modal auxiliaries; in addition, the combinations of these four features were discussed in a further section. Finally, a section was devoted to a type of progressive which was becoming obsolete in 19th-century English, viz. the *being* + present participle construction.

The investigation of the tense variable showed that there was no consistent diachronic trend in the material as a whole in the distribution of present vs. past progressives. For the individual genres Debates and History, in contrast, the percentage of present-tense progressives increased and decreased respectively. In addition, the percentage of present-tense progressives in Fiction more than doubled between periods 2 and 3, when the overall frequency of the progressive in this genre declined unexpectedly. Similarly, there was a trend towards a positive correlation between, on the one hand, the overall frequency of the progressive in Trials, and, on the other hand, the percentage of past progressives in this genre. These correspondences led me to hypothesize that the past progressive has clearly defined functions in narrative genres, and that this functional distribution, and, consequently, the overall frequency of the construction, is easily upset by tense shifts. The results can also be taken as support for Hatcher's (1951) claim that the progressive behaves differently, from a functional perspective, in different syntactic and semantic environments. Specifically, the not-solely-aspectual functions of the progressive may be more common in the present than in the past tense.

Perfect progressive verb phrases formed the topic of the next section. Given that perfect progressives have occurred in English since the late Middle English period, no dramatic development was expected in terms of the percentage of the progressives in the material that were in the perfect. Nor were any clear diachronic trends discernible in the overall data, although Drama, Fiction, and Trials displayed decreases over the century, and Science exhibited a clear decrease between periods 2 and 3.

The issue of how voice was expressed in progressive verb phrases is more complicated, since there was a formal innovation in late Modern English: the passive progressive largely replaced the passival progressive. In previous research, theories have connected the emergence and diffusion of the new construction to the grammaticalization of the progressive, the variation between BE and HAVE as auxiliaries in perfect verb phrases of intransitive verbs, formal developments in English auxiliaries, the tendency for the progressive/non-progressive paradigm to become symmetrical, the increasing incidence of the progressive with inanimate subjects, and social network theory; these theories were presented and discussed. Although the raw frequencies were low, the data from CONCE suggested that the passive progressive passed the passival progressive in frequency sometime in the middle of the century, and dominated the scene almost totally in the last three decades. This impression was supported by the results yielded by the analysis of Arnaud's data. The cross-genre distribution in CONCE indicated that the passive progressive spread first to informal and/or speech-related written genres and from there to formal written genres, although, somewhat surprisingly, there were passival progressives, but no passive progressives, in Drama and Trials. However, the raw frequencies of non-active progressives were quite low, and the distribution should thus be treated with a great deal of caution.

The section which followed dealt with modal auxiliaries in progressive verb phrases. Modals have combined with the progressive since Old English, but the combination was not very frequent even around 1700; the investigation of modal auxiliaries in progressive verb phrases thus started out from the assumption that we would see either a continued low frequency or a rise in the frequency of such verb phrases. The frequency of progressives with modal auxiliaries turned out to be both low and decreasing, however. Several possible reasons were suggested for this unexpected decrease: a possible general decrease in the frequency of modal auxiliaries in 19th-century English; the development of modal functions inherent in the progressive itself; and the possibility that the constraints on which meanings of the modals the progressive was compatible with became gradually more rigid during the 19th century. As for the individual modal auxiliaries, SHALL was the most frequent modal in CONCE, followed by WILL, MAY, MUST, and CAN. The results from Arnaud's database indicated a similar relative distribution of modals in progressive verb phrases; in addition, the frequency of progressive verb phrases with modal auxiliaries was low in Arnaud's data as well.

The next step was to combine the parameters of tense, the perfect, voice, and the presence of modal auxiliaries into a unified analysis. Each period sample was broken down into 16 subsets, representing the possible combinations of present/past, perfect/non-perfect, active/passive, and presence/absence of modal auxiliaries. (However, some of these slots were empty.) The results showed that, with the exception of the increase in the frequency of the passive progressive, there was no evidence of the average progressive verb phrase becoming more complex by incorporating a larger number of auxiliaries.

Finally, a separate section was devoted to the *being* + present participle construction, which was on its way out of the English language in the 19th century. The findings based on data from CONCE agree with what has been suggested in the literature: the only two instances of *being* + present participle come from period 1. In contrast, there are instances of *being* + present participle as late as 1840 in Arnaud's data. Although this may be a mere accident of the sampling, the analysis of Arnaud's data points to the value of investigating private letters, as well as other types of colloquial and private texts, when looking at linguistic features on their way out of (or into) printed language.

In Chapter 3, I discussed the concept of the integration of the progressive into English grammar in some detail, and described "integration" as subsuming both matters of frequency and of diffusion across linguistic and extralinguistic parameters. As can be seen from the results presented above, the rise in frequency of the progressive during the 1800s was not accompanied by the progressive verb phrase becoming more complex on average.[25] Instead, the overall results indicate that the frequency increase occurred mainly in syntactic areas where there are no other auxiliaries in the progressive verb phrase. Recent research (see e.g. Mair and Hundt 1995) has indicated that the progressive may be becoming a less marked alternative to the non-progressive in Present-Day English. Against this background, it would be interesting to see if such changes were preceded or accompanied by an increase in the frequency of more complex progressive verb phrases in 20th-century English. Studies such as Smith (2002) give valuable indications in this respect.

---

25   The introduction of the passive progressive made the progressive paradigm more complete, and also caused the progressive to occur in more complex verb phrases. At the same time, however, the near-disappearance of the *being* + present participle construction made the paradigm less complete.

Chapter 6

Variation with linguistic parameters

In the present chapter, I examine five linguistic variables that previous research has identified as important to the development and distribution of the progressive. First, a survey of what main verbs occur most frequently in progressive verb phrases will be given. In this section, I will also devote some space to the occurrence of the verbs BE and HAVE in the progressive, since the late Modern English period appears to have witnessed their re-emergence (or, for BE, possibly emergence) as main verbs in progressive verb phrases. The second variable is the Aktionsart value (e.g. [±stative], [±durative]) of the situation in which the progressive occurs; the third is the agentivity of the subjects of progressive verb phrases. These three parameters can be said to be "situational" because they influence the classification of situations, in the sense 'verb-denoted phenomena' (see Quirk et al. 1985: 177). For instance, a situation can be said to be agentive or non-agentive, and stative or non-stative; the semantics of individual verbs play an important part in these classification processes.

In addition, I will consider the modification of the progressive by temporal adverbials and the type of clause (e.g. main, adverbial) in which the progressive occurs. As the results will show, on these two parameters, the distribution of the progressive exhibits clearer tendencies towards diachronic change than it does on the three situational parameters. The chapter will conclude with a section that discusses the results in the light of what has been reported in previous research; the results will also be related to the issue of the integration of the progressive into late Modern English grammar.

6.1   Main verbs

The issue of what main verbs occur in the progressive in 19th-century English is of interest for two main reasons. On the one hand, common semantic denominators of verbs that are frequent in progressive verb phrases can give indications of what meanings the progressive tends to co-occur with. On the other hand, a study of verbs that occur in the progressive with a low frequency may also be valuable: in particular, main verbs that started to occur in the progressive only recently are important as indicators of the potentiality of the progressive.

Reflecting these two research questions, the present section is divided into two subsections. In Section 6.1.1, I will look at what main verbs are the most frequent in progressive verb phrases, and consider variation with time and genre. In Section 6.1.2, I will focus on the occurrence of the important verbs BE and HAVE. Since progressives of BE and HAVE are rare in 19th-century English, I will also take Arnaud's database into account in this analysis.

6.1.1   Frequent main verbs in progressive verb phrases

In studies of what main verbs commonly occur in progressive verb phrases, these verbs have often been divided into semantic classes and/or Aktionsart categories.[1] (These two classifications are not independent of each other, since the classification of a verb as belonging to a given Aktionsart category is influenced by the semantics inherent in the verb.) These divisions, then, function as indications of the semantics of the progressive itself, with the rationale that the meaning of the progressive is more compatible with some verb meanings and/or Aktionsart categories than with others. In the present study, however, Aktionsart values will be considered as properties of whole situations rather than of verbs in isolation (see Section 6.2), and although I will comment on the lexical meaning of the main verbs that are common in the progressive, the exact meaning of a verb form may depend on contextual factors, and even the presence of the progressive itself.[2] In addition, the subject matter of the texts in the material will affect the distribution and frequency of main verbs in progressive verb phrases; this factor should also be borne in mind when the results of the analysis undertaken in the present section are interpreted.

In the CONCE corpus as a whole, 544 different main verbs are used in progressive verb phrases. Of these, 312 occur only once, 84 twice, 33 three times, 22 four times, and 16 five times. The verbs that occur more than 20 times, in decreasing order of frequency, are given in Table 49.

---

[1]   In this context, the main verb of a progressive verb phrase is defined as the base form of the last verb form of the verb phrase.

[2]   For instance, the presence of adverbial/prepositional particles was not taken into account when the main verbs were classified: this means, for instance, that RUN *out* would be classified as an instance of RUN. Since such particles frequently affect the Aktionsart status of the situation, however, they have been taken into account in Section 6.2.

Table 49. Main verbs with more than 20 occurrences in progressive verb phrases in CONCE (percentages of all progressive verb phrases in the material within brackets)

Main verb	Occurrences (%)	Main verb	Occurrences (%)
GO	265 (11%)	LIVE	38 (2%)
COME	102 (4%)	MAKE	33 (1%)
DO	73 (3%)	GROW	29 (1%)
GET	62 (3%)	TAKE	29 (1%)
SPEAK	59 (2%)	TRY	27 (1%)
WRITE	58 (2%)	STAND	26 (1%)
STAY	52 (2%)	THINK	26 (1%)
SIT	50 (2%)	BEGIN	25 (1%)
READ	46 (2%)	SUFFER	23 (1%)
TALK	43 (2%)	SAY	22 (1%)
LOOK	42 (2%)	EXPECT	21 (1%)
WAIT	40 (2%)	LIE	21 (1%)
WALK	39 (2%)		

As shown in Table 49, the commonest main verbs in progressive verb phrases are GO and COME.[3] As regards GO, this result is all the more significant because all instances of BE *going to* + infinitive constructions with future meaning have been excluded from the data (see Section 2.2.2.4). In addition, progressives of GO and COME occur in stage directions in Drama, but such progressives were also excluded from the counts. It may be that the development of the BE *going to* + infinitive construction with future reference and the development of progressives of GO have reinforced each other, since both of these constructions contain the sequence BE *going*. Another possible reason for the dominance of these verbs is that GO and COME may have been very common as main verbs in verb phrases overall in late Modern English, as they are in the present day: in Biber et al.'s (1999: 373) corpus, consisting of Present-Day English conversation, fiction, news text, and academic prose, GO is the third most common and COME the eighth most common lexical verb. Finally, Kytö (1997: 45) points out that COME and GO favour auxiliary BE rather than auxiliary HAVE longer than other main verbs in perfect intransitive verb phrases. Although factors such as the functional load of auxiliary BE are also relevant here, it is possible that this tendency to favour auxiliary BE in perfect verb phrases also contributed to the frequent co-occurrence of COME and GO with auxiliary BE in progressive verb phrases.

If we look at the other verbs listed in Table 49, a few semantic groups can be observed. Movement verbs seem to be common in the progressive: apart from

---

3   Note that GO and COME were also the two most frequent main verbs in Rydén and Brorström's (1987) and in Kytö's (1997) investigations of the BE/HAVE paradigm with intransitives, despite the differences between the studies in terms of what genres were drawn on for data.

GO and COME, WALK also belongs to this group. Both GO and COME are frequently used to refer to future events: this function accounts for 97 (37%) of the 265 instances of GO, and 37 (36%) of the 102 instances of COME. An example is (44):

(44)   I am more Jellyby than ever now, for Mrs. Dymond *is coming* out in March or April, and I had a regular stage fright last week.
(Letters, Thackeray Ritchie, 1870–1900, p. 190)

In contrast, progressives of WALK are never used with future reference in the data. It may be that the non-specific meaning of COME and GO makes them more suitable for the expression of an unspecified future event. Another group of verbs that occur in the progressive frequently is connected with the activity of communication. To this group belong SPEAK, WRITE, READ, TALK, and SAY. A third group consists of stance verbs, i.e. verbs that denote bodily posture, represented by SIT, STAND, and LIE (referring to bodily position). This group could also be widened to include LIVE, as done by Quirk et al. (1985: 205f.), since progressives of LIVE, like progressives of SIT, STAND, and LIE, denote temporary states, whereas non-progressives describe permanent states. Some verbs seem to involve change in one way or another: to this group belongs BEGIN, and also GET and GROW when the latter two are used as linking verbs, as in (45):

(45)   The spring evenings *were getting* bright and long, when three or four ladies in calashes met at Miss Barker's door.
(Fiction, Gaskell, 1850–1870, p.130)

It is also worth noting that THINK, SUFFER, and EXPECT are among the verbs that occur in the progressive most often. These are all so-called private verbs, that is, verbs that often "denote 'private' states which can only be subjectively verified: *ie* states of mind, volition, attitude, etc." (Quirk et al. 1985: 202).[4] Most other verbs in Table 49 typically denote activities of one type or another, with DO as a special case: DO is often used to stand for another, more specific verb, which either has been mentioned or will be mentioned, as in (46):

(46)   [$The ATTORNEY-GENERAL:$] You say you were several hours with him, partly in the quadrangle, and partly, as you describe it, under cover. What *were* they *doing* in the quadrangle? – Walking in and out of the stables, looking at the different chargers.
(Trials, Tichborne, 1870–1900, p. 2,414)

---

4   Ota (1963: 73) defines largely the same group as "*I*-verbs" on the grounds that "[t]hey occur much more frequently with *I/we* as subject (both in statement and in question) or *you* as subject (in question) than with *you* as subject (in statement) or a third person subject (both in statement and in question)".

In other cases, the specific verb that DO stands for is never mentioned explicitly but can be inferred from the context.

There has been a great deal of previous research on what main verbs are common in progressive verb phrases. Wright (1994: 475f.) found that, in her corpus of early Modern English plays, the progressive favoured verbs of movement (COME and GO) and verbs of saying, i.e. much the same groups that could be identified in the CONCE data. Núñez Pertejo (2001: 342ff.), looking at the early Modern English section of the Helsinki Corpus, found that the movement verbs COME and GO, activity verbs, and verbs of resting, living, dwelling, and saying were all common in the progressive. Scheffer (1975: 117) investigated a corpus consisting of Present-Day English novels and radio commentaries. If the BE *going to* + infinitive construction is excluded, the ten commonest verbs in the progressive in Scheffer's corpus were GO (146 occurrences), followed by COME (97), DO (83), LOOK (72), THINK (55), TALK (54), WEAR (52), SAY (50), TRY (48), and GET (44). Although the dominance of GO is less pronounced in Scheffer's material than in CONCE, it is clearly the most frequent verb in progressive verb phrases in both corpora; moreover, COME and DO come second and third in both corpora. Looking at the other verbs on the list, we find that all of the ten commonest verbs in the progressive in Scheffer's corpus except WEAR are also present in Table 49. Considering the differences between Wright's, Núñez Pertejo's, and Scheffer's corpora, and CONCE in terms of periods covered and genre structure, there seems to be a good deal of continuity between early Modern English and Present-Day English in the distribution of main verbs in progressive verb phrases.[5]

Biber et al. (1999: 471ff.) approach the issue of what main verbs occur frequently in progressive verb phrases partly from another angle. Using a corpus consisting of conversation, fiction, news texts, and academic prose, they start out from the individual verbs and investigate what percentage of the occurrences of each verb is accounted for by progressives. In this way, they are able to take the factor of how common a verb is in English as a whole into account. However, the number of occurrences per one million words is also used as an indication of how frequent different main verbs are in the progressive. Biber et al. show that many semantic domains contain both verbs that occur in the progressive most of the time (>80% or >50% of all occurrences) and verbs that rarely occur in the progressive at all (<2% of all occurrences). The exception is the semantic domain of "facilitation/causation or obligation", including e.g. CONVINCE, INSPIRE, and PROMISE, where only verbs rarely occurring in the progressive are listed. Some verbs in this group, notably GUARANTEE and PROMISE, are sometimes used in

---

5   There is even some continuity with Old English in this respect. Scheffer (1975: 168) investigated what verbs (including compounds) occurred most often in the progressive in *Gregory's Dialogues*, and found that they were GANGAN (24 occurrences), LIFIAN and SPRECAN (both 14), FYLGAN (11), FARAN (10), WUNIAN and SWELTAN (both 8), and WEAXAN (6). Verbs of movement and communication thus account for many of the most common progressive patterns in Old English, early Modern English, late Modern English, and Present-Day English alike.

performative utterances in the present tense, where the non-progressive is the norm (see e.g. Quirk et al. 1985: 180).[6]

None of the verbs that occur in the progressive >80% of the time in the corpus used by Biber et al. (1999) is present in Table 49; of the verbs that occur in the progressive >50% of the time, only TALK is present in the table.[7] Among the verbs listed as occurring in the progressive more than ten times per million words can be found COME, DO, GO, LIVE, LOOK, MAKE, SAY, SIT, SPEAK, STAND, STAY, TAKE, THINK, WAIT, and WALK. This leaves BEGIN, EXPECT, GET, GROW, LIE, READ, SUFFER, TRY, and WRITE to be accounted for of the verbs in Table 49. There are at least two possible reasons why the lists do not agree more completely. First, all of Biber et al.'s lists of verbs that occur frequently in the progressive are not exhaustive, so it is possible that some of the verbs in Table 49 were not included in their examples. Moreover, the absence of some of these verbs may be explained by their being frequent in genres that were not part of the corpus used in Biber et al. (1999): for instance, as will be shown below, WRITE is characteristic of Letters and GET of Letters and Drama, and neither genre was part of Biber et al.'s corpus.[8]

Turning to period and genre breakdowns, owing to the size of the database and to limitations of space I will only give the five most frequent verbs in each period and genre subsample. (When several verbs occur equally frequently in the progressive, all of these main verbs will be given.) For most genres, results for period/genre subsample levels are not reliable, as the low raw frequencies decrease the likelihood that the sample distribution of main verbs in the progressive reflects that of the sample universe. I will therefore focus on period and genre totals in what follows.

The period breakdown is given in Table 50.

---

6   The semantic domains listed are "activities and physical events", "communication acts", "mental/attitudinal states or activities", "perceptual states or activities", "static physical situations", and "facilitation/causation or obligation" (Biber et al. 1999: 471f.). Some of the results are only valid for parts of the corpus; in particular, verbs that occur >80% of the time in the progressive can only be found in conversation, and verbs that occur >50% of the time in the progressive were only attested in conversation and fiction.

7   However, LOOK *forward* is listed by Biber et al. as occurring >50% of the time in the progressive, and LOOK is listed in Table 49 (as pointed out above, the presence of adverbial or prepositional particles in the verb phrase was not taken into account when the main verbs were classified for the present study).

8   Note, however, that, as stated above, GET was one of the most frequent verbs in the progressive in Scheffer's (1975) study, which was based on a corpus of fiction texts and radio commentaries. Moreover, GET is one of the twelve commonest lexical verbs in Biber et al.'s (1999: 373) corpus, so a high frequency of progressives of GET might have been expected when raw frequencies were normalized to a given number of words.

Table 50. The most frequent main verbs in progressive verb phrases in CONCE per period (percentages of all progressive verb phrases in each period subsample within brackets)

Period 1		Period 2		Period 3	
GO	73 (12%)	GO	112 (12%)	GO	80 (8%)
WALK	20 (3%)	COME	42 (5%)	COME	42 (4%)
COME	18 (3%)	DO	28 (3%)	GET	31 (3%)
SPEAK	17 (3%)	GET	25 (3%)	DO	29 (3%)
WRITE	17 (3%)	WRITE	24 (3%)	STAY	28 (3%)

The dominance of GO as a main verb in progressive verb phrases is further emphasized in Table 50 by the fact that this verb is the most frequent in all three periods. Moreover, COME and GO belong to the three most frequent main verbs in progressive verb phrases in all three periods. However, it seems that GO becomes slightly less dominant over the century: in both period 1 and period 2, GO accounts for 12% of all progressives, but in period 3, only for 8%. Another circumstance worth noting is that all of the verbs in Table 50 belong to one of the semantic groups mentioned above: movement (COME, GO, WALK), activity (DO, STAY), communication (SPEAK, WRITE), and change (some realizations of GET).[9] However, there are no private verbs on the list.

Another way of looking at the diachronic distribution of main verbs across the progressive paradigm is to consider type/token ratios. In such an analysis, the types consist of all different main verbs that occur in progressive verb phrases in each period; the tokens correspond to the total number of progressives per period. Increasing ratios would indicate greater diversity as regards what main verbs occur in progressive verb phrases, whereas a decrease in the ratio implies the opposite. The type/token ratios for CONCE do not indicate greater diversity in diachrony, however: the ratio is 0.38 in period 1, 0.35 in period 2, and 0.30 in period 3. It thus appears that the increase in the frequency of the progressive in 19th-century English was chiefly due to an increase in the use of main verbs that were already established in the progressive, rather than to an extension of the progressive paradigm to cover new ground in this respect.

If we proceed to consider individual genres, there is more variation in the distribution of main verbs. The results are presented in Table 51a–b: Table 51 was split so that non-expository and expository genres were kept apart. Given the low raw frequencies for some genres, I will not present percentages in Table 51.

---

9   It would perhaps also be possible to classify STAY with stance verbs such as SIT and STAND, as LIVE was added to this group. However, because STAY in the sense 'reside' has a connotation of temporariness even in the non-progressive, the progressive/non-progressive difference between temporary and permanent position is not as clear as with LIVE; STAY was therefore classified as an activity verb.

Table 51a. The most frequent main verbs in progressive verb phrases in the
expository genres Debates, History, and Science (raw frequencies
within brackets)

Debates	History	Science
GO (3)	LOOK (4)	RISE (5)
SEEK (3)	MAKE (4)	DEAL (4)
FIGHT (2)	DO (3)	APPROACH (4)
OBJECT (2)	GO (3)	INCREASE (4)
BRING (2)	GROW (3)	TRAVEL (3)
SIT (2)	WAIT (3)	
WAIT (2)		

Table 51b. The most frequent main verbs in progressive verb phrases in the non-
expository genres Drama, Fiction, Letters, and Trials (raw
frequencies within brackets)

Drama	Fiction	Letters	Trials
GO (34)	GO (27)	GO (130)	GO (66)
COME (20)	THINK (9)	WRITE (54)	SPEAK (38)
GROW (12)	SIT (8)	COME (42)	COME (30)
GET (11)	COME (7)	GET (38)	LIVE (29)
SAY (8)	SPEAK (7)	DO (34)	SIT (26)
WAIT (8)			

Of the main verbs listed in Table 51a, SEEK, FIGHT, OBJECT, and BRING in
Debates, and all the verbs in Science, are missing from Table 49 above. Debates
and Science are thus less typical than History with respect to what verbs
commonly occur in progressive verb phrases in these expository genres. It is
possible that some of this difference is due to Debates and Science containing
fewer verbs that commonly occur in progressive verb phrases than History. In
other words, one of the reasons why the progressive is comparatively rare in
Debates and Science may be partly lexical.

Turning to the four non-expository genres in CONCE, we find that these
genres exhibit a more expected pattern of main verbs, with GO as the most
common verb in the progressive in all genres. Moreover, none of the verbs in
Table 51b is absent from Table 49. As the general frequency of the progressive is
higher in these genres, it is also possible to discern some genre-specific factors
that may influence the distribution of main verbs in texts. In Drama, the entrances
and exits of characters, both on and off the stage, are frequently commented on,
which may help to explain the high frequency of COME and GO (Wright
1994: 475). An example is (47):

(47)   [$Fer.$] Will she? Well, if she will I shall be much obliged – [$Exit Mrs.
         Ferment into the house.$] – Gone! Oh I shall go mad! – I wish I could hate
         her. – Now must I abandon all my delicious plans, or I shall never get
         another word from her – [$listens$] – She's *coming* back: oh ho! she
         relents – now I must manage this in my best manner – I won't condescend
         to look at her. –
         (Drama, Morton, 1800–1830, p. 31)

In both Fiction (especially in dialogue) and Trials, the act of speaking is of
importance, often in contexts where an effort is made to clarify something
previously stated, and SPEAK is consequently among the commonest main verbs
in progressive verb phrases in these two genres. Consider (48):

(48)   Did you know of his tongue having been sore? No, sir. – You never heard
         him complain of that? I have seen him with a loaded tongue, I believe,
         about once or so. You mean a foul tongue? Yes. – I *am* not *speaking* of
         that: did he ever complain in your hearing of the tongue being sore, so as
         to render it difficult for him to swallow?
         (Trials, Palmer, 1850–1870, p. 42)

In contrast, THINK is one of the most frequent verbs in progressive verb phrases in
Fiction, but not in Trials. The difference can probably be attributed to the
importance of characters' thoughts in the Fiction genre, while Trials texts rather
focus on observable actions; moreover, the possible presence of an omniscient
narrator in Fiction may give the reader access to characters' thoughts. Other main
verbs in Fiction and Trials in Table 51b seem to occur in the progressive with a
high frequency because they are often part of narrative description (in Geisler
2002, Trials and Fiction were shown to be the two most narrative genres in
CONCE): that is, these main verbs occur frequently in progressive verb phrases
because they are used to describe ongoing action or temporary state in narrative
passages, typically providing a type of background to the action that brings the
plot forward, as in (49) and (50):

(49)   What was the next thing you saw? – I *was coming* downstairs and saw Mrs
         Maybrick on the landing.
         (Trials, Maybrick, 1870–1900, p. 86)

(50)   The boarders *were* all *sitting* there, just as usual, and the supper cloth was
         removed; Mr. Maliphant had his long pipe fixed in the corner of his
         mouth, but he held it there with an appearance of constraint, and he had let
         it go out.
         (Fiction, Besant, 1870–1900, p. I.80–I.81)

In Letters, finally, the high frequency of WRITE parallels that of SPEAK in Fiction
and Trials, reflecting the change of medium. Most progressives of WRITE occur in

the first person, and either describe or comment on the letter (or circumstances surrounding its production) of which the progressive is a part, as in (51):

(51)   But your letter this morning really did me good, and put me in good spirits, and I *am* only *writing* to tell you so.
(Letters, Jewsbury, 1850–1870, p. 386)

The dominance of GO in Letters is even more pronounced than in the other non-expository genres. This dominance is chiefly due to the use of this verb in present-tense progressive verb phrases with future reference, similar to (44) above with COME, as in (52):

(52)   The Evelyns returned our visit on saturday; we were very happy to meet, & all that; they *are going* tomorrow into Gloucestershire, to the Dolphins for ten days.
(Letters, Austen, 1800–1830, p. 53)

This future use of the progressive will be further commented on in Section 6.2.

The above brief cross-genre investigation of CONCE has shown that genre-specific factors may affect what main verbs commonly occur in progressive verb phrases. For instance, although the dominance of COME and – particularly – GO in the whole corpus may seem overwhelming, it may partly be an effect of these two verbs being especially common in genres where the progressive itself is frequent.

6.1.2   The development of BE and HAVE as main verbs in the progressive

The appearance of BE and HAVE as main verbs in progressive verb phrases meant that two important verbs, both of which frequently occur in stative situations, were added to the late Modern English progressive paradigm. CONCE yields too few data to enable detailed studies on these constructions. However, given their relevance to the general development of the progressive and the importance of the 19th century in these respects, I will present the CONCE data together with short surveys of some relevant research on this topic. In addition, I will use Arnaud's database (see Chapter 5) to obtain further examples of these two types of progressive verb phrases.

Progressives of HAVE occurred in Old and Middle English (Visser 1973: 1966), but appear to be near-absent in early Modern English (Warner 1993: 217). The status of BE as main verb in progressive verb phrases is less clear-cut, but the available evidence, though scarce, suggests parallels to the development of HAVE. Visser (1973: 1954) mentions three possible 15th-century progressives of BE; but as Denison (1993: 395) points out, at least one of them is dubious. Söderlind (1951: 101) found no progressives of either BE or HAVE in his investigation of verb syntax in Dryden's prose. Visser (1973: 1966) claims that there has been a restriction on what meanings of HAVE could take the progressive from Modern English on (viz. "the sense of 'to enjoy', 'to endure', 'to partake of', 'to experience', 'to go through', etc.", which developed later), and that HAVE could occur as a main verb in progressive verb phrases in Modern English only after these senses had developed. Warner (1993: 217), however, points out that "HAVE is found in both Middle and early Modern English in nonstative senses"; Warner's suggestion is instead "that progressive and passive participles of auxiliaries became unavailable (or marked) at this period".[10] As for the occurrence of progressives of BE and HAVE in late Modern English, Warner (1997) claims that the formal transparency (*be* + *ing*) which caused *being* to be reanalysed as a non-auxiliary in the 18th century and thus made the sequence BE *being* possible (see Section 5.3), both as part of the passive progressive and as a progressive with BE as main verb, had the same effect on *having* and BE *having*.

The first attested late Modern English instance of BE *being* + adjectival complement dates from 1819 (Denison 1998: 146). Examples with nominal complements are slightly later: Denison (1998: 147) gives an example from 1834. Thus, the sequence BE *being* is attested as part of the passive progressive several decades before its first late Modern English appearance as a progressive of BE (as pointed out in Section 5.3, the first wholly convincing example of a passive progressive is from 1772). Instances with BE *having* have been attested earlier: Warner (1997: 168) gives an example from 1787. As can be expected against this background, progressives with HAVE as main verb are more common than progressives with BE as main verb in CONCE: there are ten instances of the former against only one of the latter. Moreover, progressives of HAVE are represented in all three periods (1 instance in period 1, 3 in period 2, and 6 in period 3), while the sole progressive of BE comes from period 3. If Warner's account is correct, one of the reasons why the diffusion of BE *being* took more time than that of BE *having* may be that the former met with more negative prescriptive evaluation (see Section 5.3); Warner (1995: 546) also lists a negative 19th-century comment on BE *having*, but it still appears that BE *being* attracted more negative criticism.

Given the earlier appearance of late Modern English progressives of HAVE and the higher frequency of this pattern in the data, I will begin the presentation of my results by looking at progressive verb phrases with HAVE as main verb. In the CONCE data, progressives of HAVE are especially common in Letters: eight of the ten occurrences come from this genre. Moreover, the remaining two instances (one from Fiction and one from Trials) are both from period 3, the last period covered by CONCE. As mentioned in Section 5.3, most early instances of the passive progressive, which, like the progressive of BE, contains the sequence BE *being*, have also been attested in private letters. If we accept that all variants of the sequence BE *being* in progressives are related as regards their occurrence and diffusion, the corpus findings for HAVE thus agree with what has been reported in

---

10   As Warner (1997: 168n.) admits, however, these patterns were perhaps not entirely absent. For instance, Denison (1993: 432) and Elsness (1994: 15) each presents a possible passive progressive from the early Modern English period.

previous research for BE, another indication that the development of BE and HAVE as main verbs in the progressive is interconnected.

As regards the syntactic make-up of the progressives of HAVE in the CONCE data, two of the ten progressives of HAVE contain perfect auxiliaries, as in (53):

(53)   I *had been having* a horrid pain across my chest, and on Friday mamma carried me to Andrew Clark, who has put me on the strictest of diets for one week – no medicine, but soup, sweet things, fruit, and, worst of all, all green vegetables entirely forbidden, and my liquors confined to one small half-glass of brandy with cold water, at dinner.
(Letters, Arnold, 1870–1900, p. 324)

Given that the pattern HAVE *had* already existed in English, the occurrence of HAVE *been having* is not surprising in itself, but still testifies to the relatively quick diffusion of HAVE as main verb across the progressive paradigm. One instance – (41), also cited in Section 5.4 – contains a modal auxiliary:

(41)   We *shall be having* a Box of Tea from Mr. Twining's very soon, in which might be sent the piece of carpetting you have had so long in your possession – if you will please to direct it to us and send it to them.
(Letters, Wordsworth, Mary [2], 1800–1830, p. 30)

The data in Arnaud's database support the development indicated by the distribution of the CONCE data. Progressives with HAVE as main verb occur in all periods except period 0 (i.e. before 1800): there are 7 in period 1, 9 in period 1b, 53 in period 2, and 30 in period 3. (The uneven size of the period subsamples does not allow definite conclusions concerning the frequency development of HAVE as a main verb in progressive verb phrases.)

I now turn to progressives with BE as main verb. The one instance of BE in the progressive in CONCE, (54), is of special interest, as it contains a perfect auxiliary:

(54)   Minny and I stood behind a drapery, and saw the duel scene, and heard the audience roaring and roaring, and it seemed as if all the atmosphere of Hamlet were round about us. Then up came Irving looking very handsome and pale, and quite natural, as a man must be who'*s* just *been being* anything so real, and he thanked us so warmly when we said how we admired it.
(Letters, Thackeray Ritchie, 1870–1900, p. 162)

Visser (1973: 1957) emphasizes the low frequency of HAVE *been being* + nominal complement, and gives an example from 1909;[11] according to Warner (1997: 170), the earliest non-constructed instances of progressives with a non-finite form of BE before *being* that have hitherto been attested are from the period 1910–1920. The letter in which (54) occurs is dated November, 1874, however, and the context does not indicate that (54) was intended by the letter-writer as a grammar example or as a joke. Rather, it gives the impression of having been meant as a positive judgement of the performance of an actor in a play, with *who's just been being anything so real* meaning roughly 'who has just acted his part so convincingly'. If more examples of this type can be found, there may be empirical evidence for Warner's (1997: 173) claim that progressives with a non-finite form of BE before *being* may have been possible in speech before the second decade of the 20th century.

Example (54) is taken from Letters, a written genre that may often contain spoken and/or colloquial features. An investigation of private letters written in the last decades of the 19th century and the first decade of the 20th may thus be rewarding in this respect: apart from backdating the first attestation of a progressive containing *be being* or *been being*, such an investigation may also shed more light on the diffusion patterns of progressives containing the sequence BE *being* in general. Note that, in addition to taking a non-finite form of BE preceding *being*, (54) also takes a nominal complement (*anything so real*), and thus belongs to the syntactic group of progressives containing the sequence BE *being* that is attested latest, after the appearance of both passive progressives (as in *The house is being built*) and progressives of BE with adjectival complements (as in *You are being silly*).[12]

Arnaud's database contains three progressives with BE as main verb, one from period 1 and two from period 2; none of them includes a non-finite form of BE before *being*, and all of them take adjectival complements.[13] The example from period 1 is the well-known example from a letter by Keats, generally considered to be the first attested Modern English instance (*You will be glad to hear ... how diligent I have been, and am being*).

---

11 Visser mentions only *has been being* followed by nouns, but his statement presumably applies to all perfect progressives of BE followed by nominal complements.

12 Anne Thackeray Ritchie, who wrote the letter in which (54) occurs, appears to have incorporated several other features in her idiolect that were not too frequent in letters from the period. Kytö and Romaine (2000) found that two of the three adjectives that have double comparison in CONCE (e.g. *the very most delightfulest tour*) also come from her letters.

13 One possible example of a progressive of BE with a nominal complement from 1855 was excluded from the counts, as a gerundial interpretation was considered more likely (*... & owing to it's being Papa's busy day, I could not ask him to stay*).

6.2   Aktionsart

As pointed out in Section 6.1, researchers have tried to account for the common observation that the progressive occurs more frequently with some verbs, and in some types of situations, than others, by classifying the main verbs that occur in progressive verb phrases into different semantic groups. However, scholars have also started out from more general aspectual characteristics of verbs, such as whether the lexical content of the verb is stative or non-stative, and come up with Aktionsart classes of verbs or situations. I use the term "Aktionsart" to refer to "the intrinsic temporal qualities of a situation" (Brinton 1988: 3). The present section will focus on the latter type of analysis. In what follows, I will first briefly discuss some proposed Aktionsart typologies. I will then relate these typologies to the framework that will be used in the present study, before applying the classification to the data yielded by CONCE.

6.2.1   Aktionsart typologies: A selective survey and discussion

The most widely used Aktionsart typology is probably that formulated by Vendler (1967). In this analysis, four categories are distinguished on the basis of Aktionsart oppositions: state terms (e.g. LOVE), activity terms (e.g. RUN), accomplishment terms (e.g. RUN *a mile*), and achievement terms (e.g. FIND *the treasure*). Vendler's classification has been discussed extensively in the literature (see for instance Brinton 1988 and Dowty 1979). Table 52 summarizes Vendler's typology.

Table 52.   The Aktionsart features of Vendler's typology (based on Brinton 1988: 28f.)

State	Activity	Accomplishment	Achievement
[+stative]	[–stative]	[–stative]	[–stative]
[+durative]	[+durative]	[+durative]	[–durative]
[–telic]	[–telic]	[+telic]	–
[–voluntary]	[±voluntary]	[±voluntary]	[±voluntary]

Vendler's (1967) system has given rise to a number of suggested modifications and alternative proposals. A recent alternative is that proposed by Nordlander (1997). Nordlander (1997: 12) criticizes Vendler for not distinguishing "between the verbs and the situations in which they occur", and proposes a typology whose starting point is the verbal nucleus, which in most cases corresponds to a main verb in isolation.[14] This verbal nucleus has an invariant Aktionsart value. Verbal nuclei can be stative, processive, eventive, and telic, corresponding roughly to

---

14   On a similar note, Brinton (1988: 29) states that, in Vendler's (1967) account, "the role played by nominal arguments and nuclear prepositional phrases in aktionsart meaning is … neglected or passed over in silence".

Vendler's state, activity, achievement, and accomplishment terms (Nordlander 1997: 13n.). In Nordlander's account, the overall characteristics of the situation are defined by the nucleus together with tense/mood/aspect components and by peripheral elements outside the verbal constituency, e.g. adverbials.

Nordlander's treatment of the tense/mood/aspect properties of situations is novel and insightful. However, the view that a verb in isolation has a permanent Aktionsart value is controversial. Brinton (1988: 31), for instance, claims that "we must recognize that aktionsart is a feature of the entire sentence and that it is difficult to specify the 'basic' aktionsart of any verb". Similarly, Allen (1966: 75) notes that "perhaps it is not so much the verbs themselves that should be classified in different groups as the predications which they express", and Bache (1985: 123) argues that "the functional diversity of verbal lexemes with respect to actionality calls in question the validity of many traditional classes of verb". (See also Smitterberg 1999 for a critique of Nordlander's framework.) Moreover, for the purposes of the present section, the Aktionsart characteristics of the entire situation of which the progressive was a part, rather than those of the main verb of the progressive verb phrase, were of primary importance. Against this background, Quirk et al.'s (1985: 200ff.) proposed typology of situations is valuable for two main reasons. First, it recognizes the whole situation, rather than an isolated verb, as the unit of analysis; although the situation types are exemplified with individual verbs, Quirk et al. (1985: 200) note that "verb meanings can be separated only artificially, in this respect, from their complementations". Secondly, it is aimed specifically at explaining the co-occurrence of the progressive and different Aktionsart categories. Their typology, illustrated with examples taken from Quirk et al. (1985), is summarized in Table 53.[15]

Table 53.   The eleven situation types in Quirk et al.'s (1985) classification

Type	Stat.	Dur.	Tel.	Agen.	Example
A (Qualities)	+				*Mary is being a Canadian*
B (States)	+				*Mary is having a bad cold*
C (Stance)	±				*He is standing over there*
D (Goings-on)	−	+	−	−	*It is raining*
E (Activities)	−	+	−	+	*Jill was writing*
F (Processes)	−	+	+	−	*It is getting warmer*
G (Accomplishments)	−	+	+	+	*Jill is knitting a sweater*
H (Momentary events)	−	−	−	−	*A door was banging*
I (Momentary acts)	−	−	−	+	*John was nodding his head*
J (Transitional events)	−	−	+	−	*The queen was dying*
K (Transitional acts)	−	−	+	+	*He is scoring another goal*

15   All situation types are exemplified using main clauses; however, the typology is intended to cover both main and subordinate clauses. In some cases, the examples have been shortened slightly.

There are two stative situation types in Quirk et al.'s classification: type A situations, "qualities", represent more permanent characteristics (e.g. BE *tall*) than type B situations, "states" (e.g. BE *tired*). Quirk et al. (1985: 200) imply that the more permanent type A situations co-occur with the progressive less freely than type B situations (see also Mufwene 1984: 25f.). There is also a semi-stative type C, called "stance", which comprises situations with verbs such as SIT, LIVE, and STAND. Type C situations are claimed to be intermediate between stativity and non-stativity, in that they accept the progressive more easily than either of situation types A and B; the progressive usually expresses a temporary state when used in type C situations (Quirk et al. 1985: 205f.). Types A through C can thus be seen as ordered along a cline of increasing acceptability when co-occurring with the progressive. The remaining eight situation types in Quirk et al.'s framework are non-stative: they are characterized by their values on the three binary parameters of duration (i.e. whether or not the situation can have duration), agentivity (i.e. whether or not the subject refers to a "deliberate or self-activating initiator" of the situation; Quirk et al. 1985: 207), and telicity (i.e. whether or not the situation results in a change of state).[16]

A modified version of Quirk et al.'s (1985) typology of situations was adopted for the analysis of how Aktionsart categories interact with the progressive in the present work. Three changes were made to their typology. First, as mentioned above, Quirk et al. separate two kinds of stative situations; but since the borderline between types A (qualities) and B (states) appeared difficult to draw at times, and since few progressives were likely to occur in type A situations, these types were conflated.

Secondly, the inclusion of the parameter of agentivity in an Aktionsart classification is controversial. Brinton (1988: 32), for instance, states that "[f]eatures of agency or intentionality clearly intersect with aspectual features in the verb phrase, as do features of modality and causality, but these different categories should be kept distinct"; nor does Lucko (1995: 174) include the feature [±agentive] in his treatment of the interaction of the progressive with Aktionsart categories. Moreover, it has been hypothesized that the progressive has developed from occurring chiefly with animate subjects to occurring with a wider range of subjects (see Strang 1982). Since animate subjects are more likely to be agentive than inanimate subjects, the parameter of agentivity appears to be of special relevance to the development of the progressive. For these reasons, I will deal with this variable separately in Section 6.3; in the present section, only duration and telicity will be used to categorize non-stative situations, and agentive and non-agentive situations will not be distinguished.

Finally, progressives that refer to the future without the aid of modal auxiliaries, as in (55), were grouped together into a category of their own:

---

16   Quirk et al. (1985) use the terms "conclusive" and "non-conclusive" to describe these situation types. I will refer to these values as "telic" and "atelic" throughout, since the latter terms appear to be more common in previous research.

(55) 'But why not Mr Digweed?' Mrs Barker will immediately say. To that you
      may answer that Mr D. *is going* on tuesday to Steventon to shoot rabbits.
      (Letters, Austen, 1800–1830, p. 124)

There were three main reasons for creating a separate group for these
progressives. To begin with, progressives with future reference are sometimes not
included in discussions of the basic meaning of the construction (see e.g. Rydén
1997: 419), and I did not wish such progressives to skew the distribution of
Aktionsart categories. Moreover, progressives with future reference are
sometimes difficult to classify with respect to Aktionsart. Among other things,
they are problematic with respect to the standard test for telicity proposed by
Garey (1957: 105), "if one was *verb*ing, but was interrupted while *verb*ing, has
one *verb*ed?", to which the answer "yes" implies an atelic reading and the answer
"no" a telic reading. Finally, classifying progressives with future reference apart
from the other instances of the construction made it possible to compare their
occurrence with that of progressive verb phrases with WILL and SHALL indicating
future time. It should be noted, however, that the situation type "future" thus
stands apart from the other types in that it is not defined chiefly in terms of
Aktionsart values, and that this situation type contains progressives that also have
other Aktionsart values, which were not included in the classification. For this
reason, the presentation of my results will include both tables where the situation
type 'future' is identified as a separate category and tables where this category is
not recognized. In the latter tables, progressives that would otherwise belong to
the 'future' category will instead be classified as belonging to one of the other
situation types, where possible. The number of progressives that resist
classification will thus vary depending on whether or not a 'future' category is
recognized.

      After these modifications, the Aktionsart typology to be applied to the
CONCE data contained seven situation types. A summary of their characteristics is
given in Table 54.

Table 54.   The seven situation types distinguished in the present study

Situation type	Characteristics	Example
Stative	[+stative], [+durative], [–telic]	*He is being silly*
Stance	[±stative], [+durative], [–telic]	*I was standing right here*
Active	[–stative], [+durative], [–telic]	*Jill is singing*
Processive	[–stative], [+durative], [+telic]	*I am reading a book*
Momentary	[–stative], [–durative], [–telic]	*The door was banging*
Transitional	[–stative], [–durative], [+telic]	*The train is arriving*
Future	[+future]	*I am leaving tomorrow*

In my discussion, I will use single quotes around the labels in the leftmost column in Table 54 when they are used to denote situation types. The following corpus examples illustrate the different categories used:
'Stative' situations, as in (56):

(56)   This very Tuesday, the delay in forwarding the last number had been particularly aggravating; just when both Miss Pole and Miss Matty, the former more especially, *had been wanting* to see it, in order to coach up the court-news, ready for the evening's interview with aristocracy.
(Fiction, Gaskell, 1850–1870, p. 150)

'Stance' situations, as in (57):

(57)   I *am sitting* on a hassock beside Lucy, whose wheelcouch is drawn up outside the garden fence in the airy meadow, overlooking the flower-beds first, then the orchard, then the hop-oast, and then the pretty stretch of hop and wood beyond.
(Letters, Holland, 1870–1900, pp. 119–120)

'Active' situations, as in (58):

(58)   It has been very sudden! within twenty four hours of his death he *was walking* with only the help of a stick, *was* even *reading*!
(Letters, Austen, 1800–1830, p. 62)

'Processive' situations, as in (59):

(59)   "This is the most extraordinary, most providential meeting that could have been imagined," said Charles; "I *was crossing* to Richmond from Sussex, where I have been on some melancholy business; ..."
(Fiction, Hook, 1800–1830, p. III.326)

'Momentary' situations, as in (60):

(60)   The Government is steadily solving, or attempting to solve, that difficult modern problem of possible Socialism which *has been knocking* at all our heads and hearts so long.
(Letters, Barrett Browning, 1850–1870, p. 231)

'Transitional' situations, as in (61):

(61) Yesterday arrived your letter to Hannah written just as you *were reaching* Madras; and to day I read at the Athenæum an account of your landing, of the salutes, of the turning out of the bodyguard, and of the ceremony of proclaiming you Captain of Fort St George.
(Letters, Macaulay, 1850–1870, p. 210)

'Future' situations, as in (62):

(62) [$TREVOR.$] Why, not in so many words. But the truth is, all was confusion. He had a great conflux of the aristocracy at his house that winter, and – hem – in fact – I believe there was no beds. But he'*s coming* from London soon, and then –
(Drama, Marston, 1850–1870, p. 22)

The division of situations containing progressives into Aktionsart categories proved to be the most difficult classification procedure involved in the present study. To some extent, Aktionsart categories constitute an idealized representation of reality, which sometimes leads to difficulties regarding the classification of situations. For instance, Comrie (1976: 41ff.) points out that it is difficult to find situations that are strictly [–durative], or punctual, in that they completely lack duration, although this does not invalidate the recognition of punctuality as an Aktionsart category. Many instances were indeterminate between two or more situation types, and this fact is reflected in the number of progressives that were left unclassified. When 'future' situations were recognized as a separate category, 147 progressives, or 6% of all progressives in the corpus, resisted classification, leaving 2,293 progressives which were classified as belonging to a situation type; with the 'future' category removed, 116 progressives (5%) resisted classification while 2,324 were classified as belonging to a situation type. The progressives that resisted classification will be excluded from all calculations concerning the distribution of situation types in the remaining part of this section.

The two verbs that proved difficult to classify most often were DO and GO. In the case of DO, the difficulty generally consisted in knowing what verb DO stood for, and to which Aktionsart category the resulting situation would belong, as in (63):

(63) At the corners of the table were deposited the four masses of vegetable matter before mentioned, and in the interstices a pretty little saucer of currant-jelly, with an interesting companion full of horse-radish; all of which being arranged to her entire and perfect satisfaction, Mrs. Palmer again hurried up to the drawing-room, as red as a turkey cock, in order to appear as if she *had been doing* nothing at all, and to be just in time to be handed down again by the major.
(Fiction, Hook, 1800–1830, p. I.231)

With GO, the ambiguity was in many cases between a 'future' reading and a 'processive' reading.[17] Especially in Letters, in the absence of extralinguistic information, it frequently proved hard to tell whether a situation was in progress or would take place in the future at the time the letter was being written (see also Mair and Hundt 1995 on the difficulty of separating 'future' situations from 'processive' and 'transitional' situations). Consider (64):

(64)   I am glad you *are going* on walking tour in Wales; but I cannot help fearing for your ancles – for Heaven-sake give up, though it will be a grievous evil, if your ancles fail.
        (Letters, Darwin, 1850–1870, p. IX.122)

Although considerable effort went into making the classification internally consistent, it is possible that other scholars would have reached different conclusions concerning the classification of some individual cases. Mufwene (1984: 2ff.), for instance, lists cases where scholars have disagreed on what individual verbs typically belong to the Aktionsart category of 'stative' situations.

Some researchers seem to claim that the progressive changes the Aktionsart category of the situation in which it occurs: for instance, Quirk et al. (1985: 202) state that when the progressive occurs in a 'stative' situation, a change of interpretation that "can usually be explained as a transfer, or reclassification of the verb as dynamic" takes place. König (1995: 160) describes a similar point of view by stating that "according to one theory the meaning of the progressive can simply be described as an operation of changing the aspectual character of the sentence it combines with: the result is always a process (dynamic state)". According to this line of argument, the progressive in the 'stative' situation in (56) would be seen as an 'active' situation instead. Similarly, it can be argued that the progressive turns a 'momentary' situation like (60) into an 'active' situation by giving it duration. However, these claims are not universally accepted: see, for instance, Jørgensen (1990; 1991) for conflicting views. Moreover, it can be hypothesized that an imperfective marker such as the progressive should occur most easily in situations that are 'active' from the start, where it simply marks ongoing action, and additional semantic overtones such as temporariness, incompletion, or repeated action are absent: it is therefore of relevance to investigate which Aktionsart category the situation belongs to without the effect of the progressive, if any, being taken into account. For these reasons, I did not include the effect that the progressive itself may have had on the situation when classifying my data on the Aktionsart parameter.

---

17   The number of progressives of GO that resisted classification was thus lower when 'future' situations were not recognized as a separate category, as many of these progressives were reclassified as 'processive': 14 when 'future' situations were reclassified as belonging to other categories as against 34 when 'future' was recognized as a separate category.

6.2.2 The progressive and situation types: An overview of the distribution in CONCE

In this section, I will discuss the overall distribution of the progressive across the seven situation types distinguished in the present study. This overall picture will be supplemented with additional investigations where the variables of time and genre are taken into account in Sections 6.2.3–6.2.4. (Given the large number of situation types distinguished in the present study, results below the level of period and genre will not be presented, as the raw frequencies of many period/genre subsamples are too low for results to be reliable.) Table 55a–b presents the results for the entire corpus.

Table 55a. The progressives in CONCE across the parameter of situation type (column percentages within brackets); 'future' situations included as a separate category

Type	Frequency
Stative	135 (6%)
Stance	139 (6%)
Active	1,084 (47%)
Processive	687 (30%)
Momentary	33 (1%)
Transitional	69 (3%)
Future	146 (6%)
Total	2,293

Table 55b. The progressives in CONCE across the parameter of situation type (column percentages within brackets); 'future' situations reclassified

Type	Frequency
Stative	135 (6%)
Stance	139 (6%)
Active	1,091 (47%)
Processive	846 (36%)
Momentary	33 (1%)
Transitional	80 (3%)
Total	2,324

Looking at the overall distribution of situation types in the data, we find that 'active' situations account for almost half of the progressives (47%). The most frequent verb in this category is SPEAK (56 occurrences); situations containing SPEAK have usually been classified as 'active' if the verb takes a prepositional phrase with *of, about*, or *to* as complement or if it takes no complement at all, whereas situations where the verb takes a direct object have typically been classified as 'processive' (although the definiteness of the direct object, among other things, also enters into the decision). An example of an 'active' situation containing SPEAK is (65); (66) exemplifies a 'processive' situation.

(65)   Among the lesser faults I beg you to endeavour to remember not to stand between the half-opened door, either while you *are speaking*, or spoken to. (Letters, Coleridge, 1800–1830, pp. 513–514)

(66)   "Well, well, I am ready;" – and turning again to Emma, "but you must not be expecting such a very fine young man; you have only had my account you know; I dare say he is really nothing extraordinary:" – though his own sparkling eyes at the moment *were speaking* a very different conviction. (Fiction, Austen, 1800–1830, pp. II.78–II.79)

'Processive' situations, as in (66), constitute the second most frequent Aktionsart category in which progressives occur. In addition, the overwhelming majority of all 'future' situations in Table 55a correspond to 'processive' situations in Table 55b, while a number of situations that were indeterminate between a 'future' and a 'processive' reading could be classified as unambiguously 'processive' when the 'future' category was not recognized. Consequently, 'processive' situations account for 30% of all progressives in Table 55a, as against 36% in Table 55b. In this category, by far the commonest main verb is GO (77 of the 687 occurrences in Table 55a; 181 of the 846 occurrences in Table 55b). 'Processive' situations with progressives of GO often describe a situation in which the subject is moving from one place to another, with a change of state which will be accomplished when the goal is reached, as in (67).[18]

(67)   [$A.$] Mrs. Mulraine and James Bowditch *were going* into a court, but I stopped. She said, "Come in; now don't be foolish again." (Trials, Bowditch, 1800–1830, p. 27)

Most realizations of the progressive express imperfective aspect: it thus makes sense that 'active' and 'processive' situations should dominate the distribution of the construction across the parameter of situation type. 'Active' and 'processive' situations share the features [+durative] and [–stative]: hence, in these situations the progressive can contrast fully with the non-progressive. In contrast, in

---

18   This type of situation leads to the so-called "imperfective paradox". The imperfective paradox concerns how we can identify a situation – for instance that of going into a court in (67) – of which we only see a part; it has been discussed in e.g. Dowty (1977) and Landman (1992). Accounting for the imperfective paradox falls outside the scope of the present study, but it is interesting to note that Dowty (1977: 57) claims that the progressive must have modal values in addition to its aspectual functions on the basis of this paradox, as the completion of a situation in progress is only one of several possible outcomes.

'stative' situations, the aspectual difference between the progressive and the non-progressive is less pronounced or even absent, though an element of temporariness is often present in progressive verb phrases. In 'momentary' and 'transitional' situations, both of which are [–durative], it is necessary to reinterpret the situation as a description of a series of instantaneous events (with 'momentary' situations) or a period leading up to an instantaneous change of state (with 'transitional' situations) for the progressive to be possible. However, not-solely-aspectual progressives need not be subject to the above restrictions.

The occurrence of the progressive in 'stative' situations (6% of all progressives included in the counts) deserves special attention, since scholars have claimed that the progressive is impossible in 'stative' situations (see e.g. Langacker 1982: 276f.).[19] I will therefore present some hypotheses relating to this issue from previous research, and also devote some space to a discussion of what meanings the progressives in 'stative' situations in the material express, and of whether they tend to take private or non-private main verbs. Given the low frequency of progressives occurring in 'stative' situations, my discussion will be qualitative rather than quantitative.

Claims that the progressive is incompatible with 'stative' situations usually focus on the aspectual functions of the construction: since the progressive is often seen as a marker of imperfective aspect, and since a 'stative' situation is typically continuous (Comrie 1976: 51) or imperfective (Ljung 1980: 22f.), a strictly aspectual progressive can be claimed to be redundant in 'stative' situations. As 'stative' situations are not in progress, but rather obtain until they are terminated, it has also been claimed that the progressive does not co-occur with this Aktionsart category. In order to solve the problem posed by the progressive nevertheless occurring in what appear to be 'stative' situations, researchers have claimed that a situation which would otherwise be 'stative' is reinterpreted as non-'stative' when it contains a progressive (see e.g. Quirk et al. 1985: 202, cited above), or that some other change of meaning takes place. However, there is no widespread agreement on this view. Joos (1964: 116), for instance, sees the progressive as expressing increasing or decreasing intensity in 'stative' situations. Smith (1983) takes the view that progressives can occur in 'stative' situations as a result of a non-standard aspectual choice where "[p]rogressive statives present a state as an event, endowing the state with the properties of events" (Smith 1983: 497).

Jørgensen (1990; 1991) claims that the progressive may occur in 'stative' situations in Present-Day English without any change of meaning. Jørgensen (1990) discusses verbs of physical perception, viz. FEEL, HEAR, SEE, SMELL, and TASTE, used as main verbs in progressive verb phrases; he lists several cases with SEE and HEAR, but records few instances with the other verbs. In CONCE,

---

19   Langacker's (1982) terminology differs somewhat from that used in the present work: some of his statives, and all of his imperfectives, would correlate with 'stative' situations. However, both statives and imperfectives are considered to preclude the occurrence of the progressive by Langacker.

however, the only verb of perception that occurs in the progressive in 'stative' situations is FEEL (11 occurrences), as in (68):

(68)   Nay, she believed she had begun to idolize Humfrey himself, but now, at her age, chastened, desponding, with nothing before her save the lonely life of an heiress old maid, counting no tie of blood with any being, what had she to engross her affections from the true Object? Alas! Honora's heart *was* not *feeling* that Object sufficient!
(Fiction, Yonge, 1850–1870, p. I.93)

The two functions of the progressive that seem most likely to lie behind its occurrence in (68) are (a) the expression of a more temporary state than the non-progressive (much the same function that the progressive has in many 'stance' situations containing verbs such as SIT, LIVE, and STAND),[20] and (b) the expression of emotion and/or emphasis. In Jørgensen (1991), other verbs that typically occur in 'stative' situations are discussed, viz. HATE, HOPE, (DIS)LIKE, LOVE, REMEMBER, (MIS)UNDERSTAND, KNOW, MEAN, MIND, and THINK. His conclusions can be summarized in the following bullet list.

- Some of these verbs occur quite frequently in the progressive. (As pointed out in Section 6.1.1, Biber et al. 1999 also found that some stative verbs were quite common in the progressive.)
- With some of the verbs, the progressive keeps its "usual aspectual implications – and without any discernible 'change of meaning' " (Jørgensen 1991: 181).
- In other cases, the not-solely-aspectual function of conveying an impressive or dynamic effect is more prominent. This function may cut across Aktionsart distinctions "so that even verbs which, with their specific semantic value, would not be expected to occur in the progressive, may occasionally do so all the same" (Jørgensen 1991: 181).

In CONCE, apart from FEEL, which was discussed above, 38 different verbs occur in 'stative' situations. The commonest verbs are SUFFER (23 occurrences), EXPECT (21), FEEL (11), and LOOK (10).[21] 'Stative' situations with the above as main verbs typically express what Quirk et al. (1985: 202) refer to as " 'private' states which can only be subjectively verified: *ie* states of mind, volition, attitude, etc.". Quirk et al. (1985: 203) also state that some verbs denoting private states, including WANT, can occur in the progressive "when temporariness or

---

20   This function is essentially that of temporariness, which Quirk et al. (1985: 198) claim the progressive often expresses when it co-occurs with states and habits. Joos (1964: 108) takes temporary validity to be the basic meaning of the progressive regardless of the Aktionsart category to which an instance of the construction may belong: in his account, the progressive signals that the probability of the validity of the predication "diminishes smoothly from a maximum of perfect validity, both ways into the past and the future towards perfect irrelevance or falsity".

21   Many verbs may be part of both 'stative' and non-'stative' situations. For instance, LOOK can also be part of an 'active' situation, as in *I am looking at the painting*.

tentativeness is being emphasized", and that LOOK, in the sense 'have the appearance or give the impression of being' (*COD*, p. 839), even occurs commonly in the progressive (Quirk et al. 1985: 204n.). It is possible that the functions of temporariness and tentativeness can be related to the aspectual functions of ongoing action and incompletion which the progressive expresses in many non-'stative' situations.

However, there are also 'stative' situations in CONCE where progressives with shades of meaning other than temporariness or tentativeness can be discerned. For instance, as will be discussed in Section 7.1, in conjunction with adverbials such as *always*, the progressive gives a more general emotional colouring to the sentence than the non-progressive, as in (69):

(69)   "A study in extremes," said Bertha. "Their dinner was our luncheon – the
       very plainest boiled beef, the liquor given away; and at dinner, at the
       Bannermans', there were more fine things than Bevil said he could
       appreciate, and Augusta looking like a full-blown dahlia. I *was* always
       wanting to stick pins into her arms, to see how far in the bones are. I am
       sure I could bury the heads."
       (Fiction, Yonge, 1850–1870, p. II.61)

In (69), *always* appears to cancel out any connotations of temporariness or tentativeness the progressive might otherwise have had. In other instances, for instance (70), the progressive has an emotional effect in conjunction with other contextual elements that carry subjective and/or emotional connotations (*with my love*, *gratefully*, and *her sisterly kindness*).[22]

(70)   Please tell Lucy with my love how gratefully I *am feeling* her sisterly
       kindness.
       (Letters, Rossetti, 1870–1900, p. 141)

Progressives in 'stative' situations that are not private, in Quirk et al.'s (1985) sense of being only subjectively verifiable, can also be found in CONCE, though they are rarer than progressives in private 'stative' situations. Apart from progressives of BE and HAVE discussed in Section 6.1.2, 'stative' situations with progressives of the verbs LACK, SEPARATE, and TEND all occur once in CONCE. TEND occurs in (71):

---

22   It has been argued that, in these cases, the contextual elements themselves, rather than the
     progressive, express emotion and subjectivity (see e.g. Visser 1973: 1922). However, as
     Bybee et al. (1994: 25) point out, if a linguistic construction occurs frequently in contexts
     that express a certain inference, the construction may become associated with the expression
     of that inference. (See Chapter 7 for further discussion of this issue.)

(71)   The removal, the bustle, the talking things over with Miss Wells, and the sight of the children did much to restore her, and her old friend rejoiced to see that necessary occupation *was tending* to make her time pass more cheerfully than she perhaps knew.
(Fiction, Yonge, 1850–1870, p. I.91)

The progressive in (71) can perhaps be given an aspectual interpretation, or at least an interpretation that can be seen as derived from the aspectual functions of the progressive: the non-progressive might have implied a general truth in this context, whereas the progressive confines the validity of the situation to a specific occasion and emphasizes the ongoing change (see Rydén 1997 on the "situational immediacy" implied by many instances of the progressive). However, it is also possible that the progressive implies greater tentativeness compared with the non-progressive. The progressives in (72) and (73), in contrast, appear to have not-solely-aspectual functions:

(72)   And then – but it was not soon that she learnt to bear that, though she had gone through the like before, she had to read the household devotions, where every petition seemed *to be lacking* the manly tone to give it fulness and force.
(Fiction, Yonge, 1850–1870, p. I.99)

(73)   [$Q. (By MR. JUSTICE PARK.)$] *Is* this hedge *separating* the garden of Mr. Tuckett, from the road?
(Trials, Bowditch, 1800–1830, p. 94)

The progressive in (72) co-occurs with other expressions with subjective or emotional connotations (*every petition, manly tone,* and *fulness and force*). Moreover, it is possible that the presence of the verb SEEM makes this situation semi-private in emphasizing the subjective nature of an individual character's impression of the situation (see also Section 5.1). In (73), the reasons for the not-solely-aspectual connotations of the progressive are chiefly extralinguistic: the example occurs during an examination of a witness, William Warren, regarding a meeting of James Bowditch and Maria Glenn on either side of the hedge mentioned in (73).[23] James Bowditch (together with nine other suspects) is on trial for conspiracy, assault, and false imprisonment of Maria Glenn, so the encounter by the hedge is of some importance for the trial. In this context, it is also relevant that the question in (73) comes from a judge, who interrupts the

---

23   Given the syntactic make-up of (73), it is also possible that a definite article has been omitted (*Is this the hedge separating...*), which would make *separating* part of a postmodifier of *hedge* rather than of a progressive. However, there is no textual evidence of such an omission.

examination of William Warren by Mr. Serjeant Pell, presumably because he thinks his question is of special importance.[24]

The occurrence of the progressive in 'stative' situations in CONCE has interesting potential implications for the integration of the construction into late Modern English grammar. Progressives in 'stative' situations seem to fulfil one of two main functions: either they express a shade of temporariness or tentativeness, which may be related to the aspectual functions of the construction, or they denote not-solely-aspectual subjectivity in the form of emphasis, intensity, or vividness. These groups of functions may also combine in individual instances. As pointed out above, from a strictly aspectual viewpoint, progressives in 'stative' situations can be seen as redundant. However, such redundant occurrences may be indications of the increased integration of the progressive. Bybee et al. (1994: 125ff.) postulate a diachronic line of development where grammatical morphemes that start by expressing progressive meanings evolve towards the expression of imperfective or present meaning.[25] They define the English progressive as a progressive rather than an imperfective morpheme, the latter being a wider term that also subsumes habitual uses. Progressive morphemes present actions as ongoing at reference time, and typically occur in non-'stative' situations. However, following Comrie (1976), Bybee et al. also postulate an intermediate category consisting of continuous morphemes; a continuous morpheme is "more general than progressive because it can be used in progressive situations but in addition with stative predicates" (Bybee et al. 1994: 127). Continuous morphemes thus indicate that the situation, which may be dynamic or stative, is in progress at the point of temporal reference. In this light, the fact that the progressive appears to occur relatively frequently in 'stative' situations in late Modern English may be a sign of increasing integration of its aspectual functions into the language.[26] Bybee et al. (1994: 139) claim that continuous morphemes were not attested in their cross-linguistic investigation, but it seems that the English progressive may be a possible candidate.[27] Such

---

24   Mr. Justice Park also intervenes in a previous part of the interrogation of William Warren, to clarify the age of the Warrens' oldest child. William Warren had apparently been drinking before he was examined, which may have cast some doubt on his reliability as a witness.

25   Bybee et al. (1994: 2) describe grammatical morphemes as "closed-class elements whose class membership is determined by some unique grammatical behavior, such as position of occurrence, co-occurrence restrictions, or other distinctive interactions with other linguistic elements"; from a formal perspective, "grammatical morphemes may be affixes, stem changes, reduplication, auxiliaries, particles, or complex constructions such as English *be going to*".

26   However, other factors also enter into the results. Since the progressive occurred in 'stative' situations quite freely in Old English, the tendency for the construction to do so in late Modern English as well may be a result of tendencies specific to the history of the English language.

27   In an account based on Functional Grammar, Goossens (1994: 175) argues that the Present-Day English progressive is a restricted imperfective rather than a progressive marker, since it has applications outside the scope of pure progressive meaning. Goossens admits, however,

possible developments make it interesting to see whether any diachronic tendencies are discernible in the data yielded by CONCE. The next section is therefore devoted to an analysis that considers the parameter of time.

6.2.3   A diachronic account

By including the parameter of time in the discussion of how the progressive is distributed across situation types, I will be able to show whether any clear developments are discernible across the 19th century. The results of this analysis are given in Table 56a–b.

Table 56a. The progressives in CONCE across the parameters of time and situation type (row percentages within brackets); 'future' situations included as a separate category

Period	Stative	Stance	Active	Process.	Moment.	Transit.	Future	Total
1	25	37	271	175	1	12	45	566
	(4%)	(7%)	(48%)	(31%)	(0%)	(2%)	(8%)	
2	52	36	398	245	17	30	66	844
	(6%)	(4%)	(47%)	(29%)	(2%)	(4%)	(8%)	
3	58	66	415	267	15	27	35	883
	(7%)	(7%)	(47%)	(30%)	(2%)	(3%)	(4%)	
Total	135	139	1,084	687	33	69	146	2,293
	(6%)	(6%)	(47%)	(30%)	(1%)	(3%)	(6%)	

Table 56b. The progressives in CONCE across the parameters of time and situation type (row percentages within brackets); 'future' situations reclassified

Period	Stative	Stance	Active	Process.	Moment.	Transit.	Total
1	25	37	274	219	1	16	572
	(4%)	(6%)	(48%)	(38%)	(0%)	(3%)	
2	52	36	399	321	17	35	860
	(6%)	(4%)	(46%)	(37%)	(2%)	(4%)	
3	58	66	418	306	15	29	892
	(7%)	(7%)	(47%)	(34%)	(2%)	(3%)	
Total	135	139	1,091	846	33	80	2,324
	(6%)	(6%)	(47%)	(36%)	(1%)	(3%)	

The situation types that display clear signs of change in Table 56 are 'stative' situations, 'stance' situations, 'processive' situations (in Table 56b), and 'future' situations (in Table 56a). 'Stative' and 'stance' situations are lexically specified

---

that the construction can also be viewed as an extended progressive marker; the latter view seems to fit the data provided by this study.

to a greater extent than the other types, and thus more dependent on what verbs occur in progressive verb phrases; 'future' situations stand apart from the other situation types in not being based chiefly on Aktionsart criteria. The decrease in the percentage of 'processive' situations in Table 56b can probably be attributed to the inclusion of many of the progressives that are classified as occurring in 'future' situations in Table 56a. Moreover, 'stance' situations exhibit no consistent trend in diachrony: the percentage of 'stance' situations decreases between periods 1 and 2, only to increase again between periods 2 and 3.

  The classification of progressives into situation types and the distribution of these situation types in Table 56 pose a problem as regards testing the variation for statistical significance. As mentioned above, 'future' situations are not wholly comparable with the other categories, in that criteria related to tense rather than Aktionsart enter into the definition of this situation type. To solve this problem, I first tested the variation between 'future' situations and all other Aktionsart categories in Table 56a for significance. 'Future' situations were then eliminated from the counts, and a new test was performed on the remaining data in Table 56a. Finally, a test was carried out on Table 56b in its totality.

  All three tests showed that the distribution was statistically significant. The results thus indicate that the percentage of all progressives that refer to the future without the aid of modal auxiliaries decreased significantly over the period 1800–1900. This is interesting, as results presented in Section 5.4 indicated that, although the raw frequencies were quite low, the frequency of progressive verb phrases with WILL also decreased across this period (the results for SHALL were inconclusive). In addition, while Smith (2003) has shown that modal auxiliaries in progressive verb phrases are on the increase in late 20th-century British English, his analysis implies that the frequency of progressives which refer to the future without the aid of modal auxiliaries may have continued to decline during the 1900s.

  As future time can be expressed by a large number of constructions in English (see e.g. Berglund 1997), the results may indicate that the relative distribution of these constructions changed in late Modern English. However, data where the frequencies of the different expressions of futurity available are compared with one another would be needed to reach definite conclusions in this respect. The different meanings usually associated with these expressions, e.g. intention or prediction (Palmer 1988: 66) and subjectivity (Charleston 1955: 272) in the case of the progressive, would also have to be considered in the analysis. Finally, possible restrictions on the use of the expressions of futurity would have to be taken into account. As Aarts (1969) points out, the range of verbs that can be used with future reference in the present progressive has sometimes been underestimated; but the main verbs that occur in these constructions still tend to be verbs which also occur in non-'stative' rather than 'stative' situations, and main verbs that "indicate or imply motion" are especially frequent (Palmer 1988: 64). In the CONCE data, COME and GO together account for 134 (92%) of the 146 progressives in 'future' situations (there are 97 occurrences of GO and 37 of

COME).[28] As was shown in Section 6.1.1, progressive verb phrases with GO as main verb accounted for a lower percentage of all progressives in period 3 than in the other periods; this is also when the percentage of progressives in 'future' situations decreases. Given that GO is by far the commonest main verb in progressives that occur in 'future' situations, these two developments may be connected.

As regards the variation among non-'future' situations in Table 56a–b, the significance of this distribution is more difficult to interpret. The decrease in 'processive' situations in Table 56b is chiefly due to 'future' situations in Table 56a being reclassified as 'processive'. Otherwise, the only clear trend in the data is the increase in 'stative' situations. It may be that this variation is caused by changes in the overall distribution of situation types in the material; since such changes were not taken into account when the results were tested for statistical significance, a significant result need not reflect a change in the distribution of the progressive. However, the development of 'stative' and, perhaps, 'momentary' and 'transitional' situations can also be interpreted as indicative of increasing integration of the progressive across the 19th century as a whole. In all of these situation types, the percentage of progressives increases between periods 1 and 2; although the percentage of 'transitional' situations decreases between periods 2 and 3, the overall picture is still one of increase in diachrony (in Table 56a) or diachronic stability (in Table 56b). (However, the raw frequency of 'momentary' situations is very low.)

'Stative', 'momentary', and 'transitional' situations all lack one feature that is often associated with situations in which aspectual progressives occur, viz. [–stative] and [+durative] respectively. Progressives often have semi-aspectual implications of temporariness in 'stative' situations (see Quirk et al. 1985: 198); aspectual progressives in 'momentary' and 'transitional' situations typically denote repeated action and a period leading up to a change of state, respectively. The necessity of such semantic modifications may have constrained the occurrence of progressives in these situations. The tendency towards an increase in their occurrence in the CONCE data may thus indicate integration of the progressive across the parameter of situation type. Bache (1997: 124) suggests that the progressive/non-progressive distinction is being generalized to cover 'stative' situations as well in Present-Day English: it may be that the development attested in CONCE represents a previous stage in this diachronic process.

The findings presented in this section support the hypothesis (formulated in Section 6.2.2) that the occurrence of progressives in 'stative' situations, with functions related to the aspectual functions of the construction, may indicate that the progressive became more fully integrated in 19th-century English. Moreover, if the progressive became more accepted in 'stative', 'momentary', and 'transitional' situations during the 1800s, it would be a sign that the progressive was growing less marked in relation to the non-progressive. In diachrony, it is

---

28   The other verbs are WRITE (3 occurrences), SEND (2), STAY (2), CALL (1), LEAVE (1), PASS (1), RETURN (1), and TAKE (1).

possible that progressives in 'stative' situations have developed – and will develop – semantic connotations related to or derived from the aspectual functions of the construction in non-'stative' situations. Such developments may lie behind the frequent association of progressives in 'stative' situations with temporariness, and may lead to more clear-cut progressive/non-progressive oppositions developing in 'stative' situations. Finally, an increasing potential of progressive verb phrases in 'stative', 'momentary', and 'transitional' situations would also be relevant to the integration of the not-solely-aspectual functions of the construction, since an expanded paradigm that includes all situation types would mean a higher degree of applicability in the language overall. However, as mentioned above, the raw frequencies of progressives in 'momentary' situations are low, and neither 'momentary' nor 'transitional' situations exhibit a consistent diachronic trend.

6.2.4   Variation with genre

Cross-genre investigations often complement diachronic analyses: variation across the genre parameter is then seen as a cross-section of ongoing change, with more advanced genres leading the trend and conservative genres lagging behind. The distribution of situation types across the genres in CONCE can thus be expected to yield some interesting results. The results are given in Table 57a–b.

Table 57a. The progressives in CONCE across the parameters of genre and situation type (row percentages within brackets); 'future' situations included as a separate category

Genre	Stative	Stance	Active	Process.	Moment.	Transit.	Future	Total
Debates	–	3	29	15	–	–	–	47
		(6%)	(62%)	(32%)				
Drama	14	4	111	91	–	12	22	254
	(6%)	(2%)	(44%)	(36%)		(5%)	(9%)	
Fiction	18	16	128	92	3	6	12	275
	(7%)	(6%)	(47%)	(33%)	(1%)	(2%)	(4%)	
History	2	4	62	32	–	6	–	106
	(2%)	(4%)	(58%)	(30%)		(6%)		
Letters	83	29	459	283	13	35	90	992
	(8%)	(3%)	(46%)	(29%)	(1%)	(4%)	(9%)	
Science	1	3	44	29	2	3	–	82
	(1%)	(4%)	(54%)	(35%)	(2%)	(4%)		
Trials	17	80	251	145	15	7	22	537
	(3%)	(15%)	(47%)	(27%)	(3%)	(1%)	(4%)	
Total	135	139	1,084	687	33	69	146	2,293
	(6%)	(6%)	(47%)	(30%)	(1%)	(3%)	(6%)	

Table 57b. The progressives in CONCE across the parameters of genre and situation type (row percentages within brackets); 'future' situations reclassified

Genre	Stative	Stance	Active	Process.	Moment.	Transit.	Total
Debates	–	3	29	15	–	–	47
		(6%)	(62%)	(32%)			
Drama	14	4	113	109	–	14	254
	(6%)	(2%)	(44%)	(43%)		(6%)	
Fiction	18	16	129	105	3	6	277
	(6%)	(6%)	(47%)	(38%)	(1%)	(2%)	
History	2	4	62	32	–	6	106
	(2%)	(4%)	(58%)	(30%)		(6%)	
Letters	83	29	462	389	13	38	1,014
	(8%)	(3%)	(46%)	(38%)	(1%)	(4%)	
Science	1	3	44	29	2	3	82
	(1%)	(4%)	(54%)	(35%)	(2%)	(4%)	
Trials	17	80	252	167	15	13	544
	(3%)	(15%)	(46%)	(31%)	(3%)	(2%)	
Total	135	139	1,091	846	33	80	2,324
	(6%)	(6%)	(47%)	(36%)	(1%)	(3%)	

The dominance of progressives occurring in 'active' situations stands out clearly from Table 57: 'active' situations account for the highest number of percentage points in every genre in CONCE. The results presented in Table 57a imply that the distribution of the progressive across the parameter of situation type is an indicator of how fully integrated the construction is in a particular genre. In the three expository genres, History, Science, and Debates, there are no progressives in 'future' situations; in these genres, the overall frequency of the progressive was also low compared with the four non-expository genres. To some extent, however, the absence of progressives in 'future' situations from the expository genres in CONCE can be attributed to the low frequency of the construction in these genres: if there are comparatively few progressives occurring in a given sample, the absence of a situation type which accounts for a mere 6% of all progressives in the material may be an accident of the sampling. (Similarly, the absence of progressives in 'momentary' situations in Debates, Drama, and History, and of progressives in 'transitional' and 'stative' situations in Debates, need not be indicative of the construction being less integrated in these genres.) Moreover, the texts in History, which deal predominantly with past events, and those in Science, which often focus on natural laws that apply regardless of time reference, may make the need for progressives with future reference less felt in these genres. Nevertheless, the consistency of the results points to progressives in 'future' situations being characteristic of genres where the progressive is integrated to a high degree overall, despite the trend for progressives in 'future' situations to account for a lower percentage of all progressives in diachrony (see Section 6.2.3).

The four non-expository genres, Drama, Fiction, Letters, and Trials, share the trait that genre-characteristic constraints on subject matter may make the progressive particularly frequent in one or several situation types other than 'active' situations.[29] In Drama, 'processive' situations account for 36% of all progressives, as against 30% in the whole corpus; with 'future' situations reclassified, the percentage of progressives in 'processive' situations is 43 in this genre, compared with 36 in the entire corpus. Apart from progressives in 'future' situations (for which see below), this difference is largely due to the prevalence in Drama of progressive verb phrases with a limited number of main verbs indicating goal-oriented movement or change (see also Section 6.1.1), as in (74):

(74)   [$THE DEAN.$]
       Respect yourself, Georgiana – where *are* you *going*?
       (Drama, Pinero, 1870–1900, p. 63)

The percentage of progressives with future reference is high in both Drama and Letters (see Table 57a). Go and COME are the two most common verbs that have such future reference; an example is (75) with GO:

(75)   [$Lamb.$] … I'*m a goin'* into trainin' next week to fight Australian Harry, the Boundin' Kangaroo. I shall lick him, sir. I know I shall.
       (Drama, Robertson, 1850–1870, p. 17)

In Fiction and Letters (and to some extent in Drama), we find a comparatively high percentage of progressives in 'stative' situations. This distribution is often due to the privileged access the writer of the novel or letter has to the minds of the subjects of the verb phrases. In Letters, the writer and the subject are often the same person; in Fiction, an omniscient writer can present the mental processes of all characters, as in (56), also cited in Section 6.2.1:

(56)   This very Tuesday, the delay in forwarding the last number had been particularly aggravating; just when both Miss Pole and Miss Matty, the former more especially, *had been wanting* to see it, in order to coach up the court-news, ready for the evening's interview with aristocracy.
       (Fiction, Gaskell, 1850–1870, p. 150)

In Trials, finally, 'stance' situations account for 15% of all progressives, compared with 6% in the overall figures. There is a good deal of variation among the trials as to which verb accounts for most of the occurrences, depending on

---

29   Given the low frequencies of progressives in 'momentary' and 'transitional' situations, I will not include them in the discussion of genre-specific constraints.

what temporary situation is most important for each trial, but the commonest verb overall is LIVE referring to a temporary residence or lifestyle. Consider (76):

(76)   [$Q.$] During the time they *were living* there did you know a Mr. Dyson?
       – [$A.$] I saw him on two or three occasions.
       (Trials, Bartlett, 1870–1900, p. 43)

The overall effect of these genre-specific patterns is that, in the non-expository genres, a smaller proportion of the progressives occur in 'active' situations. Whereas all non-expository genres have percentages below 50, in the three expository genres 'active' situations account for >50% of the progressives. This distribution may also be related to the integration of the progressive. In many ways, 'active' situations constitute the most straightforward territory of occurrence for the aspectual functions of the progressive: the construction simply expresses ongoing action, without extra shades of meaning such as temporariness, repeated activity, or incompletion.[30] The results thus imply that a comparatively low percentage of 'active' situations in the distribution of progressives within a genre may be a sign that the construction is integrated to a high degree in this genre. In other words, the data yielded by CONCE concerning the frequency of the progressive (see Chapter 3) and the distribution of the construction across situation types point in the same direction: both sets of data indicate that the progressive is more fully integrated in non-expository than in expository genres.

However, against this background we might expect the percentage of all progressives that occur in 'active' situations to decrease over the century: the increase in the frequency of the construction should be paralleled by a more even distribution of progressives across situation types, if both of these are signs of integration. But as was shown in Section 6.2.3, the percentage of progressives in 'active' situations remained relatively stable in diachrony in the corpus as a whole. It may thus be that, despite the cross-genre differences which appear when the 19th century is considered as a synchronic whole, the increase in the frequency of the progressive in 19th-century English took place mainly in situations that were comparatively uncomplicated from an Aktionsart perspective, i.e. chiefly in 'active' situations. This would tie in with the distribution of the progressive across the combinativity patterns of the English verb phrase: as was demonstrated in Section 5.5, the increase in the frequency of the 19th-century progressive did not lead to an increased proportion of occurrence in formally complicated areas. As shown in Section 6.1.1, nor did the increase in frequency lead to higher type/token ratios as regards what main verbs occurred in progressive verb phrases.

---

30   Note, however, that the contrast between the progressive and the non-progressive varies with tense. In the past, the contrast is one between a perfective and an imperfective view of the situation. In the present, both the progressive and the non-progressive have imperfective functions: but whereas the progressive is a continuous or progressive marker, the non-progressive usually refers to a situation which is habitually or necessarily true.

A complex pattern thus emerges when the frequency of the progressive in CONCE is compared with the distribution of the construction across the parameters of verb phrase complexity, main-verb diversity, and situation type. In the next section, I will show that it may also be possible to establish a link between, on the one hand, the agentivity of the subjects of progressive verb phrases and, on the other hand, the emergence of the passive progressive (see Section 5.3).

6.3   Agentivity of subject

The present section will be devoted to the distribution of the progressive across the parameter of agentive and non-agentive subjects. This area may be relevant to the integration of the progressive into late Modern English, as regards both the distribution of the functions of the construction and the formal make-up of the progressive paradigm. According to some theories, the progressive occurred chiefly with animate/agentive subjects until the late Modern English period, during which the construction became increasingly acceptable with inanimate/non-agentive subjects as well (see e.g. Denison 1998: 149). This development has been claimed to have important consequences for the development of the passive progressive and the decrease of the passival progressive (see Section 5.3); as we shall see, there is some support for such claims in the data afforded by CONCE. As regards the functions of the progressive, Wårvik (1990b: 533) lists non-agentive subjects as one criterion for backgrounding in narrative texts. Thus, an increased occurrence potential with non-agentive subjects would have made the progressive a more generally available background marker, a function closely associated with the aspectual functions of the construction.

In the present section, I will first discuss the notion of agentivity and state how it will be applied to the data. Then follows a brief survey of previous research on the connection between agentivity and the progressive, followed by a presentation and discussion of my analysis.

6.3.1   The agentive/non-agentive distinction

As Quirk et al. (1985: 207) point out, the difference between agentive and non-agentive situations is not entirely clear. However, they take the distinction to apply chiefly to non-'stative' situations (see Section 6.2.1), which also seems to be the approach taken by Vendler (1967). Volition is recognized by some scholars as a key concept in the definition of agentivity: Quirk et al. (1985: 207), for instance, define an agentive situation as one which "implies that the subject refers to an agent or 'doer' of the action. The 'doer' is typically human, and is the deliberate or self-activating initiator of the action". Consequently, I excluded 'stative' and 'stance' situations from the classification. In order to minimize the number of instances resisting classification, the analysis was based on the classification framework where 'future' situations were not recognized as a separate category. The 2,050 progressives that had been assigned a situation type other than 'stative' or 'stance' in Table 55b were thus classified according to whether or not the subject of the verb phrase was agentive.

As indicated by the quote from Quirk et al. (1985) above, agentivity is a concept which includes several notions. Scholars often emphasize different aspects of similar and/or overlapping notions: in the quote, volition, control, cause, and animacy (or sentience) appear to be highlighted. Other notions suggested as important in previous research include movement and change (Dowty 1991: 572f.; Schlesinger 1995: 30ff.).[31] As pointed out above, Aktionsart also enters into the classification, since the concept of agentivity is often considered not to apply to 'stative' situations. In Ziegeler's (1999: 65ff.) account, however, a closer relationship between agentivity and Aktionsart is postulated, in which (in Vendler's terms) accomplishments and achievements are, in general, more likely to be agentive than activities. But following Brinton (1988: 32), who argues for a separation of Aktionsart and agentivity, I have classified these two parameters separately in the present study, and treated all [–stative] situations as potentially but not necessarily agentive in the classification procedure.

Accounting in detail for the parameter of agentivity in relation to the occurrence of the progressive would mean that the parameter would have to be realized as a continuum rather than a discrete category; moreover, the notions mentioned in the previous paragraph would have to be compared and ordered on a scale of relative importance. Such complex considerations lay beyond the scope of the present study. Instead, I focused on the feature of control, which was highlighted in Schlesinger (1995) as being of importance. A subject which is considered to have control over the situation can direct it "and may be able to terminate or obviate it" (Schlesinger 1995: 33). Schlesinger (1995: 33ff.) also lists situations where the potential agent causes the action but does not control it (as in *The Gulf War strained the economy*), or where there is change but no control (as in *John grew up*); in the present study, these features were not taken into account, as control was judged to be more prototypical of agentive situations. It should be noted that the notion of control, and thus agentivity, does not, as such, exclude inanimate subjects. Inanimate subjects can still be considered to have control over a situation, primarily because they are presented as personified, as in (77):

(77)   [$Julia.$] "Come, come, you must talk to me – The day is inviting – the air invigorates the spirits, gives wings to the fancy – the jocund spring *is chaunting* her matin song, while she gaily weaves a chaplet for her mother nature; and rosy health, encircled by her band of wanton zephyrs, beckons you to the upland lawn, anxious to join you in her happy train. – Dare you refuse, when 'tis heaven's breath invites? – Come, come. –"
(Drama, Morton, 1800–1830, p. 46)

---

31   In Section 6.3, I use terms taken chiefly from Dowty (1991) and Schlesinger (1995).

In (77), "the jocund spring" is personified, as indicated by the use of a verb and a direct object (CHAUNT *her matin song*) which would normally occur with human or animal subjects, and by the use of determiners and pronouns (*her*, *she* rather than *its*, *it*). A situation which would normally be non-agentive is by means of these features presented as agentive, and was therefore also classified as such. Conversely, an animate subject may be classified as non-agentive, if the feature of control is not present, as in (78):

(78)   I have not been so well; I feel as if I *were* all *falling* to pieces – as if my body had no substance to oppose to the 'wear and tear' of life.
(Letters, Jewsbury, 1850–1870, p. 353)

In (78), the subject is human, but the situation was still not classified as agentive, since the subject does not appear to have control over the situation.[32] In general, however, agentive subjects are more likely to be animate than inanimate.

6.3.2   Agentivity and the progressive in previous research

In this section, I will discuss three studies which comment on possible connections between the development of the progressive and the occurrence of the construction with agentive and non-agentive subjects. Strang (1982: 443ff.) found that progressive verb phrases with inanimate subjects, which are often found in non-agentive situations, became increasingly common in narrative prose from the 18th to the 20th centuries. Denison (1998: 149f.) hypothesizes that an increase in the occurrence of the progressive with non-human subjects after 1800 may have made the passival progressive (see Section 5.3) and the active progressive more ambiguous, which may have paved the way for the establishment and diffusion of the new passive progressive. Ziegeler (1999: 57) argues that agentivity has become more, rather than less, characteristic of the progressive in diachrony.

Strang (1982) investigates the development of the progressive in narrative prose from the 18th century onwards, and devotes a section to the animacy of the subject of progressive verb phrases. Strang's (1982: 443ff.) analysis indicates that the progressive was rare with non-human subjects before 1800. Strang presents figures for samples from individual prose works; I have reworked her figures to obtain conflated results for the 18th, 19th, and 20th centuries.[33] The diachronic distribution is given in Table 58.

---

32   Strictly, it is impossible to have control over a hypothetical situation such as that in (78). However, for the purposes of the present study, hypothetical and fictional situations were classified for agentivity on the same basis as real-world situations: that is, *as if I were falling to pieces* and *I was falling to pieces* would have the same agentivity value.

33   The abbreviation "Q. M." in Strang's (1982) list of novels sampled for subject type does not correspond to any novel in the list of primary material, but is probably *Old Mortality* by

Table 58.   The diachronic distribution of human, quasi-human/animal, and inanimate subjects in Strang's (1982) analysis (row percentages within brackets)

Century	Human	Quasi-human/animal	Inanimate	Total
18th	256 (96%)	8 (3%)	2 (1%)	266
19th	1,280 (89%)	28 (2%)	132 (9%)	1,440
20th	607 (90%)	15 (2%)	52 (8%)	674

As Table 58 shows, there are substantial differences between the 18th and 19th centuries, whereas the distribution is comparatively stable from the 19th century on. The overall figures indicate that 1% of all progressives had inanimate subjects in the 18th century, 9% in the 19th, and 8% in the 20th.

Ziegeler (1999) postulates a development where the progressive paradigm has gradually been extended to include accomplishments and achievements. This, Ziegeler claims, involves a rise in agentivity, as "[p]rototypical agentivity ... involves a change of state of an affected object" (1999: 95). (In this sense, Ziegeler's concept of agentivity is not identical with that adopted for the present study.) Ziegeler (1999: 88ff.) also links the development of the passival progressive (for which see Section 5.3) to the co-occurrence of the progressive with accomplishments. She argues that the appearance and disappearance of the passival progressive "may be an indication of a conflict between the meanings of imperfective grammatical aspect and the perfective lexical aspectual meanings of the verbs with which [the passival progressive] co-occurred", and that passival progressives may be "an intermediate stage in the spread of the construction to Accomplishment verbs" (Ziegeler 1999: 95). The development of the passive progressive, in contrast, is seen as a likely "indication that the increasing agentivity associated with the subject began to disallow inanimates with active verbs" (Ziegeler 1999: 95f.). As regards Strang's (1982: 443ff.) results, which point to an increased use of the progressive with inanimate subjects in late Modern English, Ziegeler (1999: 96) hypothesizes that, by this time, the progressive had become agentive and lost most constraints as regards type of subject.[34]

Walter Scott (Nimmo, London, and Edinburgh: Waverley Novels, 1876), originally published in 1816. *Old Mortality* is abbreviated "O. M." in the list of primary material, and would otherwise be absent in her subject-type analysis. The figures for the novel entitled "Q. M." have thus been included in the 19th-century figures in Table 58.

34   Ziegeler (1999: 90), referring to Scheffer (1975), claims that the passival progressive was acceptable "until the eighteenth century". However, Scheffer (1975: 261) refers to the 1700s as the "heyday" of the passival progressive, and the results based on CONCE and Arnaud's corpus (reported on in Section 5.3) rather indicate that the passive progressive did not pass the passival variant in frequency until the mid-19th century. Hundt (2004b: 104), however, presents results which indicate that the frequency of the passive progressive began to decrease even in the latter half of the 18th century.

Denison (1998: 150) claims that one possible reason why the passival progressive fell out of use was the increasing risk of ambiguity between an active and a passival reading. The chief reason for this increase was that active progressives co-occurred more frequently with non-human (and, by extension, usually non-agentive) subjects in 19th-century English compared with the language of the 1700s. Before 1800, active progressives would have occurred chiefly with human and passival progressives with non-human subjects; but when both active and passival progressives could occur with non-human subjects, this distinction was no longer enough to tell the two formally identical patterns apart. As the data yielded by CONCE have been classified for both voice and agentivity, it is possible to see if there are any connections between the two parameters.

6.3.3 The progressive and agentivity: Evidence from the CONCE corpus

As pointed out in Section 6.3.1, 2,050 [–stative] progressives in CONCE were classified according to whether they had agentive or non-agentive subjects; the most important criterion for agentivity was that the subject should be presented as having control over the situation. Table 59 provides data on the number of progressives with non-agentive subjects in period, genre, and period/genre subsamples.

Table 59. Progressives with non-agentive subjects in CONCE by period and genre (progressives occurring in 'stative' and 'stance' situations excluded from the counts; percentages of all progressives occurring in 'active', 'processive', 'momentary', and 'transitional' situations in each subsample within brackets)

Period	Debates	Drama	Fiction	History	Letters	Science	Trials	Total
1	1	4	6	1	29	10	7	58
	(12%)	(12%)	(8%)	(10%)	(14%)	(45%)	(5%)	(11%)
2	1	6	12	9	34	13	10	85
	(11%)	(6%)	(11%)	(25%)	(9%)	(57%)	(8%)	(11%)
3	6	4	4	11	36	21	9	91
	(22%)	(4%)	(7%)	(20%)	(11%)	(64%)	(5%)	(12%)
Total	8	14	22	21	99	44	26	234
	(18%)	(6%)	(9%)	(21%)	(11%)	(56%)	(6%)	(11%)

The overall figures display no change in diachrony: the proportion of the relevant progressives that have non-agentive subjects is thus constant across the 19th century. The only genres that exhibit a consistent diachronic trend are Drama, with decreasing percentages, and Science, where the percentage increases. However, the raw frequencies for some period/genre subsamples are low in Debates, Drama, Fiction, and History, and developments within these genres, as implied by the figures in Table 59, should therefore be treated with caution.

It does not seem that the distribution of agentive and non-agentive subjects in progressive verb phrases is directly linked to the integration of the construction in 19th-century English. It may be that the decisive developments in the agentive vs. non-agentive distribution took place before or around 1800. This hypothesis is partly supported by Strang's (1982) analysis of whether the subject of progressive verb phrases tends to be animate or not: as pointed out in Section 6.3.2, Strang's results indicate that the proportion of all progressives that had non-human subjects increased between the 18th and 19th centuries, but not between the 19th and the 20th.

However, there are differences between Strang's (1982) classification and that of the present study which complicate the picture. First, Strang looked at whether subjects were human, quasi-human/animals, or inanimate; although a great deal of correspondence between the parameters of animacy and agency can be expected, the two parameters cannot be equated. However, Hundt (2004a: 61) found that this difference was of lesser importance in her study of the use of the progressive in the ARCHER corpus. Secondly, Strang included all situation types in her study, but excluded passives and "idiomatic uses", such as BE *going to* + infinitive constructions (Strang 1982: 443), whereas I excluded progressives occurring in 'stative' and 'stance' situations, but included passival and passive instances.

These differences notwithstanding, a comparison of Strang's data and mine suggests that the major expansion of the progressive to inanimate and/or non-agentive subjects took place during the 18th century. Since Strang (1982) based her investigation on extended narrative prose, comparing her results with those for Fiction in CONCE may point to further similarities. In Strang's corpus, 9% of all progressives in 19th-century texts had inanimate subjects; the Fiction genre in CONCE yields the same percentage of progressives with non-agentive subjects. In addition, Hundt (2004a: 60) presents results that support the hypothesis that most of the change towards more non-agentive subjects took place before 1800. Hundt (2004a: 66) suggests that the spread of the progressive to non-agentive subjects was one of the reasons for the subsequent increase in the frequency of the construction. Hundt's results also indicate that the percentage of progressives with non-agentive subjects is higher than that found in the present study. However, this discrepancy may be due to differences in classification and genre make-up. As mentioned above, only [–stative] progressives were included in my counts. Moreover, ARCHER focuses on speech-related texts to a lesser extent than does CONCE, and as is made clear below, speech-related texts are likely to be characterized by a comparatively low percentage of progressives with non-agentive subjects (see also Hundt 2004a: 62f. for a similar result regarding progressives with inanimate subjects).

Table 59 reveals some interesting cross-genre differences that may have implications for the development of the passival and passive progressives. The genres where the percentage of progressives with non-agentive subjects is above or around the overall mean – Science, History, Debates, and Letters – are also genres characterized by early and/or comparatively frequent occurrences of passive progressives. The three expository genres in particular provide good matches: of the relevant progressives in Science, 56% have non-agentive subjects and 11% are passive; in History, 21% have non-agentive subjects and 3% are passive; and in Debates, 18% have non-agentive subjects and 8% are passive. (See Table 43 in Section 5.3 for cross-genre data concerning passive progressives.) Letters and Fiction form a middle ground: in Letters, 11% of the relevant progressives have non-agentive subjects and 1% are passive; in Fiction the corresponding figures are 9% and 1%. Drama and Trials constitute the opposite end of the continuum: 6% of the relevant progressives in Drama as well as in Trials have non-agentive subjects, and in neither genre has a passive progressive been attested in CONCE.[35] It thus seems that there is a connection between, on the one hand, the occurrence of progressives with non-agentive subjects and, on the other hand, the rise of the passive progressive; but in the 19th century, this connection appears to hold at the level of genre rather than time. The percentages of passive progressives are based on low raw frequencies as regards all genres but Science and Letters, but the closeness of the match between the percentage of passive progressives and the percentage of progressives with non-agentive subjects is nevertheless notable.

Against this background, it is possible to refine the picture afforded by the results presented in Section 5.3 somewhat. Pratt and Denison (2000: 417) hypothesize that the passive progressive may have occurred in speech before it entered standard written English. If this hypothesis is correct, it makes sense to assume that the construction should first occur in genres that either imitate speech (such as Drama) or incorporate spoken features and are not intended for publication (such as Letters), although CONCE only yields an example from the latter genre in period 1. Factors such as social networks may be crucial in the early stages of such diffusion processes. Because the passive progressive was stigmatized, however, it was unlikely to enter formal written genres before some of the force of its negative prescriptive evaluation had subsided; Letters is also the only genre in CONCE to contain a passive progressive from period 1. In contrast, in the second half of the century, the risk of ambiguity between an active progressive with a non-agentive subject and a passival progressive (whose surface subject is non-agentive by definition) may have had a greater influence on the distribution. In periods 2 and 3, we also find that the passive progressive occurs chiefly in the expository genres in CONCE; these genres contain comparatively many progressives with non-agentive subjects, which may be ambiguous between active and passival readings. In speech-related genres such as Drama and Trials, in contrast, the occurrence potential for the passive progressive may be more

---

35 These comparisons are not based on exactly the same sets of progressives, as different criteria were used to extract progressives for the voice and agentivity parameters. To some extent, the results are also connected, as passive progressives have non-agentive subjects by definition. However, given that progressives with non-agentive subjects clearly outnumber passive progressives, this overlap is unlikely to have affected the results in any significant way.

restricted, as such genres contain both few passive clauses overall and few progressives with non-agentive subjects.

6.4   Modification by temporal adverbials

The modification of the progressive by temporal adverbials is a topic that has received a great deal of attention in previous research. As temporal adverbials that modify progressive verb phrases often bring in specific meanings, frequent cases of modification of progressives by temporal adverbials may affect the functional load of the progressive itself in diachrony. For instance, the co-occurrence of the progressive with adverbials such as *always* (see Section 7.1) is often said to have emotional connotations, which may have helped the not-solely-aspectual functions of the progressive to gain ground. Similarly, modification by adverbials referring to future time may have influenced the development of progressives in 'future' situations (see Section 6.2). From a more general perspective, the extent to which progressives are modified by temporal adverbials is relevant to the integration of the aspectual functions of the progressive into English grammar. When the progressive becomes more integrated as a marker of ongoing action and imperfective aspect, it can be hypothesized that the need for explicit adverbial modification will decrease. In other words, once these functions of the progressive are well established, adverbials such as *now* or *when X happened* will no longer be needed to bring out these shades of meaning; the progressive alone will be sufficient.

Before presenting the results based on CONCE, I will give a brief survey of previous research in this field, focusing on what has been stated concerning how temporal adverbials that modify progressives should be defined and classified. Crystal (1966), who focuses on Present-Day English, pays specific attention to the role played by temporal adverbials that modify the different types of verb phrases. However, he does not deal with differences between the progressive and the non-progressive, and thus not specifically with adverbial modification of the progressive. Although Crystal (1966: 15) admits that the issue needs further research, he also claims that "[m]ost of the time ... the aspectual distinction does not seem to be important".

In Crystal (1966: 8), temporal adverbials are defined as "all adverbials which could be elicited as possible answers to the question 'when?' "; this definition is intended to include adverbials denoting frequency (e.g. *sometimes*) and duration (e.g. *for some time*) as well as those giving a time-reference (e.g. *tomorrow*). Crystal (1966: 8) claims that ambiguity between a temporal and a non-temporal reading can only arise in contexts where place or manner, rather than time, may be denoted by the adverbial; he takes up examples such as *gradually* and *in the sequel*. Following Crystal (1966: 8), I did not include such doubtful cases in the counts. Unlike Crystal, however, I did not group the temporal adverbials that modified progressives into subcategories. Such detailed classification lay beyond the scope of the present study; moreover, for many subsamples, breaking down the data into additional categories would have led to low raw frequencies and would thus have reduced the reliability of the results.[36]

Another issue relevant to the classification process concerns when a temporal adverbial can be considered to modify a progressive. Freckmann (1995: 258) claims that Crystal (1966) and Scheffer (1975) included "any adverbial in their lists that co-occurs with progressives within sentence limits", while he checked all adverbials manually to see that they had scope over the progressive, including cases where clause or tone-unit boundaries separate the adverbial and the progressive.[37] In the present study, these criteria were combined: an adverbial had to both occur in the same sentence as the progressive and be considered to have scope over that progressive in order to be classified as a modifier. The adverbial *the last two minutes* in (79), for instance, was considered to have scope over the progressive:

(79) "Why, to own the truth," cried Miss Bates, who *had been trying* in vain to be heard the last two minutes, "if I must speak on this subject, there is no denying that Mr. Frank Churchill might have – I do not mean to say that he did not dream it – I am sure I have sometimes the oddest dreams in the world – but if I am questioned about it, I must acknowledge that there was such an idea last spring; …"
(Fiction, Austen, 1800–1830, p. III.67)

The adverbial *in October* in (80), in contrast, was considered not to have scope over the progressive although *in October* and *shall be longing* occur in the same sentence, as it was deemed more likely that the adverbial modified *to be off with you again* than *shall be longing*:

(80) I never felt the delight of the thorough change that the coast gives one so much as now, and I *shall be longing* to be off with you again in October.
(Letters, Eliot, 1850–1870, p. 111)

As Freckmann (1995) points out, a temporal adverbial may have scope over a progressive even though the two are separated by clausal boundaries; but since distance is also an important factor in processing text, drawing the line at the sentence level seemed a reasonable compromise. This was also the line taken in

---

36   The only exception to this rule concerns adverbials such as *always*, which often bring out not-solely-aspectual interpretations of progressives. Such adverbials were classified together with all other temporal adverbials for the purposes of the analysis undertaken in the present section, but they will also form the basis for a separate investigation in Section 7.1.

37   Freckmann (1995) does not explicitly limit his investigation to temporal adverbials, although all his adverbial examples appear to be temporal.

Smitterberg, Reich, and Hahn (2000), where adverbial modification of progressives in 19th- and 20th-century texts was compared.[38]

The extent to which the progressives in CONCE were modified by temporal adverbials is shown in Table 60.

Table 60.   Progressives in CONCE modified by temporal adverbials by period and genre (percentages of all progressives in each subsample within brackets)

Period	Debates	Drama	Fiction	History	Letters	Science	Trials	Total
1	7	7	24	2	91	7	54	192
	(58%)	(19%)	(27%)	(20%)	(37%)	(27%)	(30%)	(32%)
2	4	18	24	10	145	9	44	254
	(36%)	(17%)	(19%)	(27%)	(34%)	(38%)	(26%)	(28%)
3	8	21	12	18	103	2	51	215
	(27%)	(18%)	(17%)	(27%)	(27%)	(6%)	(21%)	(23%)
Total	19	46	60	30	339	18	149	661
	(36%)	(18%)	(21%)	(27%)	(32%)	(21%)	(25%)	(27%)

Table 60 shows that the overall figures agree with the hypothesis: the percentage of all progressives per period that are modified by temporal adverbials decreases in diachrony, a decrease which is statistically significant. The significance of this result becomes even more striking in the light of the findings that will be presented in Section 6.5. As will be shown in Section 6.5, the percentage of progressives that occur in main clauses increases in diachrony, while the percentage of progressives that occur in subordinate clauses decreases. Progressives in main clauses are modified by temporal adverbials to a higher extent than progressives that occur in subordinate clauses (34% vs. 19%); an increase in the percentage of main-clause progressives would thus lead to a higher degree of modification by temporal adverbials even if the percentages of main-clause and subordinate-clause progressives that are modified by temporal adverbials were both constant in diachrony.

Of the seven genres in CONCE, Debates, Fiction, Letters, and Trials follow the overall pattern; Drama appears to be stable; History actually seems to go against the general trend, with an increase between periods 1 and 2; and Science displays an increase between periods 1 and 2, followed by a sharp decrease between periods 2 and 3. As regards the expository genres Debates, History, and Science, however, low raw frequencies in some period/genre subsamples make

---

38   Freckmann's study is based on the LOB and LLC corpora, and thus includes both spoken and written English. This factor may lie behind the importance placed on the scope of the adverbial in his study: in speech, where turns are typically shorter than they are in writing, the scope of a temporal adverbial may well be longer than in writing in terms of clauses and/or tone units. However, since even the language in the speech-related genres in CONCE is likely to have been edited when being transferred into written text, I applied the same criteria to all genres in the corpus, which also made the results more comparable.

results unreliable.[39] The relative stability in Drama may be due to the progressive being integrated to a comparatively high degree in this genre as early as 1800, so that the percentage of adverbial modification had gone down prior to the period covered by CONCE. In this respect, it is noteworthy that Drama exhibits a lower percentage of progressives modified by temporal adverbials than any other genre in CONCE.[40] The cross-genre differences in CONCE notwithstanding, however, the general correspondence between an increase in the frequency of the progressive and a decrease in the percentage of progressives that are modified by temporal adverbials for the corpus as a whole is supported by the data.

In a similar analysis, Scheffer (1975) investigated the modification of the progressive by temporal adverbials in a corpus consisting of 375,000 words of Present-Day English fiction, taken from six novels.[41] In order to keep the genre parameter under control, while still basing results on a subcorpus of reliable size, I will compare Scheffer's findings with results for the Fiction genre in CONCE as a whole. Scheffer classifies the progressives in his corpus according to the formal make-up of the verb phrases in which they occur (present, past, pluperfect etc.). To avoid low raw frequencies, I will restrict the comparison to present and past progressives with no perfect or modal auxiliaries, and to the total figures for all progressives taken together. It should be borne in mind that the criteria for when a temporal adverbial should be considered to modify a progressive may differ slightly between the studies; for this reason, I will not test variation for statistical significance. The results of the comparison are presented in Table 61.

Table 61. Progressives modified by temporal adverbials in Fiction (CONCE) and in Scheffer's (1975) corpus of Present-Day English fiction (percentages of all progressives in each subsample within brackets)

	Present progressives	Past progressives	All progressives
Fiction in CONCE	9 (18%)	35 (20%)	60 (21%)
Scheffer (1975)	136 (15%)	267 (22%)	523 (21%)

39 When investigating the modification of present progressives by temporal adverbials in 19th- and 20th-century academic texts, Smitterberg, Reich, and Hahn (2000: 105) showed that there was no statistically significant change in adverbial modification.

40 Fitzmaurice (2004a: 155) reached a similar result in her investigation of lexical adverbial modification of progressives in a corpus of 17th-century and 18th-century texts: the relative order of the three genres (Drama, Fiction, and Letters) that were included in both studies was the same with respect to the percentage of modified progressives in each genre. However, as Fitzmaurice included other adverbial categories than temporal adverbials in her analysis, it is difficult to compare the results.

41 Scheffer (1975) also analysed the modification of progressives by temporal adverbials in a corpus of radio commentaries and in *Gregory's Dialogues*, texts belonging to genres which lack close parallels in CONCE. In the former, 40% of all progressives had adverbial modification; in the latter, 49%.

The similarity of the results presented in Table 61 does not support the hypothesis formulated above, viz. that increased integration of the progressive should lead to a decrease in adverbial modification. However, it is possible that another factor is at work here. Scheffer (1975: 54f.) also classifies his progressives according to whether they occur in main or subordinate clauses. If we look at his figures for all progressives, we find that 23% of all main-clause progressives and 16% of all progressives in subordinate clauses have adverbial modification; the corresponding figures for Fiction in CONCE are 24% and 19% respectively. In Fiction, there thus appears to have been a slight decrease in adverbial modification of progressives in at least subordinate clauses between the 19th and the 20th centuries. Against this background, the constancy of the results presented in Table 61 can be explained by two changes that cancel each other out: on the one hand, a tendency towards less modification by temporal adverbials; on the other hand, a change towards more progressives occurring in main clauses, where such adverbial modification is more likely to appear. In Scheffer's corpus, 71% of all progressives occur in main clauses, whereas only 47% of the progressives in Fiction in CONCE do so. (I will return to the distribution of the progressive across types of clauses in Section 6.5.)

It may also be interesting to compare the results based on CONCE with what Freckmann (1995) found for past progressives in the LOB and LLC corpora.[42] For instance, Freckmann's results for the fiction (K–R) genres and the academic-prose genre (J) in LOB may be compared with the results for Fiction and Science in CONCE. However, the results imply that the classificational criteria used may be so different that the comparison is skewed. Freckmann's (1995: 259) data indicate that 33% of the past progressives in categories K–R, and 60% of the past progressives in category J have adverbial modification. In contrast, as shown in Table 61, 20% of the past progressives in Fiction in CONCE are modified by a temporal adverbial; none of the 11 past progressives in Science has such adverbial modification. Given the similarity of the results concerning fiction texts in CONCE and Scheffer's (1975) corpus, it may be that differences in classificational criteria and/or sampling strategies between Freckmann's study and the present work make the results less comparable.

As regards which temporal adverbs are the most frequent as modifiers of progressive verb phrases, owing to the heterogeneous make-up of phrases and clauses, I will limit my discussion to one-word adverbs. The most common adverb is *now* (72 occurrences), followed by *just* (28), *always* (24), *still* (22), and *then* (17). However, these adverbs do not have the same occurrence patterns. *Now* typically occurs in 'active' or 'processive' situations containing present-tense verb phrases without perfect or modal auxiliaries, thus emphasizing the ongoing action of an 'active' situation or the incompletion of a 'processive' situation, as in (81). In contrast, *just* tends to occur either in 'transitional' situations containing

---

42   Freckmann does not seem to define explicitly what he means by "past progressives"; for the purposes of the comparison, I have taken the term to refer to progressives with a past-tense finite verb form and without modal or perfect auxiliaries.

present or past verb phrases without perfect or modal auxiliaries, as in (82), or in 'processive' situations containing either a past-tense verb phrase without perfect or modal auxiliaries, or a present perfect verb phrase. *Always* and *still* both occur predominantly in 'active' situations, although situations with *always* tend to be in the present tense and situations with *still* in the past tense, as in (83) and (84). The situation-type distribution of *then* is more diverse, but most progressives modified by *then* occur in the past tense, either in 'active' situations, or in 'stance' situations, as in (85).

(81)   I *am* now *Engraving* Six little plates for a little work of Mr H's, for which I am to have 10 Guineas each, & the certain profits of that work are a fortune such as would make me independent, supposing that I could substantitate such a one of my own & I mean to try many.
(Letters, Blake, 1800–1830, p. 51)

(82)   But at the moment when England *was* just *plunging* into the Seven Years' War the enterprize of a duke and a millwright solved this problem of carriage, and started the country on a mighty course of industry which was to change both its social and its political character.
(History, Green, 1870–1900, p. IV.279)

(83)   There is a most charming little photograph coming out to you, which Henry Cameron has done of Billy, only Billy *is* always *laughing* and this looks unnaturally grave.
(Letters, Thackeray Ritchie, 1870–1900, p. 207)

(84)   … I awoke before six in the dark yesterday and I thought I *was dreaming* still, I heard cheers and cheers and music and more cheers.
(Letters, Thackeray Ritchie, 1870–1900, p. 252)

(85)   [$A.$] We all awoke at the same time, and then Jane Marke *was sitting* on a trunk, and a candle was burning on the table.
(Trials, Bowditch, 1800–1830, p. 61)

Overall, the results presented in this section support the hypothesis that an increased integration of the progressive leads to a decrease in the need for modification by temporal adverbials. However, differences in classificational criteria and, possibly, genre definitions made it difficult to reach definite conclusions when the results of the present study were compared with those presented in previous research. A qualitative analysis of some of the commonest adverbs in the corpus showed that they tend to occur in different contexts as regards tense and situation type.

    The comparison of Scheffer's (1975) results with those of the present study showed that the type of clause the progressive occurs in is an important parameter: developments in the clausal distribution of the progressive may lie behind variation among samples of data when other variables are being investigated. Moreover, the diffusion of the progressive across the parameter of clause type has implications for the integration of the construction into late Modern English grammar. The next section of this chapter will therefore be devoted to the co-occurrence of the progressive with different clause types.

6.5   Clause type

In previous research, the distribution of the progressive across main and subordinate clauses has been commented on as one area where development is discernible. Strang (1982: 441) notes that, in narrative prose from the period 1700–1750, the progressive favours subordinate clauses, in particular relative clauses and some adverbial clauses. In fictional dialogue, however, progressives in main clauses are more common (Strang 1982: 442). Strang (1982: 441f.) claims that, between the 18th and 20th centuries, this difference has disappeared, so that the progressive is as frequent in main clauses as it is in subordinate clauses. Given that the frequency of the progressive also increased during the same period, and that a high frequency is an important sign that the progressive is highly integrated in texts, an increased integration of the progressive may be linked to an increased occurrence of the construction in main clauses. To the extent that an increase in the proportion of main-clause progressives reflects the removal of a constraint on the occurrence of the construction, this link is to be expected. This hypothesis is strengthened by Smith's (2002) analysis of the progressive in the LOB and FLOB corpora. Smith (2002: 325f.) found that present progressives, but not past progressives, exhibited a change towards more main-clause occurrence in the 30 years that separate the two corpora; similarly, the frequency of present progressives, but not past progressives, increased between LOB and FLOB. However, as Smith (2002: 327) points out, the latter development may be due in part to the greater proportion of present-tense verb phrases in FLOB compared with LOB.

Strang's (1982) findings indicate that the 19th century is crucial to this development in the clausal distribution of the progressive; I will therefore complement Strang's results by analysing the clausal distribution of the progressives in CONCE.[43] As results presented in Smitterberg (2000a) indicated that the genre parameter is important when the occurrence of the progressive across the parameter of clause type is analysed, I will report on results both for the whole corpus and for individual genres.[44] Such an analysis may also shed new

---

43   The clausal distribution of the progressive is also important for the development of not-solely-aspectual functions of the construction; I will return to this issue in Section 7.2.

44   The results presented in Smitterberg (2000a) were based on an earlier version of CONCE than that used for the present work. Since the earlier version was compiled, the genres Debates and Trials have been added, and a few texts or parts of texts have been included in or excluded from Letters and Drama. Moreover, in a few cases, minor changes have been made to the classificatory scheme, when manual checking of the database has revealed erroneous

light on the integration of the progressive across the genre parameter: genres in which the progressive was integrated to a high degree may have a comparatively high proportion of progressives occurring in main clauses, whereas the opposite would be true of genres where the construction was less fully integrated. However, given that some period/genre subsamples contain few progressives, especially in the three expository genres, results for individual genres cannot be considered reliable throughout.

Owing to limitations of time, the investigation of the overall clausal distribution in CONCE lay outside the scope of the present study. Thus, I cannot say whether, for instance, a difference between two samples in the percentage of main-clause progressives is due to changes in the occurrence patterns of the progressive or to changes in the occurrence patterns of the clause types.[45] For this reason, variation in clausal distribution will not be tested for statistical significance, as it is not certain how a significant result should be interpreted.

The progressives in CONCE were classified according to whether they occurred in main, adverbial, comparative, nominal, or relative clauses. In this analysis, a clause was classified as a main clause if it was not subordinate to any other clause. The classification given in Quirk et al. (1985) was followed when the different types of subordinate clauses were distinguished. Of the 2,440 progressives in CONCE, 43, or 2%, proved difficult to classify on the clausal parameter; these will be excluded from all results presented in the present section. Many of these doubtful cases occur in colloquial and/or speech-related genres such as Drama, Letters, and Trials, where clipped syntax sometimes makes it difficult to decide whether, for instance, a given clause should be classified as main or subordinate. Consider (86):

(86)   Surely, did you not observe, *was* he *carrying* anything? – I do not suppose he was. I did not observe. I did not keep it in my mind.
(Trials, Tichborne, 1870–1900, p. 2,449)

In (86), the placement of the clause *was he carrying anything* after *did you not observe* indicates that the former is a nominal clause with the latter as its matrix clause; but the syntax of the clause *was he carrying anything*, with inversion and without a subordinator such as *if* or *whether*, rather suggests a direct question, and thus a main clause. Since cases such as (86) were quite few, I excluded them from the counts instead of imposing an uncertain classification on the data. With such

---

classifications. Finally, in Smitterberg (2000a), instances classified as doubtful with respect to clause type were listed as a category of their own, whereas in the present study such progressives have been excluded from the counts. For these reasons, the figures given in the two studies do not match exactly.

45   On the genre level, these two possible causes may work in roughly the same direction as far as the distribution of progressives across main and subordinate clauses is concerned. A high percentage of main-clause occurrences is assumed to be characteristic of genres where the progressive is integrated to a high degree; but as was shown in Chapter 3, many of these genres are speech-related, and can thus perhaps be expected to have comparatively many main clauses overall in the first place.

doubtful cases excluded, the clausal distribution in the whole CONCE corpus is given in Table 62.

Table 62.   The progressives in CONCE by period and clause type (row percentages within brackets)

Period	Main	Adverbial	Comparative	Nominal	Relative	Total
1	287	111	–	121	70	589
	(49%)	(19%)		(21%)	(12%)	
2	496	109	3	160	112	880
	(56%)	(12%)	(0%)	(18%)	(13%)	
3	515	116	1	188	108	928
	(55%)	(12%)	(0%)	(20%)	(12%)	
Total	1,298	336	4	469	290	2,397
	(54%)	(14%)	(0%)	(20%)	(12%)	

The only substantial developments in clausal distribution that appear to take place over the century are the increase in the percentage of main clauses, and the corresponding decrease in that of adverbial clauses, between periods 1 and 2. Otherwise, the diachronic picture is relatively stable: there is little change in the percentages of main and adverbial clauses between periods 2 and 3; comparative clauses are very rare in all periods;[46] and the percentages of nominal and relative clauses do not exhibit any great changes in diachrony, although there is a small decrease in the percentage of the former and an increase in that of the latter between periods 1 and 2, both of which trends are reversed between periods 2 and 3. In other words, the only safe conclusion on the basis of Table 62 appears to be that progressives became comparatively more common in main clauses and less common in adverbial clauses across the 19th century. Since the frequency of the progressive also rose during the 1800s, the results imply that there is a positive correlation between (a) the percentage of main-clause progressives in a text and (b) the overall frequency of the progressive. Both a high main-clause percentage and a high frequency may then be indicative of the progressive being integrated to a high degree in a given text. This link is supported by Núñez Pertejo's (2001) investigation of the progressive in early Modern English, a period when the progressive was less frequent and less fully integrated than in 19th-century English. Núñez Pertejo (2001: 349) found that only 30% of the progressives in the early Modern English section of the Helsinki Corpus occurred in main clauses. (However, differences in sampling strategies and genre make-up between CONCE and the Helsinki Corpus should be taken into account in this context.)

Since the total figures may mask important genre-specific developments, I will present results for the genres in CONCE one by one and comment on them

---

46   Similarly, Núñez Pertejo (2001: 352) found that, of the 178 progressives she analysed in the early Modern English section of the Helsinki Corpus, only one occurred in a comparative clause.

individually in what follows. However, as pointed out above, raw frequencies are low for some period/genre subsamples, which means that caution should be exercised in the interpretation of the results. Only the clause types in which progressives actually occur in each genre will be listed in the tables. The results for the Debates genre are given in Table 63.

Table 63. The progressives in Debates by period and clause type (row percentages within brackets)

Period	Main	Adverbial	Nominal	Relative	Total
1	1	2	2	5	10
	(10%)	(20%)	(20%)	(50%)	
2	5	–	2	4	11
	(45%)		(18%)	(36%)	
3	8	8	8	5	29
	(28%)	(28%)	(28%)	(17%)	
Total	14	10	12	14	50
	(28%)	(20%)	(24%)	(28%)	

Although the low raw frequencies in Debates make definite conclusions impossible to draw, there is one consistent trend in Table 63: the percentage of progressives occurring in relative clauses decreases over the century. The overall figures for the genre reveal that comparatively few progressives occur in main clauses, while especially the percentage for relative clauses is higher than the result for the whole corpus. The low main-clause percentage in the total figures supports the grouping of Debates as an expository genre, where the progressive is less fully integrated than in the non-expository genres in CONCE.

Table 64 presents the results for the Drama genre.

Table 64. The progressives in Drama by period and clause type (row percentages within brackets)

Period	Main	Adverbial	Nominal	Relative	Total
1	20	7	5	4	36
	(56%)	(19%)	(14%)	(11%)	
2	75	12	12	6	105
	(71%)	(11%)	(11%)	(6%)	
3	76	5	19	17	117
	(65%)	(4%)	(16%)	(15%)	
Total	171	24	36	27	258
	(66%)	(9%)	(14%)	(10%)	

Drama has a high percentage of main-clause progressives (above the overall mean) even in period 1. There is still a big increase between periods 1 and 2, although some of this increase is counteracted by a decrease between periods 2 and 3. As for the other clause types, the overall picture for nominal and relative clauses is inconclusive; progressives in adverbial clauses, however, display a consistent decrease in percentage points. The main-clause distribution thus matches a genre where the progressive is integrated to a relatively high degree even in period 1. In this respect, Drama exhibits similar patterns with regard to adverbial modification (see Section 6.4) and distribution across clause types. There is some further support for this finding in previous research. Wright (1994: 474), looking at the progressive in prose comedy during the period 1670–1710, found no significant change in clausal distribution in diachrony; she also found that the percentage of main-clause progressives was quite high (between 55.5% and 78%) even in this period. In a recent study of 17th-century and 18th-century Drama texts, the same scholar found that the proportion of main-clause progressives was 74% (Fitzmaurice 2004a: 147). Moreover, Strang (1982: 442) states that main-clause progressives were accepted in fictional dialogue in early 18th-century English. Against this background, it can be expected that Drama, which, like dialogue in Fiction, consists of constructed speech, should have a high percentage of main-clause progressives throughout the 19th century.

The next genre to be discussed is Fiction; the results for this genre are given in Table 65.

Table 65.   The progressives in Fiction by period and clause type (row percentages within brackets)

Period	Main	Adverbial	Comp.	Nominal	Relative	Total
1	38	14	–	18	18	88
	(43%)	(16%)		(20%)	(20%)	
2	57	22	1	22	21	123
	(46%)	(18%)	(1%)	(18%)	(17%)	
3	37	11	–	13	6	67
	(55%)	(16%)		(19%)	(9%)	
Total	132	47	1	53	45	278
	(47%)	(17%)	(0%)	(19%)	(16%)	

Fiction occupies an intermediate position relative to Drama and Debates concerning the percentage of main-clause progressives. The percentage is lower than in Drama, but climbs steadily throughout the century, especially between periods 2 and 3. However, unlike the developments in Drama, this increase does not correspond to a decrease in the percentage of adverbial clauses; adverbial and nominal clauses in Fiction appear to be stable across the century in this respect. Instead, the decrease comes chiefly in relative clauses, another area where Strang (1982) believed that the progressive was comparatively common in the 18th century. Most of the increase in the percentage of main-clause progressives comes between periods 2 and 3, rather than between 1 and 2 as in Drama; this may point to a slightly later integration of the progressive in Fiction than in Drama with respect to clausal distribution. This finding also matches the make-up of Fiction and Drama texts. Fiction texts consist of an amalgamation of narrative and dialogue, and Drama mainly comprises dialogue. Strang (1982) held main-clause progressives to be more characteristic of dialogue than of narrative. In Fiction, however, developments in the frequency and clausal distribution of the progressive appear to be partly independent of each other, in spite of the fact that both increasing frequency and increasing main-clause occurrence point to the progressive becoming more fully integrated. Despite the decrease in frequency noted for the progressive between periods 2 and 3 (see Section 3.2.4.3), the trend towards main clauses accounting for a greater share of all progressives continues. A comparison of Fitzmaurice's (2004a: 147) results for 17th-century and 18th-century texts with those of the present study indicates that this trend started before 1800, as Fitzmaurice's percentage of main-clause progressives in Fiction is 38%.

The division of Fiction into dialogue and non-dialogue subsamples (see Section 3.2.4.3) showed that period 3 contains more dialogue than periods 1 and 2: in period 1, 30% of the text consists of dialogue; in period 2, 27%; and in period 3, 42%. This shift towards more dialogue, where progressives in main clauses are more expected, may explain part of the change towards a higher percentage of main-clause progressives in period 3 of the Fiction genre.

The results for History are given in Table 66.

Table 66.   The progressives in History by period and clause type (row percentages within brackets)

Period	Main	Adverbial	Nominal	Relative	Total
1	3	2	3	2	10
	(30%)	(20%)	(30%)	(20%)	
2	13	7	5	12	37
	(35%)	(19%)	(14%)	(32%)	
3	30	11	7	18	66
	(45%)	(17%)	(11%)	(27%)	
Total	46	20	15	32	113
	(41%)	(18%)	(13%)	(28%)	

In History, the low raw frequencies in period 1 make diachronic comparisons difficult. However, if we disregard period 1 and instead focus on periods 2 and 3 and changes between them, we find that the picture is partly similar to that of Fiction, with an increase in the percentage of main-clause progressives. A further similarity with Fiction is that this increase chiefly corresponds to a decrease in the percentage of progressives in relative clauses (although in History, the percentage of adverbial and nominal clauses also decreases). In addition, the total percentage of main-clause progressives is 41 in History, as against 47 in Fiction; if main-clause occurrence is taken as a sign of integration, the clausal distribution of the progressive and the frequency of the construction both thus point to the progressive being more fully integrated in Fiction than in History.

Table 67 presents the results for Letters.

Table 67.   The progressives in Letters by period and clause type (row percentages within brackets)

Period	Main	Adverbial	Comp.	Nominal	Relative	Total
1	132	41	–	50	21	244
	(54%)	(17%)		(20%)	(9%)	
2	238	48	1	84	45	416
	(57%)	(12%)	(0%)	(20%)	(11%)	
3	233	34	1	74	39	381
	(61%)	(9%)	(0%)	(19%)	(10%)	
Total	**603**	123	2	208	105	1,041
	(58%)	(12%)	(0%)	(20%)	(10%)	

Developments across the clause-type parameter in Letters are similar to those in Drama, though the figures appear more stable, perhaps owing to the higher raw frequencies in the Letters genre. There is an increase in main-clause progressives from a level which is high even in period 1, and a decrease in adverbial clauses. The percentages of nominal and relative clauses are more stable in diachrony, and the percentage of comparative clauses is negligible. Letters is thus a genre where the percentage of main-clause progressives is high even in 1800, but still continues to increase through the 19th century. This development corresponds well with developments concerning the frequency of the progressive in Letters; both parameters indicate continuing integration of a construction that was already integrated to a comparatively high degree. In addition, a comparison with the results presented in Fitzmaurice (2004a) implies that the percentage of main-clause progressives in Letters has increased since the 18th century.

The Science genre exhibits a different pattern; Table 68 presents the results.

Table 68.   The progressives in Science by period and clause type (row percentages within brackets)

Period	Main	Adverbial	Comp.	Nominal	Relative	Total
1	9	9	–	4	4	26
	(35%)	(35%)		(15%)	(15%)	
2	8	3	1	5	7	24
	(33%)	(12%)	(4%)	(21%)	(29%)	
3	5	16	–	6	8	35
	(14%)	(46%)		(17%)	(23%)	
Total	**22**	28	1	15	19	85
	(26%)	(33%)	(1%)	(18%)	(22%)	

The results in Table 68 are difficult to interpret, probably owing to the low raw frequencies. (Some of the variation may also be due to the heterogeneity of the texts in Science.) The developments exhibit little consistency in diachrony; in particular, the figures for adverbial clauses display considerable variation without a clear pattern. However, the percentage of main-clause progressives decreases consistently, and the total results indicate that progressives in main clauses are comparatively rare in Science. The results thus imply that the progressive was less integrated in scientific writing than in many other genres in the 19th century. This indication would, again, be supported by the frequency data, which showed that Science was the genre with the lowest normalized frequency of progressives (see Section 3.2.3).

Finally, the results for Trials are given in Table 69.

Table 69.   The progressives in Trials by period and clause type (row percentages within brackets)

Period	Main	Adverbial	Nominal	Relative	Total
1	84	36	39	16	175
	(48%)	(21%)	(22%)	(9%)	
2	100	17	30	17	164
	(61%)	(10%)	(18%)	(10%)	
3	126	31	61	15	233
	(54%)	(13%)	(26%)	(6%)	
Total	310	84	130	48	572
	(54%)	(15%)	(23%)	(8%)	

The pattern for Trials is partly similar to those for Drama and Letters, especially the former. In both Trials and Drama there is a substantial increase in the percentage of main-clause progressives between periods 1 and 2; this increase is, then, partly counteracted in both genres by a smaller decrease between periods 2 and 3. (However, in all three periods, Drama has higher main-clause percentages than Trials.) As mentioned in Sections 3.2.4.7 and 4.2, period 2 in Trials stands out from the other two period samples with respect to normalized frequencies of progressives and dimension scores (see Geisler 2002). Similarly, all four clause types represented in Trials display either their highest or their lowest percentage of progressives in period 2. It may be that the subject matter of the proceedings affects the distribution of clause types in Trials; as pointed out in Section 3.2.4.7, the subject matter of the Trials texts in period 2 differs somewhat from that of the texts from periods 1 and 3. In terms of total figures, Trials have the third highest percentage of main-clause progressives in the corpus, after Drama and Letters. Furthermore, if period 2 is discarded, a comparison between period 1 and 3 still points to a diachronic increase in the percentage of main-clause progressives in Trials, and a decrease chiefly in the percentage of adverbial clauses.

Taken together, the results presented in this section indicate that genres where the progressive is integrated to a comparatively high degree (as indicated by the frequency of the construction) also tend to be characterized by a high and/or increasing percentage of the progressives occurring in main clauses. There are also differences across the genre parameter concerning, for instance, in which clause type(s) the percentage of progressives decreases to compensate for the increasing percentage of main-clause progressives.

6.6   Discussion of results

The first investigation in the present chapter dealt with what main verbs occurred in progressive verb phrases in CONCE. The analysis showed that GO was clearly the most frequent main verb in the progressive, although the dominance of this verb decreased in diachrony. The most common verbs in progressive verb phrases seemed to come from specific semantic areas, such as movement verbs and communicative verbs. The results were consistent with what has been claimed in previous research for both earlier periods and for Present-Day English. The genre parameter was shown to affect the distribution of main verbs. In two of the expository genres, Debates and Science, some of the verbs that occurred in the progressive with the highest frequency were not the same as the commonest verbs in progressive verb phrases in the overall results. Among the non-expository genres, some of the cross-genre variation could be attributed to general differences in subject matter in Drama, Fiction, Letters, and Trials. A separate section was also devoted to the occurrence of BE and HAVE as main verbs in late Modern English progressive verb phrases. Whereas CONCE only provided one progressive of BE, progressives of HAVE were more common, and the data implied an increase in the frequency of this pattern. Additional data taken from Arnaud's corpus supported the observations that were based on CONCE.

In the investigation of what Aktionsart categories the progressive co-occurred with, I adopted a modified version of Quirk et al.'s (1985) typology of situations. In the modified version, agentivity was not treated as a feature affecting Aktionsart classifications, and two 'stative' situations were grouped together. In addition, progressives referring to the future without the aid of modal auxiliaries were both treated as a category of their own and grouped together with other progressive verb phrases. The analysis revealed that the clear majority of all progressives occurred in 'processive' and, above all, 'active' situations. A separate analysis of progressives in 'stative' situations showed that the progressive appears to add either a shade of temporariness or tentativeness, which may be related to the aspectual functions of the construction, or some subjective, not-solely-aspectual implication. From a diachronic point of view, the clearest trends in the data were that the percentage of progressives in 'stative' situations increased, whereas progressives in 'future' situations became comparatively less frequent in diachrony. (When 'future' situations were not recognized as a separate category, most progressives referring to the future without the aid of modal auxiliaries were reclassified as occurring in 'processive' situations, and the decrease in percentage points thus occurred in this Aktionsart category instead.)

There were also indications that progressives in 'momentary' and 'transitional' situations were, possibly, becoming more frequent, though low raw frequencies and slight decreases between periods 2 and 3 precluded definite conclusions. Finally, an analysis of how the different genres patterned with respect to situation types showed that, whereas >50% of the progressives in each of the expository genres Debates, History, and Science were part of 'active' situations, the non-expository genres presented a more diversified picture. To some extent, these patterns could be related to genre-specific constraints, as was also the case with main verbs in progressive verb phrases.

The next section dealt with the issue of whether the progressives that occurred in [–stative] situations had agentive or non-agentive subjects. As with situation types in the preceding section, there was little diachronic change. Strang's (1982) analysis of whether the subjects of progressive verb phrases were human, quasi-human/animals, or inanimate indicated that the difference between the 18th and 19th centuries was considerable, while that between the 19th and 20th was small; it was therefore assumed that most of the development towards a higher incidence of progressives with non-agentive subjects had taken place prior to the period covered by CONCE. When, instead, the genre parameter was investigated, it turned out that the genres which displayed a high proportion of progressives with non-agentive subjects were also the genres where the passive progressive appeared either early or with a comparatively high frequency. (However, the raw frequencies of passive progressives were too low to allow definite conclusions in this respect.)

As regards the modification of progressives by temporal adverbials, the analysis showed that the progressive developed towards less adverbial modification over the 19th century, although there was considerable variation among genres. Scheffer's (1975) investigation of the extent to which progressives in Present-Day English fiction were modified by temporal adverbials did not at first appear to support the trend towards a decrease when the results were compared with those for Fiction in CONCE. However, when the parameter of clause type was included in the calculations, the results did point to a decrease in temporal adverbials modifying the progressive at least in subordinate clauses from the 19th century to the present day. Freckmann's (1995) data on adverbial modification of past progressives in LOB and LLC, in contrast, did not support the tendency attested in CONCE. This dissimilarity can possibly be attributed to the different classificational criteria applied to Freckmann's material and in the present study. An additional investigation of some temporal adverbs that frequently modify progressives in CONCE showed that these adverbials exhibit a good deal of variation concerning the type of verb phrase and the situation type in which the modified progressives occur.

The final results section of the present chapter was devoted to the occurrence of the progressive in different types of clause. The results reached in Strang's (1982) investigation of narrative prose, which showed that main clauses accounted for an increasingly large share of the progressives in the material, were supported by the analysis of the CONCE data. The overall figures showed that the progressive developed towards more occurrences in main clauses and fewer in adverbial clauses over the 19th century as a whole. Separate investigations of the individual genres showed that the expository genres contained few main-clause progressives compared with the non-expository genres. Among the three expository genres, History, where the progressive was also more frequent than in Debates and Science (see Section 3.2.3), showed a tendency towards increased main-clause occurrence, though not to the same degree as that of the four non-expository genres. Of these, Drama had the highest percentage of main-clause progressives, followed by Letters, Trials, and Fiction.

There are several ways in which the investigations undertaken in this chapter are relevant to the integration of the progressive into 19th-century English. As regards main verbs in progressive verb phrases, the results indicate that the increase in the frequency of the progressive did not spread equally over the verbal paradigm, since the type/token ratio for main verbs in progressive verb phrases decreased in diachrony. It thus seems that most of the increase in frequency is due to main verbs which already occurred in the progressive by 1800 becoming even more frequent in progressive verb phrases. However, there are also indications that the progressive became more fully integrated in terms of what main verbs could and did occur in progressive verb phrases over the century. The dominance of GO as the most common main verb in progressive verb phrases became less pronounced in diachrony (although this change did not result in higher type/token ratios). Moreover, the availability of BE and HAVE as main verbs in progressive verb phrases in late Modern English is very important in this context, given the centrality of these two verbs in the English language.

As for Aktionsart, the greater diversification of the progressive across situation types in the non-expository genres can be linked to the higher frequency of the construction in these genres, and thus to the integration of the progressive into English grammar. A genre where the progressive is integrated to a high degree will thus tend to have both comparatively high frequencies of progressives and a comparatively low percentage of progressives in 'active' situations. An imperfective marker such as the progressive is easy to apply to an 'active' situation, where there is typically a simple progressive/non-progressive contrast between an ongoing action and either a habitual action (in the present) or a perfective action (in the past). Later on, the progressive can spread to [+telic] and [–durative] situations, acquiring specific, situation-dependent connotations such as incompletion or repeated action in the process (see also Ziegeler 1999).

The increasing occurrence of the progressive in 'stative' situations may also be related to the integration of the construction, to the extent that occurrence in contexts where aspectual progressives can be seen as redundant (although they frequently imply temporariness) is a sign of integration. However, not-solely-aspectual functions of the progressives are also common in 'stative' situations; progressives in 'stative' situations may thus also imply that these functions became more fully integrated over the 19th century. The decrease in the percentage of progressives that occur in 'future' situations is more difficult to relate to the integration of the construction. Since the number of future expressions available has increased since Old English, it is possible that developments in the overall distribution of forms with future reference affect the occurrence of progressives in 'future' situations in CONCE.

A connection can be hypothesized between (a) the decrease in type/token ratios for main verbs in the progressive, (b) the diachronic stability of the percentage of 'active' situations, and (c) the lack of change in the distribution of the progressive across different formal types of verb phrases (see Section 5.5). In 19th-century English, most of the increase in the frequency of the progressive appears to have taken place in formal and aspectual contexts where the construction was already a common and established option, e.g. 'active' situations that contain verb phrases with no auxiliaries other than progressive BE and with main verbs that were already established in the progressive.

In diachrony, there was little development in the distribution of the progressive across the parameter of agentive vs. non-agentive subjects. However, when genre rather than time was used as the independent variable, the parameter of agentivity was found to be potentially relevant to the integration of the progressive. The data implied that progressives with non-agentive subjects correlated positively with the occurrence of passive progressives. Although the raw frequencies of passive progressives were low, the results thus implied that the proportion of progressives with non-agentive subjects is a relevant parameter when the partial replacement of the passival by the passive progressive is studied, as hypothesized by, for instance, Denison (1998). Thus, the distribution of the progressive across a semantic category may have implications for the formal make-up of the paradigm of the construction; and a complete and symmetrical paradigm is, in turn, a sign of integration. Links such as these point to the complexity inherent in processes of integration.

The decrease in the modification of the progressive by temporal adverbials can be seen as a sign that the construction, and in particular its aspectual functions, became more integrated into English. As connotations of ongoing action, incompletion, and temporariness became increasingly associated with the progressive, the need to specify the imperfective characteristics of the situation further with temporal adverbials may have decreased.

As for clausal distribution, the increased occurrence of the progressive in main clauses has been listed by Strang (1982) as a late Modern English development by which the progressive became independent of clausal environment. This development would, then, also have made the progressive more fully integrated into the English language as a whole, as a restriction on the occurrence of the construction disappeared. The CONCE data indicated (a) that the percentage of progressives that occurred in main clauses increased between periods 1 and 2, and (b) that non-expository genres had higher percentages of main-clause progressives than expository genres. The findings thus support the hypotheses that the progressive became more fully integrated into English during the 19th century, and that the construction was more fully integrated in non-expository than in expository genres.

The above results should not be taken as definite evidence that the progressive in fact developed in the directions indicated by the findings. The overall distribution of main verbs, situation types, agentive and non-agentive subjects, temporal adverbials, and clause types was not taken into consideration; thus, it cannot be claimed with absolute certainty that differences in the data are due to developments in the progressive paradigm, rather than to changes in the distribution of the five linguistic parameters under scrutiny in the present chapter. However, the likelihood of the latter type of change probably differs between the parameters. It is possible that, for instance, the English language as a whole developed towards containing relatively more main clauses and fewer subordinate clauses over the 19th century (if, for instance, non-specialist writing developed in the direction of speech); but it seems less probable that there should be pronounced changes in the occurrence of temporal adverbials or in the overall distribution of situation types. Moreover, even if, say, all of the change in the clausal distribution of the progressive were due to an increasing occurrence of main clauses in English as a whole, the effect would still have been that language users saw and heard more progressives in main clauses, which might in turn have made this type of construction more accepted and more fully integrated.

If we compare the results presented in Chapters 5 and 6, it appears that features outside the verb phrase, and outside the immediate situation, correlate better with frequency developments in the distribution of the progressive than do verb-phrase-internal and situation-internal features. Both the modification of the progressive by temporal adverbials and the clausal distribution of the construction showed signs of being linked to the increase in the frequency of the progressive. It would be an interesting question for further research to see whether the same pattern can be found for the present-day progressive; Smith's (2002) study is a valuable indicator in this respect.

In Chapters 3 through 6, the occurrence of the progressive has been analysed in terms of frequency variation with extralinguistic parameters, co-variation with sets of linguistic features, and distribution across linguistic parameters. However, the approach has largely been quantitative. Since the aspectual functions of the progressive account for most of its realizations in late Modern English, changes concerning these functions may have obscured separate tendencies in the status and development of the not-solely-aspectual functions of the construction. For this reason, I will devote the next chapter to an investigation of three types of not-solely-aspectual progressives in 19th-century English.

Chapter 7

The not-solely-aspectual progressive: An analytical approach

The not-solely-aspectual functions of the progressive are seldom discussed at length in quantitative studies of the construction. One reason for this is that, at least in late Modern English and Present-Day English, progressives with not-solely-aspectual functions are less frequent than aspectual progressives, and thus have less impact on the cumulative distribution of data. The aspectual functions of the construction are also more or less obligatory in Present-Day English.[1] However, the development of the not-solely-aspectual functions of the progressive is relevant to the integration of the construction into late Modern English, as indicated by both previous research (see e.g. Wright 1994) and results reached in the present work. In order to complement the results presented in Chapters 3 through 6, I will therefore devote the present chapter to looking at three types of progressives that express something beyond purely aspectual meaning.

There is some disagreement in previous research concerning the status of not-solely-aspectual progressives. Visser (1973: 1924; italics original) claims that all occurrences of the progressive in the history of English have the common denominator that they are *"used when the speaker chooses to focalize the listener's attention on the POST-INCEPTION PHASE of what is, was or will be going on at a point of time in the present, past or future"*, thus disqualifying not-solely-aspectual shades of meaning such as emotion.[2] Other scholars admit that the progressive has not-solely-aspectual functions, but emphasize the quantitative dominance of the aspectual functions of the construction (see e.g. Mindt 1997).

---

1   Possible exceptions include temporal *as*-clauses, where the progressive is rare even in imperfective contexts (see Övergaard 1987).

2   Scholars also disagree regarding the relation of the progressive to aspect. Zandvoort (1962: 19), Hirtle (1967: 27n.), and Visser (1973: 1923) point to differences between the Slavonic languages and English in this respect; Brusendorff (1930: 239) denies that the progressive expresses progressive aspect, instead taking the semi-aspectual meaning of simultaneity to be the core meaning of the progressive (Brusendorff 1930: 229). In contrast, Nehls (1988: 175), Söderlind (1951: 80), and Bache (1985: 303) see similarities between Slavonic and English aspect.

Hübler (1998: 92), in contrast, while he recognizes the existence of aspectual progressives, claims that the progressive can be interpreted "as a genuinely emotive language device", both historically and in Present-Day English. In Hübler's (1998: 89f.) account, the aspectual functions of the progressive have developed from the BE + preposition + gerund construction (for which see Section 2.2.2.5), while the emotional functions were inherent in the Old English progressive. The progressive is claimed to function "as an index of the speaker's emotional attitude toward the propositional context expressed" (Hübler 1998: 63).

Yet other scholars postulate a core meaning of the progressive that subsumes both aspectual and not-solely-aspectual functions.[3] According to Scheffer (1975: 40), the progressive "is used to emphasize the action, state, occurrence predicated by the verb with reference to a contextually defined moment or period in time". Scheffer intends this core meaning to subsume both aspectual and not-solely-aspectual functions. On a similar note, Åkerlund (1911: 2) claims that the core meaning which underlies all the functions of the progressive is that the construction "gives, so to speak, a stronger inner stress to the verb, makes it more sentence-stressed, by calling the interest directly to the idea of time". The division between aspectual and not-solely-aspectual functions is made more explicitly by Rydén (1997: 421), who sees the progressive as having the core meaning of "dynamic process", and as implying "situational/attitudinal immediacy and awareness"; non-progressives, in contrast, are "factual, informative, presentative rather than graphic, analytical or evaluative". This core meaning is realized in two facets, which largely correspond to aspectual and not-solely-aspectual functions, respectively. Bache (1985: 212f.) also sees a connection between the internal situational focus of imperfective aspect and shades of meaning such as intensity, vividness, and concern, and between the external focus of perfective aspect and shades of meaning such as factuality and detachment.

---

3   All researchers do not believe that such a core meaning can be found. Strang (1982: 443), for instance, claims that "it is likely that the quest for a single central function in present-day uses is a wild-goose chase", and Schousboe (2000: 115) criticizes proposed core meanings as being either vague or vulnerable to counter-examples. Nor is the border-line between presenting a core meaning of the progressive and stating the most frequent function of the construction always clear. For example, Durst-Andersen (2000) points out that Jespersen's frame-time theory is vulnerable to counter-examples, although Jespersen (1909–1949: 178) only states that his theory is applicable to the majority of the occurrences of the progressive. Moreover, all scholars have not formalized the functional load of the progressive in terms of aspectual and not-solely-aspectual uses. A few examples may suffice. Calver (1946: 323) characterizes the present non-progressive as expressing "the constitution of things", while the present progressive expresses "mere occurrence". Edgren (1985: 74) sees temporary relevance as common to all occurrences of the progressive. It is claimed by van Ek (1969) that the core meaning of the progressive is the expression of heightened temporary relevance (a core meaning which, like Scheffer's, is intended to subsume both aspectual and not-solely-aspectual functions). Stubbs (1996: 216) considers the central function of the progressive to be to encode uncertainty and change, thus connecting the progressive/non-progressive opposition to mood as well as to aspect.

Overall, a considerable number of studies include not-solely-aspectual functions in their accounts of the progressive. This is particularly true when Old and Middle English are in focus (see e.g. Kisbye 1963: 51; Nehls 1988: 180; Mustanoja 1960: 593f.); some studies claim that the expression of aspect was not the main reason for its use in these periods.[4] However, there is some disagreement concerning precisely what progressives with not-solely-aspectual functions express. The progressive is often claimed to be more subjective, emotional, vivid, tentative, descriptive, etc. than the non-progressive. What these connotations seem to have in common is that they imply an attitudinal focus from the speaker's perspective (see Rydén 1997). The exact not-solely-aspectual function conveyed is, however, in most cases dependent on the linguistic context of the progressive. Žegarac (1993: 211ff.), for instance, claims that the use of the progressive "alerts the hearer to an extra set of intended effects", and that the context plays an important part in clarifying which effect is intended.

As mentioned above, in this chapter I will examine the occurrence and development of three types of not-solely-aspectual progressives that have been addressed in previous research, as they occur in the data afforded by CONCE. The three types are:

- Progressives modified by *always* and adverbials with similar meanings (see Section 7.1), as in (87):

(87) [$A.$] James Bowditch *was* <u>continually</u> *talking* of his love to Miss Glenn, and asking me to try to make her like him.
(Trials, Bowditch, 1800–1830, p. 58)

- Potentially "experiential" progressive verb phrases, which meet several criteria that have been linked with the expression of foregrounding and/or subjectivity in previous research, viz. first- or second-person subjects, present tense, and occurrence in 'stative' situations, and in main clauses (see Section 7.2).[5] By way of exemplification, (88) meets all four criteria:

(88) I *am wanting* (yet dreading?) to see some day the additions to Sister Helen: – have even you really found it possible to augment advantageously that terse fierce masterpiece?
(Letters, Rossetti, 1870–1900, p. 100)

- "Interpretative" progressives, which are used to comment on and interpret another situation, with which the situation that includes the progressive is presented as identical (see Section 7.3), as in (89), where the progressive interprets the situation expressed by the *when*-clause:

---

4   Similarly, Brunner (1955: 221) states that most progressives in Shakespeare's works are used for situations which are considered important or interesting.

5   Section 7.2 is partly based on Smitterberg (2000b). The term "experiential" is taken from Fitzmaurice (2004a).

(89)   *Am* I *dreaming* when I think that we may derive from this much high enjoyment, and that you may see in the prospect something which is worth living for?
(Letters, Southey, 1800–1830, p. 362)

I will devote a separate section to each of the three types of not-solely-aspectual progressives under scrutiny. The types are ordered according to their dependence on explicit linguistic context. Progressives modified by adverbials like *always* can be selected using a binary classification procedure, and are thus highly context-dependent. The potentially experiential progressives were also selected on the basis of the linguistic context surrounding the progressive verb phrases, but here the interplay of four features, rather than the presence or absence of one single feature, was decisive. The interpretative progressives, in contrast, proved impossible to classify solely on the basis of discrete linguistic features whose presence or absence could be coded for in a database. Instead, close readings and decisions concerning the overall semantic content of the situation were necessary to conclude whether a progressive should be classified as interpretative or not. At the end of the chapter, the results will be summarized, and implications for the development and integration of the progressive discussed, in the light of previous research.

7.1   Progressives modified by adverbials of the ALWAYS type

The emotional, not-solely-aspectual connotations of progressives modified by adverbials such as *always* and *all the time* have often been commented on in previous research (see e.g. Jespersen 1909–1949: 191ff.; Scheffer 1975: 91f.). As Jespersen (1909–1949: 191) points out, in these cases the adverbial "does not mean 'at all times in the history of the world' … but 'at all the times we are just now concerned with' ".[6] The pattern often expresses a negative evaluation of the situation in which the progressive occurs, and the implication is then usually that the continual recurrence of the situation is a source of irritation. However, it can be seen from corpus examples such as (90) that this need not be the case (see also Bodelsen 1936: 231f.).

---

6   Bodelsen (1936: 230f.), in contrast, claims that, when *always* co-occurs with the progressive, it can only mean 'at all times', not 'at all the times we are concerned with just now'. Bodelsen (1936: 231) takes the modification of progressives by *always* to have a metaphorical meaning by which "an action which really takes place at frequent intervals is described, by a piece of picturesque exaggeration, as taking place at all times".

(90) My collector called a few days ago with his accounts (quite satisfactory). When we had gone through them, he asked me if I were writing another book. I said "of course I am – I *am* <u>always</u> *writing* books," & shewed him a lot of Manuscript.
(Letters, Butler, Samuel [2], 1870–1900, p. 122)

In this example, *am always writing* appears to lend additional emphasis to the overall statement that the subject is engaged in the process of writing another book, rather than express any negative evaluation of this process. It is also possible that there is some negative evaluation, but that it is directed at the question asked by the collector rather than at the writing process itself, and thus at another, textually adjacent situation. The fact that the subject is in the first person singular, and thus identical with the speaker, may help to indicate that the source of irritation should be shifted away from the immediate situation.

In most cases, however, it is the evaluation of the situation where the progressive occurs that seems to be intended as negative by the speaker, as in (91):

(91) … but you never did – never for an instant – trifle with me nor amuse me with what is called encouragement – a thing by the bye – which men *are* <u>continually</u> *supposing* they receive without sufficient grounds – but of which I am no great judge – as except in this instance I never had an opportunity.
(Letters, Byron, 1800–1830, p. IV.55)

In (91), the phrase *without sufficient grounds*, together with extralinguistic knowledge supposedly shared between the writer and the addressee (i.e. that a man who believes he is always encouraged can be a source of irritation), indicates that the speaker intends a negative evaluation of the situation. Charleston (1960: 229f.) sums up the situation in 20th-century English by saying that the present progressive has an emotional connotation when modified by adverbials such as *always*, and that the situation, since it is suggested that it is repeated (too) frequently, is likely to be perceived as irritating by the speaker. Charleston also comments on the modification of the past progressive by adverbials like *always* in a later section (Charleston 1960: 247f.). Killie (2004: 29) considers modification by adverbs such as *always* to be the only wholly reliable indication that a progressive has subjective functions (but cf. Fitzmaurice 2004b).

There are at least two reasons why the co-occurrence of adverbials like *always* and the progressive has been given a considerable amount of attention in previous research. First, the pattern is relatively easy to spot, as the majority of instances contain one of a quite limited, though not exclusive, set of adverbials. In the CONCE data, for instance, progressives modified by one of the five adverbials *always, constantly, continually, perpetually*, and *every day* account for more than half of the progressives that are modified by adverbials belonging to this group (see Table 70). Secondly, the modification of progressives by

212 The progressive in 19th-century English

adverbials such as *always* appears to have a long history in the English language. Scheffer (1975: 180, 219) comments on the modification of Old English progressives by adverbs like *æfre*. In Middle English, the pattern has been noticed by Scheffer (1975: 219), and also by Jespersen (1909–1949: 191), who even claims that it is "particularly frequent" in this period. Jespersen also cites early Modern English instances, as does Wright (1994).[7]

Against this background, one of two possible quantitative developments concerning progressives modified by *always* and other such adverbials can be expected. On the one hand, progressives with such modification may account for a constant proportion of all progressives through the 19th century, as such an established function will follow the general integration of the progressive into new linguistic contexts. On the other hand, the percentage may decrease in diachrony, either because the new linguistic contexts into which the progressive spread did not offer as many chances for the pattern to occur, or because it had already spread to these areas and other parts of the progressive paradigm were, so to speak, catching up with progressives modified by *always* etc. during the late Modern period.

In the present analysis, all temporal adverbials that were considered to modify progressives in Section 6.4 were gone through. Those which were classified as belonging to the same semantic field as *always* were given a specific code in the database. A relatively wide definition of this semantic field was adopted, so that longer and more specific adverbials such as *all day long* and *ever since we came* could be included in the study. Adverbials that indicated a continual occurrence of the situation which contained the progressive verb phrase were included, whether or not the situation itself was conceived of as limited in time. I will refer to members of this field as "ALWAYS-type adverbials" henceforth. The ALWAYS-type adverbials modifying progressives attested in CONCE, sorted in decreasing order of frequency, are given in Table 70.

---

7   A further reason for the attention paid to this pattern may be the seeming semantic conflict
      between a temporal adverbial indicating unlimited duration (e.g. *always*) and a verbal
      construction (i.e. the progressive) that is often taken to denote temporariness.

Table 70. ALWAYS-type adverbials modifying progressives in CONCE

Adverbial	Occurrences	Adverbial	Occurrences
always	24	*during all that time*	1
constantly	15	*each day*	1
continually	7	*eternally*	1
perpetually	5	*ever*	1
every day	4	*ever since*	1
all the time	3	*ever since I began*	1
incessantly	3	*ever since I came out*	1
all day	2	*ever since its production*	1
all day long	2	*ever since last week*	1
all the morning	2	*ever since we came*	1
almost all day long	2	*ever since we parted ...*	1
again and again	1	*ever since Wednesday*	1
all his life	1	*every day for ...*	1
all my life	1	*every minute*	1
all the afternoon	1	*every moment*	1
all morning	1	*for ever*	1
all the while	1	*forever*	1
all this fortnight	1	*nearly all the morning*	1
all through ...	1	*the whole afternoon*	1
almost all the time	1	*the whole lecture ...*	1
at all hours	1	*through the year 1613*	1
day after day	1	*unremittingly*	1

In the present section, potential not-solely-aspectual progressives were thus selected if they co-occurred with another linguistic feature, viz. ALWAYS-type adverbials; no close readings of the data were carried out to ensure that the examples actually had not-solely-aspectual functions. However, the not-solely-aspectual effect of progressives modified by ALWAYS-type adverbials has been established in previous research. It can therefore be assumed that most progressives with such modification have not-solely-aspectual connotations, in particular regarding high-frequency adverbials such as *always* and *constantly*.[8]

The period/genre breakdown of how many progressives in CONCE are modified by ALWAYS-type adverbials is given in Table 71. Note that an ALWAYS-type adverbial may have scope over more than one progressive, and that a

---

8   Some scholars have argued that not-solely-aspectual connotations of the progressive arise only from its linguistic context. This is the line taken by, for instance, Curme (1913: 176f.) and Visser (1973: 1922), although in a later work Curme (1932: 254) claims that the progressive may have emotional connotations. However, in diachrony such co-occurrences are likely to affect the meaning of the progressive. As Bybee et al. (1994: 7) point out, when a grammatical morpheme loses some of its original semantic content, "its interpretation is more and more dependent on the meaning contained in the context, and it eventually is affected by this context". Thus, collocation patterns of a linguistic feature may be a plausible indication of the future functions of the feature.

progressive may be modified by more than one ALWAYS-type adverbial; there need thus not be any exact correspondence between the total figure in Table 71 and the number of occurrences in Table 70.

Table 71.   Progressives modified by ALWAYS-type adverbials by period and genre (percentages of all progressives in each subsample within brackets)

Period	Debates	Drama	Fiction	History	Letters	Science	Trials	Total
1	3	2	1	–	14	4	6	30
	(25%)	(5%)	(1%)		(6%)	(15%)	(3%)	(5%)
2	1	4	7	3	19	5	4	43
	(9%)	(4%)	(6%)	(8%)	(4%)	(21%)	(2%)	(5%)
3	1	3	2	2	16	1	3	28
	(3%)	(3%)	(3%)	(3%)	(4%)	(3%)	(1%)	(3%)
Total	5	9	10	5	49	10	13	101
	(9%)	(3%)	(4%)	(4%)	(5%)	(12%)	(2%)	(4%)

As Table 71 demonstrates, raw frequencies are low for most period/genre subsamples. I will therefore not comment on developments within genres; results of comparisons of genre totals should also be regarded as tentative. The period results, where raw frequencies are more reliable, imply a trend towards a decrease between periods 2 and 3 in the percentage of progressives modified by ALWAYS-type adverbials. However, the decrease across the century is not statistically significant, so it is not possible to say whether the results indicate the beginning of a trend or random variation. In either case, the modification of progressives by ALWAYS-type adverbials appears to be a stable feature of 19th-century English, with roughly one progressive in 25 being modified in this way. The M-coefficients for progressives modified by ALWAYS-type adverbials do not indicate that linguistic change is taking place either: the M-coefficient is 9 in period 1, 13 in period 2, and 9 in period 3.

Turning to cross-genre variation, we find that two expository genres, Science and Debates, have the highest percentage of modification by ALWAYS-type adverbials, while the non-expository genre Trials has the lowest percentage. Given that the pattern is usually taken to express emotion, it could be expected that comparatively few progressives should co-occur with ALWAYS-type adverbials in academic writing. However, the high percentage in Science can perhaps be explained by the pattern having less emotional force in many instances in this genre. Not all progressives modified by ALWAYS-type adverbials have not-solely-aspectual functions (see Scheffer 1975: 92 and Mair and Hundt 1995: 119 for examples). Given the relatively wide range of adverbials included in the category of "ALWAYS-type adverbials" in the present study, there are likely to be a number of cases in the data where the not-solely-aspectual effect is weak or non-existent. Consider (92):

(92)   The aqueous agents *are* incessantly *labouring* to reduce the inequalities of the earth's surface to a level, while the igneous, on the other hand, are equally active in restoring the unevenness of the external crust, partly by heaping up new matter in certain localities, and partly by depressing one portion, and forcing out another of the earth's envelope.
(Science, Lyell, 1800–1830, p. 167)

On the one hand, the modification of the progressive by the ALWAYS-type adverbial *incessantly* in (92) may be said to be less emotionally loaded than those in (90) and (91) cited above, or even not to be emotionally loaded at all; since the selection process identified potential rather than actual not-solely-aspectual progressives, it may be that (92) simply does not carry not-solely-aspectual force. On the other hand, this may also be an impression readers get because academic texts contain fewer emotional expressions than, for instance, novels and private letters, particularly in Present-Day English. However, Görlach (1999: 150) claims that Science texts were less objective and impersonal in at least the early 19th century than today. The progressive in (92) can perhaps be seen as having some not-solely-aspectual connotations despite its occurring in Science: it fits well with a presentation of the "aqueous agents" as voluntary agents rather than inanimate forces of nature (as indicated by the term *agents*, as well as the verb LABOUR). As pointed out in Smitterberg et al. (2000: 112), such progressives may denote general emphasis and vividness rather than (negative) evaluation.

There are also cases in Science where a more clear-cut not-solely-aspectual shade of meaning is conveyed by the co-occurrence of the progressive and an ALWAYS-type adverbial, as in (93):

(93)   So in the Russian exchanges, owing to the enormous amount of paper money afloat, which is practically inconvertible, the most violent fluctuations *are* constantly *occurring*.
(Science, Goschen, 1850–1870, p. 65)

In (93), the presence of further features indicating a subjective attitude (*enormous amount*, *the most violent fluctuations*) places the progressive and the ALWAYS-type adverbial *constantly* in an emotionally loaded context. Such not-solely-aspectual co-occurrences of progressives and ALWAYS-type adverbials may have been more characteristic of the more personal style that, according to Görlach (1999: 150), was common during parts of the 19th century, than of the objective style with which scientific writing is usually associated in Present-Day English.[9]

---

9   It is noteworthy that four of the ten progressives modified by ALWAYS-type adverbials in Science, including (93), come from George Joachim Goschen's text, as there may have been some German influence on Goschen's English. Goschen had a German father and an English mother; the father settled in London in 1814 (Elliot 1911: 2ff.). Goschen also spent three years in a German school before being sent to Rugby (Elliot 1911: 6f.). Smitterberg et al. (2000) found that there is a greater tendency for Present-Day German verb phrases than Present-Day English verb phrases to be modified by temporal adverbials (although this

In Debates, the modification of the progressive by ALWAYS-type adverbials rather appears to fulfil a rhetorical function in the majority of cases. The not-solely-aspectual implication is also more transparent in this genre: typically, progressives modified by ALWAYS-type adverbials show that the speaker dislikes the content of the situation in which the progressive occurs, as in (94):

(94)   If lord Wellington should survive the scrapes into which he *was* constantly *bringing* his army, he might one day be entitled to distinction and rewards. (Debates, 1800–1830, p. XV.448)

Whereas Science texts tend to be monologic, Debates texts are more dialogic in nature; in addition, the speakers who take turns in Debates are typically opposed to one another's views. Because progressives modified by ALWAYS-type adverbials give speakers an opportunity to comment negatively on some aspect of the previous turn, it is not surprising that the not-solely-aspectual functions of the co-occurrence should stand out more clearly in Debates than in Science.

The low percentage of progressives modified by ALWAYS-type adverbials in Trials may also be a result of genre-specific constraints. In this genre, a rather formal speech situation, as well as a fact-oriented and narrative style, may impose constraints on the occurrence of progressives with such modification.[10] When the pattern occurs, as in (95), in most cases it seems to provide general emphasis rather than express irritation with the content of the predication.

(95)   [$A.$] I thought him to be a very religious man; when he had time he *was* always *reading* his bible or his hymn book. (Trials, Martin, 1800–1830, p. 13)

In the remaining four genres, progressives that are modified by ALWAYS-type adverbials make up between 3% and 5% of all progressive verb phrases. As pointed out above, such progressives often express a negative evaluation of the content of the situation, though there are also cases where more general emotional emphasis seems to be intended. Some of the five progressives modified by ALWAYS-type adverbials in History seem to imply more general emphasis rather than attitudinal evaluation, though these two elements are often both present, as in

---

difference was, in fact, noticeable in political but not academic language), possibly because German lacks a progressive that can make the aspectual status of a situation explicit. It is possible that Goschen's English was influenced by German in this respect and that this would account partly for his comparatively frequent use of progressives modified by ALWAYS-type adverbials.

10   On the other hand, the Trials genre came out as one of the most involved genres in CONCE in Geisler's (2002) factor score analysis of the corpus (see Chapter 4). However, it is possible that, whereas Trials may contain many involved features such as second-person pronouns and private verbs, the formality of the speech situation still keeps down the frequency of more overtly emotional features.

(96). (As pointed out above, similar instances could be found in Science, the other genre in CONCE that consists of academic prose.)

(96)   His knowledge of a soldier's art *was* always *prompting* him to observe the rules of war, which a man of genius would probably have disregarded. (History, Walpole, 1870–1900, p. VI.313)

In contrast, Drama contains several instances where the context is highly emotional and evaluative, for instance (97):

(97)   [$HANNAH.$]
        [$Shutting the oven door.$] Not me! Torturing prisoners might a' done for them Middling Ages what Noah's always *clattering* about, but not for my time o' life. I'll shut that wicket.
        (Drama, Pinero, 1870–1900, p. 108)

    In sum, the occurrence of progressives modified by ALWAYS-type adverbials appears to be stable in late Modern English. In cases where the percentage of progressives with such modification is low in a given genre, or where the shade of meaning expressed appears to vary across the genre parameter, this seems to be explicable in terms of genre-specific constraints (which may change in diachrony). The modification of the progressive by ALWAYS-type adverbials gives the impression of being a feature that is integrated to a high degree into late Modern English grammar, which is expected considering that progressives with such modification have been attested even in Old English.

7.2   Potentially experiential progressives

Progressives modified by ALWAYS-type adverbials, the topic of the preceding section, constitute an easily recognizable subset of progressive verb phrases that often have not-solely-aspectual functions. However, there are also other cases where the progressive is felt to have not-solely-aspectual connotations of subjectivity, emphasis, intensity, emotion etc., but where explicit modification by ALWAYS-type adverbials is absent. Since the formal make-up of the progressive itself does not vary between aspectual and not-solely-aspectual instances, other, less apparent, contextual features can be assumed to be at work in these cases. In the present section, I will use combinations of contextual features that co-occur with progressive verb phrases in order to identify potential not-solely-aspectual progressives in the data. I will also complement this selection procedure by checking how many of the progressives selected have overt expressions of emotion in the near context.
    As regards the question of what contextual features might be suitable candidates for inclusion in the analysis, Wright (1994) is an important study.

Wright (1994: 472) lists five features that characterize what she calls the "modal" progressive. (All features do not have to be present in every instance of a modal progressive, however.) Modal progressives have foregrounding, non-truth-conditional, and non-aspectual functions, as opposed to the backgrounding functions of aspectual progressives (Wright 1994: 472f.). The features are listed in Table 72.

Table 72.   Wright's (1994) diagnostics for the modal progressive

Diagnostic	Characteristic
Syntactic environment	Main vs. subordinate clause
Tense	Present vs. past
Verb type	Private (cognitive) vs. activity
Identity of subject	First, second, third person
Lexical support	Adverbial modification

In Wright (1995: 158f.), four of these features are explained in more detail. Main-clause occurrence is taken to be an indicator of foregrounding; lexical support is claimed to draw readers' attention to the expressiveness of the progressive; private verbs are considered more likely than activity verbs to support experiential/expressive readings; and first-person subjects are said to promote the communication of a first-hand experience. As for the present tense, this feature was suggested in Section 5.1 as more likely than the past tense to promote not-solely-aspectual interpretations. In what follows, I will develop Wright's model further and adapt it to a quantitative methodology.

Wright (1994: 468) links the modal progressive to many not-solely-aspectual functions that have been proposed for the construction in the literature, among others Ljung's (1980) interpretative function (see Section 7.3). In other words, it seems that modal progressives are hypothesized to account for a large share of the not-solely-aspectual occurrences of the construction, which makes the diagnostics important for future research. Wright (1994) illustrates her diagnostics with corpus examples, but also looks specifically at the distribution of the progressives across the parameters of clause and tense: main-clause and present-tense occurrences outnumber subordinate-clause and past-tense occurrences in her corpus. However, as aspectual progressives are usually taken to outnumber not-solely-aspectual occurrences of the construction, a progressive verb phrase that only meets one of Wright's (1994) criteria cannot be safely classified as not solely aspectual (with the possible exception of adverbial support – see below): otherwise, Drama texts would be dominated by not-solely-aspectual progressives. This is also indicated by Wright, who (1994: 472) refers to each feature as "partly instrumental" in bringing out a not-solely-aspectual function of the progressive in some of her examples. In the absence of stronger criteria, it seems that a combination of the diagnostics outlined in Table 72 may be a good starting-point for quantitative research.

Killie (2004) claims that, with the exception of modification by ALWAYS-type adverbials, Wright's (1994) criteria are not reliable indicators of subjectivity in early Modern English progressives. Killie's claim is based on an investigation of a number of ALWAYS-type adverbs that modify progressives; Killie (2004) finds that the modified progressives, which are considered subjective, do not appear to favour main clauses, first- or second-person subjects, the present tense, or cognitive verbs. However, as I show below, the special status of progressives modified by ALWAYS-type adverbials makes it possible for a subjective interpretation to arise even though the other indicators are not present (see Section 7.1 of the present study; see also example 98 below). In addition, Fitzmaurice (2004b: 183) recognizes that, even if most of the criteria she listed in Wright (1994) are present in the context of a progressive verb phrase, there is no guarantee that the progressive in question does not have primarily aspectual functions. Interestingly, Killie (2004: 43) mentions the possibility that several linguistic features in combination may trigger a subjective reading as a topic worthy of further investigation.

In a later study, Fitzmaurice (2004a) further develops the framework she described in Wright (1994), and argues that the selection of a figurative main verb by speakers is an important sign that a progressive has a subjective function. (For a comparison of Fitzmaurice's results and mine, see Smitterberg 2004.) In Fitzmaurice (2004b: 183), it is even claimed to be "the best independent indicator" of subjectivity in progressive constructions. However, Killie (2004: 42) found that, in her corpus, most progressive verb phrases which were modified by *always* and similar adverbs, and which were thus considered subjective, had main verbs that were not used figuratively, which may argue against Fitzmaurice's claim (see above for a discussion of Killie's methodology). In addition, decisions regarding when the use of a verb should be considered figurative involve a certain amount of inherent subjectivity (see Section 7.3 for a related classification). For these reasons, the criterion of figurative verb use was not included in this study.

In what follows, I will use a modified version of Wright's (1994) list of diagnostics to investigate the occurrence of not-solely-aspectual progressives in CONCE from a quantitative perspective. Wright's diagnostics were adapted to the present study in the following way. All progressives occurring in clauses that were not subordinate to any other clause were considered to meet the main-clause criterion. The tense criterion was met by progressives occurring in verb phrases with a finite verb in the present tense and without perfect or modal auxiliaries. Instead of looking at verb type, I classified all progressives that occurred in 'stative' situations (see Section 6.2.2), many of which have private main verbs such as WANT and THINK, as meeting the third criterion. As for identity of subject, this criterion was considered to be met by progressives that had a first- or second-person subject. Wright (1994) does not say that the "identity of subject" criterion should be interpreted so that first- and second-person subjects are diagnostic of modal progressives, whereas third-person subjects are not: there is no "vs." indicating opposition on this parameter in her list of diagnostics. Moreover, in Wright (1995) it rather seems that first-person subjects should indicate a subjectivity-encoding progressive, as opposed to second- and third-person subjects. However, both first- and second-person subjects are characteristic of dialogic communication, with its connotations of situational immediacy. For this reason, I grouped first- and second-person subjects together as indicators of potentially experiential progressives.

The criterion of lexical support, however, was not included in the present analysis, but instead treated separately in Section 7.1. This criterion is different from the other four criteria in three important ways. First, it is not wholly clear what adverbials should be included in the definition of this criterion: Wright (1994) includes chiefly, but not exclusively, adverbs of the ALWAYS type (see Section 7.1) in her examples. Secondly, the categories of present vs. past tense, main vs. subordinate clauses, 'stative' vs. other situations, and first- or second- vs. third-person subjects apply to almost all progressives in the data (exceptions include non-finite progressive verb phrases and progressives which could not be classified with certainty on one or more of the above parameters). In contrast, nothing requires a progressive to be modified by temporal adverbials, a subset of which (e.g. ALWAYS-type adverbials) can serve as diagnostics for a not-solely-aspectual interpretation. (As shown in Sections 6.4 and 7.1, 27% of all progressives in CONCE were modified by temporal adverbials in general, and 4% by ALWAYS-type adverbials.) Thirdly, the modification of progressives by ALWAYS-type adverbials appears to be a stronger indicator of not-solely-aspectual status than the other four criteria, given that this feature has a long history and is frequently commented on in previous research. In CONCE, cases can be found where a progressive with ALWAYS-type adverbial modification has a not-solely-aspectual function although none of the other four criteria is met, as in (98):

(98)   It was, indeed, wonderful, that, with greater means of rewarding merit, than all the combined merit and deserts of Europe could possibly exhaust, they *were* perpetually *throwing* the burden upon the people.
(Debates, 1800–1830, p. XV.456)

Progressive verb phrases that met three or four of the four remaining criteria were selected for the present study. Progressives that were modified by an ALWAYS-type adverbial were then excluded from the counts, so that this factor would not affect the results.[11] It was not easy to find a suitable term for the progressives selected. In the end, I adopted the term "potentially experiential progressives". "Experiential" is one of the terms used by Fitzmaurice (2004a) to refer to not-solely-aspectual progressives; the word "potentially" indicates that, as the selection was purely context-driven and did not involve close readings of individual instances, there is no guarantee that each progressive selected has a not-solely-aspectual function. The criteria are summarized in Table 73.

---

11   A total of 15 progressives that met three or four of the four criteria were modified by
ALWAYS-type adverbials, and were thus excluded from the counts.

Table 73.   Criteria used to select potentially experiential progressives

Criterion	Characteristic
Tense	The progressive verb phrase is in the present tense and has no perfect or modal auxiliary
Clause	The progressive occurs in a main clause
Person	The progressive verb phrase has a first- or second-person subject
Situation type	The progressive is part of a 'stative' situation

By way of exemplification, consider the potentially experiential progressives (88) and (99)–(102). Of these, (88), also cited above, meets all four criteria, whereas (99) fails to meet the tense criterion, (100) the clause criterion, (101) the person criterion, and (102) the situation-type criterion.

(88)   I *am wanting* (yet dreading?) to see some day the additions to Sister Helen: – have even you really found it possible to augment advantageously that terse fierce masterpiece?
(Letters, Rossetti, 1870–1900, p. 100)

(99)   And, added to this, I *have been hoping* and expecting to get away for England for five months past, and Mr. Chapman not arriving, Sir Alexander's importunities have always overpowered me, though my gloom has increased at each disappointment.
(Letters, Coleridge, 1800–1830, pp. 496–497)

(100)   [$Admiral.$] If I were to go down on my knees to her I couldn't express a thousandth part of the sorrow I'*m feeling* at this moment.
(Drama, Jones, 1870–1900, p. 51)

(101)   Ernest *is hoping* to get an Irish magistracy, a better thing than his post at York, though not one that I should covet.
(Letters, Butler, May, 1870–1900, p. 226)

(102)   Ye'*re ganging* fra my hairt to anither, who'll gie thee mairo' the gude things o' this world than I could ever gie 'ee, except love, an' o' that my hairt is full indeed!
(Drama, Gilbert, 1870–1900, p. 16)

The decision to draw the line at three criteria was based primarily on the distribution of the data. On the one hand, if progressives that met only two criteria were included, many progressives that were aspectual rather than not solely aspectual would be selected; on the other hand, if all four of the criteria had to be met, the material would yield too few progressives for a quantitative analysis to be meaningful, and many progressives with not-solely-aspectual functions would be left out of the analyses. (I will return to the issue of how many potentially experiential progressives failed to meet each of the criteria, and of how many met all of them, later on in the present section.)

As pointed out above, since the selection of potentially experiential progressives was thus carried out automatically (after the database had been coded manually for the relevant linguistic parameters), I cannot claim that all selected progressives in my material have not-solely-aspectual functions. Furthermore, all not-solely-aspectual progressives are not included in the category of potentially experiential progressives. First, as pointed out above, progressives modified by ALWAYS-type adverbials were excluded from the counts of potentially experiential progressives. Secondly, the category of interpretative progressives (see Section 7.3) overlaps only partly with that of potentially experiential progressives. Thirdly, there may be other not-solely-aspectual functions of the progressive which are not captured by any of the three analyses included in this chapter. The present analysis should rather be seen as an attempt to investigate a sub-group of not-solely-aspectual progressives with the aid of corpus-based, quantitative methods.[12]

The distribution of potentially experiential progressives in CONCE is given in Table 74.

Table 74.   Potentially experiential progressives in CONCE by period and genre (percentages of all progressives in each subsample within brackets)

Period	Debates	Drama	Fiction	History	Letters	Science	Trials	Total
1	–	9	4	–	38	1	8	60
		(24%)	(5%)		(15%)	(4%)	(4%)	(10%)
2	1	30	10	–	80	1	19	141
	(9%)	(28%)	(8%)		(19%)	(4%)	(11%)	(16%)
3	3	39	8	–	91	1	21	163
	(10%)	(33%)	(12%)		(24%)	(3%)	(9%)	(17%)
Total	4	78	22	–	209	3	48	364
	(8%)	(30%)	(8%)		(20%)	(4%)	(8%)	(15%)

As shown in Table 74, potentially experiential progressives account for 15% of all progressives in CONCE. In Section 7.1, it was shown that the percentage of modification by ALWAYS-type adverbials was stable in diachrony; the percentage of potentially experiential progressives, in contrast, displays a consistent, and statistically significant, increase, from 10% to 17%. Potentially experiential progressives thus account for an increasingly larger share of all occurrences of the progressive through the 1800s. The increase is even more marked in terms of normalized frequencies: the M-coefficient for potentially experiential progressives is 17 in period 1, 41 in period 2, and 55 in period 3. Thus, roughly

---

12   Note, however, that theoretical and intuitive elements are not absent from such a methodology, as decisions concerning what features in the linguistic context are relevant precede the quantitative classification of the data.

speaking, the frequency of potentially experiential progressives trebles across the 19th century.

As regards the cross-genre distribution, potentially experiential progressives are especially common in Letters and, above all, Drama. It is likely that the informal and dialogic format of Drama texts accounts for part of this high percentage: owing to these characteristics, Drama texts can be expected to contain a large number of emotional and attitudinal linguistic features.[13] In Letters, the high percentage may be due to the frequent communication of subjective, first-hand experiences in this genre. Debates, Fiction, and Trials form a middle ground, whereas there are few potentially experiential progressives in Science, and none in History.[14] (However, low raw frequencies in the three expository genres mean that results for these subsamples are not reliable.) Against the background of these results, the potentially experiential progressive seems to be frequent in genres that incorporate spoken, colloquial, and subjective features, which is in line with Wright's (1994) characterization of the modal progressive as a vehicle for encoding subjectivity in texts.[15]

Potentially experiential progressives also appear to be a feature characteristic of involved production. If the raw frequencies of potentially experiential progressives for genre subsamples in CONCE are turned into M-coefficients, these normalized frequencies can be compared with the results Geisler (2000) reached when calculating factor scores for the genres in CONCE on four of the dimensions of Biber's (1988) factor analysis. Table 75 shows the results of the comparison. As in other tables in the present work where results from Geisler's factor score analyses are presented, the order of the genres on Dimensions 3 and 5 has been reversed: high rankings on these dimensions thus correspond to situation-dependent reference and non-abstract information respectively.

---

13   The difference between dialogue and narrative in Fiction is also revelatory of the importance of dialogic, situational immediacy for the occurrence of potentially experiential progressives. Whereas 23% of all progressives in dialogue in this genre are potentially experiential, this is only true for 1% of the progressives that occur in non-dialogue (see Section 3.2.4.3 for a discussion of this division).

14   In History, the preponderance of past-tense progressives contributes to making potentially experiential progressives infrequent. To some extent, the same can be claimed for narrative passages in Fiction and Trials, and for the parts of Debates that are presented as indirect speech.

15   I use the term "subjectivity" in Finegan's (1995: 1) sense of 'expression of self and the representation of a speaker's (or, more generally, a locutionary agent's) perspective or point of view in discourse – what has been called a speaker's imprint'.

Table 75.   The order of the genres in CONCE with respect to the frequency of the
potentially experiential progressive (M-coefficients) and to
Dimensions 1 (Involved vs. informational production), 2 (Narrative
vs. non-narrative concerns), 3 (Elaborated vs. situation-dependent
reference), and 5 (Abstract vs. non-abstract information) (dimension
scores taken from Geisler 2000)

M-coefficient	Dimension 1	Dimension 2	Dimension 3	Dimension 5
Drama	Drama	Trials	Letters	Drama
(87)	(13.28)	(3.79)	(–2.38)	(–2.40)
Letters	Trials	Fiction	Trials	Trials
(61)	(11.24)	(1.98)	(–1.92)	(–2.30)
Trials	Letters	History	Drama	Fiction
(25)	(3.92)	(–0.34)	(–1.83)	(–1.12)
Fiction	Fiction	Debates	Fiction	Letters
(20)	(–2.42)	(–0.66)	(–1.53)	(–0.83)
Debates	Debates	Drama	Science	Debates
(7)	(–8.64)	(–1.05)	(2.23)	(1.79)
Science	Science	Letters	History	History
(3)	(–8.93)	(–1.56)	(3.00)	(2.93)
History	History	Science	Debates	Science
(–)	(–19.41)	(–5.52)	(3.89)	(4.32)

The potentially experiential progressive appears to have affinities above all with
linguistic features that indicate involved production: apart from Trials and
Letters, the order of the genres is identical in these two columns. However, the
patterns formed by the actual M-coefficients and dimension scores are not as
similar, and the low raw frequencies for the expository genres make the relative
order of these genres unreliable. Nevertheless, the similarity with Dimension 1 is
interesting, as such a pattern would support a characterization of the potentially
experiential progressive as an indicator of subjectivity: features indicating
involved production include subjective features such as first-person pronouns and
private verbs.[16]

Dimension 1 of Biber's (1988) factor analysis is one of the three
dimensions that separate stereotypically oral from stereotypically literate genres
(Biber and Finegan 1997: 260); the other two are Dimensions 3 and 5. In the
CONCE corpus, these dimensions separate the non-expository genres Drama,
Fiction, Letters, and Trials from the expository genres Debates, History, and

---

16   Since some features that load on Dimension 1 as indicative of involved production are partly
or wholly identical with some of the criteria used to select potentially experiential
progressives, it can be argued that it is only natural that genres should display the same
pattern with respect to potentially experiential progressives and Dimension 1. However, since
the selection of potentially experiential progressives also presupposes that these features
occur together, within or in the near context of progressive verb phrases, this cannot be taken
for granted.

Science (Geisler 2002). As Table 75 shows, the same division occurs when the frequency of potentially experiential progressives (as well as the overall frequency of the progressive – see Chapter 3) is compared across genres. The results thus indicate that the potentially experiential progressive is characteristic of non-expository texts which are speech-related and/or incorporate colloquial features.

As regards which criteria the potentially experiential progressives meet, 298 of the total of 364, or 82%, fail to meet the situation-type criterion, as in example (102), quoted above. Of the remaining 66 potentially experiential progressives, 29 (or 8% of all potentially experiential progressives) meet all four criteria, as in (88); 13 (4%) fail the tense criterion, as in (99); 13 (4%) do not meet the clause criterion, as in (100); and 11 (3%) fail the person criterion, as in (101). These results indicate that the four criteria used to select potentially experiential progressives may not be on an equal footing. Since very few of the progressives selected meet the situation-type criterion, progressives in 'stative' situations may be more marked and in this respect a stronger indication that the progressive has a not-solely-aspectual function.

There is some support for such a hypothesis in previous research on the co-occurrence of the progressive with these four linguistic features. Although results presented in Strang (1982) indicate that, at least in narrative prose, the progressive was less fully integrated in main than in subordinate clauses in 19th-century English, there do not seem to have been any severe restrictions on main-clause occurrence, as evidenced by the results presented in Section 6.5. Present-tense progressives without passive or modal auxiliaries were common even in Old English. As for the person criterion, if the late Modern English progressive still tended to occur chiefly with animate subjects, this may in fact have increased the percentage of first- and second-person subjects compared with Present-Day English, since inanimate subjects tend to occur in the third person. In contrast to these three criteria, progressives in 'stative' situations still constitute a marked feature in Present-Day English (see Quirk et al. 1985: 200).

As pointed out above, the potentially experiential progressives were selected on the basis of their co-occurrence with three or four of four linguistic features; the selected instances were not checked individually, using close readings, to ensure that they had not-solely-aspectual functions. Such a semi-automatic selectional method has the advantages that (a) it is comparatively objective in that the criteria used are defined explicitly, and (b) it does not entail the application of Present-Day English intuitions to late Modern English data. However, this type of selection process may also lead to progressives that are, in fact, mainly aspectual being selected. Thus, the results presented in Table 74 only imply that the occurrence potential of the not-solely-aspectual progressive has increased, as not all progressives selected necessarily have not-solely-aspectual status. In order to further increase the likelihood that the potentially experiential progressives in the data had not-solely-aspectual functions, I added yet another feature to the analysis, viz. the overt expression of emotion in the near context of the potentially experiential progressives. This feature was chosen because not-solely-aspectual progressives are often said to have emotional connotations; in addition, emotional expressions often encode subjectivity in texts. However, by narrowing the selection in this way I am likely to be excluding a number of not-solely-aspectual progressives from the counts, as not all potentially experiential progressives need an expression of emotion in the near context for their not-solely-aspectual function to be brought out.

In order to quantify the data, I classified all the potentially experiential progressives in CONCE according to whether or not they had at least one expression of emotion in the near context. Features counted as expressions of emotion included subjective evaluative adjectives and exclamations.[17] For exemplification, see (103) and (104):

(103) [$LILIAN.$] [$excitedly$] You *are jesting!* – oh, say that you are jesting! Send after them! part them – part them, as you value my peace – my life! (Drama, Marston, 1850–1870, p. 22)

(104) So she turned away from all Peggy's asides and signs; but she made one or two very mal-apropos answers to what was said; and at last, seized with a bright idea, she exclaimed, "Poor sweet Carlo! I'*m forgetting* him. Come down stairs with me, poor ittie doggie, and it shall have its tea, it shall!" (Fiction, Gaskell, 1850–1870, p. 132)

The extent to which the potentially experiential progressives in CONCE were modified by expressions of emotion is shown in Table 76. The table shows that there are no potentially experiential progressives modified by expressions of emotion in History or Science, nor in the first two periods of Debates and the last period of Trials; moreover, the total raw frequencies in Debates, Fiction, and Trials are low.[18] Results for these five genres are thus not reliable.

---

17   The diversity of emotional expressions is difficult to capture using discrete linguistic categories, as the emotional shade of meaning of a given expression may itself be context-dependent. For instance, repeating words or phrases may, in some contexts, provide emphasis, while in other contexts the same strategy may be used in the interest of clarity. Similarly, subjectivity and emotion can be brought out by whole expressions rather than single adjectives, and sometimes by stylistic features like non-standard language. However, subjective evaluative adjectives and exclamations were the two discrete categories that accounted for most expressions of emotion co-occurring with potentially experiential progressives in the data.

18   As there are no potentially experiential progressives in History, nor in period 1 of Debates, five cells are empty by definition in Table 76. This also means that it is not possible to calculate percentages for these cells, since doing so would entail division by zero.

Table 76. Potentially experiential progressives modified by expressions of emotion by period and genre (percentages of all potentially experiential progressives in each subsample within brackets)

Period	Debates	Drama	Fiction	History	Letters	Science	Trials	Total
1	–	2	1	–	8	–	1	12
		(22%)	(25%)		(21%)		(12%)	(20%)
2	–	11	3	–	15	–	1	30
		(37%)	(30%)		(19%)		(5%)	(21%)
3	1	10	1	–	19	–	–	31
	(33%)	(26%)	(12%)		(21%)			(19%)
Total	1	23	5	–	42	–	2	73
	(25%)	(29%)	(23%)		(20%)		(4%)	(20%)

In the two remaining genres, Drama and Letters, 29% and 20% respectively of the potentially experiential progressives have expressions of emotion in the near context. If we turn to period totals, the percentage of all potentially experiential progressives that have expressions of emotion in the near context exhibits no consistent pattern through the 19th century; the picture is rather one of stability in diachrony. Of all potentially experiential progressives in CONCE, 20% have expressions of emotion in the near context, corresponding to 3% of all progressives in the corpus. In other words, potentially experiential progressives with expressions of emotion in the near context are only slightly less common than progressives modified by ALWAYS-type adverbials, which account for 4% of all progressives in CONCE (see Section 7.1). As it can be assumed with relative safety that potentially experiential progressives with expressions of emotion in the near context have not-solely-aspectual functions in addition to or instead of their aspectual functions, this result shows that the potentially experiential progressive may be an important subtype of not-solely-aspectual progressives.

7.3 The interpretative progressive

In this section, I will focus on what Quirk et al. (1985: 198n.) refer to as a possible fourth component of the meaning of the progressive, viz. "that the event described has an interrelationship or identity with another simultaneous event". Many scholars have noted that the progressive frequently presents two situations as simultaneous, with one of them overlapping the other (as in *They were leaving when I arrived*), where the non-progressive would present them as following each other (as in *They left when I arrived*); Jespersen (1909–1949) even considered this expression of a time-frame to be the most important function of the progressive. In some cases, however, the progressive suggests that the two situations are identical rather than simultaneous (see e.g. Ota 1963: 63 and Edgren 1971: 131); it is these latter cases that will be analysed in the present section. Charleston (1960: 246) notices the similarity between the two functions, and claims that in the latter case the progressive is "not parallel with, but identical with, another activity or state. This is a form of interpreting the implications of one activity or state in terms of another".[19]

In these contexts, a not-solely-aspectual interpretation of the progressive may arise. Instead of looking at two actions as simultaneous (a statement that is often objectively verifiable), the speaker presents the actions as identical (a statement that is dependent on subjective judgement). By way of exemplification, consider (105) and (106):

(105)   One must not jump to conclusions, but I believe that man to be such an utter scoundrel that I do not think I *am doing* him much wrong <u>if I suspect that the story of his wife's death was a pure fabrication of his own.</u>
(Letters, Butler, Samuel [2], 1870–1900, p. 228)

(106)   [$Sir R. [Carelessly.]$] What was the name of the church?
[$Lucien.$] Saint – Saint – Something.
[$Sir R.$] What was the church like?
[$Lucien.$] The inside?
[$Sir R.$] Yes.
[$Lucien.$] The inside? [$Beginning to flounder.$] There was nothing remarkable about the inside.
[$Sir R.$] Was it a large church?
[$Lucien.$] Yes – rather – rather a large church – a medium sized church – [$Catches SIR RICHARD'S eye.$] You'*re pumping* me!
(Drama, Jones, 1870–1900, p. 53)

In (105), the writer expresses an identity between the situation containing the progressive *am doing* and the content of the following *if*-clause; the situation containing the progressive may be said to provide a subjective interpretation of the situation described in the *if*-clause (the subjectivity is further underscored by the verb THINK, which precedes the interpretative progressive). In (106), the connection between the two situations is less explicit. Lucien realizes that Sir R. may be trying to obtain information from him, and interprets the entire preceding exchange using a progressive. Unlike (105), (106) contains no overt mention of the situation that the progressive interprets, but a non-finite clause like *by asking me all these questions* could be inserted before or after the clause containing the progressive with little change of meaning. According to Ljung (1980: 77), the interpreted situation is frequently thus omitted. Following Ljung, I have adopted the term "interpretative progressives" to refer to progressives such as those in

---

19   Charleston (1960) discusses the past progressive in the above quote; however, she (1960: 229) notes a similar function of the present progressive.

(105) and (106), which have not-solely-aspectual implications of this kind instead of or, more commonly, in addition to their aspectual functions.[20]

One of the first scholars to pay attention to this function of the progressive appears to have been Smith (1917). He considers this function to be related to that expressed by progressives of BE (see Section 6.1.2) and by gerundial constructions (as in *That is putting it mildly*). The semantic relation with progressives of BE is also pointed out by Ljung (1980: 69ff.). Buyssens (1968: 136) notes that progressives in examples like (105) are not required by the aspectual characteristics of the situation: in (105), the action described by the progressive and that described in the *if*-clause are taken to be identical, and yet the former is in the progressive but the latter in the non-progressive.

The occurrence of the interpretative progressive is also of interest from a diachronic perspective. König (1980: 281), basing his hypothesis on Buyssens's (1968) investigation, assumes that the interpretative progressive "is a more recent phenomenon in the history of English". If König's assumption is true, the frequency of interpretative progressives should be low and/or rising in late Modern English. However, Arnaud (2002) lists several 19th-century instances, and Jespersen (1909–1949: 187) and Buyssens (1968: 317f.) both give some early Modern English examples, which raises the question of what status interpretative progressives had in 19th-century English.

There are some differences in the criteria that have been used to identify interpretative progressives in previous research. Wright (1994: 468ff.), for instance, implies that the modal progressive (see Section 7.2) is similar to Ljung's (1980) interpretative progressive. However, a pilot study based on parts of CONCE revealed that only slightly more than half of the interpretative progressives in the data were also either potentially experiential progressives or progressives modified by ALWAYS-type adverbials. (Differences between Wright's classificatory framework and that of the present study may underlie this discrepancy.) Based on the results of this pilot study, I undertook a separate investigation of the interpretative progressive in the data afforded by CONCE. I took the interpretative function to be more specific than, and thus separate from, the more general not-solely-aspectual functions of the progressive analysed in Sections 7.1 and 7.2. This functional separation should make it possible for a progressive to be both interpretative and potentially experiential, or both

---

20   All scholars do not seem to agree that this is a not-solely-aspectual function. Ljung (1980: 85), for instance, claims that the progressive still expresses imperfective aspect in these cases, but that its interplay with other linguistic features may create special effects, such as the interpretative progressive (see also Huddleston and Pullum 2002: 165). However, in some examples, such as (105), the progressive could not be replaced with a non-progressive without loss of interpretative meaning: a non-progressive (*...I do him much wrong...*) would not make sense in (105), and the closest non-progressive option, *will do*, would express consequence rather than identity. In some cases, the progressive is thus necessary for an interpretation to arise: and this interpretation, i.e. the expression of identity of two situations, is not ultimately an aspectual function, although identity presupposes simultaneity. Against this background, it can be assumed that the interpretative progressive has a not-solely-aspectual, context-dependent function.

interpretative and modified by an ALWAYS-type adverbial. Consequently, I did not classify interpretative progressives that were also potentially experiential progressives or modified by ALWAYS-type adverbials apart from other interpretative progressives, although I will comment on the extent to which these selections overlap in the data.

A closely related issue concerns what types of progressive verb phrases should be considered interpretative. Ljung (1980: 69, 89) appears to consider progressives in 'stative' situations and progressives of verbs of sensation as interpretative by default.[21] Ljung (1980: 78f.) also claims that interpretative progressives chiefly occur with human subjects. König (1980) and Wright (1994), however, seem to consider other parameters, such as main-clause occurrence and syntactic environment, potentially important in bringing out the interpretative function of the progressive. Since there is, then, no complete agreement on how interpretative progressives should be selected, I went through the progressives in CONCE example by example and classified them according to whether they were interpretative or not, without imposing any constraints such as those mentioned above on the data prior to classification.

As close readings were necessary to decide whether the progressives in CONCE had interpretative connotations, the classification process was more subjective than when potentially experiential progressives and progressives modified by ALWAYS-type adverbials were selected. I looked at each progressive in CONCE to see whether the situation it described could be seen as identical with another situation, mentioned explicitly or inferred from the context, and whether the progressive would, then, provide an interpretation of this other situation. Progressives that met these criteria were classified as interpretative. The distribution of interpretative progressives is given in Table 77. The table groups the progressives into period, genre, and period/genre subsamples; however, given the low overall frequency of the interpretative progressive, results for period/genre subsamples, and for some genre subsamples, should be treated with caution.

---

21   However, as was discussed in Section 6.2, progressives in 'stative' situations may also, for instance, imply temporariness or general emphasis. But since subjective close readings are often necessary to identify interpretative progressives, scholars are likely to classify some such constructions in different ways.

Table 77.   Interpretative progressives by period and genre (percentages of all
            progressives in each subsample within brackets)

Period	Debates	Drama	Fiction	History	Letters	Science	Trials	Total
1	1	4	2	1	5	1	6	20
	(8%)	(11%)	(2%)	(10%)	(2%)	(4%)	(3%)	(3%)
2	2	7	10	–	3	1	25	48
	(18%)	(6%)	(8%)		(1%)	(4%)	(15%)	(5%)
3	5	14	–	2	5	5	21	52
	(17%)	(12%)		(3%)	(1%)	(14%)	(9%)	(6%)
Total	8	25	12	3	13	7	52	120
	(15%)	(10%)	(4%)	(3%)	(1%)	(8%)	(9%)	(5%)

Of the 120 interpretative progressives in the material, 67 (or 56%) are also potentially experiential progressives, and one (1%) is modified by an ALWAYS-type adverbial. There are thus 52 interpretative progressives (43%) which belong to neither of the other types of not-solely-aspectual progressives investigated in the present chapter.

Table 77 also shows that the percentage of interpretative progressives increases over the 19th century, from 3% in period 1, via 5% in period 2, to 6% in period 3. This increase is not statistically significant, however. Another way of looking at the interpretative progressive is to consider its normalized frequency per number of words, thus taking into account the fact that the overall frequency of the progressive in CONCE nearly doubled between periods 1 and 3 (see Section 3.2.2). The results of such a calculation indicate that interpretative progressives were considerably more frequent at the end of the 19th century than they were at the beginning: the raw frequencies correspond to M-coefficients of 6 in period 1, 14 in period 2, and 17 in period 3. This result is consistent with a view of the interpretative progressive as being relatively new. On the other hand, the relative stability in the proportion of all progressives that are interpretative, as well as the occurrence of interpretative progressives in all genres in CONCE even in period 1, indicates that the interpretative progressive was an established feature of English grammar as early as 1800.

As mentioned above, in many subsamples the raw frequency of interpretative progressives is low, and cannot form the basis for reliable conclusions. Nevertheless, some interesting trends emerge when the genre parameter is considered. The percentage of interpretative progressives is the highest in the three genres that are based entirely on speech which has either been constructed (Drama) or written down (Debates and Trials). This points to situational immediacy as being important for the occurrence of the interpretative progressive. In these genres, interpretative progressives are frequently used to call attention to what has been stated in a previous turn of speech, in order either to re-interpret or to clarify what has been said (in which case the speaker may interpret his/her own utterance). Consider (107) and (108):

(107)   "I cannot express the repugnance with which I view the dual vote. It seems to me to be more invidious than anything which can be devised. You *are raising* up a sham sort of oligarchy to control and overbalance the will of the people. I will not associate the giving of power with any shabby expedient to counteract it."
(Debates, 1870–1900, p. IV.1183)

(108)   [$Mr. Serjeant Shee.$] ... Don't you know there were a great many tradesmen whose claims on the chapel were unpaid? – I heard so; but as I was not the first chaplain, I never attached –
[$Mr. Baron Platt.$] That was no blame to him.
[$Mr. Serjeant Shee.$] I *am* not *imputing* it as the least blame to this gentleman.
(Trials, Boyle, 1850–1870, p. 68)

In (107), the speaker uses an interpretative progressive to communicate what he believes is the significance of the dual vote. The textual function of the interpretative progressive in (107) is thus similar to that of the progressive modified by an ALWAYS-type adverbial in (94), cited in Section 7.1. In these examples, both of which come from Debates, a speaker uses a progressive as part of a rhetorical strategy in order to cast a shadow on the contents of a previous speech. In (108), in contrast, an interpretative progressive is used by Mr. Serjeant Shee to explain the significance of his own question, asked before the witness was interrupted by Mr. Baron Platt. Example (108) also shows that the interpretative progressive can be negated, in which case an interpretation is excluded rather than invited.

However, whether the interpretative progressive is affirmative or negative, and whether the speaker's or somebody else's behaviour is being interpreted, the situational immediacy of conversation is still important in the examples. This also means that one of the reasons why the interpretative progressive has been considered a recent phenomenon in English may be that researchers' access to speech-related texts from historical periods remains limited.[22] The importance of conversation is also emphasized by a look at the Fiction genre. Ten of the twelve interpretative progressives in Fiction, or 83%, occur in dialogue, even though only 33% of all progressives do so.[23] (However, the raw frequencies are so low

---

22   If we accept that dialogues, in which speakers can interpret both their own and one another's utterances and actions, will usually contain more interpretative progressives than monologues, the shortage of suitable historical texts becomes even more notable. Some speech-related genres to which researchers have turned for insights into the spoken language of the past, such as sermons and speeches, are monologic in nature and thus less likely to yield occurrences of the interpretative progressive.

23   Moreover, both of the interpretative progressives in non-dialogue are from the same text, Elizabeth Gaskell's *Cranford*, and both are in the first person, which leaves more space for subjective interpretation than third-person narrative.

that the division of interpretative progressives in Fiction into dialogue and non-dialogue occurrences cannot be considered reliable.)

Against this background, it may seem peculiar that Science, a genre which is not characterized either by subjectivity or by conversational, situational immediacy, should contain a high percentage of interpretative progressives. However, it should be noted that five of the seven instances come from one and the same text, viz. Norman J. Lockyer's *The Chemistry of the Sun*, which means that idiosyncratic writing strategies may be at work. Moreover, four of these five interpretative progressives contain the prepositional verb DEAL *with*, as in (109):

(109)   ... but if on the disk of the sun itself – take a spot, for instance, in the very middle of the disk – we get any change of wave-length such as I have referred to, it is perfectly clear that we *shall* no longer *be dealing* with what we can justly call a wind, it will really be an upward or downward current.
(Science, Lockyer, 1870–1900, p. 134)

In this and other examples from Lockyer's text, the interpretative progressive is used to explain the significance of instrument readings and observations to the reader; in (109), this observation is made explicit in the preceding conditional clause. In addition, the use of *we* may indicate that the author has his readers in mind, which may help to explain the occurrence of a linguistic feature characteristic of the situational immediacy of conversation.

In the remaining two genres, History and Letters, the interpretative progressive is less frequent, accounting for only 3% and 1% of all progressives respectively.[24] The History texts are largely monologic in nature, and, unlike the authors of Fiction texts, History writers in CONCE do not, as a rule, try to involve the reader by using e.g. first-person subjects in sentences. The interpretative progressives that do occur in History serve to give the writer's interpretations of historical people's actions, as in (110):

(110)   The demand of England was that all things in the realm, courts, taxes, prerogatives, should be sanctioned and bounded by law. The policy of the King was to reserve whatever he could within the control of his personal will. James in fact *was claiming* a more personal and exclusive direction of affairs than any English sovereign that had gone before him. England, on the other hand, *was claiming* a greater share in its own guidance than it had enjoyed since the Wars of the Roses.
(History, Green, 1870–1900, p. III.81)

---

24   Similarly, Arnaud (2002) found that the number of interpretative progressives was small in his corpus of late Modern English private letters.

In Letters, interpretative progressives occur predominantly with subjects in the first person singular, usually to clarify a point that has previously been raised by the letter-writer, as in (111):

(111) But pray believe that <u>in venturing such an ignorant suggestion</u> I *am* only *trying* to make matters easy, pleasant, manageable; I *am* not *attempting* to meddle where you have and I have not rights.
(Letters, Rossetti, 1870–1900, p. 132)

In some cases, where the letter-writer comments on his/her own letter, it is difficult to determine whether a progressive should be classified as interpretative or not, particularly when the situation which may be being interpreted is not mentioned explicitly. Consider (112):

(112) My dearest Fanny, I *am writing* what will not be of the smallest use to you.
(Letters, Austen, 1800–1830, p. 173)

In (112), it is possible that the writer is interpreting her own performance; the implied interpreted situation might then be something along the lines of *when I produce this letter*. However, the writer could also simply be describing what she is currently doing, rather than interpreting an situation with which that containing the progressive is identical. Ambiguous instances such as (112) were not classified as interpretative, which may help to explain the low percentage of interpretative progressives in Letters. As for the second and third person, there are two interpretative progressives with third-person subjects in Letters. Interpretative progressives with second-person subjects, in contrast, are conspicuous by their absence from the Letters genre, which may suggest that this particular dialogic feature was not frequently transferred to communication via private letters in 19th-century English. (The longer stretch of time that separates an exchange of letters, compared with an exchange of turns in conversation, may be important in this context.)
    Another way of looking at the interpretative progressive is to investigate the linguistic contexts in which the construction occurs in the material. König (1980: 275f.) lists seven syntactic environments where, he claims, the interpretative progressive is likely to occur.[25] The environments tend to have the interpretative progressive in a main clause; they differ as regards how, and whether, the interpreted situation is expressed explicitly. The environments listed are: main clauses with the interpreted situation in participial clauses following *in* (1) or *by* (2); main clauses with the interpreted situation in conditional (3), temporal (4), or relative (5) clauses; and what König refers to as "parataxis", where the interpretative progressive may occur either in non-dialogue (6) or in direct speech (7). In categories (6) and (7), there is no explicit link between the

---

25   See also Behre (1961) for a related, but less explicit, syntactic classification.

interpretative progressive and the interpreted situation; rather, the connection must be inferred.

For the present study, I adopted a modified version of König's classification. First, paratactic occurrences were not subdivided into those occurring within and outside direct speech, as this distinction would only be valid in Fiction. Moreover, CONCE also provided examples of interpretative progressives occurring in subordinate clauses, and König's categories only cover main-clause progressives. (However, when the interpreted situation is in a relative clause, König does give examples of interpretative progressives in nominal clauses.) In my analysis, interpretative progressives in subordinate clauses were classified together with those occurring in main clauses, and the classification was based on the same criteria. Interpretative progressives in subordinate clauses were thus grouped together with the paratactic occurrences if the interpreted situation was not stated explicitly in a subordinate clause in the near context of the interpretative progressive (see below). Since "parataxis" is not a suitable name for interpretative progressives which may occur in both main and subordinate clauses, I will instead refer to members of this group as having the interpreted situation in a removed context. If, in contrast, the interpreted situation was mentioned explicitly in a subordinate clause in the near context of the interpretative progressive, the interpretative progressive was placed in one of groups (1)–(5) above, depending on the type of subordinate clause in which the interpreted situation occurred. The resulting groups, illustrated with corpus examples, are:

Participial clauses following *in*, as in (113):

(113)   But I *am getting* on too fast, <u>in describing the dresses of the company</u>. I should first relate the gathering, on the way to Mrs. Jamieson's.
        (Fiction, Gaskell, 1850–1870, p. 149)

Participial clauses following *by*, as in (114):

(114)   He believed that <u>by refusing the people their rights</u>, <u>by continuing the representation of the country on its present narrow basis</u>, they *were acting* a most dangerous part.
        (Debates, 1850–1870, p. CXII.1163)

Conditional clauses, as in (105), also cited above:

(105)   One must not jump to conclusions, but I believe that man to be such an utter scoundrel that I do not think I *am doing* him much wrong <u>if I suspect that the story of his wife's death was a pure fabrication of his own</u>.
        (Letters, Butler, Samuel [2], 1870–1900, p. 228)

Temporal clauses, as in (89), also cited above:

(89)   *Am* I *dreaming* when I think that we may derive from this much high enjoyment, and that you may see in the prospect something which is worth living for?
(Letters, Southey, 1800–1830, p. 362)

Relative clauses, as in (115). The italicized progressive in (115) was the only example where an interpretative reading was suggested with the interpreted situation in a relative clause.

(115)   "Robin was telling Lucy he wanted some one to teach him to be good, and she said she would, but I think she is not old enough."
"Any one who is good *is teaching* others, my Owen," said Honor. "We will ask in our prayers that poor little Robin may be helped."
(Fiction, Yonge, 1850–1870, p. I.111)

The interpretative status of (115) is, on first reading, less clear than that of the other examples, perhaps because the interpreted situation is 'stative'. In contrast, in all of König's (1980) examples belonging to this category, the interpreted situation is non-'stative', which may make the interpretative reading easier to discern.

The final category comprises interpretative progressives with the interpreted situation in a removed context, as in (116):

(116)   [$Court.$] She observed her Master the second time, but as you put the question, it seems as if she had seen him both times.
[$Mr. Topping.$] No, my Lord, I *am inquiring* about a different thing – this was when she first came down in the morning.
(Trials, Angus, 1800–1830, p. 47)

Interpretative progressives belonging to the last category do thus not co-occur with any formal linguistic features which might indicate that an interpretative reading is intended. Indeed, in occurrences such as (116), the situation that is interpreted by the progressive is frequently not mentioned explicitly, but has to be inferred from the context of the utterance, which also complicates the selection of interpretative progressives. Nor are the five subordinate clauses listed above safe indicators that a progressive in the near context is interpretative; as pointed out above, close readings were necessary to distinguish interpretative from non-interpretative progressives.

The analysis of syntactic environments revealed that interpretative progressives with the interpreted situation in a removed context accounted for

102 out of the 120 instances, or 85%.[26] As for the other types, there were eight instances (7%) where the interpreted situation occurred in a participial clause following *in*, five where it occurred in a participial clause following *by* (4%), two instances each where it was part of a temporal or a conditional clause (2% each), and one instance when the situation being interpreted occurred in a relative clause (1%). However, the data imply that interpretative progressives with the interpreted situation in a removed context may account for a smaller share of all interpretative progressives in diachrony: in period 1, they constitute 90% of all interpretative progressives, in period 2, 85%, and in period 3, 83%. Although raw frequencies are too low to allow definite conclusions, this apparent decrease may be a sign that the interpretative progressive began as a possible, not-solely-aspectual inference which was sometimes appropriate when the progressive presented two actions as simultaneous, and which was especially likely to occur in face-to-face conversation. When interpretative progressives started to occur in writing, a need may then have arisen for making this inference explicit syntactically.[27] Another possible influence on the emergence of the interpretative progressive is the occurrence of the progressive in clauses introduced by *as if* or *as though*, where the subordinators make the hypothetical identity of the situations in the subordinate clause and its matrix clause explicit (see Söderlind 1951: 84 for examples; see also Behre 1961: 309, who includes progressives in clauses introduced by *as if* and *as though* in his examples).

7.4   Discussion of results

The results of the investigations carried out in this chapter indicate that important developments concerning the occurrence of progressives with not-solely-aspectual functions took place during the 19th century. However, there were also considerable differences between the three types of not-solely-aspectual progressives, differences which might be taken to indicate that these types cover partially different functional domains.

The analysis of progressives modified by ALWAYS-type adverbials showed that there was no statistically significant change in the percentage of all progressives that had such modification. Since the modification of progressives by ALWAYS-type adverbials has been recognized by scholars investigating periods

---

26   It is possible that some researchers have not considered such instances interpretative. Arnaud (2002), for instance, claims that interpretative progressives, though rare in his material, are easy to recognize since the interpreted situation "is so clearly identified that we are verging on syntax proper".

27   The large proportion of interpretative progressives with the interpreted situation in a removed context may perhaps also be due to a greater semantic difference between the progressive and the non-progressive in such cases. Substituting a non-progressive for an interpretative progressive when the interpreted situation is not mentioned explicitly may result in a general statement, as opposed to one valid only at the time in question (see Goedsche 1932: 469 for exemplification); but this effect is often cancelled if the interpreted situation is specified in a subordinate clause.

both preceding and following the 19th century, the result was interpreted as an indication that this type of progressive is a stable feature of 19th-century English. The cross-genre distribution revealed that Debates and Science had high percentages of progressives modified by ALWAYS-type adverbials, while the percentage in Trials was low. One possible explanation for the distribution in Science is that the pattern had less not-solely-aspectual force (or sometimes none at all) in this formal genre, providing general emphasis rather than subjective evaluation; another is that Science texts have become more impersonal between the 19th and 20th centuries, so that progressives modified by ALWAYS-type adverbials were more frequent in 19th-century scientific writing. In Debates, another expository genre, progressives modified by ALWAYS-type adverbials rather appeared to be part of a rhetorical strategy used by speakers to provide a previous utterance with a negative evaluation. In Trials, the low percentage is possibly attributable to the formality of the speech situation and the fact-oriented style of most dialogues in this genre. As in Science, progressives modified by ALWAYS-type adverbials in Trials often appeared to express general emphasis rather than (often negative) evaluation. Overall, the commonest function of the progressives modified by ALWAYS-type adverbials in the data was to express a negative evaluation of the situation in which the progressive occurred, although there were also instances where a more general emphasis on the situation seemed to be intended.

The section that followed dealt with what I have called potentially experiential progressives, the selection of which was based on the co-occurrence of the progressive with four different linguistic features. Progressives selected as potentially experiential met three or four of the following four criteria: they were present-tense verb phrases with no perfect or modal auxiliaries, or occurred in main clauses, in verb phrases with first- or second-person subjects, or in 'stative' situations. In addition, progressives modified by ALWAYS-type adverbials were excluded from the counts of potentially experiential progressives. The classification was based partly on that found in Wright (1994). The distribution of potentially experiential progressives across the three periods in CONCE showed a statistically significant increase: in terms of normalized frequencies, potentially experiential progressives were roughly three times as common in period 3 as in period 1. They were most frequent in Drama and Letters, and least frequent in History and Science, which supports the hypothesis that the construction is characteristic of non-expository texts where there is room for the communication of subjective attitudes; however, the low raw frequencies of potentially experiential progressives in expository genres make it impossible to draw definite conclusions in this respect. The presence of spoken features in texts also appeared to promote the occurrence of potentially experiential progressives. This assumption was further supported by the similar patterns that the relative order of the genres in CONCE displayed with respect to, on the one hand, the frequency of potentially experiential progressives and, on the other hand, the scores on Dimension 1 of Geisler's (2000) factor score analysis. As regards which criterion, if any, the potentially experiential progressives in the data did not meet, the situation-type criterion was by far the commonest.

In order to increase the likelihood that the selected constructions had not-solely-aspectual functions, the potentially experiential progressives were classified for whether or not they had expressions of emotion in the near context in an additional analysis. There was no consistent development in diachrony in this respect. In the CONCE corpus as a whole, roughly 3% of all progressives were potentially experiential and had expressions of emotion in the near context. If we accept that all such progressives have not-solely-aspectual functions in addition to their aspectual functions, these constructions constitute a subset of all progressives which is almost as large as (though less conspicuous than) that consisting of progressives modified by ALWAYS-type adverbials.

The investigation of interpretative progressives, finally, showed that the percentage of these progressives in CONCE did not increase significantly across the 19th century. However, given the overall increase in the frequency of the progressive, the results imply that interpretative progressives became considerably more common in English between periods 1 and 3. Of the three subgroups of not-solely-aspectual progressives investigated, interpretative progressives showed the clearest affinities with genres where conversational turn-taking occurs, such as Debates, Drama, Trials, and dialogue in Fiction. The surprisingly high percentage of interpretative progressives in Science appeared to be explainable by (a) idiosyncratic tendencies peculiar to one text and (b) a slightly different use of the interpretative progressive in this genre in order to explain the scientific significance of instrument readings and observations to the reader. In History and Letters, there were comparatively few interpretative progressives, perhaps owing to an absence of dialogic features characteristic of face-to-face interaction in these genres. (The low percentage of interpretative progressives in Letters may also be due to a number of ambiguous instances with the letter-writer as the subject of the progressive verb phrase.) An investigation of the different types of interpretative progressives that occurred in the data showed that the overwhelming majority of instances did not have the interpreted situation mentioned explicitly in a subordinate clause; in most cases, the situation was either mentioned in a separate sentence or had to be inferred from the context. However, there were small signs that the dominance of interpretative progressives with the interpreted situation in a removed context was becoming less pronounced in diachrony.

The analyses carried out in the present chapter have shown that not-solely-aspectual progressives appear to account for a substantial share of all progressives, although it must be remembered that many, if not all, not-solely-aspectual progressives also have aspectual functions.[28] If we add up the number of progressives that are either interpretative, potentially experiential, or modified

---

28   As implied by Buyssens (1968), some interpretative progressives may not have any aspectual function at all, as many such progressives have a non-progressive in the interpreted situation, which is supposedly identical to the situation in which the interpretative progressive occurs.

by an ALWAYS-type adverbial, we find that such constructions account for 517, or 21%, of the 2,440 progressives in CONCE. On the one hand, owing to the methods used to select potentially experiential progressives in particular, there is no guarantee that all of these 517 progressives have not-solely-aspectual functions; on the other hand, nor have all not-solely-aspectual functions of the progressive been explored in the present chapter. For instance, since it was hypothesized in Section 7.2 that the situation-type criterion was stronger than the other three criteria when it came to selecting potentially experiential progressives, close readings of progressives that occur in 'stative' situations might yield further occurrences. (However, trying to select all not-solely-aspectual progressives by means of close readings would have been an overwhelming enterprise.) Another type of not-solely-aspectual function which could be explored further is the use of the progressive as a politeness strategy, a function which, as Ljung (1980: 76) points out, is closely related to the interpretative progressive.[29]

Since many of the features used to select potentially experiential progressives, notably 'stative' situations, first- or second-person subjects, and present-tense verb phrases, can be related to the expression of subjectivity and the speaker's perspective, there may be connections between the general integration of the progressive into late Modern English grammar and the significantly larger share of all progressives that are potentially experiential progressives across the 19th century. Traugott (1995) proposes that grammaticalization processes typically involve a tendency for grammaticalized forms to become more subjective in diachrony. Although, as pointed out in Section 3.2.1, there may be some complications involved in applying the concept of grammaticalization to the development of the progressive, there are also parallels between the integration of the construction into late Modern English and the process of grammaticalization. In both cases, the process results in generalization across some paradigms (in the case of the progressive, evidenced by for instance the emergence of the passive progressive, the appearance of progressives of BE and HAVE, and the increasing occurrence of the progressive in main clauses) and in increases in the frequency of the grammaticalized or integrated form. Against this background, it can be hypothesized that, if the progressive became more fully integrated in English during the 19th century, its subjectivity should also have increased. The dramatic increase in the frequency of potentially experiential progressives is one indication that this is the case.

---

29   It is also possible that the diversity of not-solely-aspectual functions of the progressive available varies across the parameters of time and genre. For instance, Paccaud (1988) and Toolan (1983) both discuss not-solely-aspectual, subjective functions of progressives in fiction written by Joseph Conrad and William Faulkner respectively. Ehrlich (1990: 81ff.) discusses the use of the progressive to convey events from a character's point of view in fiction, and hypothesizes that such linguistic devices are more likely to occur in modern novels, where the representation of a character's consciousness is often of primary importance (Ehrlich 1990: 104f.). Couper-Kuhlen (1995), finally, discusses a possible new use of the progressive as a foregrounding device in American conversational narrative.

The diversity that the three types of not-solely-aspectual progressives exhibit with respect to their distribution across the genre parameter suggests that they do not fulfil exactly the same function in texts. The percentage of progressives modified by ALWAYS-type adverbials was the highest in Science and Debates; an analysis of the occurrences in these genres pointed to their having functions such as providing general emphasis (in Science) and conveying a negative evaluation of the situation described by the progressive verb phrase (in Debates). The percentage of potentially experiential progressives, in contrast, was much higher in Drama and Letters than in other genres. Both private letters and speeches in plays provide many opportunities for characters and writers to express their subjective points of view, and many of the features used to select the potentially experiential progressive have subjective connotations. It thus makes sense to assume that the potentially experiential progressive emphasizes the subjective aspects of the situations in which it occurs; the situations are, then, seen as filtered through the speaker's consciousness. The percentage of interpretative progressives, finally, was high primarily in Debates, Drama, dialogue in Fiction, and Trials, genres where conversational turn-taking, though often formalized or constructed, is central.[30] Interpretative progressives thus seem to depend for many of their attestations on contexts where situations to be interpreted subjectively occur a short while preceding the use of the progressive. In sum, different types of context may bring out varying shades of not-solely-aspectual meaning in progressive verb phrases, and the meaning expressed may also be of a general or specific nature. However, what all of the functions investigated in the present chapter have in common is that, by choosing to use a progressive, the speaker assumes a subjective attitude towards the situation described by the progressive verb phrase.[31]

---

30 As mentioned above, the high percentage of interpretative progressives in Science could be explained partly in terms of idiosyncratic writing strategies.

31 Smith (1983: 480; 1997: 6ff.) points out that aspectual progressives also involve speaker choice, as speakers decide to present a situation as, for instance, imperfective or perfective. However, Smith (1997: 6) also states that "[a]spectual choice is limited by conventional categorization, pragmatics, and the constraint of truth". Not-solely-aspectual progressives have less formalized and more speaker-dependent functions, and are thus more open to speaker choice, than aspectual progressives.

Chapter 8

Concluding discussion

Despite the impressive amount and depth of previous research on the progressive, we have so far lacked a cross-genre, corpus-based study of its use and development across the entire 19th century. The present study has attempted to fill this gap. In this concluding chapter, I first connect the results of the study in order to describe the integration of the progressive into late Modern English grammar in Section 8.1. The results will be discussed roughly in the order they were presented in previous chapters. As stated in Section 1.2, the concept of integration is closely related to the main aim of the present study, viz. to account for the use and development of the progressive in 19th-century English English; Section 8.2 addresses the four secondary aims subsumed by that main aim. Section 8.3, finally, suggests some areas where further research would be valuable.

8.1   Interrelating the results: The integration of the progressive

The frequency of a linguistic construction is an important indicator of how fully integrated the construction is: a frequency increase is often a reliable sign that the construction is becoming more integrated into the language variety under scrutiny. There are at least two reasons for the importance placed on frequency in this respect. First, in processes of grammaticalization, an increase in frequency often accompanies semantic bleaching and widened syntactic applicability. The concept of integration is not identical with that of grammaticalization (as pointed out in Chapters 1 and 3), but as the two processes have a great deal in common, it can be assumed that both are likely to result in increasing frequencies. In addition, a low frequency compared with that of another paradigmatic option (the non-progressive, in the case of the progressive) has been listed as a sign of markedness, although frequency need not be suitable as a markedness criterion for members of semantic categories such as aspect (Comrie 1976: 116f.); nevertheless, an increasing frequency may indicate that a construction is becoming a less marked choice. The validity of this argument increases if the frequency of the construction has been measured from a variationist perspective, i.e. in comparison with the other paradigmatic option(s).

In terms of frequency, the data clearly indicate that the progressive became more fully integrated into English grammar during the 19th century. The results pointed to a nearly doubled frequency between the periods 1800–1830 and 1870–1900, as measured in occurrences per number of words. Moreover, the investigation into the relation between the progressive and the non-progressive showed that the progressive manifested a statistically significant increase. These findings tie in with the background provided by previous research, where rising frequencies have been reported from late Middle English up to and including Present-Day English. However, two circumstances complicate the picture somewhat. First, the development of obligatory aspectual functions of the progressive, which has been postulated to have taken place in the mid-19th century (see Nehls 1988), might be expected to lead to a more even distribution of progressives across the genre parameter. As the progressive developed into an obligatory, grammaticalized marker of imperfective aspect, situational differences in usage should have decreased rather than increased; but instead, genres became more diversified in diachrony with respect to the frequency of the progressive. The same holds for letters written by women and by men: these two groups exhibited no statistically significant difference in period 1, whereas the difference in period 3 was significant. Secondly, some, but not all genres manifested statistically significant frequency increases. This also speaks against a theory of the progressive that postulates a consistent increase in English as a whole.

The insights gained from comparing the frequency of the progressive with dimension scores obtained by Geisler (2000; 2001; 2002; 2003) on some of Biber's (1988) dimensions of variation may help to explain some of the increase in genre diversity. Biber and Finegan (1997) showed that Modern English genres have become more diversified in their linguistic make-up: the contrast between stereotypically oral and stereotypically literate language has increased, thus making the linguistic differences between expository and non-expository genres more pronounced. The progressive has been listed as an oral and/or colloquial feature in previous research, something which was supported in the present study by the comparison of the frequency of the progressive with factor scores obtained by Geisler (2002) on Dimensions 1, 3, and 5 of Biber's (1988) factor analysis. The expository genres were separated from the non-expository genres with respect to the frequency of the progressive as well as factor scores on these dimensions, so that genres where oral features could be found also had high frequencies of progressives.[1] It is thus probable that an increasing polarization of oral and literate genres led to greater genre diversity in the frequency of features characteristic of oral and literate discourse respectively. As results presented in Biber (2003) and in this study identify the progressive as an oral feature, it makes sense that the distribution of the construction should become more diversified

---

1   As pointed out in Chapter 4, the extent to which a text exhibits narrative concerns on Dimension 2 may also be important; in CONCE, this factor separates History, with more narrative concerns and higher frequencies of progressives, from the other two expository genres.

across the genre parameter. Taken together, the results show that the genre parameter is important when processes of integration are studied, and that the integration of a linguistic feature may be too complex a process to study without access to a range of genres that represent a broad spectrum of the language variety under scrutiny. For instance, in terms of frequency, the progressive was more fully integrated in many non-expository genres in period 1 than it was in some expository genres in period 3.

The lack of significant increases, and, in this sense, clear signs of integration, in some genres is more difficult to account for. One possible reason is that a low-frequency feature such as the progressive will not display a reliable pattern unless more material is considered. However, developments and heterogeneity within genres may also lie behind part of the results. In Science, the only expository genre in which the frequency of the progressive does not increase significantly, an increasingly impersonal or literate style may be a factor (see Görlach 1999: 150).[2] In addition, academic writing encompasses a wide variety of traditions, subject matter, and styles (see Biber 1988: 171), which may affect the results. Fiction and Trials, the other genres that do not manifest significant increases in frequency, are also genres that may subsume a large number of different styles, in terms of the subject matter, the level of formality, the degree of editorial intervention, and (in Fiction) the proportion of dialogue to non-dialogue.

As regards the difference between women and men letter-writers, women have been claimed by Labov (2001: 292f.) to conform less than men linguistically when the relevant sociolinguistic norms are not overtly prescribed, and to be leaders in linguistic change from below. As this holds true for most manifestations of the 19th-century progressive, it makes sense that women are ahead of men in this integration process. It is also possible that high frequencies of progressive verb phrases in private letters were part of a female gender style in 19th-century English. In this context, there is a connection back to multi-feature/multi-dimensional approaches: Geisler (2003) showed that women letter-writers were, on the whole, closer than men to the oral poles of Dimensions 1 and 3 (the difference on Dimension 5, the third dimension that correlates with an oral/literate distinction, was not statistically significant).

The above exceptions notwithstanding, the overall impression is still that the progressive clearly became more fully integrated into English grammar during the 19th century. However, a look at the diffusion of the construction across a number of linguistic parameters revealed that an increase in the frequency of a linguistic feature does not necessarily entail greater complexity or a more even distribution across syntactic and semantic parameters. The complexity of the average progressive verb phrase, in terms of how many auxiliaries it incorporated, did not increase in diachrony. In addition, the *being* + present participle construction largely disappeared in the course of the 19th century. It thus seems that the integration of the progressive was the most pronounced in

---

2   However, in Geisler's (2002) factor score analysis, the Science genre did not change to a statistically significant degree across the periods covered by CONCE.

formally simple contexts, where additional formal and/or semantic distinctions did not complicate the progressive/non-progressive contrast. A notable exception is the diffusion of the passive progressive, which increased the potential complexity of the progressive verb phrase. (As we shall see below, however, there may have been other reasons why the passive progressive increased in frequency in the 1800s.)

On the three situational parameters investigated (main verbs, situation types, and agentive vs. non-agentive subjects), different patterns manifested themselves. I will first comment on the diachronic tendencies in the data. The type/token ratio for main verbs in progressive verb phrases decreased, which ties in with the finding that progressive verb phrases did not become more complex and diversified on average during the 19th century. However, there were also tendencies in the other direction: the dominance of GO became less pronounced, and the important verbs BE and HAVE became available and increased in frequency, respectively. As for situation types, the most important changes were that the percentage of progressives in 'stative' situations increased, whereas the percentage of progressives in 'future' situations decreased; when 'future' situations were not recognized as a separate category, the decrease occurred among progressives in 'processive' situations instead. It is difficult to interpret the consequences of the latter change for the integration of the progressive without access to figures for other means of expressing future time in English. The former change, however, is clearly relevant to the issue of integration, as the progressive has been claimed to be rare, or even impossible, in 'stative' situations. The occurrence of both aspectual and not-solely-aspectual progressives in stative situations may be important in this context. Aspectual progressives in 'stative' situations would indicate that the progressive is developing into a more general imperfective marker. As regards not-solely-aspectual progressives, 'stative' situations often express states which can only be subjectively verified. The occurrence potential of the progressive as an encoder of subjectivity in texts would thus increase if the construction began to occur more freely in 'stative' situations.[3] On the third situational parameter, agentive vs. non-agentive subjects, the overall results did not imply diachronic change. Against the background of previous research, notably Strang (1982), we can assume that the progressive was already integrated to a relatively high degree with non-agentive subjects by 1800, which would explain the lack of change in the CONCE data. If so, the parameter of agentivity may have been one of the first contexts to be affected by a postulated late 18th-century grammaticalization of the progressive (see Denison 1998: 155f. for an account of such a grammaticalization process). Brinton (1988: 161f.) claims that, in grammaticalization, semantic processes may precede syntactic

---

3   Note that the progressive occurred in 'stative' situations quite freely in Old and Middle English, when its main function has also been claimed not to have been aspectual (Mustanoja 1960: 593f.; Nehls 1988: 180).

developments.[4] If this order of appearance can be extended also to cover processes of integration, Brinton's claim may help to explain the comparatively early extension of the progressive to occurrence with non-agentive subjects. Extending the progressive paradigm in this way requires no syntactic change, but is chiefly a semantic process.

The genre parameter revealed further interesting results of relevance to the integration of the progressive. The investigations of main verbs, situation types, and agentive vs. non-agentive subjects all pointed to differences between expository and non-expository genres. The commonest main verbs of progressive verb phrases in non-expository genres also tended to be frequent in the progressive in the material as a whole, while these verbs were not as frequent in progressives in expository genres. Lexical factors may thus affect the integration of the progressive in texts: if verbs that rarely take the progressive dominate in a given genre, the progressive will be comparatively infrequent in this genre.[5] The analysis of situation types showed that, in non-expository genres, comparatively high percentages of the progressives occurred in genre-specific situation types, for example 'stance' situations in Trials. In contrast, the expository genres in CONCE were all characterized by high percentages of the progressives occurring in 'active' situations, which should constitute the most straightforward context of occurrence for aspectual progressives. As for agentivity of subject, finally, the proportion of all progressives that had non-agentive subjects was higher in expository genres than in non-expository genres. This difference does not, at first, seem to be linked to the integration of the progressive. The results presented in Strang (1982) would rather lead us to expect the opposite pattern, since non-expository genres should have been ahead in the integration process, and since the change had gone from agentive to non-agentive subjects. The explanation may rather be that expository genres had a higher proportion of non-agentive subjects overall. This postulated difference would, then, affect the distribution of the progressive. However, the results are still relevant to the integration of the progressive, as genres where progressives with non-agentive subjects were common also yielded early occurrences and/or high frequencies of passive progressives. In other words, passive progressives tended to occur in genres where passival progressives, whose surface subjects are always non-agentive, would be most likely to cause ambiguity, owing to the many active progressives with non-agentive subjects (as pointed out in Sections 5.3 and 6.3, other factors, such as negative prescriptive reaction to the passive progressive, also enter into the picture). Although the raw frequencies of passive progressives were too low

---

4   Brinton (1988) focuses on the development of aspectualizers in English; however, she argues that her study may be of general relevance to the study of grammaticalization (Brinton 1988: 162).

5   To reach safe conclusions in this respect, however, the frequency of different main verbs in both progressive and non-progressive verb phrases would have to be examined. Moreover, as the non-expository genres account for a larger share of CONCE than the expository genres, the distribution of main verbs in progressive verb phrases in the former has a greater impact on the cumulative figures.

to be reliable, the consistency of the results implies that genre-characteristic traits affected the integration of the progressive in terms of the formal make-up of the construction.

On the parameters of (a) modification by temporal adverbials and (b) clause type, the diachronic correspondences with frequency developments were more pronounced: the results implied a decrease in the percentage of all progressives that were modified by temporal adverbials, and an increase in the percentage that occurred in main clauses. These results are both linked to the integration of the progressive. As aspectual progressives became more fully integrated into English grammar, it can be assumed that the need to specify the aspectual meaning further (using temporal adverbials) decreased. As for clausal distribution, the results are in line with Strang's (1982) findings: as part of the integration of the progressive, the construction became less dependent on clausal environment, and less confined to occurrence in subordinate clauses. However, there are differences between the two features regarding their relation to the integration process. Modification by temporal adverbials is chiefly relevant to the aspectual functions of the progressive (exceptions include progressives modified by ALWAYS-type adverbials, which will be commented on later on in this section), and aspectual progressives often function as background markers in texts. In contrast, occurrence in main clauses has been listed as a sign that a situation is foregrounded (Wårvik 1990b: 533), and foregrounding is mentioned by Wright (1994: 468) as a characteristic of many not-solely-aspectual progressives.

From a cross-genre perspective, the modification of the progressive by temporal adverbials revealed no obvious patterns concerning what percentage of the progressives had such modification. Across the parameter of clause type, however, the by-now familiar division between expository and non-expository genres appeared. Non-expository genres had higher percentages of main-clause progressives than expository genres. Like the analysis of normalized frequencies, the investigation of the clausal distribution of the progressive thus showed (a) that there was development in the direction of the progressive becoming more fully integrated across the century and (b) that non-expository genres were ahead in this development.[6]

In the final results chapter, special attention was paid to the integration of three not-solely-aspectual types of progressives: progressives modified by ALWAYS-type adverbials, potentially experiential progressives, and interpretative progressives. The diachronic analyses revealed differences among the three types. Progressives modified by ALWAYS-type adverbials exhibited no clear trend in diachrony, either regarding the percentage of all progressives they accounted for or concerning their normalized frequency. In contrast, there was a significant increase in the proportion of potentially experiential progressives; in addition, the normalized frequency of potentially experiential progressives roughly trebled between periods 1 and 3. Interpretative progressives held an intermediate position: the increase in the percentage of interpretative progressives was not

---

6   Note, however, that the overall clausal distribution in the material was not studied.

statistically significant, but the normalized frequency of the interpretative progressive nevertheless nearly trebled over the period covered by CONCE. The diachronic stability of progressives modified by ALWAYS-type adverbials points to their being a well-integrated feature of late Modern English, a hypothesis which is supported by the long history of the pattern attested in previous research. Interpretative progressives, in contrast, have been claimed to be a relatively new addition to the progressive paradigm (see König 1980). The increase in the frequency of interpretative progressives provides partial support for this claim in that the type appears to be undergoing integration into 19th-century English, although the comparatively high frequencies even in period 1 indicate that interpretative progressives must have been in existence for some time prior to 1800.[7] If grammaticalization and integration can be taken to share a number of characteristics, the overall increase in potential not-solely-aspectual progressives indicated by the results is in line with Traugott's (1995) hypothesis that the grammaticalization of a linguistic feature typically entails an increase in subjectivity.

The cross-genre comparison showed that the distributional patterns of the three types were different. Progressives modified by ALWAYS-type adverbials accounted for larger proportions of all progressives in Science and Debates than in the other genres. (However, as the progressive was rare in these genres, the normalized frequency of this type of progressive was higher in, for instance, Letters than in Science.) The percentage of potentially experiential progressives, in contrast, exhibited the expected division between expository genres (with low percentages) and non-expository genres (with high percentages); Drama and Letters, with high percentages, also stood out from all other genres. Interpretative progressives exhibited high percentages chiefly in Debates, Drama, and Trials, genres characterized by more or less dialogic turn-taking. The diversity of the genre patterns indicated that the three types of not-solely-aspectual progressives may have different functions; moreover, the types appear to be integrated to varying degrees in different genres.

The present study has shown that the genre parameter is a very influential extralinguistic variable regarding the integration of the progressive into late Modern English. In terms of frequency, the synchronic cross-genre distribution of the progressive resembles a cross-section of ongoing change, with non-expository genres representing a more advanced stage in the development. Moreover, the genre parameter accounts for increasingly more variation in the frequency of the progressive in diachrony. (However, not all features investigated showed the expected genre spread, with non-expository genres being further ahead in the integration process.)

The present study has also shown that investigating the diachronic integration of a linguistic feature into a language variety requires a broad scope, both concerning the material on which the analyses are based and as regards

---

7   As pointed out in Section 7.3, Jespersen (1909–1949: 187) and Buyssens (1968: 317f.) provide early Modern English examples of interpretative progressives.

methodology. Since integration is a multi-faceted concept, an analysis of one aspect of the feature under scrutiny may indicate that the feature is integrated to a high degree, while an investigation of another aspect may indicate that the integration is still underway, or that it has not yet begun. In the case of the progressive, all three types of results are to be expected, as previous research has shown that the frequency of the construction had been rising before 1800 and that it continued to increase after 1900. In other words, some aspects of the integration process had taken place by 1800 (e.g. the extension of active progressives to occurrence with non-agentive subjects and the not-solely-aspectual effect of progressives modified by ALWAYS-type adverbials); some aspects had begun but were still in process in the 19th century (e.g. the rise in the overall frequency of the progressive and the increasing percentage of potentially experiential progressives); yet others may not have started by 1900. In this respect, the present study has pointed to the complexity inherent in processes of integration, in which two variables that are both relevant to the process may exhibit different, sometimes seemingly conflicting developments. In addition, the features under scrutiny may be related in ways that can only be revealed by studying the influence of several features on the data at the same time, something which requires a large corpus for the results to be reliable.

8.2   The secondary aims of the study: A selective overview

As outlined in Chapter 1, the main aim of the present work was to account for the use and development of the progressive in 19th-century English English. By relating the results presented to the integration of the progressive into 19th-century English, Section 8.1 has addressed that main aim. However, the main aim also subsumed four secondary aims: to address methodological issues with a bearing on, among other things, how the progressive should be defined and its frequency measured; to correlate the use of the progressive with the extralinguistic features of time, genre, and the sex of the letter-writer; to analyse the make-up of progressive verb phrases; and to investigate what kinds of linguistic features co-occur with the progressive. In this section, I will state where those four secondary aims have been addressed. The aims will be treated in roughly the order of appearance, although some overlap has been necessary.

The first secondary aim to be addressed concerned methodology. The diversity of approaches to the progressive in previous research and the broad concept of integration applied in the present work prompted me to adopt a wide perspective in terms of analytical frameworks in Chapter 1. The methodological discussion undertaken in Chapter 2 pertained to the selection of material, the definition of the progressive, and the retrieval of progressives from the material. In order to certify the validity of the results, I adopted a comparatively narrow definition of the progressive, excluding some patterns that have been considered progressives in previous research. Chapter 3 contained a further discussion focusing on methodology. Four different ways in which the frequency of the progressive can be measured were dealt with, and two of these selected for the present study.

The next secondary aim to be treated concerned variation with extralinguistic features in the frequency of the progressive. The analyses, which can be found in Chapter 3, revealed that time, genre, and the sex of the letter-writer (and the addressee) were all important independent variables when the frequency of the progressive was considered as the dependent variable. The variables of (a) time and genre and (b) time and sex were also considered in combination.

Chapter 5 addressed the make-up of progressive verb phrases, the analysis of which constituted the third secondary aim of the present work. The distribution of the progressive was analysed across the parameters of tense, voice, and the presence of perfect and modal auxiliaries; these parameters were also considered in combination. In addition, the near-disappearing *being* + present participle pattern was considered. Finally, Section 6.1 was devoted to the related question of what main verbs occur in the progressive.

The fourth secondary aim was to investigate the co-occurrence of the progressive with other linguistic features. This wide topic covered two separate types of analyses carried out in the present study. On the one hand, on the textual level, subsamples of CONCE were compared with respect to the frequency of the progressive and the results of Geisler's (2000; 2001; 2002; 2003) factor score analyses of the corpus. These comparisons were made in Chapter 4. On the other hand, the extent to which individual progressives co-occurred with other relevant linguistic features was analysed. These contextual features fell into two groups, which were analysed in separate chapters. The first group, addressed in Chapter 6, consisted of features identified as relevant to the occurrence of the progressive in previous research: two situational parameters (situation types and agentive vs. non-agentive subjects) and two features where clear diachronic patterns could be observed (the modification of progressives by temporal adverbials and the types of clauses in which the progressive occurred). Chapter 7 discussed the second group, which consisted of linguistic contexts that may help to bring out not-solely-aspectual interpretations of progressive verb phrases. Three analyses of such contexts were conducted. The first analysis considered progressives modified by ALWAYS-type adverbials; the second, potentially experiential progressives; and the third, interpretative progressives.

8.3   Suggestions for further research

Despite the wealth of previous studies on the progressive, more research on the development of the construction through the history of English is necessary. There is a need for studies that consider the co-occurrence of the progressive with other relevant linguistic features, either one by one, or as they co-occur in texts (e.g. multi-feature/multi-dimensional approaches). As regards Old English, given the connection between aspect, grounding, and Aktionsart, investigating how the progressive covaries with markers of grounding and Aktionsart (see e.g. Fischer

1992: 251f.; Hopper 1979; Aristar and Dry 1982; Wårvik 1990a) would be valuable; the tendency for the progressive to occur with intransitive verbs (Traugott 1992: 187) also deserves further examination. Regarding early Modern English, many scholars have commented on a possible connection between the increase in the frequency of the progressive and the decrease in that of periphrastic DO in affirmative clauses (see e.g. Samuels 1972; Rissanen 1991; Nurmi 1996). As regards multi-feature/multi-dimensional approaches, a new factor analysis adapting Biber's (1988; 2003) sets of features to early periods in the history of English would be of great value.

In research on the progressive – and on other linguistic features – in late Modern English, sociolinguistic approaches offer interesting prospects. As pointed out in Section 1.2, assuming sameness of socioeconomic status for informants across the 19th century is problematic. Nevertheless, the increasing levels of literacy and availability of texts that can be correlated with socioeconomic data may make studies of the progressive within this framework worthwhile, provided that corpora are compiled with the aim of sampling socioeconomically stable informant groups in mind. The sex of the speaker/writer is another parameter that clearly affects the distribution of the progressive. Correlations between biological sex and the frequency of the progressive in texts could be extended to genres other than private letters, such as witness depositions and constructed speech in plays and novels.

Another important field of research comprises studies of genre diversity and development, both concerning the extralinguistic conditions under which the texts were produced and as regards linguistic differences between texts from different genres, or texts from the same genre sampled at different times. For instance, the effects that the enlargement of the franchise and the increasing level of literacy had on the language of 19th-century written texts produced for general distribution deserve further study. Given that the progressive has been shown to be more common in informal than in formal texts, a postulated colloquialization of some written genres in 19th-century English in response to political and socioeconomic developments may have had important consequences for the integration of the construction. Studies of varieties other than English English may be very valuable in this context, as political and socioeconomic changes need not have affected all varieties of English simultaneously (see Hundt 1998: 75, 206 for data on the frequency of the progressive in different regional varieties of Present-Day English).

Looking forwards, we also need more research on the use of the progressive in the first half of the 20th century. Few corpora cover the period 1900–1960 (ARCHER is an exception): as a result, this period is underrepresented in quantitative studies. The political changes mentioned in Section 2.1.1 continued into the early 20th century, and may have contributed to a further colloquialization of many written genres. Moreover, this period yields more genuine spoken data in the form of, for instance, radio broadcasts. Although the situations in which these spoken texts were produced cannot be termed "unmonitored" or "informal", early 20th-century evidence of spoken English may shed new light on the occurrence of the progressive in late Modern English speech.

Finally, the present study has not exhausted the topic of the progressive in 19th-century English English. The aspects of the progressive that were investigated were chosen largely on the basis of what previous research has indicated as being of interest and, when possible, on the basis of pilot studies. It is possible that other parameters could be fruitfully investigated. For instance, a comprehensive study of expressions of future in late Modern English may explain why the proportion of all progressives that refer to the future, with or without the aid of modal auxiliaries, diminished during the 1800s.

In the present investigation, limitations of time and material made it necessary to restrict the scope of the study to those areas that seemed the most promising. The consistency of the results reached has confirmed the relevance of the investigations undertaken. The present work has thereby furthered our knowledge of both the development of the progressive and the comparatively neglected field of late Modern English syntax. Moreover, it is to be hoped that some of the findings concerning the integration of the progressive can be applied to research on other features that have undergone similar processes in the history of the English language.

References

Aarts, F. G. A. M. 1969. "On the Use of the Progressive and Non-Progressive Present with Future Reference in Present-Day English". *English Studies* 50, 565–579.

Adamson, S., V. Law, N. Vincent, and S. Wright (eds.). 1990. *Papers from the 5th International Conference on English Historical Linguistics.* (Current Issues in Linguistic Theory 65.) Amsterdam and Philadelphia: John Benjamins.

Aitchison, J. 1991 [1981]. *Language Change: Progress or Decay?* 2nd ed. Cambridge, New York, and Melbourne: Cambridge University Press.

Åkerlund, A. 1911. *On the History of the Definite Tenses in English.* Lund and Cambridge: Ph. Lindstedts universitetsbokhandel and W. Heffer & Sons.

Åkerlund, A. 1914. "A Word on the Passive Definite Tenses". *Englische Studien* 47, 321–337.

Allen, R. L. 1966. *The Verb System of Present-Day American English.* The Hague and Paris: Mouton & Co.

Allerton, D. J., E. Carney, and D. Holdcroft (eds.). 1979. *Function and Context in Linguistic Analysis: A Festschrift for William Haas.* Cambridge: Cambridge University Press.

Altick, R. D. 1957. *The English Common Reader: A Social History of the Mass Reading Public 1800–1900.* Chicago and London: The University of Chicago Press.

Andersen, H., and K. Koerner (eds.). 1990. *Historical Linguistics 1987: Papers from the 8th International Conference on Historical Linguistics.* (Current Issues in Linguistic Theory 66.) Amsterdam and Philadelphia: John Benjamins.

Anderson, J. (ed.). 1982. *Language Form and Linguistic Variation: Papers Dedicated to Angus McIntosh.* (Current Issues in Linguistic Theory 15.) Amsterdam: John Benjamins.

Archer, D., P. Rayson, A. Wilson, and T. McEnery (eds.). 2003. *Proceedings of the Corpus Linguistics 2003 Conference.* (UCREL Technical Papers 16.) UCREL, Lancaster University.

Aristar, A., and H. Dry. 1982. "The Origin of Backgrounding Tenses in English". In: Tuite, K., R. Schneider, and R. Chametzky (eds.), 1–13.

Arnaud, R. 1973. *La forme progressive en anglais du XIXe siècle.* Lille. (No publisher.)

Arnaud, R. 1983. "On the Progress of the Progressive in the Private Correspondence of Famous British People (1800–1880)". In: Jacobson, S. (ed.), 83–94.

Arnaud, R. 1998. "The Development of the Progressive in 19th Century English: A Quantitative Survey". *Language Variation and Change* 10, 123–152.

Arnaud, R. 2002. *Letter-Writers of the Romantic Age and the Modernization of English (A Quantitative Historical Survey of the Progressive).* Accessed at http://www.univ-pau.fr/ANGLAIS/ressources/rarnaud/index.html   during 2003.

Bache, C. 1985. *Verbal Aspect: A General Theory and Its Application to Present-Day English.* (Odense University Studies in English 8.) Odense: Odense University Press.

Bache, C. 1997 [1995]. *The Study of Aspect, Tense and Action: Towards a Theory of the Semantics of Grammatical Categories.* 2nd ed. Frankfurt am Main: Peter Lang.

Bailey, R. W. 1996. *Nineteenth-Century English.* Ann Arbor: The University of Michigan Press.

Barber, C. L., F. Behre, U. Ohlander, Y. Olsson, S. Stubelius, J. Söderlind, and R. W. Zandvoort. 1962. *Contributions to English Syntax and Philology.* (Gothenburg Studies in English 14.) Gothenburg, Stockholm, and Uppsala: Almqvist & Wiksell.

Behre, F. 1961. "On the Principle of Connecting Elements of Speech in Contemporary English". In: Bonnard, G. A. (ed.), 303–316.

Berglund, Y. 1997. "Future in Present-Day English: Corpus-Based Evidence on the Rivalry of Expressions". *ICAME Journal* 21, 7–19.

Bermúdez-Otero, R., D. Denison, R. M. Hogg, and C. B. McCully (eds.). 2000. *Generative Theory and Corpus Studies: A Dialogue from 10 ICEHL.* (Topics in English Linguistics 31.) Berlin and New York: Mouton de Gruyter.

Biber, D. 1988. *Variation across Speech and Writing.* Cambridge: Cambridge University Press.

Biber, D. 2003. "Variation among University Spoken and Written Registers: A New Multi-Dimensional Analysis". In: Leistyna, P., and C. Meyer (eds.), 47–70.

Biber, D., and E. Finegan. 1992. "The Linguistic Evolution of Five Written and Speech-Based English Genres from the 17th to the 20th Centuries". In: Rissanen, M., O. Ihalainen, T. Nevalainen, and I. Taavitsainen (eds.), 688–704.

Biber, D., and E. Finegan. 1997. "Diachronic Relations among Speech-Based and Written Registers in English". In: Nevalainen, T., and L. Kahlas-Tarkka (eds.), 253–275.

Biber, D., S. Johansson, G. Leech, S. Conrad, and E. Finegan. 1999. *Longman Grammar of Spoken and Written English.* Harlow: Pearson.

Blake, N. (ed.). 1992. *The Cambridge History of the English Language.* Vol. II: 1066–1476. Cambridge, New York, and Melbourne: Cambridge University Press.

Bodelsen, C. A. 1936. "The Expanded Tenses in Modern English. An Attempt at an Explanation". *Englische Studien* 71, 220–238.

Bøgholm, N., A. Brusendorff, and C. A. Bodelsen (eds.). 1930. *A Grammatical Miscellany Offered to Otto Jespersen on His Seventieth Birthday.* Copenhagen: Levin & Munksgaard.

Bolinger, D. 1971a. "The Nominal in the Progressive". *Linguistic Inquiry* 2, 246–250.

Bolinger, D. 1971b. "A Further Note on the Nominal in the Progressive". *Linguistic Inquiry* 2, 584–586.

Bolinger, D. 1979. "The Jingle Theory of Double -*ing*". In: Allerton, D. J., E. Carney, and D. Holdcroft (eds.), 41–56.

Bonnard, G. A. (ed.). 1961. *English Studies Today: Second Series*. Bern: Francke Verlag.

Braaten, B. 1967. "Notes on Continuous Tenses in English". *Norsk tidsskrift for sprogvidenskap* 21, 167–180.

Bringas López, A., D. González Álvarez, J. Pérez Guerra, E. Rama Martínez, and E. Varela Bravo (eds.). 1999. 'Woonderous Ænglissce': *SELIM Studies in Medieval English Language*. (Colección Congresos 14.) Vigo: Servicio de Publicacións da Universidade de Vigo.

Brinton, L. J. 1988. *The Development of English Aspectual Systems: Aspectualizers and Post-Verbal Particles*. (Cambridge Studies in Linguistics 49.) Cambridge: Cambridge University Press.

Brown, P., and S. C. Levinson. 1987 [1978]. *Politeness: Some Universals in Language Usage*. 2nd ed. (Studies in Interactional Sociolinguistics 4.) Cambridge: Cambridge University Press.

Brunner, K. 1955. "Expanded Verbal Forms in Early Modern English". *English Studies* 36, 218–221.

Brusendorff, A. 1930. "The Relative Aspect of the Verb in English". In: Bøgholm, N., A. Brusendorff, and C. A. Bodelsen (eds.), 225–247.

Buyssens, E. 1968. *Les deux aspectifs de la conjugaison anglaise au XXe siècle: Étude de l'expression de l'aspect*. (Université libre de Bruxelles: Travaux de la Faculté de Philosophie et Lettres 37.) Brussels and Paris: Presses Universitaires de Bruxelles and Presses Universitaires de France.

Bybee, J. L., and Ö. Dahl. 1989. "The Creation of Tense and Aspect Systems in the Languages of the World". *Studies in Language* 13, 51–103.

Bybee, J., R. Perkins, and W. Pagliuca. 1994. *The Evolution of Grammar: Tense, Aspect, and Modality in the Languages of the World*. Chicago and London: The University of Chicago Press.

Calver, E. 1946. "The Uses of the Present Tense Forms in English". *Language* 22, 317–325.

Chambers, J. K. 1995. *Sociolinguistic Theory: Linguistic Variation and Its Social Significance*. (Language in Society 22.) Oxford and Cambridge: Blackwell.

Charleston, B. M. 1955. "A Reconsideration of the Problem of Time, Tense, and Aspect in Modern English". *English Studies* 36, 263–278.

Charleston, B. M. 1960. *Studies on the Emotional and Affective Means of Expression in Modern English*. (Swiss Studies in English 46.) Bern: Francke.

COD = Pearsall, J. (ed.). 1999. *The Concise Oxford Dictionary*. 10th ed. Oxford: Oxford University Press.

Comrie, B. 1976. *Aspect: An Introduction to the Study of Verbal Aspect and Related Problems*. Cambridge: Cambridge University Press.

Couper-Kuhlen, E. 1995. "On the Foregrounded Progressive in American Conversational Narrative: A New Development?". In: Riehle, W., and H. Keiper (eds.), 229–245.

Crystal, D. 1966. "Specification and English Tenses". *Journal of Linguistics* 2, 1–34.

Culpeper, J., and M. Kytö. 2000. "Gender Voices in the Spoken Interaction of the Past: A Pilot Study Based on Early Modern English Trial Proceedings". In: Kastovsky, D., and A. Mettinger (eds.), 53–89.

Curme, G. O. 1913. "Development of the Progressiv [*sic*] Form in Germanic". *Publications of the Modern Language Association of America* 28, 159–187.

Curme, G. O. 1932. "Some Characteristic Features of Aspect in English". *The Journal of English and Germanic Philology* 31, 251–255.

Curzan, A., and K. Emmons (eds.). 2004. *Studies in the History of the English Language II: Unfolding Conversations*. (Topics in English Linguistics 45.) Berlin and New York: Mouton de Gruyter.

Dal, I. 1952. "Zur Entstehung des englischen Participium praesentis auf *-ing*". *Norsk tidsskrift for sprogvidenskap* 16, 5–116.

Danchev, A., and M. Kytö. 1998. "The Construction *Be Going to + Infinitive* in Early Modern English". In: Rydén, M., I. Tieken-Boon van Ostade, and M. Kytö (eds.), 145–163.

Denison, D. 1985. "Some Observations on *Being Teaching*". *Studia Neophilologica* 57, 157–159.

Denison, D. 1993. *English Historical Syntax: Verbal Constructions*. London and New York: Longman.

Denison, D. 1998. "Syntax". In: Romaine, S. (ed.), 92–329.

Denison, D. 1999. "Slow, Slow, Quick, Quick, Slow: The Dance of Language Change?". In: Bringas López, A., D. González Álvarez, J. Pérez Guerra, E. Rama Martínez, and E. Varela Bravo (eds.), 51–64.

Dennis, L. 1940. "The Progressive Tense: Frequency of Its Use in English". *Publications of the Modern Language Association of America* 55, 855–865.

Dorodnikh, A. 1989. "The English Progressive and Other Verb Forms in a Historical Perspective". *Folia Linguistica Historica* 9, 105–116.

Dowty, D. R. 1977. "Toward a Semantic Analysis of Verb Aspect and the English 'Imperfective' Progressive". *Linguistics and Philosophy* 1, 45–77.

Dowty, D. R. 1979. *Word Meaning and Montague Grammar: The Semantics of Verbs and Times in Generative Semantics and in Montague's PTQ*. (Texts and Studies in Linguistics and Philosophy 7.) Dordrecht: Reidel.

Dowty, D. R. 1991. "Thematic Proto-Roles and Argument Selection". *Language* 67, 547–619.

Durst-Andersen, P. 2000. "The English Progressive as Picture Description". *Acta Linguistica Hafniensia* 32, 45–103.

Eckert, P. 1993. "Cooperative Competition in Adolescent 'Girl Talk' ". In: Tannen, D. (ed.), 32–61.

Edgren, E. 1971. *Temporal Clauses in English*. (Studia Anglistica Upsaliensia 9.) Uppsala: Almqvist & Wiksell.

Edgren, E. 1985. "The Progressive in English: Another New Approach". *Studia Linguistica* 39, 67–83.

Ehrlich, S. 1990. *Point of View: A Linguistic Analysis of Literary Style*. London and New York: Routledge.

van Ek, J. A. 1969. "The 'Progressive' Reconsidered". *English Studies* 50, 579–585.

Elliot, A. D. 1911. *The Life of George Joachim Goschen, First Viscount Goschen, 1831–1907*. Vol. I. London: Longmans, Green, and Co.

Elsness, J. 1994. "On the Progression of the Progressive in Early Modern English". *ICAME Journal* 18, 5–25.

Erdmann, A. 1871. *Essay on the History and Modern Use of the Verbal Forms in -ing in the English Language*. Part I. Old Anglo-Saxon Period. Stockholm: P. A. Nyman.

Fanego, T. 1996. "The Gerund in Early Modern English: Evidence from the Helsinki Corpus". *Folia Linguistica Historica* 17, 97–152.

Finegan, E. 1995. "Subjectivity and Subjectivisation: An Introduction". In: Stein, D., and S. Wright (eds.), 1–15.

Fischer, O. 1992. "Syntax". In: Blake, N. (ed.), 207–408.

Fitzmaurice, S. M. 2004a. "The Meanings and Uses of the Progressive Construction in an Early Eighteenth-Century English Network". In: Curzan, A., and K. Emmons (eds.), 131–173.

Fitzmaurice, S. M. 2004b. "A Brief Response". In: Curzan, A., and K. Emmons (eds.), 183–188.

Freckmann, N. 1995. "The Progressive and Adverbial Collocations: Corpus Evidence". In: Riehle, W., and H. Keiper (eds.), 255–267.

Fries, U., V. Müller, and P. Schneider (eds.). 1997. *From Ælfric to the New York Times: Studies in English Corpus Linguistics*. (Language and Computers: Studies in Practical Linguistics 19.) Amsterdam and Atlanta: Rodopi.

van der Gaaf, W. 1930. "Some Notes on the History of the Progressive Form". *Neophilologus* 15, 201–215.

Garey, H. 1957. "Verbal Aspect in French". *Language* 33, 91–110.

Geisler, C. 2000. Investigating Register Variation in Nineteenth-Century English: A Multi-Dimensional Comparison. Paper presented at the Second North American Symposium on Corpus Linguistics and Language Teaching, Flagstaff.

Geisler, C. 2001. Gender-Based Variation in Nineteenth-Century English Letter-Writing. Paper presented at the Third North American Symposium on Corpus Linguistics and Language Teaching, Boston.

Geisler, C. 2002. "Investigating Register Variation in Nineteenth-Century English: A Multi-Dimensional Comparison". In: Reppen, R., S. M. Fitzmaurice, and D. Biber (eds.), 249–271.

Geisler, C. 2003. "Gender-Based Variation in Nineteenth-Century English Letter Writing". In: Leistyna, P., and C. Meyer (eds.), 87–106.

Goedsche, C. R. 1932. "The Terminate Aspect of the Expanded Form: Its Development and Its Relation to the Gerund". *The Journal of English and Germanic Philology* 31, 469–477.

Goldsmith, J., and E. Woisetschlaeger. 1982. "The Logic of the English Progressive". *Linguistic Inquiry* 13, 79–89.

Goossens, L. 1994. "The English Progressive Tenses and the Layered Representation of Functional Grammar". In: Vet, C., and C. Vetters (eds.), 161–177.

Görlach, M. 1991. *Introduction to Early Modern English*. Cambridge, New York, and Oakleigh: Cambridge University Press.

Görlach, M. 1999. *English in Nineteenth-Century England: An Introduction*. Cambridge: Cambridge University Press.

Grund, P., and T. Walker. Forthcoming. "The Subjunctive in Adverbial Clauses in Nineteenth-Century English". In: Kytö, M., M. Rydén, and E. Smitterberg (eds.).

Grzega, J. 1999. "A New View on Why, How and in How Far *-ing* Prevailed over *-ind*". *Views: Vienna English Working Papers* 8, 34–43.

Gustafsson, L. O. 2002. *Preterite and Past Participle Forms in English 1680–1790: Standardisation Processes in Public and Private Writing*. (Studia Anglistica Upsaliensia 120.) Uppsala: Acta Universitatis Upsaliensis.

Harvie, C. 1992. "Revolution and the Rule of Law (1789–1851)". In: Morgan, K. O. (ed.), 419–462.

Hatcher, A. G. 1951. "The Use of the Progressive Form in English: A New Approach". *Language* 27, 254–280.

Heine, B. 1994. "Grammaticalization as an Explanatory Parameter". In: Pagliuca, W. (ed.), 255–287.

Hewson, J., and V. Bubenik. 1997. *Tense and Aspect in Indo-European Languages: Theory, Typology, Diachrony*. (Current Issues in Linguistic Theory 145.) Amsterdam and Philadelphia: John Benjamins.

Hirtle, W. H. 1967. *The Simple and Progressive Forms: An Analytical Approach*. (Cahiers de psychomécanique du langage 8.) Québec: Les presses de l'Université Laval.

Hogg, R. M. (ed.). 1992. *The Cambridge History of the English Language*. Vol. I: The Beginnings to 1066. Cambridge: Cambridge University Press.

Holmberg, J. 1916. *Zur Geschichte der periphrastischen Verbindung des Verbum Substantivum mit dem Partizipium präsentis im Kontinentalgermanischen*. Uppsala: Almqvist & Wiksell.

Hopper, P. J. 1979. "Some Observations on the Typology of Focus and Aspect in Narrative Language". *Studies in Language* 3, 37–64.

Hopper, P. J. (ed.). 1982. *Tense-Aspect: Between Semantics & Pragmatics*. (Typological Studies in Language 1.) Amsterdam and Philadelphia: John Benjamins.

Hopper, P. J., and E. C. Traugott. 1993. *Grammaticalization*. Cambridge: Cambridge University Press.

Hübler, A. 1998. *The Expressivity of Grammar: Grammatical Devices Expressing Emotion across Time*. (Topics in English Linguistics 25.) Berlin and New York: Mouton de Gruyter.

Huddleston, R., and G. Pullum. 2002. *The Cambridge Grammar of the English Language*. Cambridge: Cambridge University Press.

Hundt, M. 1998. *New Zealand English Grammar – Fact or Fiction? A Corpus-Based Study in Morphosyntactic Variation*. (Varieties of English around the World 23.) Amsterdam and Philadelphia: John Benjamins.

Hundt, M. 2004a. "Animacy, Agentivity, and the Spread of the Progressive in Modern English". *English Language and Linguistics* 8, 47–69.

Hundt, M. 2004b. "The Passival and the Progressive Passive: A Case Study of Layering in the English Aspect and Voice Systems". In: Lindquist, H., and C. Mair (eds.), 79–120.

Hundt, M., and C. Mair. 1999. " 'Agile' and 'Uptight' Genres: The Corpus-Based Approach to Language Change in Progress". *International Journal of Corpus Linguistics* 4, 221–242.

Jacobs, A., and A. H. Jucker. 1995. "The Historical Perspective in Pragmatics". In: Jucker, A. H. (ed.), 3–33.

Jacobson, S. (ed.). 1983. *Papers from the Second Scandinavian Symposium on Syntactic Variation*. (Stockholm Studies in English 57.) Stockholm: Almqvist & Wiksell.

Jespersen, O. 1909–1949. *A Modern English Grammar on Historical Principles*. Part IV: Syntax (3rd Vol.). London and Copenhagen: George Allen & Unwin and Ejnar Munksgaard.

Joos, M. 1964. *The English Verb: Form and Meanings*. Madison and Milwaukee: The University of Wisconsin Press.

Jørgensen, E. 1990. "Verbs of Physical Perception Used in Progressive Tenses". *English Studies* 71, 439–444.

Jørgensen, E. 1991. "The Progressive Tenses and the So-Called 'Non-Conclusive' Verbs". *English Studies* 72, 173–182.

Jucker, A. H. (ed.). 1995. *Historical Pragmatics: Pragmatic Developments in the History of English*. (Pragmatics and Beyond 35.) Amsterdam and Philadelphia: John Benjamins.

Karlsson, F., A. Voutilainen, J. Heikkilä, and A. Anttila (eds.). 1995. *Constraint Grammar: A Language-Independent System for Parsing Unrestricted Text*. (Natural Language Processing 4.) Berlin and New York: Mouton de Gruyter.

Kastovsky, D. (ed.). 1991. *Historical English Syntax*. (Topics in English Linguistics 2.) Berlin and New York: Mouton de Gruyter.

Kastovsky, D. (ed.). 1994. *Studies in Early Modern English*. (Topics in English Linguistics 13.) Berlin and New York: Mouton de Gruyter.

Kastovsky, D., and A. Mettinger (eds.). 2000. *The History of English in a Social Context: A Contribution to Historical Sociolinguistics*. (Trends in

Linguistics: Studies and Monographs 129.) Berlin and New York: Mouton de Gruyter.

Killie, K. 2004. "Subjectivity and the English Progressive". *English Language and Linguistics* 8, 25–46.

Kirk, J. M. (ed.). 2000. *Corpora Galore: Analyses and Techniques in Describing English. Papers from the Nineteenth International Conference on English Language Research on Computerised Corpora (ICAME 1998).* (Language and Computers: Studies in Practical Linguistics 30.) Amsterdam and Atlanta: Rodopi.

Kisbye, T. 1963. *An Historical Survey of English Syntax.* Part I: The Non-Finite Forms of the Verb (Sections A–B–C–D). Århus: Akademisk boghandel.

Klegraf, J., and D. Nehls (eds.). 1988. *Essays on the English Language and Applied Linguistics on the Occasion of Gerhard Nickel's 60th Birthday.* (Studies in Descriptive Linguistics 18.) Heidelberg: Julius Groos.

König, E. 1980. "On the Context-Dependence of the Progressive in English". In: Rohrer, C. (ed.), 269–291.

König, E. 1995. "On Analyzing the Tense-Aspect System of English: A State-of-the-Art Report". In: Riehle, W., and H. Keiper (eds.), 153–169.

Korninger, S. (ed.). 1957. *Studies in English Language and Literature Presented to Professor Dr. Karl Brunner on the Occasion of His Seventieth Birthday.* (Wiener Beiträge zur Englischen Philologie 65.) Wien and Stuttgart: Wilhelm Braumüller.

Kytö, M. 1996. *Manual to the Diachronic Part of the Helsinki Corpus of English Texts: Coding Conventions and Lists of Source Texts.* 3rd ed. Helsinki: Department of English, University of Helsinki.

Kytö, M. 1997. "*Be/Have* + Past Participle: The Choice of the Auxiliary with Intransitives from Late Middle to Modern English". In: Rissanen, M., M. Kytö, and K. Heikkonen (eds.), 17–85.

Kytö, M., and S. Romaine. 2000. Exploring Variation in Adjective Comparison in CONCE: "The Very *Most Delightfulest* Tour". Paper presented at the International Symposium on Determinants of Grammatical Variation in English, Paderborn, 23–24 June, 2000.

Kytö, M., J. Rudanko, and E. Smitterberg. 2000. "Building a Bridge between the Present and the Past: A Corpus of 19th-Century English". *ICAME Journal* 24, 85–97.

Kytö, M., J. Rudanko, and E. Smitterberg (comps.). Forthcoming. *Manual to A Corpus of Nineteenth-Century English (CONCE): Coding Conventions and Lists of Source Texts.*

Kytö, M., M. Rydén, and E. Smitterberg (eds.). Forthcoming. *19th-Century English: Stability and Change.*

Labov, W. 2001. *Principles of Linguistic Change.* Vol. II: Social Factors. (Language in Society 29.) Malden and Oxford: Blackwell.

Landman, F. 1992. "The Progressive". *Natural Language Semantics* 1, 1–32.

Langacker, R. W. 1982. "Remarks on English Aspect". In: Hopper, P. J. (ed.), 265–304.

Lass, R. (ed.). 1999. *The Cambridge History of the English Language*. Vol. III: 1476–1776. Cambridge: Cambridge University Press.

Lehmann, W. P., and Y. Malkiel (eds.). 1968. *Directions for Historical Linguistics: A Symposium*. Austin and London: University of Texas Press.

Lehmann, W. P., and Y. Malkiel (eds.). 1982. *Perspectives on Historical Linguistics*. (Current Issues in Linguistic Theory 24.) Amsterdam and Philadelphia: John Benjamins.

Leistyna, P., and C. Meyer (eds.). 2003. *Corpus Analysis: Language Structure and Language Use*. (Language and Computers: Studies in Practical Linguistics 46.) Amsterdam and New York: Rodopi.

Lindblad, I., and M. Ljung (eds.). 1987. *Proceedings from the Third Nordic Conference for English Studies*. Vol. I. (Stockholm Studies in English 73.) Stockholm: Almqvist & Wiksell.

Lindquist, H., and C. Mair (eds.). 2004. *Corpus Approaches to Grammaticalization in English*. (Studies in Corpus Linguistics 13.) Amsterdam and Philadelphia: John Benjamins.

Ljung, M. 1980. *Reflections on the English Progressive*. (Gothenburg Studies in English 46.) Gothenburg: Acta Universitatis Gothoburgensis.

Ljung, M. (ed.). 1997. *Corpus-Based Studies in English: Papers from the Seventeenth International Conference on English Language Research on Computerized Corpora (ICAME 17)*. (Language and Computers: Studies in Practical Linguistics 20.) Amsterdam and Atlanta: Rodopi.

Lucko, P. 1995. "Between Aspect, Actionality and Modality: The Functions of the Expanded Form". In: Riehle, W., and H. Keiper (eds.), 171–182.

Lyons, J. 1977. *Semantics*. Vol. II. Cambridge: Cambridge University Press.

Mair, C., and M. Hundt. 1995. "Why Is the Progressive Becoming More Frequent in English? A Corpus-Based Investigation of Language Change in Progress". *Zeitschrift für Anglistik und Amerikanistik* 43, 111–122.

Matthew, H. C. G. 1992. "The Liberal Age (1851–1914)". In: Morgan, K. O. (ed.), 463–522.

Matthews, P. H. 1997. *The Concise Oxford Dictionary of Linguistics*. Oxford and New York: Oxford University Press.

Melchers, G., and N.-L. Johannesson (eds.). 1994. *Nonstandard Varieties of Language*. (Stockholm Studies in English 84.) Stockholm: Almqvist & Wiksell.

Milroy, J. 1992. *Linguistic Variation and Change: On the Historical Sociolinguistics of English*. (Language in Society 19.) Oxford and Cambridge: Blackwell.

Milroy, L. 1994. "Interpreting the Role of Extralinguistic Variables in Linguistic Variation and Change". In: Melchers, G., and N.-L. Johannesson (eds.), 131–145.

Mindt, D. 1997. "Complementary Distribution, Gradience and Overlap in Corpora and in ELT: Analysing and Teaching the Progressive". In: Fries, U., V. Müller, and P. Schneider (eds.), 227–237.

Mitchell, B. 1976. "No 'House Is Building' in Old English". *English Studies* 57, 385–389.

Mitchell, B. 1985. *Old English Syntax.* Vol. I: Concord, the Parts of Speech, and the Sentence. Oxford: Clarendon Press.

Mittendorf, I., and E. Poppe. 2000. "Celtic Contacts of the English Progressive?" In: Tristram, H. L. C. (ed.), 117–145.

Moessner, L. 1989. *Early Middle English Syntax.* (Linguistische Arbeiten 207.) Tübingen: Max Niemeyer.

Morgan, K. O. (ed.). 1992. *The Oxford Illustrated History of Britain.* London, New York, Sydney, and Toronto: BCA.

Moskowich-Spiegel Fandiño, I., and B. Crespo García (eds.). 2004. *New Trends in English Historical Linguistics: An Atlantic View.* Spain: Universidade da Coruña.

Mossé, F. 1938. *Histoire de la forme périphrastique être* + participe présent *en germanique.* Vols. I–II. (Collection linguistique publiée par la Société de linguistique de Paris 42–43.) Paris: Librairie C. Klincksieck.

Mufwene, S. S. 1984. *Stativity and the Progressive.* Bloomington: Indiana University Linguistics Club.

Mustanoja, T. F. 1960. *A Middle English Syntax.* Part I: Parts of Speech. (Mémoires de la Société Néophilologique de Helsinki 23.) Helsinki: Société Néophilologique.

Nakamura, F. 1998. A Word on the History of the English Passive Progressive. Paper presented at the Tenth International Conference on English Historical Linguistics, Manchester, 21–26 August, 1998.

Nehls, D. 1974. *Synchron-diachrone Untersuchungen zur Expanded Form im Englischen: Eine struktural-funktionale Analyse.* (Linguistische Reihe 19.) Munich: Max Hueber.

Nehls, D. 1988. "On the Development of the Grammatical Category of Verbal Aspect in English". In: Klegraf, J., and D. Nehls (eds.), 173–198.

Nevalainen, T. 1996. "Social Stratification". In: Nevalainen, T., and H. Raumolin-Brunberg (eds.), 57–76.

Nevalainen, T., and L. Kahlas-Tarkka (eds.). 1997. *To Explain the Present: Studies in the Changing English Language in Honour of Matti Rissanen.* (Mémoires de la Société Néophilologique de Helsinki 52.) Helsinki: Société Néophilologique.

Nevalainen, T., and H. Raumolin-Brunberg (eds.). 1996. *Sociolinguistics and Language History: Studies Based on the Corpus of Early English Correspondence.* (Language and Computers: Studies in Practical Linguistics 15.) Amsterdam and Atlanta: Rodopi.

Nickel, G. 1966. *Die expanded Form im Altenglischen: Vorkommen, Funktion und Herkunft der Umschreibung* beon/wesan + *Partizip Präsens.* (Kieler Beiträge zur Anglistik und Amerikanistik 3.) Neumünster: Karl Wachholtz.

Nickel, G. 1967. "An Example of a Syntactic Blend in Old English". *Indogermanische Forschungen* 72, 261–274.

Nordlander, J. 1997. *Towards a Semantics of Linguistic Time: Exploring Some Basic Time Concepts with Special Reference to English and Krio.* (Umeå Studies in the Humanities 134.) Uppsala: Swedish Science Press.

Núñez Pertejo, P. 1999. *"Be Going to* + Infinitive: Origin and Development. Some Relevant Cases from the *Helsinki Corpus". Studia Neophilologica* 71, 135–142.

Núñez Pertejo, P. 2001. *The Progressive in the History of English with Special Reference to the Early Modern English Period: A Corpus-Based Study.* Departamento de Filoloxía Inglesa, Facultad de Filoloxía, Universidad de Santiago de Compostela (CD-ROM).

Nurmi, A. 1996. "Periphrastic DO and BE + ING: Interconnected Developments?". In: Nevalainen, T., and H. Raumolin-Brunberg (eds.), 151–165.

OED = Oxford English Dictionary. Revised 2nd ed., as accessed on the Internet, at http://dictionary.oed.com, during 2001. Oxford University Press.

Ota, A. 1963. *Tense and Aspect of Present-Day American English.* Tokyo: Kenkyusha.

Övergaard, G. 1987. "Duration, Progression, and the Progressive Form in Temporal *As*-Clauses". In: Lindblad, I., and M. Ljung (eds.), 265–280.

Paccaud, J. 1988. "The Metaphorical and Narrative Function of the Progressive Form in *Under Western Eyes". Language and Style* 21, 107–118.

Pagliuca, W. (ed.). 1994. *Perspectives on Grammaticalization.* (Current Issues in Linguistic Theory 109.) Amsterdam and Philadelphia: John Benjamins.

Palander-Collin, M. 1999a. *Grammaticalization and Social Embedding: I THINK and METHINKS in Middle and Early Modern English.* (Mémoires de la Société Néophilologique de Helsinki 55.) Helsinki: Société Néophilologique.

Palander-Collin, M. 1999b. *"I Think, Methinks*: Register Variation, Stratification, Education and Nonstandard Language". In: Taavitsainen, I., G. Melchers, and P. Pahta (eds.), 243–262.

Palmer, F. R. 1979. *Modality and the English Modals.* (Longman Linguistics Library 23.) London and New York: Longman.

Palmer, F. R. 1988 [1974]. *The English Verb.* 2nd ed. London and New York: Longman.

Paradis, C. 2000. *"It's Well Weird*: Degree Modifiers of Adjectives Revisited: The Nineties". In: Kirk, J. M. (ed.), 147–160.

Peters, P., P. Collins, and A. Smith (eds.). 2002. *New Frontiers of Corpus Research.* (Language and Computers: Studies in Practical Linguistics 36.) Amsterdam and New York: Rodopi.

Phillipps, K. C. 1970. *Jane Austen's English.* London: André Deutsch.

Poutsma, H. 1926. *A Grammar of Late Modern English for the Use of Continental, Especially Dutch, Students.* Part II, Section II: Parts of Speech, the Verb and the Particles. Groningen: P. Noordhoff.

Pratt, L., and D. Denison. 2000. "The Language of the Southey–Coleridge Circle". *Language Sciences* 22, 401–422.

Quirk, R., S. Greenbaum, G. Leech, and J. Svartvik. 1985. *A Comprehensive Grammar of the English Language.* London and New York: Longman.

Raumolin-Brunberg, H. 1988. "Variation and Historical Linguistics: A Survey of Methods and Concepts". *Neuphilologische Mitteilungen* 89, 136–154.

Raumolin-Brunberg, H. 2002. "Stable Variation and Historical Linguistics". In: Raumolin-Brunberg, H., M. Nevala, A. Nurmi, and M. Rissanen (eds.), 101–116.

Raumolin-Brunberg, H., M. Nevala, A. Nurmi, and M. Rissanen (eds.). 2002. *Variation Past and Present: VARIENG Studies on English for Terttu Nevalainen.* (Mémoires de la Société Néophilologique de Helsinki 61.) Helsinki: Société Néophilologique.

Raybould, E. 1957. "Of Jane Austen's Use of Expanded Verbal Forms: One More Method of Approach to the Problems Presented by These Forms". In: Korninger, S. (ed.), 175–190.

Reppen, R., S. M. Fitzmaurice, and D. Biber (eds.). 2002. *Using Corpora to Explore Linguistic Variation.* (Studies in Corpus Linguistics 9.) Amsterdam and Philadelphia: John Benjamins.

Reynolds, H. T. 1984 [1977]. *Analysis of Nominal Data.* 2nd ed. (Quantitative Applications in the Social Sciences 7.) Newbury Park, London, and New Delhi: Sage Publications.

Riehle, W., and H. Keiper (eds.). 1995. *Anglistentag 1994 Graz: Proceedings.* (Proceedings of the Conference of the German Association of University Teachers of English 16.) Tübingen: Max Niemeyer.

Rissanen, M. 1986. "Variation and the Study of English Historical Syntax". In: Sankoff, D. (ed.), 97–109.

Rissanen, M. 1991. "Spoken Language and the History of *Do*-Periphrasis". In: Kastovsky, D. (ed.), 321–342.

Rissanen, M. 1999. "Syntax". In: Lass, R. (ed.), 187–331.

Rissanen, M., O. Ihalainen, T. Nevalainen, and I. Taavitsainen (eds.). 1992. *History of Englishes: New Methods and Interpretations in Historical Linguistics.* (Topics in English Linguistics 10.) Berlin and New York: Mouton de Gruyter.

Rissanen, M., M. Kytö, and K. Heikkonen (eds.). 1997. *English in Transition: Corpus-Based Studies in Linguistic Variation and Genre Styles.* (Topics in English Linguistics 23.) Berlin and New York: Mouton de Gruyter.

Rissanen, M., M. Kytö, and M. Palander-Collin (eds.). 1993. *Early English in the Computer Age: Explorations through the Helsinki Corpus.* (Topics in English Linguistics 11.) Berlin and New York: Mouton de Gruyter.

Rohrer, C. (ed.). 1980. *Time, Tense, and Quantifiers: Proceedings of the Stuttgart Conference on the Logic of Tense and Quantification.* (Linguistische Arbeiten 83.) Tübingen: Max Niemeyer.

Romaine, S. 1982. *Socio-Historical Linguistics: Its Status and Methodology.* Cambridge: Cambridge University Press.

Romaine, S. 1984. "On the Problem of Syntactic Variation and Pragmatic Meaning in Sociolinguistic Theory". *Folia Linguistica* 18, 409–437.

Romaine, S. (ed.). 1998. *The Cambridge History of the English Language*. Vol. IV: 1776–1997. Cambridge: Cambridge University Press.

Romaine, S. 1999. *Communicating Gender*. Mahwah: Lawrence Erlbaum Associates.

Rydén, M. 1979. *An Introduction to the Historical Study of English Syntax*. (Stockholm Studies in English 51.) Stockholm: Almqvist & Wiksell.

Rydén, M. 1997. "On the Panchronic Core Meaning of the English Progressive". In: Nevalainen, T., and L. Kahlas-Tarkka (eds.), 419–429.

Rydén, M., and S. Brorström. 1987. *The Be/Have Variation with Intransitives in English: With Special Reference to the Late Modern Period*. (Stockholm Studies in English 70.) Stockholm: Almqvist & Wiksell.

Rydén, M., I. Tieken-Boon van Ostade, and M. Kytö (eds.). 1998. *A Reader in Early Modern English*. (University of Bamberg Studies in English Linguistics 43.) Frankfurt am Main: Peter Lang.

Samuels, M. L. 1972. *Linguistic Evolution: With Special Reference to English*. Cambridge: Cambridge University Press.

Sankoff, D. (ed.). 1986. *Diversity and Diachrony*. (Current Issues in Linguistic Theory 53.) Amsterdam and Philadelphia: John Benjamins.

Scheffer, J. 1975. *The Progressive in English*. (North-Holland Linguistic Series 15.) Amsterdam and Oxford: North-Holland.

Schlesinger, I. M. 1995. *Cognitive Space and Linguistic Case: Semantic and Syntactic Categories in English*. Cambridge, New York, and Melbourne: Cambridge University Press.

Schousboe, S. 2000. "The Endless Progressive". *Acta Linguistica Hafniensia* 32, 105–119.

Short, M. 1996. *Exploring the Language of Poems, Plays and Prose*. London and New York: Longman.

Smith, A. 1917. "Über eine bisher unbeachtete Funktion der progressiven Form". *Beiblatt zur Anglia* 28, 244–251.

Smith, C. 2004. "Use of Progressive Aspect in 18ht-Century [*sic*] English: A Study of Personal Letters". In: Moskowich-Spiegel Fandiño, I., and B. Crespo García (eds.), 151–186.

Smith, C. S. 1983. "A Theory of Aspectual Choice". *Language* 59, 479–501.

Smith, C. S. 1997 [1991]. *The Parameter of Aspect*. 2nd ed. (Studies in Linguistics and Philosophy 43.) Dordrecht: Kluwer.

Smith, N. 2002. "Ever Moving On? The Progressive in Recent British English". In: Peters, P., P. Collins, and A. Smith (eds.), 317–330.

Smith, N. 2003. "A Quirky Progressive? A Corpus-Based Exploration of the *Will + Be + -ing* Construction in Recent and Present Day British English". In: Archer, D., P. Rayson, A. Wilson, and T. McEnery (eds.), 714–723.

Smitterberg, E. 1999. Review of: Nordlander (1997). *Studia Neophilologica* 71, 115–117.

Smitterberg, E. 2000a. "The Progressive Form and Genre Variation during the Nineteenth Century". In: Bermúdez-Otero, R., D. Denison, R. M. Hogg, and C. B. McCully (eds.), 283–297.

Smitterberg, E. 2000b. Pragmatic Functions of the Progressive Form in the 19th Century. Paper presented at the Eleventh International Conference on English Historical Linguistics, Santiago de Compostela, Spain, 7–11 September, 2000.

Smitterberg, E. 2004. "Investigating the Expressive Progressive: On Susan M. Fitzmaurice's 'The Meanings and Uses of the Progressive Construction in an Early Eighteenth-Century English Network' ". In: Curzan, A., and K. Emmons (eds.), 175–182.

Smitterberg, E., S. Reich, and A. Hahn. 2000. "The Present Progressive in Political and Academic Language in the 19th and 20th Centuries: A Corpus-Based Investigation". *ICAME Journal* 24, 99–118.

Söderlind, J. 1951. *Verb Syntax in John Dryden's Prose.* Vol. I. (Essays and Studies on English Language and Literature 10.) Uppsala: Lundequistska bokhandeln.

Stein, D., and S. Wright (eds.). 1995. *Subjectivity and Subjectivisation: Linguistic Perspectives.* Cambridge, New York, and Melbourne: Cambridge University Press.

Strang, B. M. H. 1982. "Some Aspects of the History of the *Be + Ing* Construction". In: Anderson, J. (ed.), 427–474.

Stubbs, M. 1996. *Text and Corpus Analysis: Computer-Assisted Studies of Language and Culture.* (Language in Society 23.) Oxford and Cambridge: Blackwell.

Sume, A. 1995. Time Evolution of Expanded Form Occurrence in Shakespeare's Plays: Comparison of Three Frequency Measures. D-Level Thesis, Linköping University, Department of Language and Literature (unpublished).

Sweet, H. 1898. *A New English Grammar: Logical and Historical.* Part II: Syntax. Oxford: Clarendon Press.

Taavitsainen, I., G. Melchers, and P. Pahta (eds.). 1999. *Writing in Nonstandard English.* (Pragmatics and Beyond 67.) Amsterdam and Philadelphia: John Benjamins.

Tannen, D. (ed.). 1993. *Gender and Conversational Interaction.* New York and Oxford: Oxford University Press.

Toolan, M. 1983. "The Functioning of Progressive Verbal Forms in the Narrative of *Go Down, Moses*". *Language and Style* 16, 211–230.

Traugott, E. C. 1982. "From Propositional to Textual and Expressive Meanings: Some Semantic-Pragmatic Aspects of Grammaticalization". In: Lehmann, W. P., and Y. Malkiel (eds.), 245–271.

Traugott, E. C. 1992. "Syntax". In: Hogg, R. M. (ed.), 168–289.

Traugott, E. C. 1995. "Subjectification in Grammaticalisation". In: Stein, D., and S. Wright (eds.), 31–54.

Tristram, H. L. C. (ed.). 2000. *The Celtic Englishes.* Vol. II. (Anglistische Forschungen 286.) Heidelberg: C. Winter.

Tuite, K., R. Schneider, and R. Chametzky (eds.). 1982. *Papers from the Eighteenth Regional Meeting: Chicago Linguistic Society*. Chicago: Chicago Linguistic Society.

Vendler, Z. 1967. *Linguistics in Philosophy*. Ithaca: Cornell University Press.

Vet, C., and C. Vetters (eds.). 1994. *Tense and Aspect in Discourse*. (Trends in Linguistics: Studies and Monographs 75.) Berlin and New York: Mouton de Gruyter.

Virtanen, T. 1997. "The Progressive in NS and NNS Student Compositions: Evidence from the International Corpus of Learner English". In: Ljung, M. (ed.), 299–309.

Visser, F. Th. 1973. *An Historical Syntax of the English Language*. Part III, 2nd Half: Syntactical Units with Two and with More Verbs. Leiden: E. J. Brill.

Warner, A. R. 1993. *English Auxiliaries: Structure and History*. (Cambridge Studies in Linguistics 66.) Cambridge, New York, and Oakleigh: Cambridge University Press.

Warner, A. R. 1995. "Predicting the Progressive Passive: Parametric Change within a Lexicalist Framework". *Language* 71, 533–557.

Warner, A. R. 1997. "Extending the Paradigm: An Interpretation of the Historical Development of Auxiliary Sequences in English". *English Studies* 78, 162–189.

Wårvik, B. 1990a. "On Grounding in English Narratives: A Diachronic Perspective". In: Adamson, S., V. Law, N. Vincent, and S. Wright (eds.), 559–575.

Wårvik, B. 1990b. "On the History of Grounding Markers in English Narrative: Style or Typology?" In: Andersen, H., and K. Koerner (eds.), 531–542.

Weinreich, U., W. Labov, and M. I. Herzog. 1968. "Empirical Foundations for a Theory of Language Change". In: Lehmann, W. P., and Y. Malkiel (eds.), 95–195.

Woods, A., P. Fletcher, and A. Hughes. 1986. *Statistics in Language Studies*. Cambridge: Cambridge University Press.

Wright, S. 1986. Tense, Aspect and Text: Processes of Grammaticalisation in the History of the English Auxiliary. PhD Dissertation, Cambridge University (unpublished).

Wright, S. 1994. "The Mystery of the Modal Progressive". In: Kastovsky, D. (ed.), 467–485.

Wright, S. 1995. "Subjectivity and Experiential Syntax". In: Stein, D., and S. Wright (eds.), 151–172.

Zandvoort, R. W. 1962. "Is 'Aspect' an English Verbal Category?" In: Barber, C. L., F. Behre, U. Ohlander, Y. Olsson, S. Stubelius, J. Söderlind, and R. W. Zandvoort, 1–20.

Žegarac, V. 1993. "Some Observations on the Pragmatics of the Progressive". *Lingua* 90, 201–220.

Ziegeler, D. 1999. "Agentivity and the History of the English Progressive". *Transactions of the Philological Society* 97, 51–101.

Appendix 1. Primary material: The CONCE corpus

In the list of texts included in CONCE that follows below, the texts are sorted first according to period and secondly according to genre. Within the period/genre subsamples, the texts are sorted alphabetically according to the name they are given in examples in the study; as there is only one Debates text per period/genre subsample, these are listed without names both in examples in the running text and in this appendix. Texts included in the S-coefficient subcorpus are listed with an asterisk (*) at the beginning of the entry.

Each entry includes information on the title and, where relevant, the author or editor of the work sampled. The word count given at the end of each entry was obtained using the computer program Hcount. Full bibliographical information on the texts in CONCE will be given in Kytö, Rudanko, and Smitterberg (forthcoming); additional information is also available at the Departments of English at Uppsala University and the University of Tampere.

Period 1 (1800–1830)

Debates
The Parliamentary Debates from the Year 1803 to the Present Time: Forming a Continuation of the Work Entitled "The Parliamentary History of England from the Earliest Period to the Year 1803." Vol. 15. Word count: 19,908.

Drama
*Holcroft = Holcroft, T. *The Vindictive Man*. Word count: 13,639.
*Morton = Morton, T. *The School of Reform; Or, How to Rule a Husband*. Word count: 8,829.
*Poole = Poole, J. *Lodgings for Single Gentlemen*. Word count: 8,843.

Fiction
*Austen = Austen, J. *Emma*. Word count: 9,975.
*Hook = Hook, T. E. *Maxwell*. Word count: 22,077.
*Shelley = Shelley, M. W. *The Last Man*. Word count: 9,980.

History
*Hallam = Hallam, H. *The Constitutional History of England from the Accession of Henry VII. to the Death of George II*. Word count: 10,142.
*Lingard = Lingard, J. *A History of England from the First Invasion by the Romans to the Accession of Henry VIII*. Word count: 10,373.
*Milman = Milman, H. H. *The History of the Jews*. Word count: 10,389.

Letters

*Austen = *Jane Austen: Selected Letters 1796–1817* (ed. R. W. Chapman). Word count: 10,321.

*Blake = *The Letters of William Blake with Related Documents* (ed. G. Keynes). 3rd ed. Word count: 8,101.

Byron = *Byron's Letters and Journals* (ed. L. A. Marchand). Word count: 12,327.

Coleridge = *Letters of Samuel Taylor Coleridge* (ed. E. H. Coleridge). Word count: 9,086.

*Hutchinson = *The Letters of Sara Hutchinson from 1800 to 1835* (ed. K. Coburn). Word count: 19,987.

Keats = *The Letters of John Keats: Complete Revised Edition with a Portrait Not Published in Previous Editions and Twenty-Four Contemporary Views of Places Visited by Keats* (ed. H. B. Forman). Word count: 9,084.

Shelley = *The Letters of Mary W. Shelley* (ed. F. L. Jones). Word count: 11,725.

*Southey = *Letters of Robert Southey: A Selection* (ed. M. H. Fitzgerald). Word count: 13,755.

Wordsworth, Mary (1) = *The Love Letters of William and Mary Wordsworth* (ed. B. Darlington). Word count: 12,203.

Wordsworth, Mary (2) = *The Letters of Mary Wordsworth 1800–1855* (ed. M. E. Burton). Word count: 15,035.

Science

*Lyell = Lyell, C. *Principles of Geology, Being an Attempt to Explain the Former Changes of the Earth's Surface, by Reference to Causes Now in Operation.* Word count: 11,898.

*Malthus = Malthus, T. R. *An Essay on the Principles of Population; Or, a View of Its Past and Present Effects on Human Happiness; With an Inquiry into Our Prospects Respecting the Future Removal or Mitigation of the Evils Which It Occasions.* 5th ed. Word count: 10,472.

*Ricardo = Ricardo, D. *On the Principles of Political Economy, and Taxation.* Word count: 15,667.

Trials

*Angus = *The Trial of Charles Angus, Esq., on an Indictment for the Wilful Murder of Margaret Burns, at the Assizes Held at Lancaster, on Friday, 2d September. 1808.* 2nd ed. Word count: 17,812.

*Bowditch = *Abduction of Maria Glenn. The Trial of James Bowditch and Nine Others, at the Suit of the King, and on the Prosecution of George Lowman Tuckett, Esq. for Conspiracy, Assault, and False Imprisonment. At the Late Summer Assizes for the County of Dorset, July 25, 1818.* Word count: 24,736.

*Martin = *Report of the Trial of Jonathan Martin, for Having, on the Night of the First of February, 1829, Set Fire to York Minster. Which Trial Took Place at the Yorkshire Spring Assizes, on Tuesday, March 31st, 1829, Before Mr. Baron Hullock.* Word count: 19,812.

Period 2 (1850–1870)

Debates
Hansard's Parliamentary Debates: Third Series, Commencing with the Accession of William IV. 13° & 14° Victoriæ, 1850. Vol. 112. Word count: 19,385.

Drama
Marston = Marston, W. *A Hard Struggle.* Word count: 6,756.
Robertson = Robertson, T. W. *Society.* Word count: 11,756.
Taylor = Taylor, T. *The Ticket-of-Leave Man.* 2nd ed. Word count: 11,031.

Fiction
Dickens = Dickens, C. *The Personal History of David Copperfield.* Word count: 11,584.
Gaskell = Gaskell, E. *Cranford.* Word count: 11,166.
Yonge = Yonge, C. M. *Hopes and Fears; Or, Scenes from the Life of a Spinster.* Word count: 16,295.

History
Froude = Froude, J. A. *History of England from the Fall of Wolsey to the Death of Elizabeth.* Word count: 10,007.
Grote = Grote, G. *History of Greece.* Word count: 10,426.
Macaulay = Macaulay, T. B. *The History of England from the Accession of James the Second.* Word count: 10,071.

Letters
Barrett Browning = *The Letters of Elizabeth Barrett Browning* (ed. F. G. Kenyon). Word count: 13,970.
Browning = *New Letters of Robert Browning* (eds. W. C. DeVane and K. L. Knickerbocker). Word count: 7,841.
Darwin = *The Correspondence of Charles Darwin* (eds. F. Burkhardt and S. Smith). Word count: 19,349.
Dickens = *The Letters of Charles Dickens* (Vol. 6, eds. G. Storey, K. Tillotson, and N. Burgis). Word count: 11,577.
Eliot = *The George Eliot Letters* (ed. G. S. Haight). Word count: 10,247.
Gaskell = *The Letters of Mrs Gaskell* (eds. J. A. V. Chapple and A. Pollard). Word count: 10,795.
Jewsbury = *Selections from the Letters of Geraldine Endsor Jewsbury to Jane Welsh Carlyle* (ed. A. Ireland). Word count: 10,896.
Macaulay = *The Letters of Thomas Babington Macaulay* (ed. T. Pinney). Word count: 13,672.
Thackeray = *The Letters and Private Papers of William Makepeace Thackeray* (ed. G. N. Ray). Word count: 16,337.
Wilson = *The Collected Works of Walter Bagehot* (ed. N. St John-Stevas). Word count: 16,432.

Science
Darwin = Darwin, C. *On the Origin of Species by Means of Natural Selection, or the Preservation of Favoured Races in the Struggle for Life.* Word count: 10,694.
Faraday = Faraday, M. *Experimental Researches in Chemistry and Physics.* Word count: 10,084.
Goschen = Goschen, G. J. *The Theory of the Foreign Exchanges.* Word count: 10,901.

Trials
Boyle = *Boyle v. Wiseman. Verbatim Report of the Trial Boyle v. Wiseman. Tried at Kingston, April 3, 1855.* Word count: 15,605.
Hill = *An Account of the Trial of John Singleton Copley Hill, Clerk in the British Mercantile Agency, 13, Old Jewry Chambers, London, (Sole Conductor, Mr. George Caster,) for an Attempt to Obtain Money under False Pretences.* Word count: 11,205.
Palmer = *The Queen v. Palmer. Verbatim Report of the Trial of William Palmer at the Central Criminal Court, Old Bailey, London, May 14, and Following Days, 1856, before Lord Campbell, Mr. Justice Cresswell, and Mr. Baron Alderson.* Word count: 25,258.
Smith = *A Full and Correct Report of the Trial of Mr. Jeremiah Smith for Wilful and Corrupt Perjury, at the Central Criminal Court, March 2nd, 1854.* Word count: 8,502.

Period 3 (1870–1900)

Debates
*The Parliamentary Debates: Authorised Edition. Fourth Series: Commencing with the Sixth Session of the Twenty-Fourth Parliament of the United Kingdom of Great Britain and Ireland. 55 Victoriæ, 1892. Vol. 4. Word count: 19,947.

Drama
*Gilbert = Gilbert, W. S. *Engaged.* Word count: 11,438.
*Jones = Jones, H. A. *The Case of Rebellious Susan.* Word count: 9,210.
*Pinero = Pinero, A. W. *Dandy Dick.* Word count: 8,442.

Fiction
*Besant = Besant, W. *All Sorts and Conditions of Men: An Impossible Story.* Word count: 9,698.
*Braddon = Braddon, M. E. *Hostages to Fortune.* Word count: 10,390.
*Hardy = Hardy, T. *Far from the Madding Crowd.* Word count: 10,025.

History

*Gardiner = Gardiner, S. R. *History of England from the Accession of James I. to the Outbreak of the Civil War 1603–1642*. Word count: 10,121.
*Green = Green, J. R. *History of the English People*. Word count: 10,208.
*Walpole = Walpole, S. *A History of England from the Conclusion of the Great War in 1815*. New and revised ed. Word count: 10,235.

Letters

Arnold = *Letters of Matthew Arnold 1848–1888* (ed. G. W. E. Russell). Word count: 8,641.
*Butler, Samuel (1) = *The Family Letters of Samuel Butler 1841–1886* (ed. A. Silver). Word count: 11,520.
Butler, Samuel (2) = *The Correspondence of Samuel Butler with His Sister May* (ed. D. F. Howard). Word count: 11,020.
*Butler, May = *The Correspondence of Samuel Butler with His Sister May* (ed. D. F. Howard). Word count: 8,385.
Hardy = *Thomas Hardy: Selected Letters* (ed. M. Millgate). Word count: 4,419.
*Holland = *Letters of Mary Sibylla Holland* (ed. B. Holland). Word count: 12,686.
*Huxley = *Life and Letters of Thomas Henry Huxley* (ed. L. Huxley). Word count: 5,137.
Rossetti = *The Family Letters of Christina Georgina Rossetti with Some Supplementary Letters and Appendices* (ed. W. M. Rossetti). Word count: 10,303.
Thackeray Ritchie = *Letters of Anne Thackeray Ritchie with Forty-Two Additional Letters from Her Father William Makepeace Thackeray* (ed. H. Ritchie). Word count: 18,780.

Science

*Bateson = Bateson, W. *Materials for the Study of Variation Treated with Especial Regard to Discontinuity in the Origin of Species*. Word count: 10,141.
*Galton = Galton, F. *Natural Inheritance*. Word count: 10,315.
*Lockyer = Lockyer, J. N. *The Chemistry of the Sun*. Word count: 10,147.

Trials

*Bartlett = *The Trial of Adelaide Bartlett for Murder Held at the Central Criminal Court from Monday, April 12, to Saturday, April 17, 1886* (ed. E. Beal). Word count: 20,926.
*Maybrick = *The Necessity for Criminal Appeal As Illustrated by the Maybrick Case and the Jurisprudence of Various Countries* (ed. J. H. Levy). Word count: 24,033.
*Tichborne = *Tichborne v. Lushington. Before Lord Chief Justice Bovill and a Special Jury*. Word count: 22,629.

Appendix 2. Text-level codes used in CONCE

In the table below, the different codes that are used within the corpus texts are explained. In the table, the underscore (_) stands for "any text".

Code	Legend
_(^_^)_	"Font other than main font": to be used for italics, typeface variation etc. in the final version of the corpus.
_[_\]_	"Editor's comment": used to indicate text inserted by the editor of the work from which the corpus text was taken.
_[^_^]_	"Our comment": used to give information about the text, and to indicate omissions in the text.
_[$_$]_	"Metatextual material": used for text that is not part of the recorded/constructed speech in speech-related genres, e.g. question/answer indications in Trials, and stage directions in Drama; also used around emendations added by the compilation team.
_{_\}_	"Letter heading": used around information about addressees, addresses, and dates in Letters, whether or not this information was part of the actual letter or an editor's comment.

Appendix 3. Tests for statistical significance

In this Appendix, the chi-square tests for statistical significance carried out in the present study are sorted according to the number of the table with which the test was associated. Descriptions of the type of variation tested replace the titles of the tables. Degrees of freedom, chi-square values, and p-values are given for each test below the relevant table.

Table 9: Variation between periods 1 and 3 in the distribution of progressive and non-progressive verb phrases (non-finite verb phrases, imperative verb phrases, and BE *going to* + infinitive constructions with future reference excluded from the counts)

Period	Progressive VPs	Non-progressive VPs
1	427	30,085
3	689	28,148

d.f. = 1; Chi-square = 78.729; $p < 0.001$

Table 11: Variation across the genre parameter in the distribution of progressive and non-progressive verb phrases (non-finite verb phrases, imperative verb phrases, and BE *going to* + infinitive constructions with future reference excluded from the counts; genres ordered in decreasing order of S-coefficients in order to facilitate comparisons between adjacent genres)

Genre	Progressive VPs	Non-progressive VPs
Trials	410	18,218
Letters	229	10,260
Drama	151	7,303
Fiction	155	7,952
History	76	5,219
Debates	40	3,699
Science	55	5,582

Overall distribution: d.f. = 6; Chi-square = 60.495; $p < 0.001$
Science vs. Debates: d.f. = 1; Chi-square = 0.198; $p = 0.656$
Debates vs. History: d.f. = 1; Chi-square = 2.310; $p = 0.129$
History vs. Fiction: d.f. = 1; Chi-square = 4.295; $p = 0.039$
Fiction vs. Drama: d.f. = 1; Chi-square = 0.261; $p = 0.610$
Drama vs. Letters: d.f. = 1; Chi-square = 0.521; $p = 0.471$
Letters vs. Trials: d.f. = 1; Chi-square = 0.010; $p = 0.921$

Table 13:   Variation between period 1 and period 3 in the S-coefficient subcorpus regarding the distribution of progressive and non-progressive verb phrases in Debates (non-finite verb phrases, imperative verb phrases, and BE *going to* + infinitive constructions with future reference excluded from the counts)

Period	Progressive VPs	Non-progressive VPs
1	11	1,819
3	29	1,880

d.f. = 1; Chi-square = 7.440; p = 0.007

Table 14:   Variation between period 1 and period 3 in the S-coefficient subcorpus regarding the distribution of progressive and non-progressive verb phrases in Drama (non-finite verb phrases, imperative verb phrases, and BE *going to* + infinitive constructions with future reference excluded from the counts)

Period	Progressive VPs	Non-progressive VPs
1	37	3,812
3	114	3,491

d.f. = 1; Chi-square = 45.436; p < 0.001

Table 15:   Variation between period 1 and period 3 in the S-coefficient subcorpus regarding the distribution of progressive and non-progressive verb phrases in Fiction (non-finite verb phrases, imperative verb phrases, and BE *going to* + infinitive constructions with future reference excluded from the counts)

Period	Progressive VPs	Non-progressive VPs
1	86	4,483
3	69	3,469

d.f. = 1; Chi-square = 0.049; p = 0.825

Table 19:   Variation between period 1 and period 3 in the S-coefficient subcorpus regarding the distribution of progressive and non-progressive verb phrases in History (non-finite verb phrases, imperative verb phrases, and BE *going to* + infinitive constructions with future reference excluded from the counts)

Period	Progressive VPs	Non-progressive VPs
1	10	2,479
3	66	2,740

d.f. = 1; Chi-square = 35.465; p < 0.001

Table 20: Variation between period 1 and period 3 in the S-coefficient subcorpus regarding the distribution of progressive and non-progressive verb phrases in Letters (non-finite verb phrases, imperative verb phrases, and BE *going to* + infinitive constructions with future reference excluded from the counts)

Period	Progressive VPs	Non-progressive VPs
1	84	5,907
3	145	4,353

d.f. = 1; Chi-square = 39.917; p < 0.001

Table 21: Variation between period 1 and period 3 in the S-coefficient subcorpus regarding the distribution of progressive and non-progressive verb phrases in Science (non-finite verb phrases, imperative verb phrases, and BE *going to* + infinitive constructions with future reference excluded from the counts)

Period	Progressive VPs	Non-progressive VPs
1	23	2,998
3	32	2,584

d.f. = 1; Chi-square = 3.096; p = 0.079

Table 22: Variation between period 1 and period 3 in the S-coefficient subcorpus regarding the distribution of progressive and non-progressive verb phrases in Trials (non-finite verb phrases, imperative verb phrases, and BE *going to* + infinitive constructions with future reference excluded from the counts)

Period	Progressive VPs	Non-progressive VPs
1	176	8,587
3	234	9,631

d.f. = 1; Chi-square = 2.850; p = 0.092

Table 25:   Variation in the S-coefficient subcorpus regarding the distribution of
progressive and non-progressive verb phrases in women's and men's
letters (non-finite verb phrases, imperative verb phrases, and BE *going
to* + infinitive constructions with future reference excluded from the
counts)

Period	Progressive VPs (women)	Non-progressive VPs (women)	Progressive VPs (men)	Non-progressive VPs (men)
1	57	3,546	27	2,361
3	100	2,366	45	1,987
1, 3	157	5,912	72	4,348

Women (periods 1 and 3) vs. men (periods 1 and 3): d.f. = 1; Chi-square = 10.990; p < 0.001
Women (period 1) vs. women (period 3): d.f. =1; Chi-square = 35.533; p < 0.001
Men (period 1) vs. men (period 3): d.f. = 1; Chi-square = 8.049; p = 0.005
Women (period 1) vs. men (period 1): d.f. = 1; Chi-square = 2.116; p = 0.146
Women (period 3) vs. men (period 3): d.f. = 1; Chi-square = 12.097; p < 0.001

Table 41:   Variation across time in the distribution of active and non-active
progressive verb phrases

Period	Active progressive VPs	Non-active progressive VPs
1	588	5
2	885	13
3	925	17

d.f. = 2; Chi-square = 2.374; p = 0.306

Table 44:   Variation across time in the distribution of progressive verb phrases
with and without modal auxiliaries

Period	Progressive VPs with modal auxiliaries	Progressive VPs without modal auxiliaries
1	31	553
2	23	861
3	11	917

d.f. = 2; Chi-square = 23.150; p < 0.001

Table 48:   Variation across time between progressive verb phrases with and
without auxiliaries other than progressive BE

Period	Only progressive BE	Additional auxiliary/-ies
1	463	114
2	712	165
3	784	142

d.f. = 2; Chi-square = 5.983; p = 0.051

Table 56a: Variation across time between progressives in 'future' and non-'future' situations

Period	Future	Non-future
1	45	521
2	66	778
3	35	848

d.f. = 2; Chi-square = 13.923; p = 0.001

Table 56a: Variation across time among progressives in non-'future' situations

Period	Stative	Stance	Active	Processive	Momentary	Transitional
1	25	37	271	175	1	12
2	52	36	398	245	17	30
3	58	66	415	267	15	27

d.f. = 10; Chi-square = 21.260; p = 0.021

Table 56b: Variation across time among progressives in different situation types

Period	Stative	Stance	Active	Processive	Momentary	Transitional
1	25	37	274	219	1	16
2	52	36	399	321	17	35
3	58	66	418	306	15	29

d.f. = 10; Chi-square = 23.046; p = 0.012

Table 59: Variation across time between progressives in [–stative] situations with non-agentive and agentive subjects

Period	Non-agentive	Agentive
1	58	452
2	85	687
3	91	677

d.f. = 2; Chi-square = 0.269; p = 0.874

Table 60: Variation across time between progressive verb phrases with and without modification by temporal adverbials

Period	Temporal adverbial present	Temporal adverbial absent
1	192	405
2	254	646
3	215	728

d.f. = 2; Chi-square = 17.145; p < 0.001

Table 71:   Variation across time between progressive verb phrases with and without modification by ALWAYS-type adverbials

Period	ALWAYS-type adverbial present	ALWAYS-type adverbial absent
1	30	567
2	43	857
3	28	915

d.f. = 2; Chi-square = 5.359; p = 0.070

Table 74:   Variation across time between potentially experiential progressive verb phrases and other progressive verb phrases

Period	Potentially experiential progressive VPs	Other progressive VPs
1	60	537
2	141	759
3	163	780

d.f. = 2; Chi-square = 15.706; p < 0.001

Table 77:   Variation across time between interpretative and non-interpretative progressive verb phrases

Period	Interpretative progressive VPs	Non-interpretative progressive VPs
1	20	577
2	48	852
3	52	891

d.f. = 2; Chi-square = 4.188; p = 0.124